D0915527

Toward a Usable Past

Toward a Usable Past

Liberty Under State Constitutions

EDITED BY

Paul Finkelman and Stephen E. Gottlieb

The University of Georgia Press

Athens and London

© 1991 by the University of Georgia Press
Athens, Georgia 30602
All rights reserved

Designed by Kathi L. Dailey
Set in Palatino by Tseng Information Systems, Inc.
Printed and bound by Thomson-Shore, Inc.
The paper in this book meets the guidelines for
permanence and durability of the Committee on
Production Guidelines for Book Longevity of the
Council on Library Resources.

Printed in the United States of America

95 94 93 92 91 C 5 4 3 2 1

Library of Congress Cataloging in Publication Data

Toward a usable past : liberty under state constitutions /
    edited by Paul Finkelman and Stephen E. Gottlieb.
        p.   cm.
    Includes bibliographical references and index.
    ISBN 0-8203-1305-x (alk. paper)
        1. United States—Constitutional law, State—History.
    I. Finkelman, Paul, 1949–   . II. Gottlieb, Stephen E.
    KF4550.Z95T69   1991
    342.73′02—dc20
    [347.3022]   90-49667
                                                  CIP

British Library Cataloging in Publication Data available

Contents

Part Five   **Assessments**

Acknowledgments

This book had its genesis in a conference "In Search of a Usable Past," held at Albany Law School on October 13–15, 1988. This volume has benefited considerably from that event. We are indebted to Chief Judge Sol Wachtler of the New York Court of Appeals, who gave the keynote address, and to the chairs and commentators at the sessions for their many insights: Akhil Reed Amar, Anthony R. Baldwin, Hon. Richard J. Bartlett, Michal R. Belknap, Dean Martin H. Belsky, Robert J. Cottrol, Robert Dykstra, Tyll Van Geel, Calvin Jillson, Kathryn D. Katz, Sanford Levinson, William E. Nelson, R. Kent Newmyer, Peter Preiser, Donald M. Roper, and Stephen L. Schechter.

We are also indebted to Albany Law School of Union University, the New York State Commission on the Bicentennial of the United States Constitution, and the Albany Commission on the Bicentennial of the United States Constitution for funding the conference. West Publishing Company made its Westlaw available for substantial additional hours during preparation of this work.

Malcolm Call of the University of Georgia Press has been helpful throughout with suggestions for the ultimate shape of this book. Professor Finkelman would like to thank Brooklyn Law School for providing financial support for final manuscript preparation, and Charles Krause, Degna Levister, Elayna Nacci, Marni Schlissel, Jordan Tamagni, and Rae Trisciuzzi for their help on this book. Professor Gottlieb would like to thank his research assistants, Jennifer C. Hickox, Maryanne E. Low, and Michele M. Walls, and the editors of the *Albany Law Review*, for assistance in innumerable ways. The editors, finally, wish to thank the contributors, not only for making this possible, but for prompt and genial response to numerous editorial requests and suggestions on our introduction and the overall project.

Toward a Usable Past

Introduction

State Constitutions and American Liberties

Paul Finkelman and Stephen E. Gottlieb

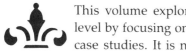 This volume explores the history of liberty at the state level by focusing on both common traditions and specific case studies. It is neither a celebration nor a condemnation. The essays explore states' successes and failures in protecting liberties. Necessarily they also explore the promise and the risks of turning to state constitutions for the development of those rights and liberties.

The Challenge Confronting State Judges Interpreting State Constitutions

There is a complex historical relationship between constitutional liberty and state government. The states, through their bills of rights, can, but need not, provide greater protection for individual liberty than is required by the federal Constitution and the United States Supreme Court. The views of two members of the United States Supreme Court help frame this issue.

In 1977 Justice William J. Brennan, Jr., warned that "our liberties cannot survive if the states betray the trust the Court has put in them."[1] Brennan, the most important advocate of civil liberties on this Court in the last three decades,[2] naturally hoped that the state courts would enthusiastically follow the precedents of the United States Supreme Court in helping to nationalize liberty. Implicit in

Brennan's remarks is the understanding that in the past states have flaunted, ignored, or only narrowly applied the rulings of the United States Supreme Court. Brennan wished the states would do more than pay mere lip service to those decisions that have expanded the protections of individual and political liberty, due process, and civil rights.[3]

Brennan has also long been on record as advocating that the states expand individual liberty and rights beyond what the United States Constitution and the Supreme Court demand, if the constitutions of the states require or allow them to do so. Thus, as early as 1961, Justice Brennan happily noted that at least some state bills of rights "have been applied by 'state courts' to an extent beyond that required of the national government by the corresponding federal guarantee."[4] Brennan, whose views may have been shaped by his experience on the New Jersey Supreme Court, clearly saw the state courts as potential allies in his lifelong commitment to expanding and protecting individual liberty.

In 1983 Chief Justice Warren E. Burger offered a quite different view of the role of the states in interpreting their own bills of rights. Burger was concerned that the state courts might actually take up Brennan's call to go beyond the United States Supreme Court in protecting liberties based on state constitutions. Burger did not see this as a welcome expansion of liberty. In fact, he feared that "state courts" would "interpret state law to require *more* than the Federal Constitution" and in the process undermine "rational law enforcement."[5] He suggested that the states amend their own constitutions to bring their bills of rights in line with the federal Constitution.

The hopes and fears of Justice Brennan and Chief Justice Burger suggest that state constitutions and state courts may be forces for progressive change or they may erect roadblocks to the expansion of liberty. Justice Brennan hoped for the former result while Chief Justice Burger hoped that the states would simply follow the guidelines of the Supreme Court, without adding to or subtracting from them.

The Role of State Constitutional History

Whatever a judge's jurisprudential views—whether a devotee of Brennan or a follower of Burger—the federal courts have traditionally avoided interpreting state constitutions. In *Murdock* v. *Memphis* (1874)[6] the Court asserted that short of explicit congressional authorization,[7] it would not overturn state decisions reached on separate state grounds, as long as those decisions did not conflict with the federal Constitution.

Since *Murdock* the Court has developed a fairly clear standard of "adequate and independent state grounds." Under this doctrine a state court's interpretation of a state law or a state constitution is "adequate" if this interpretation is sufficient to support the judgment and does not violate the federal Constitution. It is "independent" if the result is reached on the basis of interpretation that is not dependent on federal constitutional law.[8] For practical purposes, this means that a state supreme court has the power to expand liberties within its jurisdiction well beyond the standards required by the United States Supreme Court under the federal Constitution and federal laws. But the state courts cannot restrict rights under the state constitution to the point that they violate federally protected rights. Put simply, under "adequate and independent state grounds" a state court may give someone more rights than a federal court would grant, but the state court may not give people fewer rights than they have under the United States Constitution.[9]

"Adequate and independent state grounds" would seem to be a total victory for the Brennan position. But state constitutional history can undermine, as well as aid, the development of independent state grounds. In states whose traditions uphold standards of liberty that exceed federal levels, state judges are able to draw on their own independent history when asserting independent state grounds to protect rights beyond federal requirements. They will also find it easier to state their conclusions as independent state grounds.[10] Even if states have a history of expanding rights, however, scholarly inattention to state constitutional developments may make it harder for lawyers and judges to find this history.

State constitutional history, or more properly the lack of a history of independent state-protected liberties, may work against the future development of independent state protections of liberty in two ways. Where there is no tradition of liberty from which to draw, state judges who wish to assert "independent" state grounds will have a more difficult, although not impossible, task of developing a state tradition of expressing their conclusions as independent state grounds as new cases arise. Such judges may also find it difficult to overcome a nonlibertarian tradition. State jurists may be reluctant to break new paths toward liberty and instead may choose to adhere to precedent and the continuity of a state culture that gave relatively little protection to civil rights and liberties. Indeed, some jurists may feel that it is inappropriate for them to develop new paths that stray from the constitutional and common law traditions of their state, even if they think such a new direction is desirable. History, rather than a guide to expanded liberties, may become an albatross that slows down the growth of liberty in some states.

How have the states—through their legislatures, courts, and constitutions—responded to questions of liberty, fairness, and due process? Does the history of state-protected liberty provide a usable past for those who support the Brennan model? Does the history of state bills of rights justify Chief Justice Burger's concerns?

An Evaluation of State Constitutional Traditions

Most scholars have focused their attentions on the history of the federal Constitution. Little has been written on the history of state constitutions, and even less has been said about state protections of liberty.[11] Yet the states have extensive constitutional histories of their own. As Justice Brennan has noted, "the drafters of the federal Bill of Rights drew upon corresponding provisions in the various state constitutions. Prior to the adoption of the federal Constitution, each of the rights eventually recognized in the federal Bill of Rights had previously been protected in one or more state constitutions."[12]

That there has been so little study of the state constitutions and the state bills of rights might astound the founding generation because the founders looked to the states as the essential guarantors of individual liberty. During the Constitutional Convention, Oliver Ellsworth, who would one day become chief justice of the United States Supreme Court, declared that "he turned his eyes" to the state governments "for the preservation of his rights." Ellsworth expressed the views of most eighteenth-century Americans when he asserted that it was "from these [the state governments] alone he could derive the greatest happiness he expects in this life."[13] In opposing the addition of a bill of rights to the Constitution, Roger Sherman of Connecticut argued that "the State Declarations of Rights are not repealed by this Constitution; and being in force are sufficient." A majority of the delegates sustained Sherman on this point, and the Convention defeated the efforts of George Mason, Elbridge Gerry, and others to add a bill of rights to the Constitution that would have restricted the actions of the federal government.[14]

When the federal Bill of Rights was finally appended to the Constitution, it restricted only the national government because so many Americans feared that the new centralized government would undermine their liberty. James Madison would have made some of the federal Bill of Rights applicable to the states, but the Senate refused to go along with this proposal, in part because of state jealousy and in part because many senators believed that the state bills of rights were more than sufficient to protect the liberty of the people from state infringement.

To put all this into the language of modern constitutional law, many of the framers assumed there would be an adequate and independent state tradition of protecting liberty. Some of the essays in this volume address this question.

Whatever position the Philadelphia framers took on the necessity of a federal Bill of Rights, many eighteenth-century state bills of rights grew out of a shared culture. As Donald Lutz describes, republican traditions shaped state constitutions during the founding period. He argues that this tradition broadened participation in government to include a wider electorate and was expressed as well in the role of jury service.[15] Moreover, as Peter Onuf describes, it stressed the sovereignty of the people and limited the power of government over the political process.

This tradition equated liberty with popular majority rule and happiness with a close relationship between people and their government. Local government seemed a better guarantor of liberty than distant government, and bills of rights were designed to protect "the people" against the neglect or abuse of officialdom, not the excesses of popular majorities.

The senators in the first Congress who rejected Madison's proposals to insert limitations on state regulation of expression into the federal Bill of Rights[16] did not fully understand the "tyranny of the majority" or anticipate its consequences at the state level.[17] This is ironic, of course, because there already existed a great deal of tyranny by the electoral majority in many of the states[18] in the form of slavery and limitations on the franchise or officeholding based on race, religion, economic status, and gender.

Today's state constitutions are, for the most part, quite different from those of the founding period. Most state constitutions and their bills of rights have been repeatedly rewritten and vastly altered in both content and purpose from their eighteenth- and nineteenth-century predecessors.[19]

As James Henretta shows, republican traditions within the states were quickly supplemented by the "democratic" tradition of the mid-nineteenth century. Both the republican tradition and the democratic tradition gave way in the late nineteenth century, however, which was an active period of state constitutional revision, to elite ways of thinking. Constitution makers of this period sought to limit participation in government, to replace democracy with progressive management of government. The progressives made common cause between those who wanted to "perfect" democracy by eliminating corruption and other democratic excesses and those who wanted to limit, or exclude, large portions of the population from the governmental process on political or class grounds. State constitutional provisions can be much less libertarian when informed by such elitist traditions.

These tensions were played out in arenas beyond the ballot box or the courtroom. The decay in republicanism led to the establishment of a Protestant religious consensus in the development of the public school system, in ways that Thomas James makes clear. The popular "republican" assumption described by Peter Onuf, that government cannot properly instruct the people, was replaced with the assumption that government must shape the minds of the public by inculcating the cultural-religious values of the dominant Protestant majority. In fact, Jefferson and Madison's "wall of separation" between church and state was not erected at the state level until much later. Thus state traditions following the founding period are ominous for late twentieth-century notions of political and religious liberty.

The implications of these developments are affected by the interpretive modes current in state courts. State courts sometimes expanded textual provisions by drawing on the tradition of natural law in state constitutional interpretation, as Suzanna Sherry demonstrates. It is a tradition that empowers the judiciary to develop the content of individual liberty. Not all state traditions implied that courts ignored substantive precedent when they sought to expand liberty. The common law, as Connecticut Chief Justice Ellen Peters points out, was an important source of libertarian traditions which informed constitutional law. But not all traditions are so expansive. Donald Lutz argues that eighteenth-century courts could ignore provisions of bills of rights. On the contrary, H. Jefferson Powell argues that traditions which permitted the judiciary to exercise some latitude have been subordinated to a narrower understanding of positive law. To the extent that state constitutional traditions may have narrowed, the "sail," as Kermit Hall describes it, may have been taken out of state constitutional law.

Federal law can also be impoverished by the escape to state constitutional law. State constitutional law, as Lawrence Friedman persuasively argues, is part of the development of federal constitutional law rather than a separate enclave of thought. And the very attempt to isolate state constitutional law, as J. Morgan Kousser argues, is costly because it robs state cases of value as precedent in national developments. He also raises the prescient perspective of James Madison, who had pointed out the protection afforded by a national pluralist culture by contrast to what Madison described as the "faction" prevalent in state and local government. There is good reason to believe that federal courts in general will provide more protection to individuals and minorities than will state courts.

Indeed, state courts have often fallen far short of their responsibilities in handling of issues of race. Charles Ogletree demonstrates that many states have failed to provide fair trials for blacks. J. Morgan Kousser's essay chronicles the success of the segregationists in Louisiana well before the infamous decision in *Plessy* v. *Ferguson*.

Racial minorities are, of course, not the only Americans to be denied equality through state constitutional law. Mary Dudziak demonstrates how the rights of women were easily ignored by both the Connecticut legislature and the state supreme court. Her essay, on the anti-birth-control laws in Connecticut, demonstrates the promise and the dangers of relying on state constitutional protections of liberties. In most states, birth control, which had once been illegal, was legalized through the political process. But in Connecticut, women seeking to plan their parenthood could turn neither to the state legislature nor to the state courts to vindicate their rights of privacy and liberty. Only in the federal Supreme Court could they eventually find protection.

The Connecticut experience, so richly detailed by Dudziak, underscores the reasoning behind Burt Neuborne's contention that, as a civil liberties litigator, he finds that resort to state constitutional law is a strategic second choice for the enforcement of civil libertarian claims, largely because of the majoritarian character of state courts. Nevertheless, he finds improvements in state courts and opportunities to use those courts more effectively.

Charles Ogletree also finds that jury discrimination has not been universal in the states. Similarly, J. Morgan Kousser's essay demonstrates that even while the nation and many states were rushing to segregate blacks, there have been times and places, such as Kansas in the late nineteenth century, where some state courts have exceeded national standards in providing more racial equality than their neighbors. William Wiecek notes this was true for New York as well, which abolished slavery in 1827 and provided some rights for blacks that were not found in other free states. State courts, interpreting state constitutions, as Wiecek lays out, have clearly made important contributions to American constitutional law. He sees state constitutional history as full of innovation.

Kermit Hall, however, sees state constitutional history as weighed down with restrictions and filled with little energy. Despite the many occasions when state constitutional traditions have protected constitutional liberties, many of the essays in this volume, then, present an indictment of the assumption that state constitutional law is an adequate substitute for federal. The view that state courts can be laboratories of experiment is formally correct but rarely borne out.

The Need for Strong State Traditions

Evaluations are relative, however, and the federal alternative has not always been much more encouraging. The federal courts have often refused to enforce rights against either state or federal governments.

Questions were raised about the role of federal courts in protecting liberty as early as the Constitutional Convention. James Wilson asserted that it was the purpose of the states "to preserve the rights of individuals."[20] Most of the states adopted bills of rights well before the federal Constitution was written, and indeed the presence of such bills enabled Federalists to argue that a national bill of rights was unnecessary. At the Constitutional Convention George Mason of Virginia was skeptical of this position, noting that the Constitution's supremacy clause might undermine the power of the states to preserve liberty.[21] Subsequent history has shown that Mason's fears were probably unjustified because the national legislature and the federal courts have rarely restricted the states in their development of basic liberty. But Mason's opponents also erred in their expectation that the state bills of rights would be sufficient to protect civil liberties, as many of the essays in this volume demonstrate. Mason was also correct in his expectation that the addition of a federal Bill of Rights would protect civil liberties at the national level.

The federal Bill of Rights, adopted in 1791, reflects the assumptions that the states were the main guarantors of liberty. The Bill of Rights prohibited the national government, not the states, from infringing basic liberties. Thus before the Civil War the Supreme Court rarely interfered with state actions that infringed on the liberty of individuals. In *Barron* v. *Baltimore* (1833)[22] the Supreme Court held that the Bill of Rights limited only the actions of the national government and that the states were largely free to treat their citizens as they wished, with few exceptions. In *Barron* the Supreme Court refused to interfere with the state taking private property without just compensation because the Court determined that the Fifth Amendment was a limitation only on the national government. In the same term, in *Livingston's Lessee* v. *Moore*,[23] the Court refused to apply the jury trial requirements of the Bill of Rights to the states. A dozen years later a Court made up almost entirely of new members refused to apply the free exercise clause of the First Amendment to the states.[24]

Not all Americans liked these decisions. By the 1850s many lawyers and politicians in the Republican party argued that *Barron* and its progeny had been wrongly decided. This was, nevertheless, the rule of law for the era. Since most questions of liberty were handled at the state level, *Barron* meant that state protections of liberty were more relevant to most people than the protections in the federal Bill of Rights.

The only exceptions to this trend involved some property rights and explicit powers that were granted to Congress under the Constitution. For example, the Supreme Court protected some vested economic interests under the clause that specifically prohibited the impairment of the obligation of contracts by states.[25] As the proprietors of the Charles River Bridge found out, however, only specific contract provisions were protected, while implied rights and interests were subject to state law and state constitutions.[26]

In the antebellum period the Supreme Court also limited the right of states to interfere with interstate commerce, and to some extent this enhanced economic opportunity at the expense of state action.[27] But even in this area, where Congress seemed to have plenary power, the Supreme Court often deferred to the states and allowed state law, not the national Constitution, to determine the boundaries of liberty.[28]

In only one area involving individual liberty did the Supreme Court and Congress almost always impose federal rules on the states. This area of the law, ironically, involved the denial of personal liberty to people claimed as fugitive slaves. Ambiguity in the fugitive slave clause of the Constitution (Article IV, Section 2, Par. 3) and the federal law of 1793 could easily have been interpreted to allow state laws on fugitive slave rendition to operate consistently with the supremacy clause of the Constitution. But the Supreme Court ruled otherwise. In *Prigg* v. *Pennsylvania*[29] the Court struck down the personal liberty laws of Pennsylvania, which were designed to prevent the kidnapping of free blacks. Here the Court supported the liberty to own property and gave it federal protection, at the expense of individual freedom, even for people who were not slaves.[30] Thus in the most important area of individual liberty in the antebellum period, the Court rejected state constitutional law which supported freedom in favor of federal law which protected property rights. In 1850 Congress passed a new fugitive slave law which codified the proslavery direction of the Court.

Not until Reconstruction did the federal government begin to protect individual liberty, and then only in the states of the defeated Confederacy. At this time the Congress and the Court overruled state laws that limited individual liberty and expanded liberty under the umbrella of federal statutes and three new constitutional amendments. The Fourteenth Amendment was, in the words of Senator Jacob M. Howard of Michigan, adopted to protect "the personal rights guaranteed . . . by the first eight amendments of the Constitution."[31] Very quickly, however, the Court seemed to forget the purpose of the new amendments.[32] By the 1880s the Court was no longer willing to interfere in state actions involving questions of personal liberty. In *Hurtado* v. *California* (1884)[33] the Supreme Court held that the Fourteenth Amendment did not require the states to follow the dictates of the Bill of Rights. The Court reaffirmed this idea in *Maxwell* v. *Dow* (1900)[34] and *Twining* v. *New Jersey* (1908).[35] Thus on the eve of World War I most questions involving individual liberty remained in the hands of state legislatures and courts, to be decided on the basis of state laws and state constitutions.

The major exceptions to the Court's general refusal to impose national standards of liberty on the states were in cases involving private property and liberty of contract. In *Chicago, Burlington & Quincy Railroad Co.* v. *Chicago* (1897)[36] the Court held that under the due process clause of the Fourteenth Amendment the states could not take private property without just compensation. In cases such as *Lochner* v. *New York* (1905)[37] the Court further held that the due process clause of the Fourteenth Amendment could be applied to freedom of contract. Here the Court struck down a state law which limited the hours a baker could work and thus, in the Court's view, unreasonably denied him his liberty of contract. This theory was reaffirmed in *Muller* v. *Oregon* (1908),[38] although there the Supreme Court upheld the state law regulating the hours women could work as a reasonable restriction on contract rights.

A dramatic change in constitutional law took place in the years following World War I. In *Meyer* v. *Nebraska* (1922)[39] the Supreme Court overturned a state law that denied people their "liberty, or property, without due process of law." Here the Court found that the states could not abridge such basic freedoms as "the right . . . to acquire useful knowledge, to marry, establish a home and bring up children, to worship God according to the dictates of his own conscience, and generally to enjoy those privileges long recognized at common law as essential to the orderly pursuit of happiness by free men." The Court reaffirmed this concept in *Pierce* v. *Society of Sisters* (1925).[40]

A week after deciding *Pierce,* the Court began the process of incorporating the Bill of Rights into the Fourteenth Amendment through the due process clause, thereby applying the Bill of Rights to the states. In upholding New York's criminal anarchy statute the Court said, almost casually, "For present purposes we may and do assume that freedom of speech and of the press—which are protected by the First Amendment from abridgment by Congress—are among the fundamental personal rights and 'liberties' protected by the due process clause of the Fourteenth Amendment from impairment by the States."[41]

For the next fifty years the history of constitutional liberty in this country was shaped almost entirely by the United States Supreme Court. The states followed, more or less, the path laid out by the Court.

Since about 1970, however, states have increasingly become the battlegrounds for determining the meaning of the basic rights in our society. Increasingly state courts, interpreting state constitutions, are shaping our rights to life, liberty, property, due process, and equal protection of the laws.[42] It is a difficult transition.[43] The essays in this volume illustrate the complexity of state constitutional history. They puncture the simple optimism that state courts will save us from federal neglect. They also reveal that if the past is prologue, the history of state constitutional liberty is certainly an important, if not always a usable, past.

Notes

1. William J. Brennan, Jr., "State Constitutions and the Protection of Individual Rights," *Harvard Law Review* 90 (1977): 489, 503.
2. See Mark Tushnet, "The Optimist's Tale," review of *The Burger Court: The Counter-Revolution That Wasn't*, ed. Vincent Blasi, *University of Pennsylvania Law Review* 132 (1984): 1257, 1263 (describing Brennan's role as a coalition builder on the Court).
3. See Charles J. Ogletree, "Supreme Court Jury Discrimination Cases and State Court Compliance, Resistance, and Innovation," in this volume.
4. William J. Brennan, Jr., *The Bill of Rights and the States* (Santa Barbara: Center for the Study of Democratic Institutions, 1961), 20.
5. *Florida* v. *Casal*, 462 U.S. 637, 639 (1983) (Burger, C.J., concurring).
6. 87 U.S. (20 Wall.) 590, 633 (1874).
7. The Court might, and probably would, find such authorization unconstitutional. See Martha Field, "Sources of Law: The Scope of Federal Common Law," *Harvard Law Review* 99 (1986): 881, 919–21.
8. A state court decision relying on "independent grounds" may quote previous United States Supreme Court decisions for their ideas, analysis, and reasoning in the same way that it might use the decisions of a sister state, but will not be independent if its decision is logically dependent on rather than merely persuaded by what the state court finds in the United States Constitution, federal laws, or U.S. Supreme Court precedents.

9. Examples include additional protection under the equal protection clause, the First Amendment, and the guarantee of jury trials, some of which are discussed in the essays in this volume by Charles Ogletree, "Supreme Court Jury Discrimination Cases," Burt Neuborne, "The Search for a Usable Present," and J. Morgan Kousser, "Before *Plessy*, Before *Brown:* The Development of the Law of Racial Integration in Louisiana and Kansas." Mary L. Dudziak, "Just Say No: Birth Control in the Connecticut Supreme Court before *Griswold* v. *Connecticut*," underscores that almost all states, except Connecticut, had protected reproductive freedom in an era when the United States Supreme Court persistently declined to consider the issue.

10. See *Michigan* v. *Long*, 463 U.S. 1032, 1040–41 (1983).

11. For examples of the recent interest in state constitutional law and history, see "Symposium on the Revolution in State Constitutional Law," *Vermont Law Review* 13 (1988): 11–346; "Symposium: The Emergence of State Constitutional Law," *Texas Law Review* 63 (1985): 959–1339; and Hans Linde, "E Pluribus—Constitutional Theory and State Courts," *Georgia Law Review* 18 (1984): 165. A journal, *Emerging Issues in State Constitutional Law*, was inaugurated in 1988.

12. Brennan, "State Constitutions and the Protection of Individual Rights," 501.

13. *The Records of the Federal Convention of 1787*, Max Farrand, ed. (New Haven: Yale University Press, 1966), 1:492.

14. Ibid., 2:588, 618, 632.

15. One of Donald S. Lutz's important contributions is to remind us of the importance of jury service as an aspect of political participation in the eighteenth century. Ogletree, "Supreme Court Jury Discrimination Cases," writing about the modern period, illustrates nicely that the breakdown of political participation for minorities has led to denial of representative juries.

16. "No state shall infringe the right of trial by Jury in criminal cases, nor the rights of conscience, nor the freedom of speech, or of the press." This amendment would have limited the ability of the states to undermine religious liberty, freedom of expression, and due process of law. Such an amendment would have radically altered the federal structure of the new government. Charlene Bangs Bickford and Helen E. Veit, eds., *Documentary History of the First Federal Congress of the United States of America: Legislative Histories* (Baltimore: Johns Hopkins University Press, 1986), 4:39. At the Constitutional Convention Madison had tried, and failed, to incorporate greater limitations on the states by giving Congress the power to overrule state legislation. Charles Hobson, "The Negative on State Laws: James Madison, the Constitution,

and the Crisis of Republican Government," *William and Mary Quarterly* 3d Ser., 36 (1979): 215. See also Lance Banning, "James Madison and the Nationalists, 1780–1783," *William and Mary Quarterly* 3d Ser., 40 (1979): 227, for a discussion of Madison's early nationalism, and Lance Banning, "The Hamiltonian Madison," *Virginia Magazine of History and Biography* 92 (1984): 7, on Madison's fear, "as late as 1789," that "the necessary powers of the central government would prove vulnerable to the encroachments by the states." The Fourteenth Amendment finally incorporated these concepts into the Constitution by limiting the power of the states to infringe on the privileges and immunities of the citizens, liberty, and due process. See generally Michael Kent Curtis, *No State Shall Abridge: The Fourteenth Amendment and the Bill of Rights* (Durham: Duke University Press, 1986), and Richard Cortner, *The Supreme Court and the Second Bill of Rights: The Fourteenth Amendment and the Nationalization of Civil Liberties* (Madison: University of Wisconsin Press, 1981).

17. James Madison seems to be an exception to the views prevailing in the Senate. *Federalist* No. 10 indicates his fears that "factions" might control states, to the detriment of good government. His article examines the possibility that "a majority is included in a faction." In his first draft of the Bill of Rights, Madison wanted to limit state action that might limit freedom of expression. These may be the first clear expressions in American politics that the majority might become tyrannical, though it was a view which Madison shared with many of the delegates to the Convention. The Congress deleted this provision from the amendments, however, and left them limited to the states.

18. Since the electorate in most states excluded women, slaves, and some propertyless men, it frequently reflected a minority of the adult population.

19. The two notable exceptions are Massachusetts and Vermont, which have kept their constitutions, of 1780 and 1793 respectively, to the present day. Significantly, both documents begin with a Declaration of Rights that was written *before* the federal Bill of Rights. The Massachusetts declaration was written in 1780 and became part of the constitution of that year. The Vermont declaration was written in 1777, before the rest of the nation recognized the existence of what became the fourteenth state or its independence from New York and New Hampshire. It was repeated in the 1786 constitution of Vermont, still before national recognition of that state's existence, and finally it was part of the 1793 constitution of the state. On Vermont see Peter S. Onuf, *The Origins of the Federal Republic: Jurisdictional Controversies in the United States, 1775–1787* (Philadelphia: University of Pennsylvania Press, 1983), 127–45.

20. *Records of the Federal Convention of 1787*, ed. Farrand, 1:356.
21. Ibid., 2:588.
22. 32 U.S. (7 Pet.) 243, 247 (1833).
23. 32 U.S. (7 Pet.) 469, 551–52 (1833).
24. *Permoli v. New Orleans*, 44 U.S. (3 How.) 589, 609 (1845).
25. Art. I, § 10. For examples, see *Fletcher v. Peck*, 10 U.S. (6 Cranch) 87 (1810), and *Dartmouth College v. Woodward*, 17 U.S. (4 Wheat.) 518 (1819).
26. *Charles River Bridge Co. v. Warren Bridge Co.*, 36 U.S. (11 Pet.) 420 (1837).
27. *Gibbons v. Ogden*, 22 U.S. (9 Wheat.) 1 (1824); *The Passenger Cases*, 48 U.S. (7 How.) 283 (1849).
28. See, for example, *Mayor of the City of New York v. Miln*, 36 U.S. (11 Pet.) 102 (1837); *Cooley v. Board of Wardens of the Port of Philadelphia*, 53 U.S. (12 How.) 299 (1851); *License Cases*, 46 U.S. (5 How.) 504 (1847).
29. 41 U.S. (16 Pet.) 539 (1842).
30. One of the blacks seized by Prigg, in violation of Pennsylvania law, and taken back to Maryland, had been conceived and born in Pennsylvania and was clearly free under Pennsylvania law and probably under Maryland law. Nevertheless, this person was enslaved. See also Paul Finkelman, "*Prigg v. Pennsylvania* and Northern State Courts: Anti-Slavery Use of a Pro-Slavery Decision," *Civil War History* 25 (1979): 5–35.
31. U.S. Congress, Senate, *Globe*, 39th Cong., 1st sess. (1865–66), 2765, quoted in Richard C. Cortner, *The Supreme Court and the Second Bill of Rights: The Fourteenth Amendment and the Nationalization of Civil Liberties* (Madison: University of Wisconsin Press, 1981), 5. See also Michael Kent Curtis, *No State Shall Abridge* (Durham: Duke University Press, 1986). For a different view, which seems historically cramped and wrong, see Raoul Burger, *Government by Judiciary: The Transformation of the Fourteenth Amendment* (Cambridge, Mass.: Harvard University Press, 1977).
32. *Slaughterhouse Cases*, 83 U.S. (16 Wall.) 36 (1873), and *Civil Rights Cases*, 109 U.S. 3 (1883), though stating the purpose of the Reconstruction amendments as protection of the freedmen, began the narrowing construction of these amendments which largely excluded the former slaves and their descendants from its benefits for the next three-quarters of a century.
33. 110 U.S. 516 (1884).
34. 176 U.S. 581 (1900).
35. 211 U.S. 78 (1908).
36. 166 U.S. 226, 241 (1897).
37. 198 U.S. 45 (1905).
38. 208 U.S. 412 (1908).

39. 262 U.S. 390, 399 (1923).
40. 268 U.S. 510 (1925).
41. *Gitlow* v. *New York,* 268 U.S. 652, 665–66 (1925).
42. See *Webster* v. *Reproductive Health Services,* 57 U.S.L.W. 5023 (1989).
43. As Chief Justice Peters analyzed the problem in a letter to the authors, dated November 7, 1989: "There is a discontinuity in our current effort to recapture state constitutional rights that arises out of the fact that these constitutional provisions have so long remained essentially moribund. One of the side effects of the federal incorporation of the Bill of Rights is that state courts, for many years, had few incentives to explore state constitutional law. The resulting hiatus means that we are trying to update the few pre-incorporation cases that expressly deal with state constitutional provisions without the gradual period of expanding constitutional rights that came to full fruition in the Warren era. In Connecticut, for example, we are better off with the common law cases than with the early 20th century cases which are as restrictive as case law was all over the United States at that same time. The difficulty of updating rapidly, of bridging the gap suddenly between the 1920s and the 1980s is, of course, exacerbated by the political climate that is increasingly hostile to the protection of many fundamental constitutional rights."

Part One

Republicanism and

State Constitutions

Political Participation in Eighteenth-Century America

Donald S. Lutz

Political participation today revolves around citizenship, and the protection of political participation is, in effect, the protection of the rights of citizenship. The framers in 1787 inherited a somewhat different concept of citizenship, one that was embodied and functioning in the constitutions of the thirteen states. These constitutions were the culmination of American colonial constitutional development, a development at considerable variance with the British model from which they derived.[1] Among the critical variances was a theory of citizenship tied to the concept of popular sovereignty rather than to parliamentary sovereignty.[2]

Political participation was not so much protected legally as it was encouraged by constitutional and legal means. The ability to engage in political participation, the effectiveness of participation, and the attempts to enhance participation rested ultimately upon the level of commitment among the people and their leaders to popular control of government. Participation was linked to the creation and effective power of majorities rather than to the enhancement of minority rights or the protection of individuals. Still, the overall tendency was toward inclusiveness.

The approach worked best in states that were larger and more heterogeneous, that is, where there were no natural majorities and the population was grouped into towns and cities and therefore easily mobilized. It worked least well in the southern states, where the white majority was least heterogeneous, the population most dispersed across the countryside, and the leadership elite thus disposed to keep popular participation relatively low.[3] It is perhaps no accident that later American history would see resort to a more legalistic approach for the protection of individual and minority rights of participation limited most severely, but not only, in the South.

The American theory of citizenship in the 1780s differed considerably from the British version from which it emerged, yet it also differed from the view of citizenship which we hold today.[4] Most obviously, the American theory of citizenship during the founding era had not yet been linked fully with constitutionalism, as was reflected in the rights of political participation being protected more by public sentiment than by legal and constitutional means. This resulted in part from constitutions that were not accorded full status as a higher law and were not viewed as legalistically as they are today.

On one hand, eighteenth-century concepts gave stronger support to rights of political participation than is apparent from legal provisions, but on the other hand the protection of the universality of these rights, and their distribution within the population, was narrower and more restrictive than has been achieved through twentieth-century legalism. The strength of these rights resulted from American insistence that citizenship rested upon individual consent rather than upon loyalty and obligations connected with long association.[5] The logic of the American position required that everyone who gave individual consent had to be considered a citizen and be protected equally in the right of participation. Americans were still using elements of the British approach, however, which denied that all persons had sufficiently independent wills to give individual consent. Americans resisted the logical implication of their new theory by not automatically including certain categories of individuals among the citizenry.[6] Thus, whereas today we use the term *citizens* interchangeably with *Americans,* during the founding era distinctions were still maintained similar to those the classical Greeks held among classes of citizens, free inhabitants who were not citizens, and unfree inhabitants.

While Americans were struggling with this aspect of their theory of citizenship during the founding era, they also had to struggle with another problem. The thirteen states were functioning polities. They could not simply be destroyed. How, then, could a national citizenship be created without destroying state citizenship? The solution was dual citizenship. The Articles of Confederation distinguished between the privileges and immunities of citizens of the various states and citizens of the United States, thereby creating a dual citizenship. The United States Constitution, when it replaced the Articles of Confederation, retained the distinction between national and state citizenship.

Dual citizenship as originally practiced had several distinctive features. One was the understanding that the ability of a government directly to affect the lives of individuals was linked to the ability of those individuals to exercise their rights of political participation upon the government. Dual citizenship thus required a linkage between government power and political participation—one could not exist without the other for the simple reason that government power rested on popular sovereignty and its expression through popular participation.[7]

Another feature was that aside from listing a few age and residency requirements, the national Constitution left the regulation of political participation, and thus the definition of both parts of dual citizenship, to the states. Certainly the federal government retained the ability to regulate most aspects of federal elections, but the framers, too split on the topic to reach agreement, either felt no need to define the content of national citizenship or left the matter alone so as to enhance the prospects for ratification.[8]

A third feature of the American definition of citizenship in state constitutions and political practice was its paradoxical nature. Specification of citizens' rights in state constitutions and bills of rights significantly strengthened them, but such statements of rights were not viewed legalistically the way they are today. Whereas constitutionalism in Britain was essentially a matter of reverence for precedent as a means of limiting arbitrary government, in America there were actual, single documents called constitutions, which focused attention upon the document rather than upon a tradition. Citizens' rights of participation, therefore, were protected by a publicly defined, widely understood set of rights, rules, and procedures.

Even so, the first state constitutions were not used legalistically the way Americans use constitutions today. That is, political conflicts were not susceptible to resolution on the basis of the precise wording in a constitution. For example, constitutional provisions requiring that a person belong to a certain religion to hold office were often ignored, not because the provision was considered erroneous, but because it was considered more admonitory than determinative.[9] Similarly, property requirements for voting could be ignored, and often were, if the person in question was known locally to be productive and of sound character.[10] Bills of rights especially were viewed as providing a statement of broad principles rather than a set of legally enforceable rights. For this reason, they were more often than not couched in admonitory language using words like *should* and *ought* rather than the legally binding *shall* and *will*.[11] As central as political participation was to the operation of American institutions and practices, it thus operated paradoxically. No nation had ever had stronger constitutional protection for political participation, but these constitutional provisions were not the primary basis for protecting political participation. Instead, a constitutional "attitude" among elites and popular expectations that the people be consulted or included in some way on all political matters were the primary protections.

Patterns of Participation

Popular sovereignty was a robust notion during the founding era, and consequently political participation was both widely practiced and diverse in its manifestations. A complete discussion of political participation in eighteenth-century America would be too lengthy and complex for the purposes of this essay. Instead, political participation will be sorted into several categories as a means of simplifying the presentation.

The first category is formal electoral participation and includes voting in elections, running for office, or voting in referenda. A second related category is activist participation and includes working or organizing for political candidates, giving public speeches, engaging in political discussions on the streets or in taverns, writing letters or essays on political topics for publication in newspapers or as pamphlets, sending or signing letters of petition or instruction to elected officials, attending political meetings or rallies, and engaging in peaceful or violent demonstrations. In short, this second category includes everything that a person might do during elections or between elections to influence public opinion or the actions of decision makers.

A third category, preconditions for participation, includes those rights on which the activities in the second category are based. Preconditions for participation include freedom of speech, press, assembly, and petition. This category is easier to discuss than the others not only because the list is shorter but also because these four rights were treated in a standard fashion by state constitutions in the 1780s.

A fourth category includes only one form of political participation and thus adopts its name—jury duty. Often overlooked today as a form of political participation, jury duty was so important then and carried with it such a different set of possibilities than it does today that no discussion of eighteenth-century political participation in America can avoid the subject.

Formal Electoral Participation

It was once fashionable to argue that suffrage restrictions in the late 1700s excluded most people from the polls and resulted in government by the few.[12] As it turns out, the preponderance of evidence does not support the interpretation of rule by elites. This is not to say that the states were without elites. Rather, the number who could vote or run for office was not restricted to a small percentage of the people.

Bernard Bailyn estimates that between 50 and 75 percent of adult, free, or, in some states, white males in America were eligible to vote in the 1770s and 1780s.[13] Bailyn's broad estimate reflects the diversity among historians. The lower estimate matches that of Lee Soltow, who concludes that 49 percent of free or white adult males qualified for the suffrage.[14] Using tax and probate records to estimate income and property, Jackson Turner Main suggests that about 75 percent of free or white adult males could meet their respective state property requirements for voting.[15]

Robert Dinkin concludes that as a result of reductions in the property requirements for voting, the electorate in the thirteen states expanded from a range of 50 to 80 percent of adult free or white males in 1776 to a range of 60 to 90 percent in the mid-1780s. In Pennsylvania, North Carolina, Georgia, New Hampshire, and New Jersey, voter eligibility approached 90 percent; in South Carolina, Delaware, and Massachusetts it approached 80 percent; in Maryland and Virginia, between 70 and 75 percent; in New York and Rhode Island, between 60 and 70 percent; and in Connecticut, about 60 percent.[16]

Chilton Williamson estimates the size of the electorate in relation to the total adult male population from an examination of tax lists.

He concludes that between 50 and 75 percent of free or white adult males were qualified to vote.[17] Despite the broadly defined suffrage, however, actual electoral turnout typically ranged between 20 and 45 percent of free or white adult males, and only about 25 percent of these men voted in the elections to select the state ratifying conventions for the U.S. Constitution.[18]

Furthermore, plentiful evidence indicates that property requirements for voting found in state constitutions were frequently ignored. That is, the ownership of property was used as a minimal test, not the sole test. For example, Albert E. McKinley found that in 1769 about 40 percent of those who voted in New York City did not own land but voted on the basis of freemanship.[19] A referendum in Massachusetts in 1778 on whether to accept a proposed state constitution required only freemanship, which established virtual manhood suffrage, including free blacks.[20]

Using the midpoints of these various electoral studies, 65 to 75 percent of free or white adult males arguably were qualified to vote in state and local elections during the 1780s. Compared to the far lower suffrage of adult males in England,[21] the American suffrage rates were sensational.

The Theory of Participation in the State Constitutions

At first blush, the relevant state constitutional provisions appear designed to exclude potential voters. During the 1780s, six states required the ownership of fifty acres or more,[22] four states required personal wealth of between ten and sixty pounds in real or personal property,[23] and three states required that one have paid taxes in order to vote for the lower house of the legislature.[24] These provisions do not seem to have excluded many men from the electorate.[25] A more careful consideration of the reasoning behind the provisions reveals that the intent was often to make the electorate more inclusive.

Property requirements were generally seen as a valid requirement for voting on several grounds. First, property ownership demonstrated a stake in the community such that the person, caring about the outcome, would not be frivolous in casting his vote but instead would act responsibly.[26] For example, article VII of the Declaration of Rights in the 1776 Pennsylvania Constitution provided "that all elections ought to be free; and that all free men having a sufficient evident common interest with, and attachment to the community, have a right to elect officers, or to be elected into office."[27] Similar provisions in other state constitutions show that the logic was widely shared among Americans in all regions.[28] The 1776 Virginia Constitution's Bill of Rights provided "that elections of members to serve as representatives of the people, in assembly, ought to be free; and that all men, having sufficient evidence of permanent common interest with, and attachment to, the community, have the right of suffrage, and cannot be taxed or deprived of their property for public uses, without their own consent, or that of their representatives so elected, nor bound by any law to which they have not, in like manner, assembled, for the public good."[29]

It is important that the attachment is to the community, and ownership of property is assumed to involve one with the commonwealth. The very definition of political virtue at that time was to seek the common good rather than personal good only, and thus attachment to the commonwealth was an important indication of political virtue.[30] Also, ever since the Magna Carta, "no taxation without representation" had been a part of English law.[31] Ownership of property gave one the right to vote for representatives, and whereas this principle in England enfranchised a relatively few large landowners, in America the principle was used to apply to a level of property ownership that was commonly found and thus ended up being widely inclusive rather than exclusive. The balance between property as entitling one to a vote and as showing a stake in the community was interpreted in America to allow a small stake as sufficient. Furthermore, this was the minimum electorate. If one were known locally as a person of independent will, despite a lack of property, one could still vote. There were even constitutional provisions that recognized an entire class of such people. Thus article VII in the New York Constitution of 1777 provided "that every person who now is a freeman of the city of Albany, or who was made a freeman of the city of New York . . . and shall be actually and usually resident in the said cities, respectively, shall be entitled to vote for representatives in assembly within his said place of residence."[32] This passage directly follows a part of the article that prescribes a property requirement for the rest of the state, although a low one of twenty pounds, and reflects a recognition that most city dwellers owned property other than land.

Another major reason for linking the right to vote with property was that the ownership of a certain amount of property gave one an independent will in the sense of having a base from which to resist bribery or economic sanctions when casting one's vote. Propertyless people were not viewed as inherently untrustworthy, but it was generally believed that they could not freely pursue their own wills in the face of potential economic loss.[33] For example, since elections in America did not yet use the secret ballot, tenant farmers were subject to pressure from large landowners.

Among those running for office the greater danger was from the possibility of gain. Officeholders ought to be independent in their means of livelihood so they did not need the office to make a living, could resist bribes, and could withstand the economic loss from neglecting one's livelihood that holding office almost always entailed. According to this logic, officeholders should own even more property than was required to vote. This is exactly what was required by the early state constitutions, and the higher the office, the more property that was required.

A widespread connection was also made between accumulated wealth and virtue. Calvinist-based religions saw economic success as a sign that the person was virtuous, and it was common to conclude that greater accumulated wealth was a sign of greater virtue. The purpose of elections was thus to elevate men of greater virtue to public office, to identify the elect, and the level of economic success was not an unreasonable surrogate measure of virtue.[34] The connection between these various property requirements is illustrated in Section 36 of the 1776 Pennsylvania Constitution: "As every free man to preserve his independence, (if without a sufficient estate) ought to have some profession, calling, trade, or farm, whereby he may honestly subsist, there can be no necessity for, nor use in establishing offices of profit, the usual effects of which are dependence and servility unbecoming freemen."[35]

By 1793 three more states had lowered the property requirement to vote for the lower house of the legislature to simply paying taxes.[36] A taxpayer presumably was a property owner, and the amount of property was not considered important. The payment of taxes indicated enough devotion to the common good and enough need to be represented. New Hampshire took this logic to its conclusion in 1784 and instituted a poll tax.[37] Unlike the later use of the poll tax to exclude blacks from voting, the intent of the New Hampshire poll tax was to enlarge the electorate. It included those who did not own land and therefore did not normally pay taxes.[38] Willingness to come to an election and pay a minimal tax demonstrated a sufficient psychological stake in the community, and payment of the poll tax made one a taxpayer and activated the principle of no taxation without representation. The provision had the effect of producing almost universal manhood suffrage, including the free blacks in the state.[39] In 1791 Vermont became a state,[40] and it was the first one to eliminate any property or taxpaying requirement.[41] The reason was simple. In a state where virtually all males paid taxes, the requirement that all voters be taxpayers was redundant.[42] In an America whose future lay in this direction, the elimination of property or taxpaying requirements was inevitable, but on grounds of irrelevance as well as justice.

Surprisingly, state senate elections used essentially the same electorate. Of the thirteen states, two did not have an upper house,[43] Maryland used an electoral college rather than popular elections,[44] and eight of the remaining ten states used suffrage requirements for senate elections identical to those used in house elections.[45] Thus, though those elected to upper houses were significantly wealthier than those elected to lower houses, they were beholden to the same electorate and therefore tended to be indistinguishable from the lower houses in the policies they supported.[46]

Another notable constitutional provision allowed citizens to make an affirmation rather than take an oath when voting.[47] This enabled members of certain sects like the Quakers to vote who might otherwise have been excluded by their refusal to take oaths. There were also provisions for equal districting and periodic redistricting to maintain voting equality.[48] These examples illustrate how constitutional provisions were used to include rather than exclude.

To put the matter most simply, during the 1780s state constitutions did not protect the right to vote, but rather contained an explicitly stated theory of voting, had provisions in line with that theory which encouraged a broadly defined electorate, and frequently eliminated barriers to voting. Property requirements could be ignored if doing so would further the principles upon which the theory of voting rested. In other words, state constitutions did not define who could and who could not vote. Rather, they established a set of principles that were inclusive and extremely liberal for the time, guaranteed a basic electorate based on property ownership who could not be denied the vote because they were clearly identified, and left to local officials the determination of who else met the guidelines implicit in the theory of voting. Even at its worst, then, and without much in the way of constitutional protection, state electorates strained toward a high level of democracy and defined a historic high in the percentage who voted. These same state requirements also defined who could vote in national elections after the adoption of the U.S. Constitution.

If voting in referenda defined the widest form of formal electoral participation, the requirements for holding office defined the narrowest. In 1784, to run for the lower house of the legislature, Connecticut, Delaware, Massachusetts, New Hampshire, Rhode Island, South Carolina, and Virginia required that the candidate own property ranging from a minimum freehold to fifty acres or an estate worth 100 pounds.[49] New York and Pennsylvania specified no property requirements.[50] Georgia, Maryland, New Jersey, and North Carolina specified a freehold in excess of one hundred acres or an estate in excess of 250 pounds.[51]

Property requirements for the upper house were stiffer. South Carolina required a freehold worth at least 2,000 pounds.[52] Maryland and New Jersey required at least 1,000 pounds in real and personal property.[53] Massachusetts, New Hampshire, and North Carolina also specified higher property requirements for election to the upper house.[54] Only Virginia and Delaware required the same minimum freehold as they did for candidates to the lower house.[55] Running for office therefore had the most restrictive qualifications of the three forms of formal electoral participation.

Property requirements in state constitutions, on average, excluded about half of adult free or white males from the upper house and about 25 percent of adult free or white males from the lower house. Jackson Turner Main shows that after 1776, 62 percent of the representatives in New Hampshire, New Jersey, and New York had wealth amounting to between 500 and 2,000 pounds.[56] Hardly drawn from the common man, they were not the elite either, but came from the top third in wealth. They were farmers, did not come from socially prominent families, and had not gone to college. The other 38 percent came from the social and economic elites. Massachusetts displayed a similar pattern. In Maryland, Virginia, and South Carolina only 30 percent came from the nonelites, reflecting the more socially stratified southern pattern.[57]

Today we are inclined to believe that anyone can run for office, although the truth, for practical reasons, is otherwise. In the 1780s the constitutional provisions regarding this form of participation did not protect any right of participation, but it did leave open a much wider door than was used. That is, the percentage of the population eligible to run was more than twice as broad as the cross section of men that actually ran. About 75 percent of free or white adult males were eligible to run for the lower house, but only those in the top 33 percent in wealth actually did so. Ironically, whereas today every adult is in theory eligible to run for office, the sector of the population drawn upon is, if anything, narrower in wealth. Provisions in the early state constitutions did not protect any right of participation in this regard, but then they did not seem to hurt either.

Activist Participation

Political participation includes far more than voting or running for office. Indeed, empirical research suggests that in twentieth-century America, activist participation is a highly effective means for citizens to achieve political goals,[58] and there is no reason to think that this was any different during the eighteenth century.[59]

With the Stamp Act crisis in the 1760s and the onset of the independence movement in the 1770s, activist participation reached unprecedented levels. Historians refer to the "people out of doors"[60] and note the importance of this general phenomenon during the era running from roughly 1763 to 1795.[61] There is no way to derive satisfactorily reliable statistics,[62] but I estimate that of the adult free or white male population numbering about five hundred thousand in 1776[63] at least thirty-six thousand (7 percent) had engaged in complex forms of activism such as giving public speeches, writing letters or essays, or signing letters of petition or instruction to representatives. These figures are probably conservative. Assuming that in 1776 there were at least eight thousand elective offices at the local, state, and national levels,[64] assuming that half of the elections were contested, and further assuming each candidate had two activist supporters who worked for him in the campaign but not for anyone else, then at least thirty-six thousand adult free or white males, or about 7 percent of the relevant population, engaged in activist participation.[65] The assumptions can be changed in a variety of ways, but the number of elective offices makes 7 percent a likely minimum for this level of activism.

I estimate that at least seventy-two thousand (14 percent) engaged in lesser forms of activism, including political discussions on the streets or in taverns, attending public meetings or rallies, or engaging in peaceful or violent demonstrations. My estimate is derived in part from research on crowd sizes at various political rallies or demonstrations.[66] In 1778 and 1780 the town meetings that discussed and voted on the proposed Massachusetts Constitution involved more than twelve thousand citizens.[67] Also, copies of petitions to legislators with numerous signatures on each and one from Anne Arundel County in Maryland with 885 are extant.[68] Furthermore, as many as 100,000 men served in the Continental army during the war, with more serving in the militia.[69] If one counts voluntary military service as a form of political participation,[70] estimating this level of activism to have included 14 percent of free or white adult males is probably overly conservative.

In sum, a free or white adult male population that increased from approximately five hundred thousand in 1776 to about seven hundred thousand in 1787[71] not only successfully prosecuted a war of national liberation but also wrote and adopted two national constitutions, adopted an average of three state constitutions every two years during the period, published at least thirteen hundred pamphlets and newspaper articles per year on political and constitutional subjects,[72] and every year elected men to about eight thousand political offices. It is safe to say that the "people out of doors," excluding those holding office, achieved an unprecedented level of activist participation and compare favorably with the level of activist participation in contemporary America.[73]

Rights as Preconditions for Participation

This maelstrom of political participation was undergirded by, but not dependent on, a set of constitutional provisions supporting rights that were preconditions for participation. As of 1784, six states still did not have bills of rights,[74] but nine contained in their constitutions explicit guarantees for freedom of the press,[75] four guaranteed freedom of assembly,[76] six explicitly mentioned the right of petition,[77] and two mentioned freedom of speech.[78]

Several key points need to be made concerning these constitutional provisions. First, the language used in the bills of rights was invariably admonitory rather than legalistic, as has already been mentioned. Thus these rights were not protected in the sense that this term is used in our legal system today. Second, even though the admonitions were meant to have a strong moral force, that moral force was not generally intended as protection for the rights of minorities, although it sometimes had that effect, as much as for the rights of the majority to maintain control over the government.[79] That is, government was viewed as resting on a relatively direct form of popular consent, and preserving popular control of government required maintaining the ability of popular majorities to form and act. Thus constitutional provisions protecting speech, press, assembly, and petition were designed more to facilitate majority rule than to protect minority rights as we are inclined to use them today.

Third, the presence or absence of such constitutional provisions seemed to make little difference in practice. The people of Connecticut, Rhode Island, New York, and New Jersey were about as free to exercise these rights in the absence of a state bill of rights as were those in Pennsylvania, Massachusetts, Virginia, and New Hampshire with their lovingly wrought, excruciatingly detailed bills of rights. This is tied to a fourth point—that these rights did not rest on constitutional protection but on broadly shared attitudes among both the masses and the elites.[80] This is how politics was conducted in America, and a constitutional provision protecting the right of assembly was not necessary for people to assemble. Participation in eighteenth-century America rested much more on a "civic culture" than on a legalistic set of protected rights. For this reason, bills of rights read more than anything else as "celebrations" of rights, reminders rather than protections.[81]

Fifth, given what has been said thus far, it should come as no surprise that courts did not actively protect these rights in any substantive sense. As Leonard Levy was first to point out, the levels of individual liberty to which we have become accustomed did not exist in late eighteenth-century America.[82] Rights were generally secure unless an individual found himself on the margin of society—the very type of person for whom we now assume bills of rights were written.

Sixth, the relative frequency with which a right was mentioned in the state bills of rights is itself interesting. Although nine state constitutions explicitly protect freedom of the press, this guarantee was far from absolute because, for example, the courts did not always protect newspapers from censorship.[83] Still, beginning with the Stamp

Act crisis, newspapers had demonstrated that they were an efficient and effective means for providing information and generating political organization. The American Revolution was almost coterminous with the spread of relatively fast and cheap printing presses,[84] and not only were Americans the first to use the press to organize mass political behavior, but their experiences in this regard led them to invent freedom of the press.[85] Because this freedom was linked to the organizing of political majorities, relatively little thought was given to the press as an instrument for advancing or protecting minority viewpoints.

Freedom of speech, by contrast, was an old issue in English law.[86] Because the English and American courts limited the freedom of speech by prohibiting slander,[87] among other things, there was no easy way to characterize the right of freedom of speech in a constitution. The result was not so much severe limitations on freedom of speech as a reluctance to protect with constitutional admonitions something that was ill-defined legally.[88] Freedom of speech was the most tenuous of the preconditions for participation.

One would expect the same problem to arise with respect to the press because of the prohibition on libel, but the problem was largely mitigated by the use of pseudonyms. We are inclined today to view the frequent use of pen names by eighteenth-century Americans writing political tracts as a means of avoiding the wrath of British authorities or perhaps as a clever means of identifying political positions, but in fact this practice was widely used both before the onset of the Revolution and after its successful prosecution.[89] The pseudonym was used most often to shield one from being sued for libel[90] or to separate the arguments from the known political attachments of the author. The American press was nothing if not colorful. Thoroughly scurrilous, even vicious, letters and essays were published[91] by editors claiming that the pieces had come over the transom. An editor could truthfully say that he had no basis for thinking a piece true, untrue, or even damaging. By contrast, it is in the nature of speech that one knows who did the speaking.

Effective political participation rests to a significant degree upon the availability of information. Freedom of the press is only a part of what is required. Almost every state had a legal provision, if not a constitutional one, that meetings of the legislature be open to the public and that proceedings be published.[92]

The state of Pennsylvania was especially advanced in this regard and required that "all bills of public nature" be available to the public for scrutiny, except in cases of "public necessity."[93] The Pennsylvania Constitution of 1776 required that for legislation to be passed it had to be approved by two consecutive sessions of the legislature. Between sessions the bills that had been passed once were printed for the consideration of the people. Although this provision represented an impressive commitment to direct popular consent and control, practical problems limited its effectiveness.[94]

The Pennsylvania Constitution also created the Council of Censors.[95] Contrary to what its name implies today, this council, which was elected every seven years as a kind of statewide grand jury, was empowered to review all legislation as well as all acts of government for fidelity to the constitution as well as for general effectiveness and fairness.[96] The council could not pass or veto any legislation, but it could demand any information it wished from any branch of government.[97] The Council of Censors was also empowered to ensure that taxes had been assessed fairly, to call a constitutional convention, to recommend constitutional amendments or new legislation, and to censure or impeach particular officials. It is an interesting point relevant to the thesis of this essay that the 1776 Pennsylvania Constitution, which required that amendments and proposals for new constitutions originate in the Council of Censors, was replaced in 1790 through a process that contravened, indeed ignored, this constitutional provision.[98] Constitutions did not yet have full status as a higher law and were not viewed as legalistically as they are today.

Jury Duty as Political Participation

In one sense, the connection between jury duty and political participation is obvious. A juror performs a duty of citizenship by assisting in two basic political functions—the adjudication of disputes and the administration of laws. Looked at politically rather than legalistically, jury duty is participation in both a judicial and an executive function. A key question, however, is where the law originates. Some laws are judge-made, and in constitutional matters we are used to focusing on the opinions of judges as central. Most of the laws enforced or executed, however, are made by the legislature.

A jury trial always implies at least the determination of the facts by a group of one's "peers." This notion of peers contains a fundamental paradox. On one hand, it means a group of people who have no inherent biases toward the defendant as a result of their own life experiences. On the other hand, it refers to a group of people who do share certain biases—those shared by the accused or by the parties to the controversy by reason of geographical proximity and common experiences.[99] Both are part of the traditional English notion of peers, although they lead in different directions—the former toward a jury that lacks connectedness or empathy with the trial principals, the latter toward a jury that shares a certain connectedness or empathy in certain respects. Thus the jury is expected to represent the judgment of the community, carrying out its expectations and establishing standards, which requires connectedness, while at the same time reaching decisions that are impartial and fair, which requires a significant measure of disconnectedness.

This seeming digression illuminates what was in eighteenth-century America a fundamental difficulty for those wishing to enhance popular control of government through political participation. Did the community speak through the legislature, which was elected by the majority, or did it speak through the jury, which was supposedly a random, diminutive, yet direct representation of the community? Put in terms that are familiar to almost every juror today, if a jury determines the facts and those facts require the application of a law that is considered either unfair or inappropriate to the situation, may the jury substitute its will for that of the legislature? The answer in eighteenth-century America, more often than not, was yes.[100]

To the extent that this occurred, a jury was directly involved with the legislative function as well. Ever since ancient Athens, juries had been the primary means for the lower socioeconomic orders to protect themselves from the wealthy and powerful.[101] Magna Charta's famous provision for jury trials was also so motivated.[102] With a member of the aristocracy sitting as judge and commoners sitting as jury, class accommodation replaced class will, and fair procedures replaced arbitrary judgment. By the 1770s, English common law had evolved so it severely restricted the ability of juries to substitute their will for established precedent.[103] Indeed, the whole point of precedent was to limit the discretion in both judges and juries by demonstrating that many earlier judges and juries had established a clear and fair decision-rule which, barring unusual circumstances, stood as the considered opinion of the community of all classes.

With the coming of the Revolution, the attitudes spawned by an activist "people out of doors" could not be so easily restricted. The possibility that juries would substitute their will for established precedent became very real, making jury duty an important form of political participation and the courts an important avenue for the lower orders to protect their interests. When judges or legislatures in some parts of the new nation managed either to stack juries to prevent such sympathy or to avoid jury trials altogether, the results were dramatic. For example, in western Massachusetts, the inability of farmers and other debtors to use either the courts or the legislature, in which they were sorely underrepresented, to protect themselves resulted in Shays' Rebellion.[104] The first act of the rebellion was to close down the courts.[105] Interestingly, the state legislature reacted by enacting a law that prohibited those who had taken part in the rebellion from either voting or serving on juries,[106] which clearly reflects the perception of jury duty as a form of political participation.

Likewise, the denial of jury trials under the Stamp Act helped precipitate the revolutionary war.[107] The deprivation of trial by jury was one of the enumerated reasons for revolution specified in the Declaration of Independence. Later, both the framers of the United States Constitution and the Anti-Federalists variously described the right to jury trial as "the morning star of liberty which . . . revolutionized America"[108] and a "valuable safeguard to liberty . . . [or] the very palladium of a free government."[109]

Finally, although in some parts of the country jurors were selected from the lists of voters or taxpayers, such implicit tests of property ownership were frequently ignored. Systematic records of jurors' characteristics are not available, but it appears that jury duty had the fewest restrictions of any form of political participation.

Conclusion

Even though we stand in a relationship of direct descendance with eighteenth-century America, much of our constitutional heritage is irretrievable. We are still a people given to relatively high levels of political participation, especially outside the polling booth, but we no longer have the strong civic culture that Americans had in the 1780s. For better or for worse, we now rest political participation upon a legalistic defense of the ability to participate rather than upon the insistent desire of the people to be heard in every way possible.

Shall we conclude, then, that there is nothing usable to be gleaned from the foregoing historical analysis? The answer lies not in attempting to reproduce an earlier time or even to borrow intact an idea from that era. Rather, the answer is to use whatever lessons that era holds out to us, and of lessons there are several.

First, political participation was central to American institutions during the founding era. We should not conclude that because means different than our legal protection of rights were used participation was honored in the breach. It was because participation was so clearly important to Americans of the late eighteenth century, and because Americans tended to participate without invitation or legal guarantees, that such constitutional protections were not deemed important. Though our current legalistic approach focusing on rights has moved us to a stronger position constitutionally, it is in fact a measure of the weakness of our current commitment to political participation. Holding up the mirror of eighteenth-century America, we should recognize the continuing importance of participation to the health of our political system, as well as the importance of current legal protections in the absence of a strong civic culture.

Second, we learn that during the founding era the states led the way. They invented, developed, and defined political participation, just as they did citizenship. The approach developed by the states has been eclipsed by one developed at the national level, but there is no reason why the states should not lead the way again in fostering, enhancing, and protecting political participation in its various guises.

Third, the centrality of First Amendment rights for a large set of participation categories becomes apparent. We too often look upon these rights as ends in themselves, primarily because we now tend to view them as individual rights. But the rights to freedom of press, speech, assembly, and petition were originally intended to undergird the ability of the majority to maintain popular control over government, as means to a collective end. Rejecting the individual rights concept is not required for us to use these rights once again to protect the various forms of political participation. If the states are to lead the way, they might do well to reemphasize the political implications of these rights.

Fourth, our "usable past" shows us that protecting our rights and extending them to protect the various forms of participation will require us to take a broader and more consistent view of participation. If we can define what is now an adequate test for a "stake in the community," we then need to make our laws inclusive with respect to those who pass the test. If we now view all citizens, by virtue of mere residence, as having a sufficient stake, then we need to reexamine laws that are exclusive of this test rather than inclusive.

Regarding jury service as a form of political participation may lead us to ask if using voter registration lists or tax rolls is an appropriate approach. In any case, our usable past must show us that political participation is only minimally defined by voting. Instead, political participation is defined by citizenship, an active citizenship that expresses itself not because it has the right to, but because it cannot be denied its natural tendencies.

Notes

1. Donald S. Lutz, *The Origins of American Constitutionalism* (Baton Rouge: Louisiana State University Press, 1988), 50–69.
2. See Edmund S. Morgan, *Inventing the People: The Rise of Popular Sovereignty in England and America* (New York: Norton, 1988), 55–77.
3. The participatory patterns reflect three political subcultures—the New England moralistic political subculture, the middle state individualistic political subculture, and the southern traditionalistic political subculture. See Daniel J. Elazar, *American Federalism: A View from the States*, 3d ed. (New York: Harper & Row, 1984), 114–22. The moralistic political culture, predominant in New England towns and agrarian communities, emphasized the "duty of every citizen to participate in the political affairs of his commonwealth." Ibid., 117. The individualistic agrarianism characteristic of the middle states viewed political activity as "essentially the province of professionals . . . with no place for amateurs to play an active role." Ibid., 116. Traditionalistic southern plantation culture reflected a paternalistic and hierarchical conception of the commonwealth and confined political participation to "a relatively small and self-perpetuating group drawn from an established elite." Ibid., 119. See also Sidney Verba and Norman Nie, *Participation in America* (New York: Harper & Row, 1972), 229–47 on twentieth-century America.
4. For a thorough discussion of American citizenship and its origins, see

James H. Kettner, *The Development of American Citizenship, 1608–1870* (Chapel Hill: University of North Carolina Press, 1978).

5. See Donald S. Lutz, *Popular Consent and Popular Control: Whig Political Theory in the Early State Constitutions* (Baton Rouge: Louisiana State University Press, 1980), 23.

6. In part this stemmed from the still evolving notion of equality current at the time, as well as from the attachment to traditional British views on representation, the purpose of elections, and how to define a person's stake and place in the community. See John Phillip Reid, *The Concept of Liberty in the Age of the American Revolution* (Chicago: University of Chicago Press, 1988), 109–13; and Gordon S. Wood, *The Creation of the American Republic, 1776–1787* (Chapel Hill: University of North Carolina Press, 1969), 167–72, 398–403; and Dennis J. Mahoney, "The Declaration of Independence as a Constitutional Document," in *The Framing and Ratification of the Constitution*, eds. Leonard W. Levy and Dennis J. Mahoney (New York: Macmillan, 1987), 54, 58.

7. See Lutz, *Origins of Constitutionalism*, 153. Dual citizenship provided a direct relationship between the people and the national government, which was essential to both the establishment of a republican form of national government and to the preservation of state governments.

8. There is no compelling evidence in anyone's notes on the Constitutional Convention that defining citizenship was a central concern for the Federalists. Instead, the substantial debates on citizenship at the Convention centered on how long a person must be a citizen in order to run for the Senate and the need for some uniformity in naturalization laws. Nor is there much evidence that the Federalists stayed their hand in an effort to ease ratification. Instead, there seemed to be a lack of consensus on the topic, one that was not bitterly divisive but prevented any proposal from winning. See, for example, Kettner, *Development of American Citizenship*, 224–32.

9. Since America was overwhelmingly Protestant, the elimination of religious barriers mainly involved allowing Protestants not of the dominant sect or those not from "approved" Protestant churches such as Baptists, Quakers, and Mennonites to run for office. Catholics were widely excluded from holding public office before 1776, but with the onset of the Revolution they became generally eligible. Even where Catholics were explicitly disqualified, the laws were often ignored. Jews were prohibited from running for office in many places, although a few successfully ran for town and county offices anyway, because most state constitutions continued to require that officeholders be Christian. See, e.g., Md. Const. of 1776, Declaration of Rights, art. XXXXV, reprinted in *Sources and Documents of United States Constitutions*, ed.

William F. Swindler (Dobbs Ferry, N.Y.: Oceana Publications, 1973–78), 4:372, 375; N.C. Const. of 1776, Declaration of Rights, art. XXXII, ibid., 7:402, 406. Few Jews complained, and they constituted a small percentage of the population. It is an open question whether more complaints and a larger Jewish population might not have produced the same ignoring of legal requirements which happened for the Catholics. See Robert J. Dinkin, *Voting in Revolutionary America* (Westport, Conn.: Greenwood Press, 1982), 47–48. For a different view, see Morton Borden, *Jews, Turks, and Infidels* (Chapel Hill: University of North Carolina Press, 1984).

10. Lutz, *Popular Consent*, 100–101. The essential requirement for suffrage was that the person have an "independent will." This excluded children, slaves, prisoners, women, and men who were not financially independent. See also Chilton Williamson, *American Suffrage from Property to Democracy, 1760–1860* (Princeton: Princeton University Press, 1960), 10–11.

11. See, for example, Md. Const. of 1776, Declaration of Rights, art. XV ("no *ex post facto* law ought to be made"); art. XX ("no man ought to be compelled to give evidence against himself"); art. XXII ("excessive bail ought not to be required"); art. XXXVIII ("the liberty of the press ought to be inviolably preserved"), in *Sources and Documents*, ed. Swindler, 4:373–75. See also Lutz, *Popular Consent*, 67 (for a table on the use of *shall* and *ought* in Bills of Rights).

12. A good example is Courtland Bishop, *History of Elections in the American Colonies* (1893; rpt. New York: Burt Franklin, 1968), 69–90.

13. Bernard Bailyn, *The Origins of American Politics* (New York: Knopf, 1969), 87.

14. Lee Soltow, "Wealth Inequality in the United States in 1798 and 1860," *Review of Economics and Statistics* 66 (August 1984): 444, 448.

15. Jackson Turner Main, *The Social Structure of Revolutionary America* (Princeton: Princeton University Press, 1965), 68–114, 272–77. Main suggests that multiplying a 1780 pound by fifty gives the equivalent in 1965 dollars. Ibid., 9 n. 3. Then multiply that number by three to approximate the equivalent in 1989 dollars. See Bureau of the Census, U.S. Department of Commerce, *Statistical Abstract of the United States, 1989*, 109th ed. (Washington, D.C.: Bureau of the Census, 1989), 462. Thus, 50 pounds translates into roughly $7,500, 250 pounds into $37,500, and 500 pounds into $75,000. Main notes that in 1785 a bachelor could be supported by a yearly income of 25 pounds ($3,750), ibid., 115, a family of four could live in relative comfort on 100 pounds ($15,000) a year, ibid., 118, and an average house on an average lot cost about 100 pounds. Ibid., 132. The average middle-class house-

hold (these constituted over 50 percent of the population) possessed an accumulated wealth of 300 pounds in real estate ($45,000) and 100 pounds in personal estate ($15,000). See Lutz, *Popular Consent*, 103. This estimate seems reasonable by today's standards, although it is a bit misleading because families then were more likely to have more than one adult male from more than one generation in the same household. See Philip Greven, "The Average Size of Families and Households in the Province of Massachusetts in 1764 and in the United States in 1790: An Overview," in *Household and Family in Past Time*, ed. Peter Laslett (London: Cambridge University Press, 1972), 545, 548. Another 15 to 20 percent were in the upper middle class, with estates of between 500 and 1,000 pounds ($75,000 to $150,000), and almost 10 percent were in the upper class, with estates worth more than 1,000 pounds ($150,000 plus). Lutz, *Popular Consent*, 103.

16. Dinkin, *Voting in Revolutionary America*, 39.
17. Williamson, *American Suffrage*, 22–39.
18. Dinkin, *Voting in Revolutionary America*, 107–8, 129–30.
19. Albert E. McKinley, *The Suffrage Franchise in the Thirteen English Colonies in America* (1905; rpt. New York: Burt Franklin, 1969), 217–18.
20. In Massachusetts in 1777, the property requirements for voting were waived, and every male over the age of twenty-one was enfranchised to ratify the constitution. The constitution was voted on in 1778 in a referendum election open to all adult male citizens. The new constitution failed to win approval in that election. Every male inhabitant over twenty-one was again enfranchised in 1779 to elect representatives to form a convention for the purpose of framing a new constitution which was to be ratified by two-thirds of the same electorate. This was accomplished, and the new constitution took effect in 1780. See Willi Paul Adams, *The First American Constitutions* (Chapel Hill: University of North Carolina Press, 1980), 90–93; Wood, *Creation of the American Republic*, 341.
21. Since 1430, the right to vote in England was confined to "40 shilling freeholders," whose land earned at least 40 shillings per year in rent or income. Williamson, *American Suffrage*, 5. This usually required between forty and sixty acres of land. Lutz, *Origins of Constitutionalism*, 51. In England, where land was not as plentiful as in America and was frequently tied to ancient feudal claims, this rule enfranchised 6 percent of the adult males. But see John Cannon, *Parliamentary Reform, 1640–1832* (Cambridge: Cambridge University Press, 1973), 30, 41–42. Cannon estimates that between one in six and one in ten adult males had the right to vote in England and Wales in 1754. The British electorate then declined in relation to the increase in population.

22. The Delaware Election Act of 1734 required a freehold of fifty acres or more to vote for the lower house, unless the voter possessed a personal estate worth 50 pounds. Adams, *First American Constitutions*, 301; McKinley, *Suffrage Franchise*, 270. This law was unchanged in the 1776 constitution. Del. Const. of 1776, art. 5, in *Sources and Documents*, ed. Swindler, 2:199, 200. Maryland required a fifty-acre freehold or 30 pounds worth of personal estate. Md. Const. of 1776, art. II, ibid., 4:376. South Carolina required a freehold of fifty acres, or possession of a town lot, or the payment of taxes equivalent to the tax on fifty acres. S.C. Const. of 1778, art. VIII, ibid., 8:468, 471. The Virginia Election Act of 1762 required a freehold of fifty acres unsettled, or twenty-five acres with a settled plantation, or a town lot with a house. Adams, *First American Constitutions*, 303; McKinley, *Suffrage Franchise*, 40–41. This law was unchanged in the 1776 Constitution. Va. Const. of 1776, in *Sources and Documents*, ed. Swindler, 10:51, 53. The Rhode Island Election Law of 1762, which remained in effect until 1798, required possession of real estate worth 40 pounds, or with a rental value of 40 shillings per year. Adams, *First American Constitutions*, 297; McKinley, *Suffrage Franchise*, 461. This usually required between forty and sixty acres of land. See Lutz, *Origins of Constitutionalism*, 51. The Connecticut Election Law of 1715 required possession of either a freehold with a rental value of 40 shillings per year or possession of 40 pounds in personal estate. This requirement was retained throughout the eighteenth century. Adams, *First American Constitutions*, 296; McKinley, *Suffrage Franchise*, 413–14.

23. Georgia required the possession of 10 pounds, plus the payment of taxes, unless the voter was "of the mechanic trade." Ga. Const. of 1777, art. IX, in *Sources and Documents*, ed. Swindler, 2:443, 445. Massachusetts required a minimum freehold, or an annual income of 3 pounds, or a personal estate of 60 pounds. Mass. Const. of 1780, ch. I, § 3, art. IV, ibid., 5:92, 100. New Jersey required a net worth of 50 pounds. N.J. Const. of 1776, art. IV, ibid., 6:449, 450. New York required a freehold valued at 20 pounds, or an annual rental payment of 40 shillings plus the payment of taxes, except that all free men residing in Albany and New York City were also entitled to vote. N.Y. Const. of 1777, art. VII, ibid., 7:168, 174.

24. N.C. Const. of 1776, art. VIII, ibid., 7:404; Pa. Const. of 1776, § 6, ibid., 8:277, 279. In 1770, New Hampshire lowered its 20-pound real property requirement to one of having paid taxes. McKinley, *Suffrage Franchise*, 378. In 1784, this requirement was eliminated and a poll tax was initiated. N.H. Const. of 1784, pt. II, in *Sources and Documents*, ed. Swindler, 6:344, 349–50.

25. Aside from the significant reduction in property qualifications, in Penn-

sylvania, North Carolina, and New York free black males joined the electorate on the same terms as whites. Blacks began voting in Massachusetts after 1780, and in Maryland free blacks could vote in elections for the lower house. In New Jersey the 1776 Constitution gave the vote to unmarried women, a right they held until 1807. Slaves and Indians, of course, were not included in the expanding electorate. Dinkin, *Voting in Revolutionary America*, 41–42.

26. See Adams, *First American Constitutions*, 208–9; Williamson, *American Suffrage*, 5; see also Lutz, *Popular Consent*, 101–2.

27. Pa. Const. of 1776, Declaration of Rights, art. VII, in *Sources and Documents*, ed. Swindler, 8:278.

28. See, e.g., Md. Const. of 1776, Declaration of Rights, art. V, ibid., 4:373.

29. Va. Const. of 1776, Declaration of Rights § 6, ibid., 10:49.

30. See Adams, *First American Constitutions*, 5; Wood, *Creation of the American Republic*, 65–70.

31. See William McKechnie, *Magna Carta*, 2d ed. (New York: Burt Franklin, 1914), 232.

32. N.Y. Const. of 1777, art. VII, reprinted in *Sources and Documents*, ed. Swindler, 7:174.

33. See Adams, *First American Constitutions*, 209–12; Morgan, *Inventing the People*, 156–59.

34. See Lutz, *Origins of Constitutionalism*, 75, 82, 87.

35. Pa. Const. of 1776, § 36, in *Sources and Documents*, ed. Swindler, 8:284.

36. Del. Const. of 1792, art. IV, § 1, ibid., 2:205, 210; Ga. Const. of 1789, art. IV, § 1, ibid., 2:452, 454; S.C. Const. of 1790, art. I, § 4, ibid., 8:476.

37. N.H. Const. of 1784, pt. II, ibid., 6:349, 350.

38. The 1727 New Hampshire election law required possession of real estate valued at 50 pounds. In 1770, a taxpaying qualification was substituted. McKinley, *Suffrage Franchise*, 377–78. Thus the poll tax requirement of 1784 was designed to make the right of suffrage more inclusive.

39. "Every male inhabitant" who paid the poll tax had the right to vote. N.H. Const. of 1784, pt. II, in *Sources and Documents*, ed. Swindler, 6:349.

40. Act of Feb. 18, 1791, ch. VII, 1 Stat. 191 (1791).

41. Vt. Const. of 1793, ch. II, § 21, in *Sources and Documents*, ed. Swindler, 9:507, 512 (giving the vote to all free males over age twenty-one who would take the Freeman's Oath).

42. But see Williamson, *American Suffrage*, 98, who concludes that since Vermont lacked a state tax-collecting mechanism, a taxpaying qualification would have resulted in universal disfranchisement.

43. Georgia and Pennsylvania had no upper house. Adams, *First American Constitutions*, 300, 307; James Dealey, *Growth of American State Constitutions* (1915; rpt. New York: Da Capo Press, 1972), 37–39; Lutz, *Popular Consent*, 88.

44. Md. Const. of 1776, art. XIV, in *Sources and Documents*, ed. Swindler, 4:377. All persons qualified to vote for the lower house were qualified to elect delegates to the electoral college.

45. Only New York and North Carolina had higher property requirements to vote for the upper house. New York required a freehold valued at 100 pounds. N.Y. Const. of 1777, art. X, ibid., 7:174. North Carolina required a fifty-acre freehold. N.C. Const. of 1776, art. VII, ibid., 7:404.

46. See Wood, *Creation of the American Republic*, 242–44; Lutz, *Popular Consent*, 108.

47. See, e.g., Md. Const. of 1776, Declaration of Rights, art. XXXVI, in *Sources and Documents*, ed. Swindler, 4:375; N.Y. Const. of 1777, art. VIII, ibid., 7:174.

48. See, e.g., N.Y. Const. of 1777, art. V, ibid., 7:173; Pa. Const. of 1776, §§ 17, 18, ibid., 8:281. Redistricting and reapportioning provisions reflected strong demands for voting equality. See Lutz, *Popular Consent*, 109.

49. Connecticut required a freehold with an annual rental income of 40 shillings or a personal estate of 40 pounds. Adams, *First American Constitutions*, 296. Delaware required a minimum freehold. Del. Const. of 1776, art. III, in *Sources and Documents*, ed. Swindler, 2:199. Massachusetts required a freehold valued at 100 pounds or a personal estate of 200 pounds. Mass. Const. of 1780, ch. I, § 3, art. III, ibid., 5:99. New Hampshire required an estate of 100 pounds, one-half of which must have been a freehold. N.H. Const. of 1784, pt. II, ibid., 6:350. Rhode Island required a freehold with a value of 40 pounds or an annual rental income of 40 shillings. Adams, *First American Constitutions*, 297. South Carolina required a fifty-acre freehold for residents. S.C. Const. of 1778, art. XIII, in *Sources and Documents*, ed. Swindler, 8:471. Nonresident candidates, however, were required to own a settled estate and freehold valued in excess of 3,500 pounds. Virginia required a minimum freehold. Va. Const. of 1776, ibid., 10:53.

50. See N.Y. Const. of 1777, art. IV, in *Sources and Documents*, ed. Swindler, 7:173; Pa. Const. of 1776, § 7, ibid., 8:279–80.

51. Georgia required a freehold of 250 acres of land or any estate of 250 pounds. Ga. Const. of 1777, ibid., 2:445. Maryland required possession of real or personal property with a value in excess of 500 pounds. Md. Const. of 1776, art. II, ibid., 4:376. New Jersey required 500 pounds in real and personal estate. N.J. Const. of 1776, art. III, ibid., 6:450. North

Carolina required a freehold of 100 pounds. N.C. Const. of 1776, art. VI, ibid., 7:404.

52. S.C. Const. of 1778, art. XI, ibid., 8:470. Nonresidents were required to own a freehold valued in excess of 7,000 pounds.

53. Md. Const. of 1776, art. XV, ibid., 4:378; N.J. Const. of 1776, art. III, ibid., 6:450.

54. Massachusetts required a freehold of 300 pounds or a personal estate of 600 pounds. Mass. Const. of 1780, ch. I, § 2, art. V, ibid., 5:99. New Hampshire required a freehold of 200 pounds. N.H. Const. of 1784, pt. II, ibid., 6:346. North Carolina required a freehold of at least 300 acres. N.C. Const. of 1776, art. V, ibid., 7:404.

55. Del. Const. of 1776, art. 4, ibid., 2:200; Va. Const. of 1776, ibid., 10:53. New York, which specified no requirement for the lower house, also required a simple freehold. N.Y. Const. of 1777, art. X, ibid., 7:174. Georgia and Pennsylvania did not have upper houses. Connecticut and Rhode Island did not specify property requirements for candidates for the upper house. See Lutz, *Popular Consent*, 90.

56. See Jackson T. Main, "Government by the People: The American Revolution and the Democratization of the Legislatures," *William and Mary Quarterly* 3d ser. 23 (1966): 391, 406.

57. Ibid. The per capita net wealth was highest in the South. In the thirteen colonies in 1774, the average per capita net worth, excluding slaves and indentured servants, was 74.1 pounds. U.S. Department of Commerce, Bureau of the Census, *Historical Statistics of the United States, Colonial Times to 1970* (Washington, D.C.: U.S. Bureau of the Census, 1975), 1175. This reflected an average per capita net worth of 32.7 pounds in New England, 51.3 pounds in the mid-Atlantic colonies, and 131.9 pounds in the South.

58. See Verba and Nie, *Participation in America*, 2–15, 102–21.

59. See Dinkin, *Voting in Revolutionary America*, 135–46.

60. See Wood, *Creation of the American Republic*, 319–28. The "people out of doors" refers to people "outside of the legal representative institutions." Ibid., 320–21.

61. See ibid., 320–21. See also Gary B. Nash, *The Urban Crucible: Social Change, Political Consciousness, and the Origins of the American Revolution* (Cambridge, Mass.: Harvard University Press, 1979), 310–11, 350–68.

62. The estimates in the text are based on my own research and, though admittedly crude, should suffice for purposes of this essay.

63. The estimated total population of the thirteen colonies in 1780 was 2,725,369. U.S. Department of Commerce, *Historical Statistics*, 1168. Of this figure, 566,720 were blacks, leaving a total white population of 2,158,649. Official population estimates were not categorized by age and sex.

64. See Donald Lutz, "The First American Constitutions," in *The Framing and Ratification of the Constitution*, ed. Levy and Mahoney, 69, 72.

65. This estimate conceals wide regional variations in contested elections and almost certainly exaggerates the number in the early revolutionary years, although there were heated contests at the polls in Pennsylvania and Delaware in the 1770s. See Dinkin, *Voting in Revolutionary America*, 8. The greatest number of contested elections occurred after 1780 for most states. See ibid., 9–26.

66. For examples of political demonstrations of plebeian occupational groups or urban crowds in the 1760s and 1770s, see Robert Middlekauff, *The Glorious Cause: The American Revolution, 1763–1789* (New York: Oxford University Press, 1982), 89–93, 199–206, 254–55; Nash, *Urban Crucible*, 355–64; James Hutson, "An Investigation of the Inarticulate: Philadelphia's White Oaks," *William and Mary Quarterly* 3d ser., 28 (1971): 3; Jesse Lemisech, "Jack Tar in the Streets: Merchant Seaman in the Politics of Revolutionary America," *William and Mary Quarterly* 3d ser., 25 (1968): 371, 396–407.

67. See J. R. Pole, *Political Representation in England and the Origins of the American Republic* (Berkeley: University of California Press, 1971), 182, 211, 544.

68. See Lutz, *Popular Consent*, 15–18.

69. See Howard A. Peckham, *The War for Independence: A Military History* (Chicago: University of Chicago Press, 1958), 200.

70. The evidence of this contention is strongest for the militiamen, who "best exemplified in themselves and in their behavior the ideals and purposes of the Revolution." Middlekauff, *Glorious Cause*, 504. Political motivation for service in the Continental army was probably strongest at the outset of hostilities and waned as the war dragged on. See Charles Royster, *A Revolutionary People at War: The Continental Army and American Character, 1775–1783* (Chapel Hill: University of North Carolina Press, 1979), 23–25. Of course, some members of the militia may have served for reasons other than political participation. Possible other motives may have included monetary renumeration, community pressure, and a sense of adventure. The patriot forces also included about five thousand blacks for whom emancipation was the goal of enlistment. William M. Wiecek, *The Sources of Anti Slavery Constitutionalism in America, 1760–1848* (Ithaca: Cornell University Press, 1977), 55.

71. The estimated population of white males age sixteen and older in 1790 was 813,298. U.S. Department of Commerce, *Historical Statistics*, 16. One had to be twenty-one or older to vote.

72. See Lutz, "First American Constitutions," 72.

73. See Verba and Nie, *Participation in America*, 27–31.

74. See Ga. Const. of 1777, in *Sources and Documents*, ed. Swindler, 2:443–

52; N.J. Const. of 1776, ibid., 6:449–53; N.Y. Const. of 1777, ibid., 7:168–79; S.C. Const. of 1778, ibid., 8:468–76. Connecticut and Rhode Island, which did not have full constitutions until 1818 and 1841, respectively, also lacked bills of rights.

75. Del. Const. of 1776, Declaration of Rights, ¶ 23, ibid., 2:199; Ga. Const. of 1777, art. LXI, ibid., 2:449; Md. Const. of 1776, Declaration of Rights, art. XXXVIII, ibid., 4:375; Mass. Const. of 1780, pt. I, art. XVI, ibid., 5:95; N.H. Const. of 1784, pt. I, art. XXII, ibid., 6:346; N.C. Const. of 1776, Declaration of Rights, art. XV, ibid., 7:403; Pa. Const. of 1776, Declaration of Rights, art. XII, ibid., 8:279; S.C. Const. of 1778, art. XLIII, ibid., 8:475; Va. Const. of 1776, Declaration of Rights, § 12, ibid., 10:50.

76. Mass. Const. of 1780, pt. 1, art. XIX, ibid., 5:95; N.H. Const. of 1784, pt. 1, art. XXXII, ibid., 6:347; N.C. Const. of 1776, Declaration of Rights, art. XVIII, ibid., 7:403; Pa. Const. of 1776, Declaration of Rights, art. XVI, ibid., 8:279.

77. Del. Const. of 1776, Declaration of Rights, ¶ 9, ibid., 2:198; Md. Const. of 1776, Declaration of Rights, art. XI, ibid., 4:373; Mass. Const. of 1780, pt. I, art. XIX, ibid., 5:95; N.H. Const. of 1784, pt. I, art. XXXII, ibid., 6:347; N.C. Const. of 1776, Declaration of Rights, art. XVIII, ibid., 7:403; Pa. Const. of 1776, Declaration of Rights, art. XVI, ibid., 8:279.

78. Mass. Const. of 1780, pt. 1, art. XXI, ibid., 5:95; Pa. Const. of 1776, Declaration of Rights, art. XII, ibid., 8:279.

79. See Lutz, "First American Constitutions," 79.

80. See Lutz, Popular Consent, 159–69.

81. Donald S. Lutz, "The U.S. Bill of Rights in Historical Perspective," in Contexts of the Bill of Rights, ed. Stephen L. Schechter and Richard B. Bernstein (Albany: New York State Commission on the Bicentennial of the United States Constitution, 1990). See also Leonard W. Levy, Freedom of Speech and Press in Early American History: Legacy of Suppression (New York: Harper & Row, 1960), 313.

82. Levy, Freedom of Speech and Press, 176–248. Levy modified his position in his Emergence of a Free Press (New York: Oxford University Press, 1985), ix–xii, 173–219.

83. See, e.g., Levy, Emergence of a Free Press, 206–11 (recounting arrest of Eleazar Oswald, editor of the Independent Gazeteer, for publishing articles critical of the Pennsylvania Supreme Court in 1782 and 1788).

84. Richard L. Merritt, Symbols of American Community, 1735–1775 (New Haven: Yale University Press, 1966).

85. See, e.g., Stephen Botein, "Printers and the American Revolution," in The Press and the American Revolution, ed. Bernard Bailyn and John B. Hench (Worcester, Mass.: American Antiquarian Society, 1980), 45–49, who argues that during the Revolution printers adopted a partisan

approach to publishing, one aim of which was to influence public opinion. But see Levy, *Emergence of a Free Press*, 177–98, who notes that though freedom of the press became an issue during and after the Revolution, no state rejected the common law doctrine of seditious libel.

86. Freedom of speech initially arose in English law in the sixteenth century in the context of the privilege of members of the House of Commons to debate freely without fear of prosecution in the law courts or by the Crown. See Lois G. Schwaerer, *The Declaration of Rights, 1689* (Baltimore: Johns Hopkins Press, 1981), 81–86; J. P. Kenyon, *The Stuart Constitution, 1603–1688*, 2d ed. (Cambridge: Cambridge University Press, 1986), 24–25; G. R. Elton, *The Tudor Constitution*, 2d ed. (Cambridge: Cambridge University Press, 1982), 265–74. Freedom of speech as a civil right emerged later, probably not before the last quarter of the eighteenth century. See Levy, *Emergence of a Free Press*, 3–5, 14–15.

87. According to William Blackstone, slander was the malicious uttering of words which "upon the face of them, import such defamation as will of course be injurious" to the reputation of another person. *Commentaries on the Laws of England, a Facsimile of the First Edition of 1765–69*, vol. 3, *Of Private Wrongs* (Chicago: University of Chicago Press, 1979), *124. The treatment of slander in colonial jurisdictions in the seventeenth century owed much to prosecutions before English courts. See George L. Haskins, *Law and Authority in Early Massachusetts* (New York: Macmillan, 1960), 169, 183–84.

88. Nine state constitutions guaranteed freedom of the press in 1784, but only two guaranteed freedom of speech.

89. See Bernard Bailyn, *The Ideological Origins of the American Revolution* (Cambridge, Mass.: Harvard University Press, 1967), 11.

90. The use of a pseudonym as an attempt to shield a writer from libel may be inferred, for example, from the 1770 prosecution of Alexander McDougal, who had published a broadside, which condemned the New York Assembly, under the name "Son of Liberty." See Levy, *Emergence of a Free Press*, 76. McDougal was prosecuted, unsuccessfully, only after his identity was revealed by a journeyman printer responding to a sizable reward offer. Ibid., 76–80. Though the threat of prosecution remained, it may have been diminished by the failure of most prosecutions for seditious libel. Ibid., 63, 207–10.

91. See Janice Potter and Robert M. Calhoun, "The Character and Coherence of the Loyalist Press," in *The Press and the American Revolution*, ed. Bailyn and Hench, 239–40, 246–50; Robert M. Weir, "The Role of the Newspaper in the Southern Colonies on the Eve of the Revolution: An Interpretation," ibid., 123–25, 132.

92. See, e.g., Del. Const. of 1792, art. 2, §§ 8, 9, in *Sources and Documents*,

ed. Swindler, 2:207; N.Y. Const. of 1777, § XV, ibid., 7:175; Pa. Const. of 1776, §§ 13, 14, ibid., 8:281.

93. Pa. Const. of 1776, § 15, ibid., 8:281.

94. See Adams, *First American Constitutions,* 248 (noting the failure to define either "bills of public nature" or "sudden necessity" and the practical difficulty of gathering the views of the public); John Paul Selsam, *The Pennsylvania Constitution of 1776* (New York: Octagon Books, 1971), 185, quoting Thomas Paine's observation that the provision did not have the effect intended because " 'no given time was fixed for that consideration, nor any means for collecting its effects, nor were there any public newspapers in the state but what were printed in Philadelphia.' "

95. Pa. Const. of 1776, § 47, in *Sources and Documents,* ed. Swindler, 8:285.

96. Ibid. See Selsam, *Pennsylvania Constitution,* 199–201.

97. Pa. Const. of 1776, § 47, in *Sources and Documents,* ed. Swindler, 8:285.

98. In 1790, the Pennsylvania legislature bypassed the Council of Censors and authorized a constitutional convention, in direct contravention to the 1776 Constitution, which was still in effect. The same convention adopted the new constitution in 1790, without ratification by the voters of the state. See Lutz, *Popular Consent,* 139–40; Jackson T. Main, *Political Parties Before the Constitution* (Chapel Hill: University of North Carolina Press, 1973), 180–81. The Pennsylvania Constitution of 1790 provided "that all power is inherent in the people, and all free governments are founded on their authority and instituted for their peace, safety, and happiness. For the advancement of those ends, they have at all times an unalienable and indefeasible right to alter, reform, or abolish their government, in such manner as they may think proper." Pa. Const. of 1790, art. IX, § 2, in *Sources and Documents,* ed. Swindler, 8:286, 292.

99. See John Guinther, *The Jury in America* (New York: Facts on File Publications, 1988), 16–18, 58, concluding that most unbiased verdicts are reached when the jury is most heterogeneous.

100. See, e.g., Paul Finkelman, "The Zenger Case: Prototype of a Political Trial," in *American Political Trials,* ed. Michal R. Belknap (Westport, Conn.: Greenwood Press, 1981), 21–36. The well-known trial of John Peter Zenger in 1735 is an example of the role a jury can play in determining the law in a particular case. In 1776, ten states allowed juries to decide law. Lloyd E. Moore, *The Jury: Tool of Kings, Palladium of Liberty* (Cincinnati: W. H. Anderson, 1973), 112. Some states even guaranteed this in their constitutions. See, e.g., Ga. Const. of 1777, art. XLI, in *Sources and Documents,* ed. Swindler, 2:448 ("jury shall be judges of law as well as of fact"). The ability of a jury "when rendering a verdict [to] ignore a law it considers stupid or counterproductive" continues to have a "liberating effect" on the law today. See Guinther, *Jury in America,* 44.

101. Guinther, *Jury in America*, 2; Moore, *The Jury*, 1–9.
102. The Magna Charta provided: "No freeman shall be taken or [and] im-prisoned or disseised or exiled or in any way destroyed, nor will we go upon him nor send upon him, except by the lawful judgment of his peers or [and] by the law of the land." Magna Charta, ch. 39, in McKechnie, *Magna Carta*, 375. This chapter has been widely interpreted to guarantee trial by jury. See Moore, *The Jury*, 49. Blackstone wrote: "The trial by jury, or the country, *per patriam*, is also that trial by peers of every Englishman, which, as the grand bulwark of his liberties, is secured to him by the great charter" (referring to the Magna Charta). Blackstone, *Commentaries*, 4:*342–43. And in *Thompson v. Utah*, 170 U.S. 343 (1898), the Supreme Court stated: "When Magna Charta declared that no freeman should be deprived of life, etc., 'but by the judgment of his peers or by the law of the land,' it referred to a trial by twelve jurors." Ibid., 349. But see McKechnie, *Magna Carta*, 134 (concluding that the "judgment of his peers" could not have been meant to guaran-tee jury trials because modern jury trials were unknown in 1215).
103. See Arthur Reed Hogue, *Origins of the Common Law* (Bloomington: Indiana University Press, 1966), 188–89; Moore, *The Jury*, 81–82.
104. David P. Szatmary, *Shays' Rebellion: The Making of an Agrarian Insurrec-tion* (Amherst: University of Massachusetts Press, 1980), 34–36. Shays' Rebellion can also be seen as a reaction by Massachusetts farmers to their heavy tax burden as compared with that of city dwellers. Ibid., 42.
105. Ibid., 67–69.
106. Ibid., 106. The Disqualification Act of 1787 prohibited those who par-ticipated in or supported the rebellion from serving on juries for three years. The rebels were also prohibited from holding public office, teach-ing, and operating an inn or tavern.
107. See Guinther, *Jury in America*, 30–31.
108. Ibid., 30 (quoting Gouverneur Morris).
109. Alexander Hamilton, *Federalist* No. 83, in Alexander Hamilton, James Madison, and John Jay, *The Federalist*, ed. Jacob E. Cooke (Middletown, Conn.: Wesleyan University Press, 1961), 582.

The Rise and Decline of
"Democratic-Republicanism"
Political Rights in New York and
the Several States, 1800–1915

James A. Henretta

On August 7, 1846, George Crooker, a Whig delegate to the New York constitutional convention, sought to insert the first clauses of the Declaration of Independence into the state's basic charter. Alvah Worden, a moderate Jacksonian Democrat, immediately protested that "all men are created equal . . . endowed with certain unalienable rights," was a useless "abstraction"; "it amounted to recognition of a principle that no man dare to deny, but it was of no practical use." A more radical Jacksonian, Michael Hoffman, thought the phrase "meant something" but gave it a narrow legal definition; "it was inserted here to assert in strong and plain terms the principle that the non-voting classes in the State should hold their rights under the same laws as those who are voters." Levi Chatfield, the Democratic president of the convention, detected a more far-reaching and insidious design. To highlight this danger, he won consent to add *"without regard to color"* to Crooker's motion. Faced with the prospect of explicitly enhancing the constitutional rights of New York's black population, the convention voted 42 to 19 to delete the entire section.[1]

Despite the delegates' refusal to incorporate the natural rights philosophy of the Declaration, the New York Constitution of 1846 was a democratic document. Indeed, the charter embodied many constitutional principles associated with a new democratic-republican political regime. The architects of this system were not intellectuals or political theorists but practicing politicians immersed in the rough-and-tumble world of legislative combat. Consequently, the Constitution of 1846 lacked intellectual elegance and theoretical coherence. It consisted rather of a complex amalgam of traditional principles, contemporary doctrines, and emergent legal movements. Therein lies its value. To understand the rise of democratic-republicanism, and its subsequent decline, is to comprehend the logic of American state constitutional development in the nineteenth century.

This essay probes that logic in three ways. First, the text quotes extensively from the debates and proceedings of state constitutional conventions. The delegates speak for themselves, revealing their cultural assumptions and political goals. Equally important, this approach demonstrates that constitutional provisions are as much the product of specific historical circumstances as of coherent ideological principles.

Second, and conversely, the essay begins the task of defining a constitutional "tradition" of political rights in New York and the several states. It does so by focusing on continuities. Four continuing constitutional debates—over suffrage, apportionment, legislative power, and judicial authority—indicate the ways in which different politicians and interest groups used inherited language, concepts, and principles to secure their goals.

Finally, this analysis reveals four broad periods of American state constitutional development. The politicians of the revolutionary era devised an aristocratic-republican constitutional order that endured for a generation. Then, between 1820 and 1860, advocates of a more democratic political order rewrote many state constitutions. This egalitarian movement reached its apogee during Radical Reconstruction, when the defeated Confederate states reentered the Union with constitutions mandating political rights for black as well as white males. The triumph of democracy was fragile and fleeting. Beginning in the 1870s, southern Redeemers and northern Mugwumps contested the primacy of universal suffrage and popular rule. They proposed liberal-republican regimes ruled by "the best men." By World War I, upper-class reformers, aided and abetted both by entrenched party bosses and Progressive reformers, had curtailed the powers of state legislatures. Since the 1920s, state constitutions have become more managerial-republican in character. States now have stronger governors and more substantial bureaucracies than ever before and, to some extent, a renewed commitment to democratic values.[2] These broad transformations in the constitutional order have determined the character of the political rights enjoyed by the people of New York and the other states.

Black Suffrage

Despite the convention's repudiation of equality for blacks, the Constitution of 1846 was a rights-conscious document. Article I specified the constitutional rights of each "member of this State." The original New York Constitution of 1777 lacked such a bill of rights, and that of 1821 presented a less extensive list of rights only in Article VII. Accepting—but not extending—this rights consciousness, the constitutional conventions of 1894 and 1915 simply reiterated Article I of the charter of 1846.[3]

The definition of political rights stemmed as much from cultural practice as from abstract principles. The delegates to the convention of 1846 explicitly rejected a universalist theory of rights. "Six ladies of Jefferson county" asked the delegates to extend the franchise to women because the "end of civil government is to protect all in the exercise of all their natural rights." "The elective suffrage was a privilege, a franchise, a civil right, and not a natural right," replied John Kennedy, chair of the committee on the elective franchise, "civilized society throughout the world had, with a few excepted cases . . . limited political privileges, to mature age and the male sex." Other delegates asserted reigning cultural values in more aggressive terms. "We represent the free white citizens of this State over 21 years of age, and those negroes who have $250 worth of real estate," thundered Charles O'Conor, a New York City Democrat, "we did not represent the other classes at all. We constituted the political body, and with us resided the whole power of government. We control those classes, not by their choice, not by representation, but by reason of our mental and physical superiority. . . . It might be injustice that the men . . . should thus grasp and control all the powers of government, but they have done it." As another delegate put it, the exclusion of females and children was "natural," given their inability to undertake a "full and continuous exercise" of the sovereign power.[4]

The status of free adult black males was more problematic. The Constitution of 1777 gave the vote to all male freeholders, allowing free blacks, including those who became free under the Emancipation Act of 1799, a political voice. Despite the small number of black voters, many delegates to the constitutional convention of 1821 demanded the end to black suffrage. In reply, Chancellor James Kent and other Federalists argued that the "privileges and immunities" clause of the United States Constitution guaranteed equal suffrage for blacks. Other delegates contested this interpretation. They correctly pointed out that all migrants to New York had to conform to its franchise laws, regardless of their political privileges in their states of origin. In the end, the delegates rejected, by the narrow margin of 63 to 59, a provision restricting suffrage to whites. Instead, they used traditional constitutional principles to resolve the issue. Using the logic of classical republicanism that linked the franchise with a "stake in society," the convention limited voting privileges to blacks with $250 of property. Then, accepting the Whig principle of "no taxation without representation," it excused other blacks from paying taxes.[5]

The emergence of democratic individualism undermined the ideological foundations of this compromise. By the 1840s many Americans believed that society consisted of equal and autonomous individuals; voting was a person's inherent right, not a privilege of property holders. The committee on the franchise was "nearly unanimously adverse to the property qualification for an elector," Kennedy reported to the convention of 1846, so if the black man were to vote, it "should not depend on his possessions, but on his manhood." The new definition of political citizenship would expand black suffrage, an outcome that Democratic majority refused to accept. He and his constituents, declared John Hunt of New York County, "contend for self-government": "We want no masters, and least of all no negro masters, to reign over us. . . . Negroes were aliens—aliens, not by mere accident of foreign birth . . . but by the broad distinction of race—a distinction that neither education, nor intercourse, nor time could remove." Accepting the principles of *Herrenvolk* (our people) democracy, the committee recommended giving the vote only to "every white male citizen of the age of twenty-one years."[6]

This proposal was not unique. Since 1818 New Jersey, Pennsylvania, Connecticut, North Carolina, and Tennessee had excluded free blacks from the polls. Moreover, the Pennsylvania Supreme Court had upheld the verdict of the people. In *Hobbs* v. *Fogg* (1837), the court suggested that blacks "might be unsafe depositories of public power." Blacks might be citizens, the court reiterated in 1853, but they could not aspire to "the exercise of the elective franchise, or to the right to become our legislators, judges, and governors."[7]

The outcome in the New York convention was less clear-cut. Because of their racist values, the Democratic majority overwhelmingly rejected black manhood suffrage (63 to 32). But because of their ideology of "equal rights and equal privileges," some Democrats hesitated to disfranchise all blacks. These delegates voted with the Whigs to maintain the existing property qualification of $250 for black voters. In a final bipartisan gesture to the Whigs, the Democratic majority allowed a separate referendum on the issue of black suffrage. By the convincing margin of 224,336 to 85,406, the New York electorate rejected equal suffrage in favor of the traditional property qualification.[8]

State constitutional protection for black political rights fared little better in the coming decades. When the Supreme Court ruled in the *Dred Scott* decision of 1857 that blacks had never been citizens of the United States, the *New York Tribune* hoped for redress on the state level. The Republican-dominated New York legislature quickly proposed an equal suffrage amendment which, the *Tribune* proclaimed, would "carry back the State Constitutions to those principles of equal rights upon which they were originally established." The *Tribune*'s understanding of state constitutional history was sound, but its confidence in the electorate was not. New York's voters gave Abraham Lincoln 53.7 percent of their ballots in 1860 but soundly defeated the equal suffrage amendment by a margin of 63.7 percent to 36.3 percent.

Similar referenda on black suffrage went down to defeat in 1865 and 1866 in Connecticut, Wisconsin, and Minnesota, the District of Columbia, and the Colorado and Nebraska territories. Subsequent extensions of black political rights in Wisconsin, Minnesota, and Iowa failed to sway the New York electorate. In a new referendum in 1869, voters refused for the third time to endorse black manhood suffrage, although by the narrower margin of 53.1 to 46.9 percent. New York ratified the Fifteenth Amendment to the United States Constitution only because Republicans controlled both houses of the legislature.

As Phyllis Field has argued, "it was the logic of national events" rather than state constitutional change that brought black suffrage to New York and many other states.[9] The democratic reconstruction of the Union during Radical Reconstruction stemmed primarily from wartime hatred and the postwar vulnerability of the Republican party, not from the ideological conviction of a majority of northern voters. The democratic-republican constitutional tradition did not encompass political rights for women or blacks. It assumed, and wrote into fundamental law, the political primacy of white males.

White Suffrage: From Property to Autonomy

A different logic governed the expansion of white suffrage. The New York Constitution of 1777, like many late eighteenth-century charters, contained aristocratic-republican restrictions that imposed property qualifications for voting and officeholding. To vote in assembly elections, adult males needed a twenty-pound freehold (or had to rent and pay taxes on a forty-shilling leasehold). More onerous still, they had to possess a one-hundred-pound freehold to vote for the senate and governor, offices to which only freeholders could aspire. As Chancellor Kent explained to the convention of 1821, these elitist provisions ensured a "well balanced government" in which "the landed interest [would] . . . retain the exclusive possession of a branch of the legislature . . . [so] that their freeholds cannot be taxed without their consent. . . . Society is an association for the protection of property as well as of life," Kent argued, "and the individual who contributes only one cent to the common stock, ought not to have the same power and influence . . . as he who contributes his thousands." "If life and liberty are common to all, but the possession of property is not," his fellow aristocratic-republican Abraham Van Vechten maintained, "the owners of property have rights which . . . are separate and exclusive." "[That] is the true meaning of equal rights in relation to government."[10]

By 1821, democratic ideologues vigorously attacked this property-conscious definition of political rights within a balanced (or "mixed") government. "Our community is an association of persons, of human beings," David Buel, Jr., retorted, "not a partnership founded on property." "The true question," Martin Van Buren suggested in a more pragmatic vein, was whether seventy-five thousand freeholders with estates of less than $250 "should be wholly excluded from representation in one branch of the legislature . . . which had equal power to originate all bills, and a complete negative upon the passage of all laws." "In England, they have three estates," added Reuben Sanford, chair of the committee on the elective franchise. "Here there is but one estate—the people." His committee proposed to "abolish all existing distinctions and make the right to vote uniform." "Those who bear the burthens of the state" through the payment of taxes, militia service, or even humble labor service repairing the roads, Sanford argued, "should choose those that rule it."[11]

The debate was a familiar one. Like John Adams, Kent envisioned a society of distinct estates, each represented separately in the polity. Like other Federalists, he celebrated personal economic independence and relegated the propertyless to a dependent political status. He welcomed the fifty-acre freehold requirement for voting in the Northwest Ordinance of 1787 and the results of the restricted suffrage prescribed by the New York Constitution of 1777. In 1821, only 78 percent of adult males could vote for assemblymen in New York and only a meager 39 percent for governor and the senate.

Buel and Sanford began from somewhat different premises. Like Kent and the Federalists, they pictured political society as a single community of (more or less) equal, independent, and publicly responsible households. As heirs of the democratic Anti-Federalists of 1787–88, however, they placed less emphasis on property ownership and more on contribution to the community. As Jeffersonian Republicans, they applauded the congressional legislation of 1811 ending freehold voting in the territories and imposing a less demanding taxpaying test. Their somewhat similar proposal would allow 90 percent of New York's white adult males to vote in all statewide elections.[12]

Buel and Sanford were eighteenth-century republicans, not nineteenth-century liberal-democratic individualists. They determined political rights not on the basis of personhood but of public service or "virtue." As Judge Jonas Platt put it, "The electors were public functionaries, who had certain duties to perform for the benefit of the whole community." Even Martin Van Buren, calculating party politician and incipient Jacksonian Democrat, appreciated the appeal of personal independence and corporate virtue to the delegates. He listened carefully as Judge Ambrose Spencer warned that enfranchising poor militiamen and road workers would be an "aristocratic" act, giving their votes "to those who employ, clothe, and feed them." "The people were not prepared for universal suffrage," Van Buren declared, supporting a motion to strike out highway service as a qualification for voting. The final compromise, enfranchising highway workers with three years' residence, moved toward the liberal-democratic principle of equal rights by broadening the classical republican definition of personal independence and public virtue to include the propertyless.[13]

Republican assumptions surfaced again in state legislative provisions for local elections. The Alabama Constitution of 1819 mandated universal white male suffrage, but when the Alabama legislature incorporated the town of Dadeville in 1837, it restricted the vote in local elections to householders and freeholders. Similar qualifications bound the voters of Chicago (1837), Louisville (1832), Ashport and Memphis, Tennessee (1839, 1853), and many other cities. Albert Gallatin used the principle of "no representation without taxation" to defend this restriction of the franchise to propertied householders. Writing to Lafayette in 1833, the aging Jeffersonian Republican argued that municipal officials had no authority over persons but extensive powers over property; hence they should be selected by property holders, not by the populace at large.[14]

Beginning in the 1830s advocates of universal white male suffrage attacked taxpaying qualifications with two new sets of arguments. Each reflected newly emergent political and economic forces. In some southern states, reformers used the racist logic of *Herrenvolk* democracy to undermine traditional constitutional restraints. Giving the vote to every white man, a delegate to the Louisiana constitutional convention of 1845 declared, would make "the broad distinction between him and the slave [and] . . . raise a wall of fire . . . around our state and its institutions, against the diabolical machinations of abolitionism." Elsewhere, reformers focused attention on the constitutional implications of the increasingly dominant commercial economy. Marcus Morton, the Jacksonian Democratic governor of Massachusetts, questioned the traditional link between the franchise and tax payments on real estate. He argued that all males should have voting rights because they paid indirect taxes on dutiable items. Previously, some delegates to the Virginia constitutional convention of 1829–30 challenged the tie between freehold status and political independence. They pointed out that substantial property owners as well as poor tenants were often deeply in debt, and to exclude those "indebted to their neighbours, their merchants, to the Banks, &c., by account, by bond, and by trust deed" would cut the voting rolls by "one half or three fourths." The real test of independence was not formal freehold status but how a man "manage[d] . . . his private affairs."[15]

The rapid demise of property and tax qualifications resulted not only from changed circumstances and new arguments but also from escalating political competition. As early as 1826, Governor De Witt Clinton vied for popular favor with the future Jacksonian Democrat Martin Van Buren. Clinton won approval for a constitutional amendment removing the tax or service requirement for voting and basing the franchise solely on age, citizenship, and residence. In 1845, Democrats responded by sponsoring a constitutional amendment that removed the freehold qualification for membership in the senate. In the same year, the Connecticut and Louisiana legislatures eliminated taxpaying tests for local voting, and Ohio and Virginia followed suit in 1851.[16]

These changes signaled a shift from a democratic-republican to a liberal-individualist definition of voting rights. The essence of the new conception was not personhood per se but legal autonomy. It embraced autonomous male wage laborers but excluded impoverished men as well as legally dependent women and children. A committee of the Delaware constitutional convention of 1831 stated the new principle succinctly: "Paupers who live on the public funds, and who were under the direction of others, who might control their wills, ought not to be permitted to vote." As Robert Steinfeld has argued, the traditional "republican principle that only the self-governing should exercise political authority" was recast with "the liberal idea that the self-governing were those who owned and disposed of themselves."[17] Democratic-Republicans had replaced the propertied franchise of 1800 with a broader taxpaying qualification, only to have their constitutional assumptions challenged by the proponents and principles of liberal-republican individualism.

Representation: Government Closer to the People

Democratic-republicanism represented a creative, if tense, synthesis of traditional and emergent constitutional principles. It also represented—and aroused—strong political passions. "Universal suffrage once granted, is granted forever, and never can be recalled . . . but by the strength of the bayonet," Chancellor Kent warned the convention of 1821. Kent's fears were exaggerated. The foes of a broad franchise quickly devised legal rules to diminish its democratic implications. The New York Constitution of 1846 was a case in point. Article II, Section 1, proclaimed the triumph of white manhood suffrage. It bestowed the vote on every white adult male who had been "a citizen for ten days, and an inhabitant of this State for one year." Article II, section 4, reflected conservative fears and partisan politics. It sternly directed the legislature to make laws "for ascertaining, by proper proofs," those citizens eligible to vote. Masses of immigrant Irish and Germans in New York City might rightfully claim the franchise (in order to vote the Democratic ticket), but Whigs would demand rigorous registration laws to deter them from voting.[18]

Indeed, self-interested Whig and Republican demands for the "reform" of urban voting through registration became a staple of mid-nineteenth-century politics. To cut the size of the Democratic vote in Philadelphia, Pennsylvania Whigs enacted a Registry Act in 1836. Four years later, a Whig legislature mandated registration for voters in New York City while exempting those in the rest of the state; Democrats repealed this partisan measure in 1842. New York Republicans enacted a statewide registration act in 1859; a decade later, a Democratic legislative majority selfishly exempted New York City from its provisions. Despite these partisan reversals and the voiding of registration requirements by various state supreme courts, election laws multiplied. In 1880, they filled 150 pages of the statute books in New York alone.[19] Article II, section 4, of the Constitution of 1846 had not generated neutral rules for the democratic political game but served as an incentive for highly partisan legislation.

The contest over political democracy prompted fierce debates over legislative apportionment as well. In fact, the manipulation of voting districts gradually became the major device for denying fair representation. As a southern Democrat observed in 1881 following a massive Republican gerrymander of Pennsylvania's congressional districts, "You can deny a free ballot just as effectively by so districting a country as to mass all the voters of one political opinion in certain districts as you can by a suffrage qualification; and that is the favorite mode now."[20]

In New York, the convention of 1821 confronted the issue of equal representation in a debate over the appropriate electoral power of the growing metropolis on the Hudson. The discussion mixed high political philosophy with low partisan politics. "We ask no exclusive privileges," a city delegate told his colleagues, but only "that the county shall be represented in proportion to its population." Rural delegates retorted that the convention had already withheld the vote from various "unsound" portions of the state's population, such as aliens and untaxed blacks, many of whom lived in the city or county of New York. "Why, then, find fault with having them excluded in fixing the ratio of representation?" These delegates advocated apportionment according to the numbers of "electors," the procedure followed in the Constitution of 1777. The final provision used the language of *democratic individualism:* electoral districts were to contain "an equal number of inhabitants." Yet the result was *republican,* for the constitution defined inhabitants as male electors and their households of wives and children, thus excluding "aliens, paupers, and persons of color not taxed." [21]

The Constitution of 1846 used a similar republican (household) formula for apportionment, thereby reducing by one-third the potential political representation of New York City. As in 1821, city delegates demanded apportionment on the basis of total population. Aliens, paupers, and untaxed blacks "should be treated exactly the same as women and children for purposes of representation," Charles O'Conor argued during the convention, "they were equally members of society—equally burdens upon the electors." "It was the qualified electors of the State who constituted the government," Arphaxed Loomis replied, astutely turning O'Conor's own republican arguments (in the debate over women's suffrage) against him. As Loomis put it, using egalitarian rhetoric to achieve a less than fully democratic result, it was "those electors [who] should have an equal voice in the government." "No matter whether the [city] man had a greater burthen of taxation or not," he concluded, "for if that was the ground, it would be the representation of property. That idea was exploded in our government." [22]

Both Loomis and O'Conor were Jacksonian Democrats, yet their position on representation began from republican and patriarchal premises. They assumed male primacy within the family and the polity; women and children had a constitutional role only as legal dependents, not as autonomous individuals. "He was not against the provision that the basis of representation should include women and children," another Democrat declared, for the male household heads were "their natural protectors and guardians."[23]

The policy differences between O'Conor and Loomis stemmed from a geographic and social cleavage within the Democratic party. An Irish Catholic, O'Conor wished to enhance the power of the city populated by so many immigrants. He refused, when calculating representation, to distinguish between the wives and children of electors on one hand and other second-class citizens such as paupers, aliens, and untaxed blacks on the other. Conversely, Loomis insisted on precisely this distinction for apportionment purposes. As a delegate from the upstate county of Herkimer, he sought to preserve the political power of rural and small-town Democrats. Moreover, Loomis and many other noncity delegates instinctively thought of families as the basic social—and therefore political—unit. Within the Jacksonian fold, Loomis's constitutional position on representation stood for the republican past—a society of family farms and family businesses.

These geographical and ideological divisions suffused the entire debate on legislative apportionment. Many delegates accepted Tunis Bergen's general proposition that "in forming districts . . . justice would require them to be composed of equal constituencies." Yet only a few members applauded Alvah Worden's suggestion to disregard existing county lines, to "divide the State into 144 Assembly districts, by towns," and to have "every three assembly districts constitute a single senate district."[24] This scheme had the potential to give each citizen equal representation in both houses of the legislature, but this democratic-individualist outcome would diminish the traditional importance of county lines and governments. In the end, the convention took the county as the basic unit of representation. The delegates carefully grouped contiguous counties together to create 32 almost equally populous single-member senate districts. Then they created an assembly of 132 seats, reserving at least one seat to each of New York's 59 counties with the balance allocated on the basis of the qualified population.[25]

The liberal-democratic maxim of "one-man, one vote" received a high priority in this system of representation. For reasons of politics and principle, the delegates accorded almost equal respect to local corporate institutions, a hallmark of the Anti-Federalist republican tradition. Popular sentiment (and some nineteenth-century state jurists as well) envisioned states as "unions" of their constituent counties or towns. "He felt upon the subject of counties—as did the states right party upon the subject of States," Daniel Campbell of Schenectady County told the convention, "the counties were a sort of local government by themselves." [26] The Constitution of 1846 wrote this localist democratic-republican perspective into fundamental law. The delegates withdrew the authority to create intracounty assembly (and senate) districts from the state legislature and gave it to local boards of supervisors. This decision dismayed some Democratic politicians. Since the majority of the boards "are now Whig," Levi Chatfield ruefully remarked while unsuccessfully opposing this provision, it amounted to a "surrender of power" by his numerically dominant Democratic colleagues. In fact, the clause won approval because it served the political interests of New York City Democrats and of rural Whigs. Both groups feared a state legislature dominated by the opposition party; therefore, they opted for county control of local apportionment decisions. On other issues of representation, party interests remained paramount. Democrats stood solidly together to limit the number of senators to 32, while Whigs clamored for 48 members. Under the Democratic plan, one Whig complained, "more than one-third of the Senate would be represented by counties embracing cities, so that 11 senators would be elected by them." [27]

Even as partisanship determined many specific decisions, the spirit of the times imparted a democratic tinge to many midcentury constitutional debates. A power-minded party politician, Chatfield ridiculed the widely felt imperative to bring "every thing as near to the people as possible," but neither he nor established leaders in other states could completely stem its advance. When the Georgia legislature refused repeatedly to call a convention to reapportion the eastern-dominated legislature, discontented up-country politicians called extralegal conventions, first in 1833 and again in 1839. "The people have an undoubted right, in their sovereign capacity, to alter or change their form of government," proclaimed one extralegal Georgia agitator, "whenever in their opinion it becomes too obnoxious or oppressive to be borne." In Maryland, Democrats organized a mock "reform convention" in 1836 and then used strong-arm tactics to secure the direct election of the state senate. In Rhode Island, Thomas W. Dorr led the most famous extralegal movement for a more equitable constitutional system.[28]

Popular enthusiasm and partisan maneuvering threatened political revolution. In response, established politicians grudgingly introduced democratic principles into state constitutions dominated by entrenched eastern interests or aristocratic-republican elites. In New York and other states with a tradition of constitutional reform, this democratic idealism resulted in significant change. When Chatfield remarked that it was not the convention's "province to correct the acts of political partizans," another delegate replied sharply that it was indeed "the legitimate business of this body in preparing a Constitution to guard against the evils of such action." "In some sense we are all political partizans," Bishop Perkins observed during a debate over court reform, "but I trust there are none of us who do not desire an impartial and enlightened administration of justice."[29]

Perkins captured an important aspect of the convention's work. On many issues, there was either no obvious partisan position or the choices were sufficiently complex as to thwart an easy determination of political self-interest. The delegates could seek "impartial" solutions, experiment with traditional or innovative constitutional devices, and, most important, respond to the democratic fervor of the time. The New York Constitution of 1846 established a more equitable system of representation and apportionment. Moreover, it brought legislators "near to the people" by creating smaller single-member senate districts and by mandating annual assembly and biannual senate elections. Whatever their flaws or partisan contents, the democratic-republican constitutions of the 1840s and 1850s were hopeful documents that affirmed the wisdom and the power of the people.

Malapportionment: The Attack on Democratic-Republicanism

Products of a unique historical moment, the midcentury state constitutions institutionalized a democratic and participatory political culture. Politics became a religion and the ballot box a shrine. "The electorate voted with passion as well as in numbers," the (unfranchised) wife of United States Supreme Court Justice Morrison Waite noted with envy in 1876, "I should want to vote all day." Over 70 percent of eligible male Americans voted in presidential elections between 1840 and 1900; in northern states such as New York, 84 percent voted in 1900.[30]

Political parties played a crucial role in bringing out the vote. For more than a generation, the *Philadelphia Inquirer* remarked in 1884, party loyalties "were as strictly drawn as were the lines of religious sects, a man . . . did not merely entertain opinions, he had convictions." More often than not, the voter's convictions stemmed from the party platform, not personal reflection. The triumph of organizational politics ruthlessly subordinated the independent-minded voter to party discipline. "We are told the Republican Party is a machine," New York party boss Roscoe Conkling declared in 1876, "Yes . . . a political party is a machine. Every organization which binds men together for a common cause is a machine." Corrupt bargains with business corporations paid part of the cost of keeping the machine running, as did patronage from federal and state government offices. It had come to pass, lamented Henry Adams, that American governments "plundered the people in order to support party organizations."[31]

Upper-class spokesmen assailed "pure democracy" as a prime cause of political corruption and demanded its end. "Thirty or forty years ago it was considered the rankest heresy to doubt that a government based on universal suffrage was the wisest and best that could be devised," Jonathan Baxter Harrison observed in 1879. "Such is not now the case." As if to prove the point, that year's Lynde Debate at Princeton University addressed the topic "Resolved that it would be advantageous to the United States to abolish universal suffrage." Resurrecting the arguments of aristocratic-republicans, historian Francis Parkman decried "the flattering illusion that one man is essentially about as good as another." "It is in the cities," Parkman suggested in "The Failure of Universal Suffrage" (1878), "that the diseases of the body politic are gathered to a head. . . . Here the dangerous classes are most numerous and strong, and the effects of flinging the suffrage to the mob are most disastrous."[32]

To eliminate the threat posed by "an ignorant proletariat," these liberal-republicans advocated a constitutional order based, as in the eighteenth century, on the ownership of property. "No voter has a right to participate in the care of funds to which he does not contribute," New York Attorney Dorman B. Eaton argued in support of property qualifications for municipal elections. Eaton advocated passage of an amendment to the New York Constitution advanced in 1877 by the Tilden Commission, a twelve-man body dominated by wealthy patricians. The amendment proposed a nonpartisan, administrative system of municipal governance. Powerful boards of finance would take over the management of all New York cities and would be elected only by the tax- and rent-payers. Residents of cities with one hundred thousand inhabitants would need $500 in property or annual rent payments of $250 to qualify to vote for board members. The amendment would have disfranchised more than half of the 75.6 percent of the eligible electorate that voted in New York City's municipal election of 1885. Despite strong Republican support, this overt assault on universal suffrage failed to win approval by two successive legislatures and thus could not be submitted to the people.[33]

Unable to mount a frontal assault on universal suffrage, northern "reformers" adopted a piecemeal approach. The Massachusetts legislature, responding to widespread public dissatisfaction with machine-run "ticket" voting, instituted the Australian ballot in 1888. By 1890, thirty-five states had secret-ballot laws. Progressive era reformers were no less suspicious of universal suffrage. The idea of "the essential equality" of citizens was "pernicious," Richard T. Ely of Wisconsin declared in 1894. To curb the influence of parties over ordinary voters and the selection of candidates, Progressive-sponsored legislation subjected primary elections to mandatory state supervision. Simultaneously, Redeemer-run southern legislatures met the democratic Populist challenge by systematically disfranchising blacks and poor whites. These measures weakened party machines and caused a substantial drop in voter registration and turnout. Over "the last sixty years," James Quayle Dealey, professor of social and political science in Brown University, noted with approval in 1915, there had been "a steadily growing list of regulations and requirements . . . registration, educational qualifications . . . or a requirement of prepaid taxes, poll of property; so that the list of registered voters in some states are in per cent no larger than the voting lists of the revolutionary period." In the eyes of Progressives and Redeemers, government "by the people" meant, as Dealey put it, control by "the more intelligent and patriotic part of the body of citizens" and not the "ignorant and indifferent" masses: Negroes, naturalized foreigners, and illiterate voters. Whatever the rationale or mechanisms, the advocates of a restricted franchise were successful. By 1920, only 20 percent of the qualified electorate voted in the southern states and only 58 percent in the North, the lowest rates in nearly a century.[34]

The demand by liberal reformers for a responsible electorate had, in one sense, always been a part of American republican ideology. It recapitulated the insistence by aristocratic-republicans like Chancellor Kent and Judge Spencer that voters be genuinely "independent" and "virtuous." This sentiment likewise echoed the calls by democratic-republicans like Buel and Sanford for self-governing communities of responsible citizens. Now, however, the debate over constitutional principles took place in a society increasingly divided along lines of class and ethnicity. Liberal-republicanism emerged as the constitutional theory of native-born white Americans of respectable rank or rural residence.

Increasing legislative malapportionment was a central characteristic of the new constitutional regime. In many states Republican politicians, aided or abetted by Progressive reformers, rewrote constitutions to enhance the political power of rural counties at the expense of rapidly growing urban areas. Ohio was a case in point. The Constitution of 1851 achieved a delicate balance between republican values of corporate identity and democratic principles of equal representation. It permitted each county to have a seat in the legislature but *only* if the county had half as many inhabitants as would be required under equal apportionment. Bitter political conflicts quickly disrupted this equilibrium as Democratic- and Republican-dominated legislatures constantly redistricted the state. Indeed (as Peter Argersinger has pointed out), "From 1876 through 1886, Ohio conducted six consecutive [congressional] elections with six different districting plans." In a bid to ensure the permanent dominance of rural-based Republicans in the state legislature, the Hanna Amendment of 1903 changed Ohio's constitution to give each county a seat regardless of population. Pennsylvania Republicans pursued a similar policy. A constitutional amendment of 1873 gave each county a seat in the lower house. Another measure of 1901, devised to curb the representation of Philadelphia and Pittsburgh, specified that no more than one-sixth of the members of the senate could be elected by any city or county.[35]

The New York convention of 1894 likewise repudiated equal representation as a prime principle of legislative apportionment. "We can never have a truly representative and a truly republican government," argued Elihu Root, chairman of the judiciary committee and Republican floor leader, unless "the small and widely scattered communities, with their feeble power . . . shall, by the distribution of representation, be put on an equal footing . . . with the concentrated power of the cities." To achieve this goal, the Republican-dominated convention distributed legislative seats according to a series of complex formulas. As in 1846, it guaranteed each of the 59 existing counties a seat in the 128-member house. But the new apportionment scheme permitted some less populous counties to claim a second seat. The convention introduced a similar rural bias into the 50-member senate, declaring that, regardless of population, "no county shall have more than one-third of all the senators; and no two counties . . . more than one-half."[36] In the interests of the Republican party, rural voters, and respectable reformers, the new constitution virtually obliterated the democratic goal of equal representation.

New York politicians and judges soon admitted the impossibility of conforming to the complex provisions of the Constitution of 1894. To fulfill the mandate "that each senate district shall contain as nearly as may be an equal number of inhabitants," an act of 1907 paired Rockland and Richmond counties, thus violating the stipulation that districts "shall, at all times, consist of contiguous territory." Four years later, the Court of Appeals upheld the act, ruling that the legislature had conformed as nearly as possible to the apportionment rules. The inability of later courts to discover a "rational plan" in the constitution testified to its intellectual bankruptcy. The delegates of 1894 had manipulated the language and the concepts of democratic-republicanism to achieve a self-interested result that was foreign to its history and spirit. Like its aristocratic predecessor, the new liberal-republican constitutional regime privileged property and locality over personhood at the polls and in the halls of the legislature.[37] The delicate equilibrium of the democratic-republican order had collapsed.

The Debate over Legislative Power

Liberal-republican constitutionalists also sought to protect private property from state regulation or taxation by restraining "legislative tyranny." Their goals were new, but the "problem" of concentrated legislative power was not. The first American state constitutions vested sovereignty in the people and placed effective political authority in the legislature. These late eighteenth-century documents addressed the dangers posed by arbitrary executive power and impulsive legislative factions. They did not anticipate the appearance of disciplined political parties. Yet in the New York constitutional convention of 1821 Martin Van Buren could confidently assert that such "parties would always exist, and they would consult their interests." Aristocratic-republican delegates to the convention of 1821 reluctantly agreed. "The baneful influence of party spirit," one remarked, had been felt "in every department of the government."[38] The rise of "party spirit" forced the convention to reexamine the institutions created by the Constitution of 1777, particularly the councils of appointment and revision.

The governor, chancellor, and the judges of the supreme court sat on the Council of Revision. The council automatically reviewed all legislative bills. Those bills that it deemed "improper" could not become law unless they were reenacted by two-thirds of those voting in the assembly and senate. Like most veto-exercising bodies of the time, the council rejected relatively few laws. Uncontested evidence presented by Supreme Court Justice Jonas Platt indicated that the council had disallowed only 123 of 6,590 bills enacted between 1778 and 1821. Public dissatisfaction with the council stemmed from the presence on the supreme court of prominent politicians; of the ten justices who served between 1802 and 1823, three ran successfully for the governorship. Moreover, the council invalidated politically controversial legislation not on the grounds that it was "unconstitutional" but "as inconsistent with public good."[39]

The text of the constitution justified this broad mandate, but the council's partisan demeanor prompted sharp attacks from representatives of every ideological persuasion. "The two branches of the legislature ought to be the judges of . . . the public good," Peter R. Livingston told the convention of 1821. Livingston was a classical-republican who placed his faith in the "virtue" of the people and the integrity of "an independent and upright judiciary." "There could be no act of the legislature in violation of the constitution," he maintained, "without the intervention of this department." Once the judiciary pronounced a law to be contrary to the constitution, Livingston (like Lord Coke and James Otis before him) assumed that enlightened legislators would repeal it and enact a new ordinance. Hence he opposed a "qualified" (two-thirds override) veto power for the governor: If "the body politic [is] corrupt and rotten—it is immaterial about your checks and balances."[40]

In their attacks on the council, democratic-republicans took a less abstract and legalistic view. They stressed the political complexion of the council, particularly its elitist and potentially tyrannical features. Martin Van Buren assailed the council "as being composed of the judiciary, who are not directly responsible to the people." "It is in effect an executive council, of which the members hold their seats for life," John Duer warned: "Let its members . . . be the active leaders of your political parties . . . [and] the whole authority, legislative, executive, and judicial, will come to be vested in a single body, and you will be cursed with a constitution, republican in its form, but aristocratic in its operations and effect."[41]

"Federalist" republicans also underlined the necessity "of separating the judiciary from the legislative department," but their first line of defense against party spirit and the "omnipotence of the legislature" was neither Livingston's departmental theory of judicial review nor Van Buren's popular scrutiny. Rather, they advocated a qualified executive veto as described in "the plain and simple language" of the United States Constitution. The governor, like the president, an aristocratic-republican delegate proclaimed reassuringly, "is the man of the people—elected by their suffrage and identified with their interests. He is a watchful sentinel to guard us from evil."[42]

Delegates espousing each of these ideological positions voted unanimously to eliminate the Council of Revision. Swayed by Federalist logic, they decided (by a 100-to-17 margin) to replace the restraining function of the council with a qualified (two-thirds) executive veto.[43] The danger to representative government in New York had not come from legislative majorities, as feared by the early theorists of American republicanism and many delegates to the Philadelphia Convention of 1787, but from power concentrated in the hands of the judiciary. Nonetheless, the doctrines of separation of powers and checks and balances provided delegates with a set of Federalist constitutional solutions.

The issues posed by the Council of Appointment found their resolution in the Anti-Federalist tradition. The Constitution of 1777 vested the appointment of most state officers in the hands of the governor and a council of four senators.[44] In 1821, the council appointed no fewer than 8,287 military officers and 6,663 civil officials. Its reach extended into every county, town, and village and involved dozens of positions—justices of the peace, coroners, notary publics, commissioners of deeds, captains and lieutenants of militia units. "The people have called for the destruction of the council of appointment," Peter Sharpe told the convention of 1821, "and they expect the appointing power to be returned to the counties." The increasing power of Martin Van Buren's Albany Regency added a political dimension to this smoldering localist resentment. "The dominant party are resolved not merely to govern," protested Peter Jay, an erstwhile Federalist, "but to crush the minority [and] . . . to strip them of every office, however humble."[45]

These sentiments assured the demise of the Council of Appointment but not the fate of its patronage. To safeguard his power, Van Buren secured the chairmanship of the committee of appointments. The committee's report proposed that eight thousand minor militia appointments would be "thrown home to the people," Van Buren explained to the convention, allowing the governor to fill only seventy-eight senior military positions. The legislature would dispose of another three thousand civil offices, "as they may think proper . . . leaving but about two thousand five hundred upon which the governor will have a right to discriminate." Van Buren hoped to buy off legislators and localists with minor posts and militia appointments while preserving the bulk of the valuable patronage for the Albany Regency. "That the majority should govern, was a fundamental maxim in all free governments," he declared bitterly after listening to two days of speeches opposing his scheme, "and when his political opponents acquired the ascendency he was content that they should have it in their power to bestow the offices of government."[46]

Van Buren's candor raised the issue of the "plain and clear republican principles" (as Elisha Williams put it) that should inform the selection of state officials. The problem was especially acute with respect to important local appointees, the sheriffs and justices of the peace. "This power must be vested somewhere," Van Buren declared, and he was "for giving control to the majority of the state." In his view, popular sovereignty meant strong, centralized political institutions. "There should be some channel through which the remotest parts of the state would feel the influence of the central administration," a Van Burenite argued in support of the governor's appointment of sheriffs; to elect them locally "would make our government no better than a confederacy of counties . . . somewhat like the confederacy of these United States . . . before the present constitution was formed."[47]

Aristocratic-republicans demanded just such a localist constitutional solution. It was in their interest as influential members of the county gentry to identify popular sovereignty with local rule. They charged Van Buren and his colleagues with hypocrisy. "We are told one day that the people are capable of voting for governor, senators, and members of the assembly," the aristocratic-republican General J. R. Van Rensselaer pointed out, "and the next day they are considered incapable of electing justices of the peace in the very towns where they live." Van Burenites replied in kind, assailing former Federalists for suddenly running "foremost in the race of democracy." Nonetheless, an alliance of aristocratic-republican gentry and local-oriented delegates rejected Van Buren's centralized patronage system. Instead, the convention decreed that sheriffs and county clerks would be "chosen by the electors of the respective counties."[48]

There was strong sentiment for the local election of justices of the peace as well. "Everyone knows that heretofore the justices have been appointed . . . by leaders of [the] respective parties," declared Judge William Van Ness, "I am for restoring the people their rights. . . . Let the privilege be exercised by the people directly." Van Ness's argument did not sway many of his fellow aristocratic-republicans, who firmly opposed the popular election of judicial officers. "The officer deriving his authority in this way," protested Colonel Samuel Young, "could not, from the constitution of our nature, be an independent and impartial magistrate." This split among aristocratic-republicans resulted in the narrow defeat of a motion to elect justices of the peace (54 to 57). Nonetheless, localist and antiparty sentiment forced Van Buren to accept a compromise plan. It gave county judges and boards of supervisors the power to appoint justices; the governor could intervene only if they did not agree.[49] On the issue of appointments, the convention endorsed the localist perspective of the Anti-Federalists of 1787.

Considered as a whole, the Constitution of 1821 lacked theoretical consistency. It endorsed some democratic definitions of political "rights" by expanding the electorate for the governor and senate and giving voters the power to elect local militia officers, sheriffs, and (indirectly through boards of supervisors) justices of the peace. It also contained aristocratic-republican definitions of rights, notably the qualified veto and an appointed judiciary and magistracy. Equally significant, the convention debates indicated that various political factions did not embrace separate constitutional traditions. Rather, each group drew upon the common heritage as its interests dictated.[50] Aristocratic-republicans adopted the Anti-Federalist predilection for the local control of officeholders even as they championed the Federalist qualified veto over legislative bills. Democratic-Republicans likewise endorsed the veto but firmly repudiated the Federalist principle of an appointive judiciary. In 1821, there were both Democratic-Republican and Federalist solutions to the problems posed by "violent" political parties and excessive legislative power.

The Rise of the Judiciary: Laissez-Faire

In the convention of 1846, democratic-republican fervor forced a fundamental reevaluation of traditional constitutional restraints on popular and legislative power. "Are the people capable of self-government, or are they not?" George Patterson demanded early in the convention during a long debate on the governor's qualifications for office. Should the constitution stipulate that the chief executive be a native-born citizen? Be thirty years of age? Have resided in the state for five years? Delegates discussed these apparently trivial matters for two weeks, ostensibly seeking constitutional safeguards against a coup d'état by a young "genius" like Napoleon.[51]

In fact, the real issue under debate was of the highest importance, nothing less than constitutionalism itself. As Alvah Worden phrased the problem, whether "in the formation of a government, checks and balances should be placed on the exercise of the popular will." Such constitutional restrictions were the "last strangling efforts of dying old Federalism," he maintained. Conversely, "a Republican Democratic government . . . is best administered, when the popular will has as few restraints about it as possible. The more restraints . . . the more of an artificial machine you get, and the less advantageously it works." The people "cannot limit *their own* discretion . . . without forfeiting their sovereignty," John Hunt continued the argument; he was "certain" that the convention had "no right to impose any restrictions at all" on the popular will.[52]

This extreme (and emergent classical-liberal) constitutional doctrine alarmed many Whig delegates. "To say that *no* restriction can, or should be, placed on this elemental power [of the sovereign people], but the power itself," Charles Kirkland replied, "is to utter a political heresy, not transmitted to us by the Fathers of the Republic." Henry Nicoll pursued the point. "Undoubtedly the sovereign power resided in the whole people," he told the delegates, and "the exercise of this power is given by the whole people to the majority." Still, he believed that the whole people had "the right to say to the majority that they shall exercise this power under certain restrictions." "It was our duty," declared Richard Marvin, "to provide those safeguards which all experience and history has taught us to be proper." "Restrictions and rules of action [were necessary] . . . to prevent all from running into anarchy and confusion," Ambrose Jordan cried out in frustration, "Where is this ultra democracy to stop?"[53]

In the event, radical Jacksonian Democrats in the convention of 1846 were even more anxious than many Whigs to insist on constitutional restraints. "We find ourselves . . . with a constitution giving the supreme legislative power of the State to the Legislature—unrestricted and unlimited," complained Churchill Cambrelling. "And what has been the consequence? . . . a legislative despotism." "The constitutions of every State in the Union," the radical democratic leader Michael Hoffman pointed out, "have given the legislative power in the mass— in general terms—and then thought to restrain it . . . by express limitations." A better (and more far-reaching) procedure, he maintained, would be to specify "that all powers not granted to the legislature are the residuary, reserved powers of the people, not to be exercised unless they make an express grant of them."[54]

Significantly, Hoffman's view bore a striking similarity to the Tenth Amendment to the United States Constitution, which reserved all nondelegated powers to the states or the people. Like his Anti-Federalist ancestors, Hoffman advocated an inherently limited government. He rejected the Federalist model of a strong government restrained in its operation through internal checks and balances.

Nonetheless, radical Democrats joined with Federalist-oriented Whigs to insert restrictions on the governor's age and residency. As Robert Morris, a New York City lawyer, put it, "Why have any Constitution, but to provide . . . checks or guards"? This strange political alliance formed again during debates on the veto power. To combat "excessive legislation," Whigs and radical Democrats wanted the assent of two-thirds of those *elected* to the assembly and senate (not merely two-thirds of those present and voting) to defeat a governor's veto. Other Democrats attacked this proposal as "anti-republican" because it "made the Governor equal to two-thirds of the people." Some Democratic advocates of legislative supremacy wished to eliminate the veto entirely (the practice in eight states) or to permit an override with a "bare" (51 percent) majority, "a prominent feature in ten of the Constitutions of our sister states." Faced with disparate and strongly held positions, the delegates decided (61 to 36) to retain the veto power "as it now exists, and thereby avoid all extremes."[55]

This threefold split in the convention informed the reorganization of the judiciary as well. As in 1821, the delegates confronted the issue of a politicized judiciary. "Who selects most of your judges now?" asked Amos Wright, "the politicians of a party caucus." "The Governor was no longer left free to act in the selection of the best men," protested Richard Marvin, a Whig. "Judges were not only appointed on party grounds," added a radical Democrat, "but they were also removed to subserve party purposes." "This system . . . *must* be abolished."[56]

Whig delegates cast about for a scheme that would create an appointive but nonpartisan judiciary. One plan required the senate to approve the governor's nominations by a two-thirds vote so that "the two leading parties must concur in a choice; and they would [therefore] be compelled to select moderate men, and men of ability." Both regular Democrats and their radical colleagues refused to accept this "Federalist" device or any scheme that left judges "wholly irresponsible to the people." Radical Jacksonians demanded local or district elections to allow "individual knowledge and personal acquaintance" to influence "the action of the elector." They joined with Whigs to reject a plan to elect supreme court judges on a statewide general ticket. The Whig party "with two exceptions [stood] in phalanx against the amendment," Democratic leader Levi Chatfield complained, "whilst his own party divided." As finally written, the new constitution required the election of all judges—justices of the peace by town electors, local judges by county voters, supreme court justices by the electors of eight judicial districts, and four of the eight judges on the Court of Appeals by a statewide vote.[57]

For the radical Jacksonian Michael Hoffman, an elective judiciary was a key feature of the new democratic-republican constitutional order. Its main task was to restrain legislative spending. Between 1827 and 1846, the state government went deeply into debt. It spent $50 million to build new canals and extended $12 million in aid to various private enterprises. By diminishing canal revenues and raising the cost of new loans, the Panic of 1837 created a fiscal crisis in New York. To restore the state's credit, radical Democrats joined with New York City bankers to pass the "Stop and Tax" law of 1842. This act suspended most canal work and levied a tax to reduce the debt. The Constitution of 1846 wrote fiscal conservatism into fundamental law. Article VII set aside certain revenues to pay existing debts and mandated additional taxation "to preserve the public faith." It prohibited the state from extending its financial credit to private individuals and corporations and limited its debts to $1 million, except as funded by taxes approved by a popular referendum.[58]

Whigs strongly opposed these restrictions, both on practical and constitutional grounds. They championed an activist or "positive" state that promoted economic development, not the "negative" state favored by many radical Jacksonians. Along with some party Democrats, they argued that the popular referenda mandated by Article VII changed "our representative government into a democracy." "If we adopt such a section," Alvah Worden told the convention, "it would only be saying to the world . . . that the experiment of a republican, representative, responsible form of government, after a trial of more than 70 years, had proved a failure." "Is he unwilling that [the people] should speak their sentiments through their representatives," another delegate asked Hoffman. "Does he wish to save them from themselves?"[59]

Hoffman's reply revealed the link between the popular election of judges and the new constitutional restrictions on taxation. He "did not want this tax-creating power left with the legislature," Hoffman explained, for he knew from bitter experience "what the power of corrupt lobby black-legs could do. . . . We will not trust the legislature with the power of creating indefinite mortgages on the people's property." Hoffman had watched party politicians and logrolling localists use joint resolutions as a "mode of whipping around the constitution" to vote money in the final days of a session. Even an explicit constitutional restriction, such as that prohibiting the expenditure of state funds "except in pursuance of an appropriation by law," required judicial enforcement. "If you want a judge that can stand by the constitution against legislative usurpation," he declared, "you look in vain for a man appointed by power." "There can be no Constitution in this country, unless the judges . . . depend for their offices upon the people of the state."[60]

The constitutional theory of democratic republicanism thus enhanced both the power of the people and that of the judiciary. By placing the judiciary "on a popular foundation," Churchill Cambrelling pointed out, the New York Constitution of 1846 made it coequal with the legislature and the executive, "all of them springing directly from the people." "Elect your judges," Abner Keynes similarly advised the Massachusetts constitutional convention in 1853, "and you will energize them, and make them independent, and put them on a par with the other branches of government." Between 1846 and 1860, no fewer than nineteen state conventions wrote constitutions with an elected judiciary.[61]

The enhanced constitutional authority of the bench encouraged and justified judicial activism. Previously, judicial review was a suspect doctrine in republican political theory. As Judge John B. Gibson of the Pennsylvania Supreme Court declared in 1825, judicial review denied "a *postulate* in the theory of our government, and the very basis of the superstructure, that the people are wise, virtuous, and competent to manage their own affairs." Practical as well as ideological factors initially limited the scope of judicial review. The early state constitutions contained few specific provisions, legislatures enacted few laws, and judges had not yet fully developed the doctrine of "vested rights." Consequently, New York courts decided only 11 constitutional cases before 1821 and only 50 during the next quarter-century. The constitutional revisions of the 1840s marked a turning point in New York and many other states. Echoing the sentiments of reformers like Hoffman, Judge Gibson explicitly endorsed judicial activism in 1845. Lawyers increasingly tried cases on constitutional issues (127 in New York alone during the 1850s) and judges responded positively. By 1861, judges in various states had voided at least 150 laws.[62]

In New York, the prominence of the judiciary *in* the constitution steadily increased. The Constitution of 1821 described the judicial department in less than a page; by 1869 a constitutional amendment revising the court system and specifying its powers filled five closely printed pages. The authority of judges *over* the constitution increased accordingly. Between 1871 and 1905, New York judges heard 1,031 constitutional cases and set aside or curtailed 258 legislative acts.[63]

Judges diligently upheld the constitutional limitations inserted by

Hoffman and his colleagues. In particular, they adhered to Article III of the Constitution of 1846 by voiding private acts that embraced "more than one subject," had misleading titles, or otherwise escaped careful legislative scrutiny. An amendment of 1874 increased the number of restrictions on legislative action, as did new provisions in the Constitution of 1894. Between 1906 and 1938, the New York courts invalidated no fewer than 136 acts (of 587 considered) for transgressing various constitutional limitations. As Michael Hoffman had predicted to the delegates, your actions "will set an example . . . [in] every State of the Union and will go down with time itself, until that time will mingle with the murmurs of eternity."[64]

The judiciary likewise expanded its supervision of the political process. Courts in twenty states reviewed apportionment acts during the 1890s and struck down redistricting statutes that did not conform to the judges' view of proper constitutional standards. They also protected the rights of independent candidates for office and supervised election procedures. But state courts rarely contested laws affecting freedom of speech or the press; nor did they void constitutional provisions denying suffrage to blacks and poor whites or withholding equal representation from urban areas.[65]

The courts' refusal to guarantee equal political rights for all Americans was not accidental. It reflected the growing authority of the socially conservative, property-conscious ideology of liberal-republicanism in judicial circles. Influenced in part by Judge Thomas M. Cooley's *Treatise on the Constitutional Limitations* with regard to state legislatures, first published in 1868, jurists devised new doctrines to protect private property from state taxation or regulation. In the case of *In re Jacobs* in 1885, the New York Court of Appeals expanded the concept of vested rights into the doctrine of "substantive due process." Over the next two decades, New York jurists used this doctrine to overturn legislative acts in forty-seven court cases.[66]

The Constitution of 1846 laid the foundation for judicial protection of private property rights. Article VIII, section 3, explicitly extended to corporations many of the legal rights of "natural persons," thus bringing them under the protection of the due process clause of Article I, section 6. Likewise, Article V, section 8, diminished some of the traditional "police powers" of state governments. It abolished all state offices for "inspecting any merchandise, produce, manufacture, or commodity whatever." This laissez-faire administrative policy was the work of Jacksonian Democrats. It implemented their vision of a negative state by reducing "the patronage of government . . . [by] 500 officers." It also revealed a new confidence in the market system and in the ability of individual Americans to govern themselves in economics as well as politics. "All such evidences of antiquated ignorance should be erased from the statute book," Campbell White of New York County proclaimed. "The acuteness of the great body of the people render them perfectly capable of taking care of themselves in all the transactions of life; and we have laws to enforce the fulfillment of contracts according to their plain, obvious and honest import." [67]

The Constitution of 1846 balanced this emergent ethic of contractual individualism with traditional values of communitarian republicanism. Various clauses preserved state offices protecting public health, the regulation of weights and measures, and various government interests; forbade the legislature to "sell, lease, or otherwise dispose of any of the canals of the State"; regulated the terms of leases and grants on privately owned agricultural lands; and made stockholders in banking corporations individually liable "for all its debts and liabilities." [68]

These contradictions did not endure. By the end of the nineteenth century, corporate economic power and an activist judiciary had elevated private rights over the public welfare. This decisive transition—from an expansive legislature with a "commonwealth" ideology to a strong judiciary espousing laissez-faire principles—signaled the maturation of the new liberal-republican constitutional order. In matters of political economy as in concepts of suffrage and apportionment, the demise of democratic-republicanism was nearly complete.

Progressive Restrictions and Managerial Powers

In the final decades of the nineteenth century, as in the closing years of the twentieth, educated Americans undertook a comprehensive assessment of the state constitutional tradition. Progressive era reformers—many of them academic intellectuals—composed an impressive array of books and articles. Most authors condemned state legislatures as too responsive to local interests or dominated by business corporations; they likewise depicted urban governments as boss-ridden and corrupt. Their critique of the existing governmental system both reflected and exploited the long-standing American belief that political power meant social corruption.

Some Progressives wanted to use the power of the state to reform the social and economic order. They wanted to regulate capitalist enterprise and improve the conditions of life for middle-class Americans. But many Progressives also feared a genuinely democratic political system, for they recognized that the economic interests and cultural values of blacks, immigrants, and ordinary working people were very different from their own. They advocated honest and efficient government while espousing liberal-republican conceptions of limited government and the rights of private property. In this regard, these Progressives agreed with the sentiments of conventional state politicians such as Democratic Governor Roswell P. Flower of New York. "In America the people support the government," Flower declared in response to union leader Samuel Gompers's plea for unemployment relief during the depression of 1893, but "it is not the province of the government to support the people. Once recognize the principle that the government must supply public work for the unemployed, and there will be no end of official paternalism." [69]

To end the era of "distributive politics," especially now that political parties filled with labor unions and common citizens demanded access to government largesse, Progressives placed further Federalist-type restrictions on legislative power. The New York Constitution of 1894 required the votes of two-thirds of those *elected* to the assembly and senate to override an executive veto. Like their democratic-republican predecessors in 1846, Progressives also found innovative ways to mobilize the "people," by which they meant responsible middle- and upper-class citizens, against corrupt party politicians and legislators. Writing in 1915, J. Q. Dealey praised "the constitutional initiative and referendum" and the constitutional convention as the great agencies "through which democracy finds expression." [70] However innovative, these measures looked more to the past than to the future. They were devices designed to restrain a still-dominant party-controlled legislature or redefine its priorities.

The future of the state constitutional order lay elsewhere. Just as the judiciary enhanced its authority at the expense of the legislature in the late nineteenth century, so the executive department and its administrative bureaucracy emerged as a new center of power during the twentieth century. The past offered few precedents for this development. For aristocratic-republicans, the governor had served primarily as a negative check on legislative power. Radical democratic-republicans had feared an activist governor or an executive bureaucracy filled with incompetent party hacks. "The Governor to be elected under the Constitution," Henry Murphy reassured the convention of 1846, "would have little power or patronage. His office will be purely administrative." Moreover, the New York Constitution of 1846, like many other mid-nineteenth-century charters, forced governors to share bureaucratic authority with independently elected officials— secretaries of state, treasurers, and comptrollers. The creation of new regulatory boards and commissions further diffused executive power. In 1900, New York had eighty-one separate state boards, commissions, and departments, and Massachusetts had more than two hundred. As Woodrow Wilson observed in 1889, "The governor . . . is not the 'Executive', he is but a single piece of the executive. There are other pieces coordinated with him over which he has no direct official control."[71]

To empower state governors, early twentieth-century reformers invoked the vision of Alexander Hamilton. They celebrated his image of a purposeful managerial executive department and demanded more administrative authority for the governor. Sensing a threat to its predominance, the New York legislature rejected bills that strengthened the executive department in 1909 and again in 1910. In response, New York Progressives called a new constitutional convention. Aided by the historian Charles A. Beard and twenty other consultants from the Bureau of Municipal Research, the convention of 1915 proposed major revisions in the organization of the state government. One amendment would profoundly shift the locus of fiscal power, an upstate Republican senator complained, by taking "a long-standing function of the legislature, that of initiating the financial plan," and giving it to the executive. A "short ballot" amendment sought to reduce the number of elected state officials. As the conservative Republican corporate lawyer and national statesman Elihu Root wrote, this measure would cut the power of "party bosses" by making "one governor elected by the people the real chief executive." Beard predicted that these reforms would establish "a degree of responsible government hitherto unknown in American politics."[72]

In the short run, the electorate dashed the hopes of reformers by rejecting the amendments by a two-to-one margin. The plan "was not a response to broad outside pressure," a later scholar has concluded, but simply the handiwork of "a small group of progressive and powerful Republican reorganization advocates in the convention." In the longer run, the campaign for administrative consolidation, fewer statewide elected positions, and an executive budget succeeded in state after state. In New York, these measures won approval during the governorship of Alfred E. Smith.[73] In proposing the enhancement of the positive powers of the governor, the convention of 1915 began a new era in the constitutional history of New York and the several states.

A Complex and Ambiguous Legacy

For the previous century, constitutional debate had focused not on executive power but on other issues—popular suffrage, equal apportionment, local authority, and judicial review. Aristocratic-republicans in New York had advocated property qualifications for voting, representation by estates or interests, a federalist system of "checks and balances," and the control of appointments by local elites. Their vision of American republicanism collapsed partially in 1821 and more decisively in 1846 because it could not command popular support in an age of competitive political parties. Democratic-Republicans made the governmental system more responsive to the interests of a wider spectrum of the American people, even as they placed constitutional and judicial restraints on popularly elected legislatures and political parties. They advocated universal white manhood suffrage based not on personhood but on individual autonomy and membership in a community; a system of apportionment that balanced equal representation with geographic interests; specific constitutional limitations on legislative authority; and the popular election of all officials, including a strong, independent, and review-minded judiciary.

    The decline of democratic-republicanism stemmed from internal weaknesses and external forces. Its ideology rested on a narrow cultural foundation; it did not accept as legitimate the political rights claimed by women, blacks, or urban immigrants. Likewise, its popular electoral remedies did not break the power of political machines, and an independent judiciary proved to have a constitutional mind of its own. Equally important, middle- and upper-class reformers and businessmen had an alternative political agenda that they advanced with

considerable skill and energy. To protect class and geographic interests, liberal-republicans restricted suffrage and equal representation.
They likewise inhibited popular political participation through "nonpartisan" plans for municipal governments and judicial appointments.
Their definitions of the "people" and of the political rights of Americans differed markedly from those of their democratic-republican predecessors.

Which constitutional theory deserved to prevail? Or were they all
simply products of their time and circumstance, to be accepted as the
givens of the historical record? Which set of doctrines, of distinct and
different "original intents," best speaks to our condition in the late
twentieth century?

As always, the search for a usable past devolves into a choice
among competing constitutional values and even among rival social
classes. "We are the minority; and for us, therefore, does the Constitution exist," a group of Catholic immigrants in Philadelphia declared
during a dispute with the Protestant majority over school textbooks
in 1844: "Unless for the shield which the Constitution gives to . . . the
weaker party, this government would be a despotism." In succeeding
decades, a far more powerful minority of liberal-republican capitalists likewise sought constitutional protection for their property; "all
attempts to pillage and destroy it [by legislative majorities]," declared
corporate attorney John F. Dillon in 1895, "are as baneful as they are
illegal." Delegates to the New York convention of 1846 had confronted
similar contrasting definitions of the political rights of the American
people. "It had been gravely asserted on this floor that the majority
ought to go by law to secure the rights of the minority," George Simmons acknowledged, "but he asserted that it was to secure the rights
of the majority." "Go where law does not prevail," he concluded,
"and a minority rules."[74] A good democratic-republican, Simmons had
made his choice. And so must we all.

Notes

Research for this paper was supported by a Liberal Arts Fellowship at
the Harvard Law School, a sabbatical leave from Boston University, and
grants from the American Council of Learned Societies, the National
Endowment for the Humanities through the American Antiquarian

Society, and the American Philosophical Society. I am grateful for the criticisms and suggestions offered by Bernard Bailyn, Kermit Hall, Robert Dykstra, Calvin Jillson, J. Morgan Kousser, and members of the History Department seminar, University of Maryland—Baltimore County.

1. William B. Bishop and William H. Attree, *Report of the Debates and Proceedings of the Convention for the Revision of the Constitution of New York, 1846* (Albany: Evening Atlas, 1846), 539–41.

2. See Daniel J. Elazar, "The Principles and Traditions Underlying State Constitutions," *Publius: The Journal of Federalism* 12 (Winter 1982): 11–25, for an alternative conceptualization. Elazar identifies three constitutional "traditions" (Whig, federalist, and managerial) and six state constitutional "patterns" (commonwealth, commercial republic, southern contractual, civil code, frame of government, and managerial). My formulation relates many of these ideological perspectives and constitutional principles to the specific political factions and social groups (or classes) that espoused them.

3. For the texts of New York's nineteenth-century constitutions see *Sources and Documents of United States Constitutions,* ed. William F. Swindler (Dobbs Ferry, N.Y.: Oceana Publications, 1973–78), 10: 141–344.

4. Memorial, August 15, 1846, in Bishop and Attree, *Report,* 646; Kennedy, September 30, 1846, ibid., 1027; O'Conor, July 10, 1846, ibid., 269; Cornell, October 2, 1846, ibid., 1046.

5. Nathaniel H. Carter and William L. Stone, *Reports of the Proceedings and Debates of the Convention of 1821* (Albany: Cantine & Leake, 1821), 134, 180–202, 374. There were 1,036 free blacks in New York City in 1790 out of a total African-American population of 3,092, but 7,490 free blacks in 1810 (out of 8,918). Blacks constituted about 9.8 percent of the city's population in both years. See Shane White, " 'We Dwell in Safety and Pursue Our Honest Callings': Free Blacks in New York City, 1783–1810," *Journal of American History* 75 (September 1988): Table 1.

6. Kennedy, September 30, 1846, in Bishop and Attree, *Report,* 1027; Hunt, September 30, 1846, ibid., 1030. During the previous decade, Democratic majorities in the assembly had rejected petitions favoring equal suffrage by votes of 74 to 23, 71 to 23, and 109 to 11. See Phyllis F. Field, *The Politics of Race in New York: The Struggle for Black Suffrage in the Civil War Era* (Ithaca: Cornell University Press, 1982), 49. For the concept of *Herrenvolk* democracy, see George Frederickson, *White Supremacy: A Comparative Study of American and South African History* (New York: Oxford University Press, 1981).

7. Field, *Politics of Race,* 29; Fletcher M. Green, *Constitutional Development in the South Atlantic States, 1776–1860* (Chapel Hill: University of North

Carolina Press, 1930), 193, 226, 230–31; James H. Kettner, *The Development of American Citizenship, 1608–1870* (Chapel Hill: University of North Carolina Press, 1978), 316. Southern judges initially endorsed a similar definition of citizenship as consisting of various types of rights. "Surely the possession of political power is not essential to constitute a citizen," Judge William Gaston of North Carolina argued in 1839 (anticipating positions advanced in New York in 1846), "if it be, then women, minors, and persons who have not paid public taxes are not citizens." Ultimately, southern jurists repudiated the traditional "birthright" definition of American citizenship; they argued instead that the degraded legal circumstances of free blacks disqualified them from citizenship. It was "not the place of a man's birth, but the rights and privileges he may be entitled to enjoy, which makes him a citizen," declared the Kentucky Court of Appeals. *Amy* v. *Smith,* 11 Ky. (1 Litt.) 326, 333 (1822). See Kettner, *Development of American Citizenship,* 316–32.

8. Field, *Politics of Race,* 53, 62, 106, 126–27.

9. Ibid., 160, 183–87, 199.

10. Const. of 1777, Arts. VII, X, XVII; Kent, September 22, 1821, in Carter and Stone, *Reports,* 219–21; Van Vechten, September 22, 1821, ibid., 226–27.

11. Buel, September 22, 1821, in Carter and Stone, *Reports,* 221. To support his position, Buel called attention to the United States Constitution, one of the principles of which was "that orders and classes of men would not, and ought not, as such, to be represented." September 24, 1821, ibid., 244; Van Buren, September 25, 1821, ibid., 257; Sanford, September 19, 1821, ibid., 178.

12. Chilton Williamson, *American Suffrage from Property to Democracy, 1760–1860* (Princeton: Princeton University Press, 1960), 117, 197, 205, 213. Donald S. Lutz, *Popular Consent and Popular Control: Whig Political Theory in the Early State Constitutions* (Baton Rouge: Louisiana State University Press, 1980), distinguishes three constitutional perspectives during the revolutionary era (Whig, radical Whig, and Federalist). His instructive analysis focuses on theories of representation while my emphasis falls more on the sociopolitical goals of the constitution makers. His radical Whigs prefer a broad suffrage and government by direct popular consent as do my democratic-republicans; his Whigs and Federalists seek, by different means, to restrain popular sovereignty, hence my decision to define them both as aristocratic-republicans.

13. Platt, September 27, 1821, in Carter and Stone, *Reports,* 278; Spencer, October 20, September 22, 1821, ibid., 186–87, 218–19; Van Buren, September 26, 1821, ibid., 275; Const. of 1821, Art. II, § 1.

14. Williamson, *American Suffrage,* 220–21. Late twentieth-century United

States Supreme Court decisions that address special qualifications for local elections include *Kramer* v. *Union Free School District No. 15* 395 U.S. 621 (1969); and *Salyer Land Co.* v. *Tulare Lake Basin Water Storage District* 410 U.S. 719 (1973).

15. Williamson, *American Suffrage*, 269, 266; Robert J. Steinfeld, "Property and Suffrage in the Early American Republic," *Stanford Law Review* 41 (January 1989): 359–60.

16. Williamson, *American Suffrage*, 207, 241, 264–67.

17. Steinfeld, "Property and Suffrage," 362, 375.

18. Kent, September 20, 1821, in Carter and Stone, *Reports*, 222.

19. Williamson, *American Suffrage*, 276; Morton Keller, *Affairs of State: Public Life in Late Nineteenth Century America* (Cambridge, Mass.: Harvard University Press, 1977), 243, 525. Keller cites the following decisions voiding registration laws as unconstitutional restraints on voting rights: *Page* v. *Allen*, 58 Pa. 388 (1868); *State* v. *Swift*, 69 Ind. 505 (1879); *Dells* v. *Kennedy*, 49 Wis., 555 (1880); *Daggett* v. *Hudson*, 43 Ohio St. 548 (1885); and *Kennen* v. *Wells*, 144 Mass. 497 (1887).

20. Quoted in Peter H. Argersinger, "The Value of the Vote: Political Representation in the Gilded Age," *Journal of American History* 76 (June 1989): 67.

21. Edwards and Young, October 11, 1821, in Carter and Stone, *Reports*, 406, 408. The apportionment scheme likewise mixed democratic-individualist with corporate-republican principles. The constitution provided electors with equal representation in the senate by dividing the state into eight large, equally populous, districts, each with four seats. In the assembly, each county received at least one seat, regardless of its population.

22. O'Conor, July 21, 1846, in Bishop and Attree, *Report*, 384–85; Loomis, July 21, 1846, ibid., 386.

23. Jordan, July 21, 1846, ibid., 386.

24. Bergen, July 22, 1846, ibid., 389; Worden, July 22, 1846, ibid., 399. See also the remarks of Tilden and Morris, July 23, 1846, ibid., 413–14.

25. Delegates condemned the large, multimember senate districts created by the Constitution of 1821 because they resulted in party-run elections in which voters "were compelled by political organization to vote for men they did not know." See Morris, July 23, 1846, ibid., 412; Campbell, July 21, 1846, ibid., 402; and Wright, July 21, 1846, ibid., 379.

26. July 21, 1846, ibid., 380. See Elazar, "Principles and Traditions," 16, for the "union" theory of state polities.

27. Rhodes, July 24, 1846, in Bishop and Attree, *Report*, 426; Chatfield, July 28, 1846, ibid., 446; Wright, July 21, 1846, ibid., 379; see also the series of votes on size of the senate, July 22, 1846, ibid., 399–400.

28. Green, *Constitutional Development*, 206–9, 233–48; Patrick T. Conley, *Democracy in Decline: Rhode Island's Constitutional Development, 1776–1841* (Providence: Rhode Island Historical Society, 1977), chaps. 12–13.

29. Green, *Constitutional Development*, chap. 7; Chatfield and Young, July 24, 1846, in Bishop and Attree, *Report*, 423; Perkins, August 14, 1846, ibid., 637.

30. Waite quoted in Keller, *Affairs of State*, 242; Michael E. McGeer, *Popular Politics: The American North, 1865–1928* (New York: Oxford University Press, 1986), 5–7.

31. *Inquirer* quoted in McGeer, *Popular Politics*, 13; Keller, *Affairs of State*, 256 (Conkling), 271 (Adams), and chap. 7.

32. Harrison quoted in McGeer, *Popular Politics*, 45; Lynde Debate noted in Stanley N. Katz, "The Strange Birth and Unlikely History of Constitutional Equality," *Journal of American History* 75 (December 1988): 756; Parkman quoted in McGeer, *Popular Politics*, 46–47.

33. McGeer, *Popular Politics*, 48–49. "Reformers" at the Virginia Constitutional Convention of 1901–2 were more ruthless. Unwilling to risk a popular vote on a document that disfranchised thousands of poor whites (as well as blacks), the convention simply promulgated the Constitution of 1902, a dubious procedure that nonetheless survived challenge in state and federal courts. Margaret Virginia Nelson, *A Study of Judicial Review in Virginia, 1789–1928* (New York: Columbia University Press, 1947), 123–24.

34. Keller, *Affairs of State*, 529; Loren P. Beth, *The Development of the American Constitution, 1877–1917* (New York: Harper & Row, 1971), 117–18, 126–27; Ely quoted in Katz, "Constitutional Equality," 756; James Q. Dealey, *Growth of American State Constitutions, from 1776 to the End of the Year 1914* (Boston: Ginn and Company, 1915), 262–63; McGeer, *Popular Politics*, 6–7.

35. Argersinger, "Value of the Vote," 71; Robert G. Dixon, Jr., *Democratic Representation: Reapportionment in Law and Politics* (New York: Oxford University Press, 1968), 82–83.

36. Root quoted in Dixon, *Democratic Representation*, 84; Richard L. McCormick, *From Realignment to Reform: Political Change in New York State, 1893–1910* (Ithaca: Cornell University Press, 1981), 52–55; Const. of 1894, Art. III, § 4.

37. *Matter of Reynolds* 202 N.Y. 430 (1911). See Franklin A. Smith, *Judicial Review of Legislation in New York, 1906–1938* (New York: Columbia University Press, 1952), 217. For reapportionment litigation in New York see *WMCA v. Lomenzo*, 377 U.S. 633 (1964); *WMCA v. Simon*, 202 F. Supp. 741 (S.D.N.Y. 1962); and 208 F. Supp. 368 (S.D.N.Y. 1962); and the discussions in Dixon, *Democratic Representation*, 201–9; Ruth C.

Silva, "Apportionment in New York," *Fordham Law Review* 30 (1962): 581–604, and "Apportionment of the New York Assembly," *Fordham Law Review* 31 (1962): 1–42; Alfred de Grazia, *Apportionment and Representative Government* (New York: Praeger, 1963), 40–53. See, in general, Beth, *Development of the American Constitution*, 107–28; and J. Morgan Kousser, *The Shaping of Southern Politics: Suffrage Restriction and the Establishment of the One-Party South, 1880–1910* (New Haven: Yale University Press, 1974).

38. Van Buren, September 25, 1821, in Carter and Stone, *Reports*, 262; Van Vechten, September 6, 1821, ibid., 83.

39. Const. of 1777, Art. III; Platt, September 5, 1821, in Carter and Stone, *Reports*, 54.

40. Livingston, September 4–7, 1821, in Carter and Stone, *Reports*, 50–51, 92, 90–91. Daniel D. Tompkins, former New York Supreme Court justice, governor, vice-president of the United States, and now president of the convention, took a similar position: September 6, 1821, ibid., 79. On the "departmental theory of judicial review" implicit in Livingston's position, see William M. Wiecek, *Liberty Under Law: The Supreme Court in American Life* (Baltimore: Johns Hopkins University Press, 1988), 38–39.

41. Van Buren, September 6, 1821, in Carter and Stone, *Reports*, 71; Duer, September 8, 1821, ibid., 108.

42. Tallmadge, September 4–5, 1821, ibid., 45, 65; Edwards, September 5, 1821, ibid., 60.

43. Votes, September 9, 1821, ibid., 115, 121. Reflecting naive antiparty optimism, Chancellor Kent suggested that the qualified veto would probably not "be exercised but on constitutional grounds." September 5, 1821, ibid., 63.

44. Const. of 1777, Art. XXIII. This centralization of patronage power was controversial from its inception. The patriot committee of Tryon County pleaded with the wartime Convention of 1777 to respect "our freeholders' voices in regard to appointing the civil officers of our country"; otherwise, "the public would take it as an infringement of their liberties, wherefore . . . [they] fight." Tryon County Committee, May 8, 1777, *Journals of the Provincial Congress, Provincial Conventions, Committee of Safety and Council of Safety of the State of New York, 1775–1776–1777* (Albany: T. Weed, 1842), 2:473–74.

45. "Appointments under the Council," in Carter and Stone, *Reports*, 161–62; Sharpe, September 13, 1821, ibid., 149; Jay, October 5, 1821, ibid., 345.

46. Van Buren, October 3 and 5, 1821, ibid., 332, 353–54.

47. Williams, October 9, 1821, ibid., 385; Van Buren, October 4, 1821, ibid.,

342. This reasoning appealed to some former Federalists (King, October 9, 1821, ibid., 386). With regard to state constitutional doctrine, however, most aristocratic-republicans were localists.

48. Van Rensselaer, October 4, 1821, ibid., 332; Burroughs, October 4, 1821, ibid., 345; Const. of 1821, Art. IV, § 8.

49. Van Ness, October 4, 1821, in Carter and Stone, *Reports,* 336; Young, October 4, 1821, ibid., 343. For similar reservations about an elective magistracy, see Ross, October 3, 1821, ibid., 327, and Van Vechten, October 5, 1821, ibid., 351; Votes, October 4–5, 1821, ibid., 344, 356; Const. of 1821, Art. IV, § 7.

50. Edwards, October 16, 1821, in Carter and Stone, *Reports,* 444; Platt, October 2, 1821, ibid., 310. For a similar analysis of the pragmatic use of four distinct ideological traditions during the revolutionary era, see Isaac Kramnick, "The 'Great National Discussion': The Discourse of Politics in 1787," *William and Mary Quarterly* 3d ser., 45 (January 1988): 3–32.

51. Patterson, July 1, 1846, in Bishop and Attree, *Report,* 214. The debate lasted from the twenty-third to the thirty-second day, ibid., 172–278. A motion to eliminate all qualifications for governor failed, 41 to 56; the motion on age passed, 61 to 49. See ibid., 339.

52. Worden, June 30, July 9, June 27, 1846, ibid., 207, 260, 178; Hunt, June 29, 1846, ibid., 187.

53. Kirkland, July 8, 1846, ibid., 237; Nicoll, June 30, 1846, ibid., 199; Marvin, June 30, 1846, ibid., 203; Jordan, June 29, 1846, ibid., 188.

54. Cambrelling, July 23, 1846, ibid., 403–4; Hoffman, June 8, 1846, ibid., 58.

55. Morris, June 27, 1846, ibid., 180; Wright, July 16, 1846, ibid., 331; Penniman, July 16, 1846, ibid., 335; Nicholas, July 20, 1846, ibid., 370; Votes, ibid., 337, 370–71.

56. Wright, August 15, 1846, ibid., 651; Marvin, August 12, 1846, ibid., 594–95; Swackhammer, August 12, 1846, ibid., 613.

57. Stow, June 23, 1846, ibid., Wright, August 15, 1846, ibid., 651; O'Conor, August 25, 1846, ibid., 754; Bascom, September 1, 1846, ibid., 788; Chatfield, August 25, 1846, ibid., 757. Making a minor concession to Whig demands for an appointive judiciary, the Democratic majority allowed the indirect selection of four appeals court judges "from the class of justices of the supreme court having the shortest time to serve." Const. of 1846, Art. VI, §§ 2, 4, 12, 14, 17.

58. Const. of 1846, Art. VII; L. Ray Gunn, "The Crisis of Distributive Politics: The Debate over State Debts and Development Policy in New York, 1837–1842," in *New York and the Rise of American Capitalism: Economic Development and the Social and Political Development of an American State,*

1780–1870, ed. William Pencak and Conrad Edick Wright (New York: New-York Historical Society, 1989), 168–201.

59. Bascom, September 22, 1846, in Bishop and Attree, *Report,* 944; Worden, September 22, 1846, ibid., 945; Hawley, September 21, 1846, ibid., 916.

60. Hoffman, September 22, 23, 1846, ibid., 946–47; Hoffman, July 16, 1846, ibid., 325; Const. of 1846, Art. VII, § 8; Hoffman, August 18, 1846, in Bishop and Attree, *Report,* 672–73.

61. Cambrelling, October 9, 1846, in Bishop and Attree, *Report,* 1081. For Keynes and a persuasive analysis of judicial power as an integral feature of democratic-republican constitutions, see Kermit L. Hall, "The Judiciary on Trial: State Constitutional Reform and the Rise of an Elected Judiciary, 1846–1860," *Historian* 44 (May 1983): 350 and passim.

62. Gibson dissenting in *Eakin* v. *Raub,* 12 Serg. & Rawle 330, 343 (Pa. 1825), cited in William E. Nelson, "Changing Conceptions of Judicial Review: The Evolution of Constitutional Theory in the States, 1790–1860," *University of Pennsylvania Law Review* 120 (1972): n. 108; Edward S. Corwin, "The Extension of Judicial Review in New York, 1783–1905," *Michigan Law Review* 15 (February 1917): 284–85.

63. *Sources and Documents,* ed. Swindler, 10:209–13; Keller, *Affairs of State,* 362; Corwin, "Judicial Review," 285.

64. Charles Z. Lincoln, *The Constitutional History of New York* (Rochester: Lawyers Co-operative Publishing Company, 1906), 4:377–410; Franklin A. Smith, *Judicial Review of Legislation in New York, 1906–1938* (New York: Columbia University Press, 1952), 107, 136–44, 222–23; Hoffman, September 23, 1846, in Bishop and Attree, *Report,* 957.

65. Keller, *Affairs of State,* 359–60, 455, 519; Beth, *Development of the American Constitution,* 218–19, 234–35; Smith, *Judicial Review in New York,* 77; Nelson, *Judicial Review in Virginia,* 164–65.

66. Thomas M. Cooley, *A Treatise on the Constitutional Limitations Which Rest upon the Legislative Power of the States of the American Union* (Boston: Little, Brown, 1868); Corwin, "Judicial Review," 295–96; Keller, *Affairs of State,* 362; Beth, *Development of the American Constitution,* 84.

67. Nicoll, August 4, 1846, in Bishop and Attree, *Report,* 512; White, August 4, 1846, ibid., 513.

68. Const. of 1846, Art. V, § 8; Art. VII, § 6; Art. I, § 14; and Art. VIII, § 7.

69. Quoted in McCormick, *From Realignment to Reform,* 57.

70. The new veto provision was initially implemented in a constitutional amendment of 1874, Art. IV, § 9; Dealey, *Growth of American State Constitutions,* 257–58. Walter F. Dodd, *The Revision and Amendment of State Constitutions* (Baltimore: Johns Hopkins Press, 1910), 64, 67, notes that many Progressive era constitutions, particularly in the South, were

not submitted for popular ratification and sought to restrict popular political rights.

71. Murphy, June 26, 1846, in Bishop and Attree, *Report*, 172; Wilson quoted in Thomas Schick, *The New York State Constitutional Convention of 1915 and the Modern State Governor* (New York: National Municipal League, 1978), 11.

72. Schick, *Convention of 1915*, 22, 42–43, 91, 98, 100.

73. Ibid., 119, 121, 134–35.

74. Catholics quoted in James's essay in this volume at note 38. Dillon in Keller, *Affairs of State*, 368; Simmons, July 7, 1846, in Bishop and Attree, *Report*, 232.

State Politics and Republican Virtue

Religion, Education, and Morality in Early American Federalism

Peter S. Onuf

James Madison believed that the new federal republic could not survive without popular virtue. "The people will have virtue and intelligence to select men of virtue and wisdom," he told the Virginia ratifying convention. This was the "great republican principle." "No theoretical checks, no form of government, can render us secure" unless there was sufficient "virtue among us."[1] But where did this virtue come from? And assuming that it was not the spontaneous product of self-government itself, what steps could republican constitution writers such as Madison take to guarantee popular virtue?

These questions troubled the founders, and they remain controversial today. Contemporary commentators agree that a well-informed citizenry is essential to the preservation of republican government. Some would go an important and controversial step further, asserting that knowledge alone, unless deeply grounded in moral and religious principles, is an insufficient basis of good citizenship. These latter-day Christian republicans cite the authority of the founders themselves, noting that even some of the enlightened skeptics in their ranks acknowledged the crucial role of the churches in shaping republican character. Religion supported the new republican states, and the states—to the extent possible, given the plurality of sects and popular hostility to establishments—supported religion.[2]

Modern "nonpreferentialists," who say that government should support religion generally without favoring any particular sect, can make a plausible historical argument. First, the interdependence of piety and virtue was virtually axiomatic in the political discourse of the founding period. However much leading revolutionaries fancied themselves "classical republicans" or enlightened "liberals," few set much stock in the natural capacity of the common folk to sustain their virtuous commitment to the public good or even to know and pursue their own true interests as individual citizens. At the very least, they all recognized that the private character of republican citizens was a matter of the utmost public concern. And many were persuaded that the very survival of the American republics depended on fostering popular piety, morality, and virtue.

But what sort of government did the Philadelphia Convention create? Given the framers' views on piety and virtue, the secularity of the federal Constitution is particularly striking.[3] At this point, non-preferentialists turn to their second key premise: that the Constitution created a complicated federal regime that depended on the states to perform vital functions. The new central government *appears* secular because it does not deal directly with questions of character and citizenship; the states determine the qualifications of voters and are therefore responsible for inculcating republican principles. Constitutional recognition of individual liberties and states' rights, most notably in the Bill of Rights, was designed to secure this distinctive function *against* outside interference, *not* to facilitate secularization and disestablishment. The federal Constitution was silent on questions of character and citizenship precisely because the state constitutions committed the states to support religion and public education.[4]

This account of early American federalism seems plausible, even compelling: clearly the federal and state governments were supposed to play distinctive roles in the new system. But we should hesitate before invoking the early state charters as normative or prescriptive in our own debates about church-state relations. I have no illusions about "setting the record straight" in the following pages, nor will I offer a definitive reading of Madison's views on human nature and popular virtue. But I do want to raise some questions about what the founders thought the states should do in their new federal system. Madison, for one, did not set much store in the states as the font of virtuous citizenship; after all, the "Vices of the political system" were specifically the vices of the states.[5] Madison's distrust of the states was apparent in his unsuccessful efforts to give the new Congress veto power over state laws and later to subject the states to some of the constitutional limitations in the federal Bill of Rights. Madison and his friends were convinced that the state governments were at the root of the new nation's problems. Precisely because the states gave free reign to popular licentiousness and thereby corrupted popular virtue, the states constituted the chief threat to the survival of American republicanism.

Of course, not all the founders embraced Madison's pessimistic judgment of the states, and Madison himself eventually came to realize the advantages of federalism.[6] Certainly the Anti-Federalists, whose important role in shaping the new regime is now recognized, had good things to say about their state governments. But even if most Americans resisted Madison's conclusion that the states were the source of all evil, it did *not* follow that they believed the state governments should take an extensive, positive role in fostering popular virtue. The tendency in the years before the adoption of the federal Constitution was toward disestablishing state churches and minimizing the scope of government interference in religious life. Decreasing state support for religion was not offset by investment in public education, nor did state legislators show any enthusiasm for sumptuary laws or other measures to curb excessive consumption or moral decline. By 1787 the states had effectively withdrawn from any active effort to shape character. If popular virtue was as crucial as Madison suggested, it would have to come from some other source.

Republican Religion

Most of the founders agreed that Protestant Christianity provided the best support for republican virtue. Because, in the words of Benjamin Rush, "a Christian cannot fail of being a republican," it was obviously advisable for the American republics to promote Christianity.[7] But what sort of state support would be broadly acceptable in a pluralistic religious environment? Experience in the colonies and new states showed that religious establishments generated sectarian divisions and offended many devout Christians. Furthermore, critics of the establishments charged, state churches could not foster the authentic piety that made people truly virtuous. Church establishments thus reversed the proper relation between religion and republican government: when the state prescribed public worship it corrupted true religion and violated individual rights of conscience.[8]

The early state constitutions reveal considerable confusion about the role of the churches. Where established churches or multiple establishments already existed, the commonplace association of piety and virtue was invoked as a justification for state support of religion. In Massachusetts, the 1780 Constitution proclaimed that the "happiness of a people, and the good order and preservation of republican government" depended on "public instructions in piety, religion, and morality." "Institution of public worship of GOD" was essential to the success of America's republican experiment.[9] State-supported churches would inculcate "morality and piety, rightly grounded on evangelical principles," thus enabling citizens of New Hampshire to distinguish between liberty and license and so to submit to legitimate authority.[10] All but two of the new state charters provided religious tests for officeholders that presumably would identify the virtuous and proscribe the vicious.[11]

Outside of New England, constitution writers tended to be more circumspect about state support for religion. But even where a plurality of sects complicated or precluded state support, some of the constitutions endorsed the principle of establishment on republican grounds. In South Carolina, for instance, "the Christian Protestant religion shall be deemed, and is hereby constituted and declared to be, the established religion of this State." The 1778 Constitution set forth a series of "articles" to which all recognized religious societies had to subscribe, including acknowledgment of the "divine inspiration" of the Bible.[12] Marylanders also envisaged a multiple establishment, in this case including Roman Catholics. The 1776 Constitution empowered the Maryland legislature, at its "discretion," to "lay a general and equal tax, for the support of the Christian religion."[13]

Efforts to establish Christianity, even where sectarian diversity precluded actual state support, show how concerned constitution writers were with fostering popular piety and virtue. But most of the new charters also incorporated provisions that acknowledged individual rights of conscience and, south of New England, disavowed any preference for a particular sect. The Maryland Constitution thus stipulated that "all persons, professing the Christian religion, are equally entitled to protection in their religious liberty."[14] The establishment of Christianity presumably depended on an all-inclusive, and therefore highly improbable, interdenominational accord. Similarly, the New Jersey Constitution provided that "there shall be no establishment of any one religious sect in this Province, in preference to another."[15]

Most of the constitutions barred "preferential" establishments. Some betrayed more pervasive misgivings about establishments in general. New York's 1777 Constitution secured free exercise of religion in order to ward off "the bigotry and ambition of weak and wicked priests and princes [who] have scourged mankind."[16] New York, South Carolina, and North Carolina barred preachers from civil office. The North Carolina Constitution limited officeholding to Protestant Christians, proscribing anyone "who shall hold religious principles incompatible with the freedom and safety of the state."[17]

State constitutional provisions concerning religion and morality tended to work at cross-purposes. Guarantees of religious freedom— or at least toleration of religious dissent—and constitutional protections and admonitions against the abuse of clerical power all tended to delimit, if not nullify, any practical support for state church establishments. Yet even when guarding against potential abuses of religious authority, state constitution writers implicitly acknowledged the interdependence of Christian religion and republican politics. Most Americans agreed that good citizenship was grounded in Christian belief and sustained by public worship and instruction. But the implementation of state support for religion proved problematic. The dilemma was most eloquently set forth in the Delaware Constitution of 1792: "Although it is the duty of all men frequently to assemble together for the public worship of the Author of the universe, and piety and morality, on which the prosperity of communities depends, are thereby promoted; yet no man shall be compelled to attend any religious worship, [or] to contribute to the erection or support of [any church]."[18] Republicanism may have depended on Christianity, but respect for religious freedom and the threat of sectarian hostility precluded the new state governments from cultivating the popular piety and virtue which alone could sustain them.

The forces working toward disestablishment were most conspicuous in Virginia.[19] Section 16 of the Bill of Rights in the 1776 Constitution guaranteed "free exercise of religion," asserting that "the duty which we owe to our creator, can be directed only by reason and conviction, not by force or violence." Virginia's leaders recognized that the denial of "free exercise" endangered the safety and welfare of the state by fomenting sectarian divisions. This meant that the Anglican establishment would have to make significant concessions to evangelical dissenters. But because the establishment was not completely dismantled, sectarian differences still constituted a potential threat to social peace and good order. Therefore, "it is the mutual duty of all to practice Christian forbearance, love, and charity towards each other." In effect, the authors of the Bill of Rights were asking for the "forbearance" of the dissenters on the issue of state support; they implicitly acknowledged that preference for any denomination was a legitimate grievance.[20]

The Virginia Bill of Rights could be read as a pledge that the state would move toward disestablishment. Madison, the original author of the free exercise clause, clearly saw established religion as a source of danger to the republic. As a result, he was reluctant to invoke the conventional link between Christian piety and republican virtue that justified church establishments elsewhere. Significantly, Madison hoped that the specifically Christian virtues of "forbearance, love, and charity" would curb the sectarian tendency to divide over doctrinal positions or ecclesiastical forms. But he did *not* suggest that Christianity provided the foundation of republican government.[21] The preservation of "free government," according to the immediately preceding provision of the Bill of Rights, required "a firm adherence to justice, moderation, temperance, frugality, and virtue."[22]

The disjunction of republican morality and Christian religion, reflected in their placement in separate sections of the Virginia Bill of Rights, had momentous implications for the history of church-state relations in America. Subsequently, Thomas Jefferson and Madison developed a compelling argument for a complete "wall of separation" between the two spheres that elaborated and exploited the textual distinction. The Statute for Religious Freedom, finally adopted in January 1786, thus stipulated that "our civil rights have no dependence on our religious opinions" and guaranteed that "all men shall be free to profess, and by argument to maintain, their opinion in matters of religion, and that the same shall in no wise diminish, enlarge, or affect their civil capacities." No Virginian would be required to "frequent or support any religious worship, place, or ministry whatsoever," the logical culmination of positions tentatively staked out in 1776.[23]

The Virginia campaign for disestablishment was not repeated in other states because, outside of New England, specific denominations did not enjoy a dominant position and therefore could not command significant state support. As a result, there was no compelling need to resolve the contradictory attitudes toward church establishments that were manifest in the early constitutions. Constitutional endorsements of establishment thus had little practical effect beyond expressing the widely shared idea that piety supported virtue and that virtue was the animating principle of a healthy republic.

The history of church-state relations followed a distinctive course in New England. Preachers in New Hampshire, Massachusetts, and Connecticut who sought to defend the power and privileges of the congregational establishments against challenges from Baptists and other dissenters developed the most elaborate case for state support of religion. Defenses of established religion, a ritual theme in election day sermons in these three states, provide the richest source of contemporaneous commentary on the role of Christianity in supporting republican government. But they also reveal the difficulty of reconciling established churches with widely shared assumptions about religion and politics. The ideological and institutional tendencies that undercut establishments elsewhere were clearly at work in New England as well.[24]

Defenders of established religion argued that the preservation of order in church and state were inextricably linked. "Let the restraints of religion be once broken down," intoned Phillips Payson in the 1778 Massachusetts election sermon, "and we might well defy all human wisdom and power to support and preserve order and government in the state." It would be fatal to leave "the subject of public worship to the humors of the multitude."[25] "True virtue, and religion, and subjection to the Ordinances of God," explained Moses Hemmenway, were the only durable foundation for liberty.[26] Therefore, Zabdiel Adams added, the state must continue to enforce attendance at public worship, where "the sacred obligations of religion [were] pointed out and inculcated."[27]

These clerical republicans were concerned about the capacity of their countrymen to discharge civil as well as "sacred" obligations.

In republican regimes that were grounded in the sovereignty of the people, it was imperative that the contracting parties fulfill their commitments to each other. "There is no stronger cement in society than a sacred regard to OATHS," wrote "Worcestriensis" in 1776. Challenges to true religion—that is, to the established church—"lessen the reverence of the people for oaths . . . so shaking the foundation of good order and security in society."[28] How, asked James Dana, could nonbelievers who assumed public trusts be offered "the oath of God"? "Can it have any binding force? And if their oath is no tie, do they not dissolve the bond of society?"[29] Rulers and citizens alike must be held accountable for their words and actions. "Reverence" or "fear of God" was the only guarantee of "that sense of moral obligation, without which," election preacher Simeon Howard concluded, "there can be no confidence, no peace or happiness in society."[30]

Yet it was not clear from clerical discourses exactly how state-supported and mandated public worship fostered good citizenship. Confusion on this point revealed the contradictory tendencies in Christian republicanism that undercut church establishments. Defenders of established religion could argue that public worship was the most efficacious means of the personal renovation, or "new birth," that transformed "subjects"—of Satan or King George III—into pious citizens who were capable of governing themselves. Christianity promoted "the welfare of society," Dana thus told the Connecticut legislature, "by making it's members what they ought to be."[31] But Dana and other election day preachers were uncomfortable with a purely evangelical conception of their ministry. The great legacies of the revivals that had swept New England in the 1740s were the proliferation of dissenting sects and a powerful tendency within New Light Congregationalism to eschew state support and rely on free-will offerings. And, as Charles Chauncy and other critics of the Great Awakening had warned, the New Lights' emphasis on instantaneous conversion and the new birth negated the traditional role of the churches in fostering morality and guiding their members toward salvation. If evangelical preaching could have such profound and lasting effects on born-again Christians, the institutional state-supported church was superfluous.[32]

The underlying premise of the argument for state support was that there were large numbers of nonbelievers or false Christians who had to be taught to submit to civil and religious authority; perhaps even authentic Christians, unable to slough off remnants of the Old Adam, still needed instruction in their duties. The emphasis in defenses of the establishment's prerogatives therefore was on a punitive God, not on His gracious intercession. But few evangelical Christians were moved by such evidently self-serving arguments for hierarchy and order in church and state. As the work of Alan Heimert and Harry S. Stout suggests, the Calvinist thrust of the Great Awakening was hostile to Old Light condemnations of human nature and justifications of established order.[33] By the time of the Revolution, most established clergymen in New England had been won over to a moderate New Light stance. They were increasingly wary about invoking state power to uphold their prerogatives or to curb dissent.

Popular religiosity tended to subvert the authority of established churches, even in New England, where clergymen—the so-called black regiment—eagerly embraced the revolutionary cause. The moral authority of the clergy was not based on unthinking popular deference to the ministerial office but instead depended on their enthusiastic advocacy of civil and religious liberties and their millennial vision of national redemption. The evangelicals who most fervently proclaimed God's sovereign power held earthly authorities in considerably lower esteem and were remarkable for their own assertiveness. New England clergymen did not have to be reminded of their dependence on the goodwill of all-powerful congregations. Even when election day preachers called on the legislatures to uphold the established church, they acknowledged the wisdom of the people and their representatives. Surely the revolutionaries' success on the battlefield demonstrated the extraordinary virtue of the American people.[34]

The belief that Americans were sufficiently pious and virtuous to vindicate their rights and govern themselves constituted a radical limitation on clerical pleas for state support of religion. Certainly the state should punish vice and immorality and encourage public worship; popular piety, most commentators agreed, was the surest foundation of good citizenship. But any state interference in matters of conscience was fraught with danger: after all, the source of true piety was the unmediated experience of God's grace. Defenders of church establishments thus faced the delicate task of reconciling state support with Christian liberty. Ironically, it was much easier for secularized republicans to argue for the utility of church establishments. After all, Montesquieu had advocated state churches that could indoctrinate republicans in the principles of virtue and patriotism.[35] But many Christian republicans were reluctant to confuse sacred and secular realms or to reduce the churches to such a clearly subordinate, instrumental role.

If defenders of church establishments had to respect the scruples of pious Christians about state interference, they also had to acknowledge that piety was not the only source of virtue. The wiser, better-educated sort obviously had less need of edifying religious instruction than the humble and ignorant. In theory, the axioms of natural law and right were self-evident to the meanest capacities. But conservative republicans such as Theophilus Parsons emphasized the difficulty of enlightening the ignorant. "The spirit of a free republican constitution," Parsons wrote in the *Essex Result*, "*ought* to be political virtue, patriotism, and a just regard to the natural rights of mankind." Where the "spirit" was "wanting," however, the state must turn to "that Being, who infused the breath of Life into our first parent."[36] The invidious distinction between the enlightened few and the ignorant mass was more fully developed by Joseph Lathrop, writing in response to agrarian disturbances in western Massachusetts: "The beauty and reasonableness of virtue, and its tendency to the happiness of mankind in private and social life, though an argument of real truth and importance, yet is, in some respects, too refined to be clearly perceived, and in other respects, too disinterested to be strongly felt by men not used to such speculations, or not already formed to a benevolent temper." Only the educated and leisured upper class could be animated by this natural, political virtue. For humbler folk, fear of a "righteous" God could take the place of enlightened understanding. Threats of divine "rewards and punishments" would carry an "awful weight" and be "level to the lowest capacity."[37]

Lathrop's primary concern was to sustain civil order. The preacher performed a vital civic function by teaching common folk to submit unquestioningly to legitimate authority. Such arguments appealed to political conservatives, but many Christian republicans found them deeply offensive. Prescriptions for political religion apparently recapitulated the hierarchical order of the old regime, with educated and enlightened magistrates and clergy exercising authority over the unthinking masses. From a radical republican perspective, justifications for established religion thus seemed to repudiate the fundamental republican faith in man's natural capacity for self-government. All men, conservatives such as Parsons and Lathrop seemed to suggest, were *not* created equal. Given their pessimistic assessment of man's fallen nature, Old Light Calvinists could readily endorse such a conclusion. But New Light evangelicals, who believed the Kingdom of God was imminent, embraced the idea of equality with their characteristic enthusiasm. By the grace of God, authentic Christians were equally empowered to promote His works. Evangelical preaching helped bring sinners to Christ, thus expanding the community of believers and eliminating arbitrary distinctions among them.

The creation of new republican governments underscored the importance of popular virtue and thus led many state constitution writers to endorse established religion. Paradoxically, however, the popular religious fervor that helped sustain the revolutionary movement ultimately proved incompatible with church establishments. Many Christians concluded that state support for a particular church, or even for a variety of recognized sects, did not promote the popular piety that alone could sustain republican government.

Republican Education

Sectarian diversity and evangelical piety limited the effectiveness of established churches in fostering good citizenship. The obvious, presumably uncontroversial alternative was to support public education. Republican citizens might bridle at heavy-handed political preaching, but who could question the need to instill patriotism and respect for authority in the rising generation? The education of youth should be the highest priority in a free state. "Despotism and tyranny want nothing but wealth and force," Phillips Payson told the Massachusetts General Court, "but liberty and order are supported by knowledge and virtue."[38] In his influential *Thoughts on Government* (1776), John Adams urged the new states to provide for the "liberal education of youth, especially of the lower class of people."[39] A decade later Benjamin Rush explained the importance of "an equal diffusion of literature." "Without learning," Rush asserted, "men become savages or barbarians, and where learning is confined to a *few* people, we always find monarchy, aristocracy, and slavery."[40]

Several of the new state constitutions recognized the need for state-supported schools. Heeding Adams's advice, the authors of the North Carolina Constitution promised to support "useful learning . . . at low prices" by establishing "a school or schools."[41] Pennsylvania's 1776 Constitution projected a more elaborate system, including "a school or schools" in each county and "one or more universities."[42] The classic rationale for republican education was set forth by Adams himself, the leading draftsman of the Massachusetts Constitution of 1780. According to Chapter V, section II, the general diffusion of "wisdom and knowledge, as well as virtue," was essential for preserving the people's "rights and liberties." Therefore it was incumbent on the state's governors to spread "the opportunities and advantages of education in the various parts of the country, and among the different orders of the people."[43]

Yet despite these constitutional provisions and a general agreement on the importance of a well-informed, virtuous citizenry, the new states took remarkably few practical steps to promote public education. There are obvious explanations for this failure. First, the political and economic disruptions of the war and postwar period precluded any systematic—and expensive—efforts to establish schools. In any case, the state governments had to rely on local jurisdictions to establish local schools. But rural citizens had a low tolerance for new tax burdens, a clear message of the agrarian disturbances that swept the countryside in the mid-1780s. As a result, the legislatures could do little beyond confirming or modifying the corporate privileges of the old colonial colleges and sanctioning largely private efforts to found a few new colleges.[44]

Conservative educational reformers did not believe that practical, political obstacles to state-supported schools justified the legislatures' inaction. "Every kind of useful knowledge will be carefully encouraged and promoted by the rulers of a free state," Payson told Massachusetts legislators in 1778, *unless they should be men of ignorance themselves.*"[45] Failing to follow Payson's advice, this and succeeding legislatures demonstrated their "ignorance." Conservative commentators were predisposed toward a pessimistic verdict on America's republican rulers: according to traditional, elite standards, the immediate effect of the Revolution had been to increase the ratio of "ignorant," uneducated common folk in the legislatures.[46] The resulting "blunders in legislation" came as no surprise to Noah Webster. "If we examine the men who comprise the legislatures," Webster wrote, "we shall find that wrong measures generally proceed from ignorance either in the men themselves, or in their constituents. They often mistake their own interest, because they do not foresee the remote consequences." [47]

Educational reformers were caught in a vicious circle. The manifest deficiencies of popular government were the leading justification for state-supported schools, but how could reformers persuade ignorant men to promote learning? The impasse appeared irremediable. "Did we know *more*," a Massachusetts writer complained, "we might govern ourselves—did we know *less* we should be governed by others." [48] Without a sufficiently well-informed public, republicanism was incompatible with good government—or perhaps with any government at all.

Although reformers such as Webster and Rush were clearly committed to republican principles, their proposals for public schools constituted powerful indictments of republican government in the American states. By identifying popular ignorance as the central problem, Webster and Rush implied that further tinkering with the state constitutions would be useless. Massachusetts and other states had already adopted new charters incorporating institutional checks on popular excesses, including stronger executives and bicameral legislatures, with disappointing results. Not coincidentally, Webster and Rush simultaneously advocated the creation of a much more powerful central government. The common theme in their proposals for educational and national constitutional reform was disillusionment with the state governments.

Efforts to foster popular virtue, whether through state-supported religious or educational establishments, were premised on pessimistic assessments of the character of the American people. Popular ignorance was less a lack of information than a lack of respect for the well-informed and a natural disposition toward selfishness and licentiousness. Noah Webster's essay on education, first published in 1787–88, shows the reformers' affinity for an authoritarian, Old Light conception of church and state. For Webster, the fundamental principle of government was subordination. Because government, so defined, is not natural to men in society, "it must be supplied by the rod in the school, the penal laws of the state, and the terrors of divine wrath from the pulpit." [49] Ironically, no defender of the established churches dared go this far in impugning the natural virtue, patriotism, and piety of the American people. In any case, most preachers who emphasized the "terrors of divine wrath" did so to bring sinners to Christ, not to serve the interests of the state by creating a docile, "governable" people.

Educational reformers emphasized the natural intractability of the uneducated and ill-informed child. "Let our pupil be taught that he does not belong to himself," Rush urged, "but that he is public property."[50] Drawing inspiration from Rush and citing the authority of the great lawgiver Lycurgus, preacher-scientist-entrepreneur Manasseh Cutler proclaimed the "grand principle . . . that children belonged to the state rather than to the parents."[51] Teaching children to submit to legitimate authority and to distinguish liberty from license was essential to good order in a republic. The essential task for families, schools, and churches alike was to break the wills of children, who were naturally savage, self-centered, and shortsighted. "The government both of families and schools should be absolute," Webster explained; "strict discipline . . . is the best foundation of good order in political society."[52]

The unflattering characterization of children in their "natural" state could easily be extended to embrace the great unwashed, ill-informed mass of adults suspended in a state of perennial childhood. The class bias of these educational and religious programs is unmistakable: although it was necessary to make the common folk into "republican machines," according to Rush's infamous prescription, the better sort rationally appreciated the advantages of republican government and so displayed a more active, self-directed "virtue."[53] Public schools certainly might identify and cultivate natural aristocrats among the common people, but the primary function of republican education was to control and discipline the unruly masses.

The early public school proposals reveal growing pessimism among conservatives about the future of republicanism in America. The reformers' barely concealed contempt for the common folk guaranteed that their schemes would be defeated. The failure of educational reform also revealed the controversial character of basic republican premises and values. If Americans generally agreed about the need for a well-informed citizenry, they differed radically over what republican citizens needed to know and over the sources of that knowledge. Building new schools was not necessarily the best means of promoting popular virtue. After all, the central tenet of revolutionary ideology was that the sovereign people were capable of grasping the fundamental axioms of law and politics. The demystification of authority—in all fields—encouraged ordinary Americans to use their "common sense" to extend knowledge and promote their own and the country's welfare.[54]

Revolutionaries such as the historian David Ramsay believed that British tyranny had suppressed the arts and sciences in America. It followed that independence would give a major boost to learning. "A few years will now produce a much greater number of men of learning and abilities," he predicted in 1778, "than we could have expected for ages in our boyish state of minority, guided by the leading strings of a parent country." Ramsay thought the Revolution would lift the pall of ignorance and inspire a general pursuit of truth, as well as of happiness. "The times in which we live, and the governments we have lately adopted," he concluded, "all conspire to fan the sparks of genius in every breast, and kindle them into flame."[55]

Radical republicans believed the exigencies of war and state-making would release the latent, natural "genius" of each republican citizen. Practical knowledge of human nature was best obtained in the busy concourse of republican society, where "mankind appear as they really are, without any false coloring." By participating in the common cause, Americans would learn from each other; when they were liberated to pursue their individual and collective welfare, their ingenuity would rise to the challenges presented by a vast "untutored continent."[56]

In a republic, the native genius of each citizen was fulfilled through active engagement with other citizens and with the natural environment. Republican learning thus was identified with the challenges presented by widespread economic and political opportunity, not with the attainment of rarefied knowledge that accentuated social distances.[57] Americans rejected the claims of superior, centralized authority in the cultural as well as political realm. Knowledge, like political authority, was broadly grounded in the sovereign people. Juxtaposed to the artificiality and overrefinement of European "civilization," America's republican society was more "natural"—that is, more nearly in accord with human nature. In resisting British tyranny, American patriots had grasped the fundamental "natural laws" defining individual rights and governing political life. Similarly, by uncovering the analogous natural laws governing the material world, enterprising Americans could attain unprecedented prosperity, power, and social happiness. "Here is opened a wide and extensive field," exclaimed James Bowdoin, "which the sons of literature are invited to cultivate and improve."[58]

Republican theorists sought to offset Europe's traditional cultural authority in America by exalting the role of nature and natural law. American nature was not simply an antidote for the vices and corruption of overcivilized Europe; instead, in Joel Barlow's words, the continent's bountiful "natural resources" called forth the "enterprising genius" of the American people.[59] In mastering the wilderness, Americans would gain new knowledge, enabling them to exploit the "dormant powers of nature and the elements."[60] "A large volume of the book of nature, yet unread, is open before us," Ramsay explained, "and invites our attentive perusal."[61] Because the Revolution freed Americans to explore and exploit the vast continent before them, the arts and sciences would flourish.

Although most Americans agreed that schools were necessary to disseminate basic skills and teach young people the responsibilities of citizenship, the most visionary republicans relegated formal education to a distinctly secondary role. The purpose of republican education, they suggested, was to enable citizens to express their natural genius, not to beat them into docile submission. Thomas Jefferson believed that schools should equip the people "to know ambition under all its shapes, and [to be] prompt to exert their natural powers to defeat its purposes."[62] Popular education thus was the best safeguard against a self-aggrandizing ruling class. Republican education, so conceived, would not express or support the social and political distinctions cherished by conservative educational reformers but would instead guarantee responsible, limited government.

The most enthusiastic patriots were convinced that virtue and piety were already broadly diffused among the people and therefore did not depend on state-supported churches or schools. By declaring their independence, Americans liberated themselves from the shackles of ignorance and could now test their natural genius against the opportunities afforded by a vast continent. The new state constitutions guaranteed a vigorous public life that would itself be a source of popular enlightenment. "Demophilus" thus urged Pennsylvanians to institute "town meetings among the people" that would "raise up so many able men to improve its internal police." Expanding political participation, not schools, would guarantee that "the science of *just* and *equal* government, will shine conspicuous in Pennsylvania."[63]

The plans of educational reformers betrayed a radical and self-defeating ambivalence about the nature of education in republican society. Conservative writers such as Webster and Rush recognized that schools should help disseminate "useful knowledge" and that education in the New World should serve the interests of the many, not the few. The conservatives therefore joined in disparaging the traditional monopoly of exclusive, aristocratic schools and universities, insisting on the broadly inclusive, practical character of the arts and sciences in a republican society. In America merely "ornamental" learning should not be allowed to serve as a pretext for claims to social and political preeminence.[64] Yet educational reformers were clearly more concerned about popular ignorance than about the abuses of elite education. The schools' leading function, they suggested, was not to empower the people but to teach them to submit to authority. Although Rush's and Webster's republican credentials cannot be doubted, their obsession with controlling a licentious and unruly people was at odds with the basic republican premise that the people were capable of knowing their own true interests and therefore of governing themselves.[65] A clear idea of what schools were supposed to do was the inevitable casualty of this fundamental confusion.

If conservative commentators had ample reason to question the political character of the American people during the "critical period," representatives of the people might equally well doubt the motives of the self-proclaimed better sort. Many republicans saw the Society of the Cincinnati as a brazen move to institute an American aristocracy.[66] Similarly, common folk continued to resist the claims of lawyers and preachers who sought to overawe the people with their erudition. "Learning often serves only to make man eminently mischievous and hurtful," a South Carolina writer warned.[67] Perhaps state-supported schools would accentuate social distinctions by elevating the educated few above the ignorant mass. Jealous of their liberties and suspicious of the intentions of the elite, the people's representatives may well have concluded that it would be better for republics not to support schools at all than to allow would-be aristocrats to use them to advance their class interests at the people's expense.

Optimistic patriots were confident that most of what Americans needed to know to be a free and prosperous people could be grasped by the "meanest capacity." Similarly, as the great religious revivals showed, a "saving knowledge" of Christ was often vouchsafed to the humblest Christians. Evangelicals thus downplayed the importance of the institutional church and an educated clergy. Vital piety, not worldly knowledge, was the true wellspring of republican virtue.

Forming Minds

The revolutionaries of 1776 agreed that "the quality of private characters" was crucial to the success of America's republican experiment.[68] "Our governors have a right to take every proper method to form the minds of their subjects," clergyman Samuel West asserted in a 1776 Massachusetts election sermon. But what methods were "proper," and how much would American minds have to be formed? When West wrote, the task of educating the public did not appear as formidable as it would a decade later. West predicted that "the wisest and most experienced" would soon be recognized as America's "natural" leaders. In a "state of nature," when the "dictates of conscience and the precepts of natural law" were "uniformly and regularly obeyed, men would only need to be informed what things were most fit and prudent to be done." The primary role of republican leaders therefore was to inform and enlighten the people when a lack of knowledge and experience "left their minds in doubt." A republican government would tend to obliterate the distinction between elite knowledge and popular ignorance on which aristocratic regimes depended.[69]

West assumed that the common folk were predisposed to do good and that their character was naturally virtuous. It was imperative "that we should thoroughly study the law of nature, the rights of mankind, and the reciprocal duties of governors and governed." But it was possible for Americans to gain a "thorough acquaintance" with the principles of natural law while "remaining ignorant of many technical terms of law" and "utterly unacquainted with the obscure and barbarous Latin that was so much used in the ages of popish darkness and superstition." Schools that were devoted to cultivating these abstruse, technical branches of learning were worse than useless: they threatened the health of the republican body politic.[70]

Yet revolutionary optimism soon gave way to doubts and misgivings as political tensions and ideological contradictions began to rupture the patriot coalition.[71] As a result, efforts to shape character and form minds through churches and schools proved politically controversial. Unfortunately, many conservative commentators concluded, the common folk did not know what was good for them; their resistance to the edifying instruction of their betters suggested that they were insufficiently virtuous to sustain republican rule. The problem was already clear in 1778, when William Whiting sought to bring the fractious "inhabitants of Berkshire County" to their political senses. Although, Whiting acknowledged, "there may not . . . be a set of people in the world, who are blessed with better natural geniuses," the farmers of Berkshire were not well enough informed about "matters of a political nature . . . to distinguish the principles of a free and equal government, from those of despotism and tyranny." Echoing Samuel West, Whiting called for the reasonable deference of uninformed "natural geniuses" to wiser, more experienced natural leaders. But Whiting recognized that the people of western Massachusetts were all too prone to resist instruction, particularly from lawyers. Because many judges and lawyers had sided with the Crown and creditors had used the courts to seize the property of indebted farmers, the common folk displayed a regrettable, if understandable, "prejudice against law" and "an undue hatred and jealousy against all the men who have been appointed to administer, or have attempted to introduce, law into the country."[72]

The problem was not simply a lack of information, but rather a pervasive popular "prejudice," "hatred," and "jealousy" against the well-informed. For all their natural genius, the people seemed determined to resist all reasonable appeals. Whiting's paradoxical formulation shows how popular wisdom, piety, and virtue could be so drastically discounted in conservative polemics. The capacity of the people to govern themselves was thus transformed from an assumption to a problem. Conservatives did not abandon the republican faith: the people might learn how to govern themselves, or rather submit to the government of their natural superiors, if they were properly instructed. But the kind of instruction advocated by educational reformers and defenders of clerical establishments constituted a massive indictment of the intelligence and virtue of the people. Because they were naturally irrational, licentious, and vicious, the common people would have to be taught to submit to legitimate authority.

But the conservatives' message fell on deaf ears. For those whose faith in the people remained unshaken, efforts to create elaborate educational establishments or to preserve the privileges of established churches seemed to mask some sinister, "aristocratic" purpose. Such suspicions subverted efforts to shape republican morality. If most Americans agreed that a well-informed and virtuous citizenry was essential for the survival of the republic, they differed profoundly over how those qualities could best be fostered and sustained. As a result, there was no clear consensus on the proper role of state-supported churches and schools in shaping republican character. Those most persuaded that virtue was in decline were most inclined to advocate sumptuary legislation and state-supported schools and churches. But given the "democratic" character of state politics during the Confederation period, it was impossible for conservative "reformers" to gain significant support for programs premised on the people's lack of virtue. This was particularly true, of course, when reformers suggested that popular policies of the legislatures themselves provided the most compelling evidence of moral decline and decay. If there was "a Republican remedy for the diseases most incident to Republican Government," as James Madison promised in *Federalist* No. 10, that remedy would *not* be found in the states.[73]

Conclusion

The crucial move that James Madison and the Federalists made in 1787 was to dissociate themselves from earlier efforts of nationalist-minded reformers to shape the character of the people. To do this, of course, they had to overcome the profound skepticism about popular licentiousness and "democratic despotism" in the states that had brought many delegates to Philadelphia in the first place. But if Madison learned to live with the states, he did not expect much from them; he certainly did not rely on them to make the people virtuous. If the national government were properly constructed with the states confined to their appropriate spheres, the people would be found sufficiently virtuous to act their proper parts in the new scheme. Perhaps, in the throes of their critical period, Madison and his colleagues had made too much of the vicious and degraded character of the people and the state governments. In 1788, when he sought to persuade his fellow Virginians to join the new Union, he acknowledged that there was sufficient "virtue and intelligence" among the people to sustain republicanism. Popular virtue was an essential assumption, not the central problem, of republican government.

Was popular virtue simply to be taken for granted? What were its ultimate sources? Scholars have suggested a variety of intriguing answers. Madison thought that "extending the sphere" would curb factiousness, thus rejecting the traditional idea that virtue was a product of the civic life of small republics; some republicans hoped the spread of commerce and the growth of interlocking interests would bring Americans closer together and instill common values; and many, of course, continued to rely on the people's piety and their natural love of liberty to sustain free government. But few of them put much faith in state-supported churches or even in public education. The state governments would play important roles in the new system, most notably in checking encroachments on their own rights and in guarding the liberties of their citizens. But the founders did not rely on the states to foster virtue. Quite the contrary: for at least some of the founders, the urgency of national constitutional reform reflected the *failure* of the states to act effectively to shape the political character of the American people.

Notes

1. James Madison speech in Virginia convention, in *The Debates in the Several State Conventions on the Adoption of the Federal Constitution*, ed. Jonathan Elliot (1876; rpt. Philadelphia: Jonathan Lippincott, 1941), 3:536–37. For an incisive reading of this passage see Lance Banning, "Some Second Thoughts on Virtue and the Course of Revolutionary Thinking," in Terence Ball and J. G. A. Pocock, *Conceptual Change and the Constitution* (Lawrence, Kan.: University Press of Kansas, 1988), 194–212.

2. For good statements of this position see Richard Vetterli and Gary Bryner, *In Search of the Republic: Public Virtue and the Roots of American Government* (Totowa, N.J.: Rowman, 1987); and Jean Yarbrough, "The Constitution and Character: The Missing Critical Principle?" in *To Form a More Perfect Union: The Critical Ideas of the Constitution*, ed. Herman Belz, Ronald Hoffman, and Peter J. Albert (Charlottesville, Va., forthcoming, 1992). For an excellent critical analysis of arguments for the importance of Christianity in American republicanism see Thomas L. Pangle, *The Spirit of Modern Republicanism: The Moral Vision of the American Founders and the Philosophy of Locke* (Chicago: University of Chicago Press, 1988), 78–85, 107.

3. Stephen Botein, "Religious Dimensions of the Early American State," in *Beyond Confederation: Origins of the Constitution and American National*

Identity, ed. Richard Beeman, Stephen Botein, and Edward C. Carter II (Chapel Hill: University of North Carolina Press, 1987), 317–18. Botein adds, however, that "the constitutions of the separate states were anything but secular." Ibid., 318. My understanding of church-state relations in the founding era relies heavily on Botein's perceptive essay and on Thomas J. Curry, *The First Freedoms: Church and State in America to the Passage of the First Amendment* (New York: Oxford University Press, 1986); and William Lee Miller, *The First Liberty: Religion and the American Republic* (New York: Knopf, 1986). See also Leonard Levy's vigorous broadside against the "nonpreferentialists" in *The Establishment Clause: Religion and the First Amendment* (New York: Macmillan, 1986).

4. Gary D. Glenn, "Forgotten Purposes of the First Amendment Religion Clauses," *Review of Politics* 49 (1987): 340–67.

5. James Madison, "Vices of the Political System of the United States, [April 1787]," in *The Papers of James Madison*, ed. Robert A. Rutland et al. (Chicago and Charlottesville: University Press of Virginia, 1962–), 9:345–57. See Gordon S. Wood, *The Creation of the American Republic, 1776–1787* (Chapel Hill: University of North Carolina Press, 1969), 393–429.

6. When and why Madison came to this realization is the subject of considerable controversy. See my discussion in "Reflections on the Founding: Constitutional Historiography in Bicentennial Perspective," *William and Mary Quarterly*, 3d ser., 46 (1989): 361–63.

7. Benjamin Rush, *A Plan for the Establishment of Public Schools and the Diffusion of Knowledge in Pennsylvania* (Philadelphia, 1786), in *Essays on Education in the Early Republic*, ed. Frederick Rudolph (Cambridge, Mass.: Harvard University Press, 1965), 11.

8. This is one of the leading themes of Madison's "Memorial and Remonstrance against Religious Assessments, [1785]" in *American Political Writing during the Founding Era, 1760–1815*, ed. Charles S. Hyneman and Donald S. Lutz (Indianapolis: Liberty Press, 1983), 1:631–37. See the illuminating discussion in Rhys Isaac, " 'The Rage of Malice of the Old Serpent Devil': The Dissenters and the Making and Remaking of the Virginia Statute for Religious Freedom," in *The Virginia Statute for Religious Freedom: Its Evolution and Consequences in American History*, ed. Merrill D. Peterson and Robert C. Vaughan (New York: Cambridge University Press, 1988), 139–69.

9. Mass. Const. (1780), Declaration of Rights, § 3, in *The Federal and State Constitutions, Colonial Charters, and Other Organic Laws of the State, Territories, and Colonies: Now or Heretofore Forming the United States of America*, ed. Francis N. Thorpe (Washington, D.C.: U.S. Government Printing Office, 1909), 3:1889–90.

10. N.H. Const. (1784), Bill of Rights, § 6, ibid., 4:2454.

11. See, for instance, provisions in the Md. Const. (1776), ibid., 3:1690, and N.C. Const. (1776), ibid., 5:2793.

12. S.C. Const. (1778), § 38, ibid., 6:3248, 3255–56.

13. Md. Const. (1776), Declaration of Rights, § 33, ibid., 3:1686, 1689.

14. Ibid.

15. N.J. Const. (1776), § 19, ibid., 5:2594, 2597.

16. N.Y. Const. (1777), § 38, ibid., 5:2623, 2636–37.

17. N.C. Const. (1776), § 32, ibid., 2787, 2793. For a concise survey of such provisions in early state constitutions see Morton Borden, *Jews, Turks, and Infidels* (Chapel Hill: University of North Carolina Press, 1984), 11–15.

18. Del. Const. (1792), Art. 1, § 1, in *Federal and State Constitutions,* ed. Thorpe, 1:568.

19. See Miller, *First Liberty,* 3–150, and the essays collected in *The Virginia Statute for Religious Freedom,* ed. Peterson and Vaughan.

20. Va. Const. (1776), Bill of Rights, § 16, in *Federal and State Constitutions,* ed. Thorpe, 7:3814.

21. Madison, "Memorial and Remonstrance," 636.

22. Va. Const. (1776), Bill of Rights, § 15, in *Federal and State Constitutions,* ed. Thorpe, 7:3814.

23. For the text of the statute and illuminating commentaries see *The Virginia Statute for Religious Freedom,* ed. Peterson and Vaughan.

24. Curry, *First Freedoms,* 165–75.

25. Phillips Payson, "A Sermon [Boston, 1778]," in *American Political Writing,* ed. Hyneman and Lutz, 1:530.

26. Moses Hemmenway, *A Sermon, Preached Before His Excellency John Hancock* (Boston: Printed by Benjamin Edes & Sons, 1784), 32.

27. Zabdiel Adams, "An Election Sermon [Boston, 1782]," in *American Political Writing,* ed. Hyneman and Lutz, 1:556.

28. "Worcestriensis," *Massachusetts Spy,* September 4, 1776, ibid., 1:452.

29. James Dana, *A Sermon, Preached Before the General Assembly of the State of Connecticut . . . May 13, 1779* (Hartford: Printed by Hudson and Goodwin, 1779), 40.

30. Simeon Howard, *A Sermon Preached Before the Honourable Council . . . May 31, 1780* (Boston: Printed by John Gill, 1780), 20, 24.

31. Dana, *Sermon,* 14.

32. Edwin Scott Gaustad, *The Great Awakening in New England* (1957; rpt. Chicago: Quadrangle, 1968), 80–101 and passim.

33. Alan Heimert, *Religion and the American Mind: From the Great Awakening to the Revolution* (Cambridge, Mass.: Harvard University Press, 1966); Harry S. Stout, "Religion, Communications, and the Ideological Ori-

gins of the American Revolution," *William and Mary Quarterly* 3d ser., 34 (1977): 519–41.

34. Heimert, *Religion and the American Mind.*
35. Noah Webster, *On the Education of Youth in America* (Boston, 1790), first published in *American Magazine*, 1787–88, in *Essays on Education*, ed. Rudolph, 65, citing Montesquieu, *Spirit of the Laws*, 1:42.
36. [Theophilus Parsons], *The Essex Result* (Newburyport, 1778), in *American Political Writing*, ed. Hyneman and Lutz, 1:480, 521.
37. Joseph Lathrop, *A Miscellaneous Collection of Original Pieces* (Springfield, 1786), in *American Political Writing*, ed. Hyneman and Lutz, 1:666–67.
38. Payson, "Sermon," 527–28.
39. John Adams, *Thoughts on Government* (Boston, 1776), in *American Political Writing*, ed. Hyneman and Lutz, 1:407.
40. Rush, *Plan for Public Schools*, 3.
41. N.C. Const. § 41, in *Federal and State Constitutions*, ed. Thorpe, 5:2794.
42. Pa. Const. § 44, ibid., 5:3091.
43. Mass. Const. chap. 5, § 2, ibid., 1907–8.
44. David W. Robson, "College Founding in the New Republic, 1776–1800," *History of Education Quarterly* 23 (1983): 323–41.
45. Payson, "Sermon," 527; emphasis added.
46. Jackson T. Main, "Government by the People: The American Revolution and the Democratization of the Legislatures," *William and Mary Quarterly* 3d ser., 23 (1966): 391–407.
47. Webster, *On the Education of Youth*, 67.
48. "The Worcester Speculator," *Worcester Magazine*, October 1787, in *American Political Writing*, ed. Hyneman and Lutz, 1:700.
49. Webster, *On the Education of Youth*, 57.
50. Rush, *Plan for Public Schools*, 14.
51. Manasseh Cutler, "Sermon Preached at Camous Martius, [Marietta, North-West Territory, August 24, 1788]," in William Parker Cutler and Julia Perkins Cutler, *Life, Journals and Correspondence of Rev. Manasseh Cutler, LL.D.* (1888; rpt. Athens: Ohio University Press, 1987), 2:449.
52. Webster, *On the Education of Youth*, 57–58.
53. Rush, *Plan for Public Schools*, 17.
54. The following paragraphs are adapted from Peter S. Onuf, "The Founders' Vision: Education in the Development of the Old Northwest," in *". . . Schools and the Means of Education Shall Forever Be Encouraged*," ed. Paul H. Mattingly and Edward W. Stevens, Jr. (Athens: Ohio University Library, 1987), 4–15.
55. David Ramsay, *An Oration on the Advantages of American Independence: Delivered . . . on the Fourth of July, 1778* (Charleston: Printed by John Wells, Jr., 1778), 4.

56. Ibid., 8, 3.

57. Many revolutionaries were hostile to the pretensions of lawyers—
one of the most conspicuously "learned" classes in contemporary
America—because of the way they supposedly exploited their expert
knowledge at the expense of the public. See Joseph E. Ellis, *The Jeffersonian Crisis: Courts and Politics in the Young Republic* (1971; rpt. New York:
Norton, 1974), 111–22.

58. James Bowdoin, *A Philosophical Discourse, Addressed to the American
Academy of Arts and Sciences* (Boston: Printed by Benjamin Edes and
Sons, 1780), 9.

59. Joel Barlow, "Oration to the Cincinnati, [Hartford, July 4, 1787]," *American Museum* 2 (August 1787): 142.

60. Tench Coxe, "An address to the friends of American manufactures,
[Philadelphia, August 9, 1787]," *American Museum* 2 (September 1787):
255.

61. Ramsay, *Oration on American Independence*, 8.

62. [Thomas Jefferson], "A Bill for the More General Diffusion of Knowledge, [December 1778]," in *The Papers of Thomas Jefferson*, ed. Julian P.
Boyd et al. (Princeton: Princeton University Press, 1950–), 2:526–33.

63. "Demophilus" [George Bryan?], *The Genuine Principles of the Ancient
Saxon or English Constitution* (Philadelphia, 1776), in *American Political
Writing*, ed. Hyneman and Lutz, 1:363.

64. "In the opulent part of civilized nations" such as England, education
"is directed principally to show and amusement." Webster, *On the
Education of Youth*, 44.

65. See Richard M. Rollins, "Words as Social Control: Noah Webster and
the Creation of the *American Dictionary*," *American Quarterly* 28 (1976):
415–30.

66. Wallace Evan Davies, "The Society of Cincinnati in New England,"
William and Mary Quarterly 3d ser., 5 (1948): 2–25; Charles Royster, *A
Revolutionary People at War: The Continental Army and American Character, 1775–1783* (Chapel Hill: University of North Carolina Press, 1979),
349–57.

67. [Anonymous], *Rudiments of Law and Government Deduced* (Charleston,
1783), in *American Political Writing*, ed. Hyneman and Lutz, 1:582.

68. Ibid., 600.

69. Samuel West, *On the Right to Rebel* (Boston, 1776), in *American Political
Writing*, ed. Hyneman and Lutz, 1:413, 432.

70. Ibid., 447.

71. Royster, *Revolutionary People at War*, 295–330; Jack N. Rakove, *The Beginnings of National Politics: An Interpretive History of the Continental Congress*
(New York: Knopf, 1979).

72. William Whiting, *An Address to the Inhabitants of Berkshire County* (1778), in *American Political Writing*, ed. Hyneman and Lutz, 1:463–64.

73. Alexander Hamilton, James Madison, and John Jay, *The Federalist*, ed. Jacob E. Cooke (Middletown, Conn.: Wesleyan University Press, 1961), no. 10 (Madison), 65.

Rights of Conscience and State School Systems in Nineteenth-Century America

Thomas James

Current usage in the United States treats conscience primarily as individual freedom of thought in deciding what is right. As an example, one thinks of the conscientious objector who refuses to comply with state mandates when to do so would violate deeply held beliefs. In contrast, judicial decisions on conscience and schooling until the end of the nineteenth century virtually ignored individual conscience. Instead, they took majority rule to be the arbiter of disputes over conscience and schooling. Reasoning from that premise, they recognized a unified, collective conscience, an imputed societal consensus about the proper system of belief for learning what is right through common schooling. The policies affirmed by those decisions, such as Bible reading and corporate prayers during the school day, granted legitimacy to that collective conscience as this society's pathway to freedom and democratic citizenship.

Many issues of conscience, as we currently understand the term, did not give rise to explicit public policy in the nineteenth century. Alexis de Tocqueville was amused during his visit to the United States by a newspaper article that mentioned a judge's refusal to hear testimony from a witness in court because the man professed to be an atheist.[1] The conscience of the unbeliever, the lone dissenter without voice in a Christian nation, was hardly recognizable in the public culture of the day.

As the example of the atheist in court suggests, rights of conscience cannot be understood apart from their religious origins. Such rights took form in the struggle of dissenting Protestant sects to build communities in which they could freely and exclusively practice their corporate faith. Formal education in the United States, the tradition of cultural transmission that crystallized as schooling institutions in American society, sprang from the same origins. Nowhere is this more clear than in the experience of the Puritans, who in 1647 enacted the first comprehensive school law in the Western Hemisphere, a measure designed to counter the presumed influence of Satan among young people in the towns of Massachusetts. Puritan leaders acted decisively because they knew that literacy strengthened the cultural cohesion of dissenting communities of belief. It protected their values against the organized hierarchies of the Old World. It fortified them, not so much against the chaos and cultural amnesia of the wilderness as against competition among diverse sectarian and secular systems of value. Given the strong influence of New England community traditions on the genesis of American education,[2] the notion of conscience as an educational goal continued to reflect the deep-seated social agreements and impasses arising from the history of that region.

For the Puritans, as William G. McLoughlin explains in his study of dissent in New England, "liberty of conscience meant freedom from persecution for those who believed in and practiced the true Christian religion." Those who separated themselves from that understanding were subject to banishment from the community. Such expulsion was viewed not as "persecution" but as "punishment," suggests McLoughlin, for in the prevailing understanding of the Puritans, conscience was a faculty "capable of performing only the one function assigned to it," which was to recognize the "word of God" within the accepted beliefs and texts of the community. The separatists were banished from the community, therefore, not so much for "conscience misinformed," because that could be corrected, but for an act of will, for refusing to be "informed" properly.[3]

Against this prevailing view, separatists such as Roger Williams had defended the right to practice alternative forms of belief. Splitting off from the Puritan commonwealth to form new dissenting communities, they posited conscience as a faculty capable of developing different modes of grasping the nature of good and evil, though like others throughout the American colonies they shared the same fundamentally Protestant assumptions about the pietistic function of conscience.

Years later, Thomas Jefferson added a more familiarly modern view during the revolutionary transformation of the colonies into a nation-state. Jefferson and other Enlightenment rationalists treated individual conscience as entirely private. Freedom of conscience, though still interpreted as a religious function, was to be a natural right existing before any public sanction under a republican form of government, and thus not within the purview of political authority.[4]

Yet this ideal never came close to being realized in revolutionary America. In his *Notes on Virginia* (1787), Jefferson lamented the "religious slavery" codified in law and social practice. Still on the books in Virginia was a law passed in the eighteenth century stipulating that if someone "denies the being of a God, or the Trinity, or asserts there are more gods than one, or denies the Christian religion to be true, or the scriptures to be of divine authority, he is punishable on the first offence by incapacity to hold any office or employment ecclesiastical, civil, or military; on the second by disability to sue, to take any gift or legacy, to be guardian, executor, or administrator, and by three years' imprisonment without bail."[5] Jefferson argued vehemently against such legalized orthodoxy: "The operations of the mind, as well as the acts of the body, are subject to the coercion of the laws. But our rulers can have no authority over such natural rights, only as we have submitted to them. The rights of conscience we never submitted, we could not submit. We are answerable for them to our God. The legitimate powers of government extend to such acts only as are injurious to others. But it does me no injury for my neighbor to say there are twenty gods, or no God. It neither picks my pocket nor breaks my leg."[6]

Jefferson's most often quoted dictum on church and state denies that government should have any involvement whatsoever in matters of religious conscience. Replying to the Danbury Baptist Association at the beginning of the nineteenth century, he gave the broadest possible interpretation to the meaning of the First Amendment to the U.S. Constitution: "I contemplate with sovereign reverence that act of the whole American people which declared that their legislature should 'make no law respecting an establishment of religion, or prohibiting the free exercise thereof,' thus building a wall of separation between Church and State."[7]

Although the "wall of separation" might be said in retrospect to have become the received wisdom in American public policy, it is sobering to recall that the legalization of this dictum as a national prohibition against Bible reading and prayer in public schools is less than thirty years old. Natural rights, though central to the Declaration of Independence and the Bill of Rights, exercised less influence on legal culture and institutional practice in the nation's early decades than is often assumed.[8] Not until 1923 was state law subjected to federal constitutional provisions on religious freedom and the separation of church and state.[9] As the common school movement took hold in the nineteenth century, the rule of law followed commonsense notions of the majority about the rationale of expanding social institutions, supporting a Protestant cultural hegemony over the ultimate values that breathed life into a republican form of government. Many leaders believed that the polity itself and the natural law sustaining its cherished freedoms not only sprang directly from those values but were inconceivable without them. They believed this despite, and in part because of, the constant pressure of pluralism in a growing democracy raising up its young citizens from many ethnic communities and cultural backgrounds. The unitary view of conscience as a single-purpose faculty, or mental organ, which could be developed only through the inculcation of values drawn from Protestant Christianity, remained the dominant paradigm of moral instruction in the spread of common schools.[10]

The history of disagreements over that majoritarian consensus forms the subject of this essay. The development of schooling in the United States was a battleground for the differing forms of socialization preferred by majorities and minorities. Through a deepened understanding of the legal categories used to regulate these conflicts, it is possible to reconstruct the shifting boundaries of state-protected rights of conscience as state-sponsored common schooling expanded. The inquiry proceeds first by suggesting a frame of reference—the struggle to define the universality of common schooling—for addressing questions of conscience in the expansion of state school systems during the nineteenth century. Then it traces the development of legal reasoning in that century's most celebrated disagreement over majoritarian orthodoxy: the use of the King James Bible as a required textbook in common schools. Finally, it is suggested that compulsory attendance requirements in state law heightened the tension between state-sanctioned forms of socialization and state-protected rights of conscience. This tension remains central to the historical experience of universal popular schooling in the United States.

The Quest for Universality

Schools were anything but universal in the half-century after the American Revolution. During the first three decades of the nineteenth century, government sponsorship of schooling in the United States did little more than condone existing sectarian, voluntaristic, and charitable traditions. Where schools existed, local communities had relied upon those traditions since colonial times to transmit the fundamentals of literacy and the values controlling social participation in community life.

A momentous change occurred as new states joined the Union. States, not the federal government, had—and still have—primary constitutional authority for education. As the nineteenth century progressed, state governments began to do much more than recognize local practice and precedent. Emanating from older established states such as Massachusetts and Connecticut, then taking root before the Civil War in newer free states such as Ohio, Michigan, and California, a growing body of reform ideas, constitutional provisions, and school laws helped to shape educational expansion, accelerating some kinds of institutional development while frustrating others. The power to define schooling in the public sphere, not only to determine its governing structure but to designate public schools as such, support them with tax dollars, and prescribe necessary content, had the effect of cultivating some forms of instruction while driving others to the margins of public life.

As the nation expanded, common schooling became one of the great reform movements of the nineteenth century. Members of an organized evangelical alliance, reformers were intent on winning the West through their persuasive efforts. They spoke of common schooling in religious, even millennial terms, as a social salvation for growing communities. Schooling was conditioned to some degree by the language that people invoked when building consent for educational expansion, and school builders surrounded their institutions with explicitly pietistic language.[11] It was no accident that common schools were made to look like chapels; local citizens heard schooling depicted as a national religious quest, a search for moral authority in communities that were themselves founded as part of a religious destiny in a Christian nation. As the primary agency beyond family and church for building moral cohesion, schools were expected to implant a common

conscience across families, churches, and communities, thus ensur-
ing such cohesion on a larger scale throughout the republic. From the
letter A—which the schoolchild's speller in New England had introduced for decades with a verse on original sin, "In Adam's fall, we
sinned All"—the process of education and the influence of Protestant-
ism were inseparable in the common schools.[12]

Another stimulus for the growth of state-sponsored schooling
was the assumed connection between education, understood broadly
as a religious and moral quest, and republican institutions in a democracy. A seminal statement of that connection is to be found in the
Declaration of Rights of the Massachusetts Constitution of 1780, which
established the right of the people to instruction by "public Protestant teachers of piety, religion, and morality" and stressed the importance of this right in maintaining civil order and happiness.[13] While
Thomas Jefferson and other founders of the national government
sought to avoid encouraging established state religion in their educational proposals, others—Benjamin Rush, for example—placed religious instruction at the center of their schooling plans. Rush hoped to
use Christian training to produce "republican machines" for the new
nation. "Let our pupil be taught that he does not belong to himself,"
he argued, "but that he is public property." To be free, according to
this reasoning, a citizen belongs to a state that defines itself a priori
as the bastion of freedom. To place the citizenry on that high ground
of total freedom, reading the Bible in classrooms was essential to the
political process. Rush asked rhetorically, "When a man who is of
doubtful character offers his vote, would it not be more consistent
with sound policy and wise government to oblige him to read a few
verses in the Bible to prove his qualifications than simply to compel
him to kiss the *outside* of it?"[14]

The connection between religious education and republican institutions was usually more subtle. School reformers frequently drew
from a set of tacit assumptions about how to organize civic instruction in universalistic terms but with religious overtones. They sought
a generalized civil religion to stabilize secular values in a fractious
polity, rather than the inculcation of specific religious doctrine drawn
from sectarian practice. The disestablishment of churches in the eighteenth century, far from excluding religious language from the polity,
had made pan-sectarian Christian unity the lingua franca of civic
republicanism. Political leaders and educational reformers drew on

religious themes to establish the legitimacy of the new order they proposed. As the authority of the churches receded and that of secular governmental authorities grew in the formal education of the young, institution builders used the consensual basis of a shared religious culture to designate unity of purpose and harmony of interests amid growing state involvement in schooling. Noah Webster, who opposed Bible reading and advised Americans to "unshackle your minds and act like independent beings," nevertheless signaled the determination of the nation's educational thinkers to cement religious faith into an enduring core of republican virtues when he proposed a "Federal Catechism" to standardize the thought and language of would-be citizens.[15] The founders did not succeed in building an educational system in the early national period, but they established a strong precedent for obscuring the distinction between nationalistic and religious aims in the education of the young.[16]

The nation's founders also gave impetus to educational expansion throughout the nineteenth century by linking evangelical nationalism with the distribution of public lands to stimulate construction of schools. The Northwest Ordinance of 1787 placed schooling at the center of democratic state building in new states with the following language: "Religion, morality, and knowledge, being necessary to good government and the happiness of mankind, schools and the means of education shall forever be encouraged."[17] Setting aside a portion of new lands to the west in support of schools, the Northwest Ordinance listed religion first among the forms of culture to be transmitted by schooling. One legal issue that arose in the nineteenth century was whether the organic law of the states prohibited the exclusion of religion from public education.[18] This was no small issue because the availability of public lands through the ordinance (and through later laws modeled on it) became one of the driving forces of educational expansion in the nineteenth century. Besides making the proceeds of land sales available for common school endowments—and, regrettably, for gluttonous local corruption—the ordinance reinforced both the republican faith and the evangelical politics that pervaded school reform.[19]

The American common school of the nineteenth century was, first and foremost, an agency of moral education. The achievement of the reformers was not so much in raising the educational level of the population. Rates of literacy were already high in comparison with those of European nations. Rather, it was in projecting the ideal of unified civic conscience, a disciplined social imagination holding sway across a diverse population.[20] Powerfully declaring that unity in the organic law of new states, the hortatory language of the Northwest Ordinance reappeared in state constitutions as the nation expanded westward. Not infrequently, the constitutions preceded their articles on education with a separate preamble, stating the moral and civic aims of schooling in lofty terms.[21]

Protestant religious culture entered into the pedagogy and content of common schooling as the sine qua non of moral instruction to buttress the states' constitutional aims. In new states and the nation as a whole (though not in the South until after the Civil War), common schools aimed to create a universal civic culture in support of republican political institutions.[22] With the spread of state-sponsored schooling, the universality of the civic culture took on new social meanings, well beyond those of expanding political participation. As they became more centralized and their content more uniform within states, the public schools incorporated existing cultural and political units, sometimes in ways that threatened the collective conscience and forms of social organization those units had sought to perpetuate. Generalized patterns of resistance to the common school movement took three forms in the antebellum United States. Local officials and citizens, claiming the prerogative to control what they saw as a community institution, resisted measures promoting state centralization and funding of schools.[23] Some of the more orthodox Protestant clergy opposed trends toward secularization, as in the celebrated debates between Horace Mann and the Boston schoolmasters.[24] In parts of the country drawing new immigrants, growing numbers of Catholics resented the pan-Protestant culture of the common school, particularly the use of non-Catholic versions of Scripture in the curriculum.[25]

The last of these conflicts mirrored most distinctly the underlying struggle over rights of conscience in nineteenth-century schooling. As Catholic immigrants began to arrive in greater numbers after the 1830s, many of them joining the working class in the nation's early centers of industrialization, the drive to unify the moral teachings of the common schools intensified. So did the Catholic resistance, first to state-sanctioned use of the Protestant Bible, then to the constitutional and statutory denial of public funds for Catholic education as a legitimate alternative within the common school system. Catholics eventually resolved to build a separate and nonpublic school system beyond the cultural imperatives of public authority. Long before the last stage was reached in the latter third of the nineteenth century, imposition and resistance during the 1830s and 1840s led to political struggle in New York State,[26] Bible riots in Philadelphia,[27] and similar tensions and disturbances in other places. For decades to come, the battle over Catholic rights of conscience was highly visible in the social history of major American cities—from Boston[28] to Cincinnati[29] to Chicago[30] to San Francisco.[31]

The common school reformers filtered such controversies through a durable set of fears and obsessions. They were neither the first nor the last public figures in the United States to engage in phantasmagoric speculation about the enemy within. The nation's founders, too, had fretted about what they saw as a decline of political virtue amid growing freedom in the new nation, and they had given voice to fears of conspiracy, faction, and usurpation. But whereas the perils of more widely diffused political rights existed as possibilities in the early years of the new nation, they were real and present to reformers after the Jacksonian revolution in American politics during the 1820s. Besides the dramatic expansion of the franchise and the crumbling of stable hierarchies in the political party system, leaders who perceived themselves as keepers of the nation's collective conscience saw about them the flow of new immigrants, a wildly fluctuating economy, growing sectional conflict, and uncontrollable social ills attending urban growth and a nascent industrial economy. The place of conscience in the political culture of the Whig party—and it was the Whigs, neopuritan heirs to the lost world of intact moral community, who emerged as the most prominent educational reformers—took on heightened importance as a standardized form of self-control. Properly instructed conscience would serve as the countervailing force against unbridled self-interest and demagoguery, and it was to be secured, in large part, through education.[32]

Over and over again in the language of school reformers, then again in the stream of litigation on the use of religious Scripture in schools, advocates of educational expansion reaffirmed the religious basis of common schooling as the means to shape conscience. Such affirmations were resilient enough to survive in the decisions of lower courts well into the twentieth century, mingling freely—and without perceived contradiction—with arguments recognizing the functions of education for cultivating democratic citizenship in a religiously diverse society. Addressing the theme of Christianity and common schools in the late 1830s, Horace Bushnell, widely known Protestant minister and reform publicist, summarized the underlying strategy of this argument, which, among its proponents, changed little over time. He railed against the idea that schools might ever be viewed as non-religious institutions: "It is a divorce against law, and one that cannot continue without dishonor to both parties. Education without religion," he continued, "is education without virtue. Religion without education, or apart from it, is a cold, unpaternal principle, dying without propagation." [33]

Protestant ministers were brought into accord with secular reformers like Horace Mann by means of a consensus on the content of public instruction. Thus it was that the King James Bible retained its foothold in the moral training offered by common schools. Yet at the same time, in keeping with the general trend toward disestablishment of churches and the secularization of formal schooling under state control, sectarian indoctrination by competing Protestant groups for the most part withered away from state-sponsored schooling during the spread of common schools. The scruples of Catholics or other religious groups entering this paradoxical regime of civic instruction were frequently brushed aside in much the same way that separatists had been suppressed or banished from the old Puritan commonwealth. In some cities, conflicting groups did reach agreements to allow local discretion over which version of the Bible would be used. But in many others, and generally as the states enacted provisions specifically denying public funds to schools using Catholic instead of "nonsectarian" but pan-Protestant Scripture and prayers, the dissenters had no recourse but to build their own schools without public subsidies if they wished to maintain their alternative views of conscience.

The ire of the nativists at such resistance is evident in an editorial from the *Common School Journal* in 1852. In that year the Massachusetts legislature, pressed by the anti-Catholic Know-Nothing party, enacted the nation's first state compulsory school attendance law. The occasion for the editorial was Catholic protest against required readings of the King James Bible in the town of Cambridge:

> The English Bible, in some way or other, has, ever since the settlement of Cambridge, been read in its public schools, by children of every de-

nomination; but in the year 1851, the ignorant immigrants, who have found food and shelter in this land of freedom and plenty, made free and plentiful through the influence of these very Scriptures, presume to dictate to us, and refuse to let their children read as ours do, and always have done, the Word of Life. The arrogance, not to say impudence, of this conduct, must startle every native citizen, and we can not but hope that they will immediately take measures to teach these deluded aliens, that their poverty and ignorance in their own country arose mainly from their ignorance of the Bible.[34]

Shaped by majoritarian bias during the rise of common schools, freedom of conscience carried a narrow meaning in the political culture of American education. In the state and local worlds of common school politics, it remained fundamentally different from the natural rights posited by Thomas Jefferson, which were more admired than observed during the expansion of the educational system. Practically speaking, conscience referred to the positive freedom to develop Protestant moral values considered essential to participation by like-minded people in republican political institutions.[35] As it appeared in disputes over common schooling, the notion of conscience evolved not so much in response to minority rights as to accommodate what might be termed a bounded pluralism within the prevailing culture of the majority. Rights of conscience in state-sponsored schooling offered not secular but pan-Protestant neutrality for the socialization of the young. Such neutrality was a necessary term of social consensus for building public institutions after the disestablishment of Protestant churches and the resulting sectarian competition in the early nineteenth century as representatives of those churches created an "evangelical united front" of voluntary associations to spread their ideas and reform the social life of local communities.[36]

Two rhetorical strategies made the accommodation of secular and sectarian aims plausible to competing Protestant organizations. One was to present the state itself as a covenant with millennial aims, a righteous quest to redeem the world from evil influences. A second and less elevated strategy was simply to maintain a core of religious dogma in school content, universal enough to be acceptable to the most influential Protestant sects. Within the traditional framework of values that had given rise to this educational vision—that is, within the social compact of enclosed dissident communities, each of which formed a totality as a moral and political order, demanding consensual solidarity[37]—freedom was the right to participate in a covenant offering salvation to those who held steadfastly to its system of beliefs.

Minority Cultures and the Rule of Law

Minorities clamored to disavow the prevailing conception of freedom in American education. To pursue only the example of the Catholics is to discover the plight of many groups in American society under the rule of law. During the Philadelphia Bible-reading controversy in the 1840s, a group of Catholics published a pamphlet that set forth the key democratic argument for minority rights: "We are the minority; and for us, therefore, does the Constitution exist. The majority need not its protection, for they have the power to take care of their own interests. Unless for the shield which the Constitution gives to those who are smaller, and, therefore, the weaker party, this government would be a despotism, for the governing power would be uncontrolled. . . . UNDER NO CIRCUMSTANCES IS CONSCIENCE AT THE DISPOSAL OF A MAJORITY."[38]

The shield of state constitutional protection, behind which the Catholic minority hoped to gather before the onslaught of pan-Protestant socialization, existed as a hope but not yet as legal doctrine during the spread of common schools in the nineteenth century. Faced with a choice between legitimizing that metaphoric shield or condoning the use of the Bible in public schools, the courts of the nineteenth century sided with the Protestant majority and its values in almost every case. In most jurisdictions no litigation arose, either because of the settled attitude of judges or because the custom and practice in local schools allowed some leeway in the choice of Scriptures. In a few instances—such as the public subsidies given to two Catholic parochial schools in Poughkeepsie, New York, from 1873 until 1898—public policy and the conscience of Catholic dissenters were brought into accord, even given limited court approval in some places, such as Illinois and Pennsylvania.[39] Occasionally, as in Cincinnati after the Civil War, Catholic opponents of pan-Protestant public schooling and liberal reformers seeking more thorough secularization of public schools joined forces to sustain a prohibition against the use of Scripture in public schools.[40] Such was the dominant strategy, as well, of Jewish leaders in American cities, aiming to make school culture, if not entirely secular and universalistic, at least neutral in its effects on different ethnic groups.[41] This was not enough, however, to win public subsidies for schools using Catholic as opposed to Protestant religious materials, since obviously the secularists allied with Catholic leaders for the exclusion of Protestant religious texts would oppose them on the inclusion of other religious texts in schools under a regime of doctrinal pluralism guided by local choice. Nor was the prospect of secular neutrality sufficient to influence the tightening rules of the Catholic church during the same era, mandating religious education in separate church-controlled schools for all Catholic children as a reaction to the prejudices deeply ingrained in public schools.[42]

The first state supreme court case on Bible reading in the public schools upheld the expulsion of a Catholic student in Maine for refusing to read the King James Bible, which was used as a reader in the curriculum. The case, *Donahoe v. Richards* (1854), represents the majoritarian mandate par excellence. Against its Procrustean rule, designating exactly what religious text was to be used in the acquisition of literacy in common schools, the incremental changes in legal precedent over the rest of the century can be measured with some degree of precision. The majority opinion in the appeal to the state supreme court placed all public power over the question in the hands of the legislature or its designated local agencies under law, such as school districts:

> The legislature establishes general rules for the guidance of its citizens. It does not necessarily follow that they are unconstitutional, nor that a citizen is to be legally absolved from obedience, because they may conflict with his conscientious views of religious duty or right. To allow this would be to subordinate the State to the individual conscience. A law is not unconstitutional, because it may prohibit what a citizen may conscientiously think right, or require what he may conscientiously think wrong. The State is governed by its own views of duty. The right or wrong of the State, is the right or wrong as declared by legislative Acts constitutionally passed.[43]

The will of the majority, vested in legislatures and school boards, became the first rule in Bible-reading cases during the nineteenth century.[44] *Donahoe* epitomized positive freedom in the pan-Protestant mold, holding that "when liberty of conscience would interfere with the paramount rights of the public, it ought to be restrained." Widely cited in ensuing years, this decision revealed the tendency of public officials to use the religious values countenanced by the majority for strengthening the legitimacy of state institutions and powers. "Even Mr. Jefferson," continued the opinion, "claims no indulgence for any thing that is detrimental to society. . . . His position is, that civil government is instituted only for temporal objects, and that spiritual matters are legitimate subjects of civil cognizance no farther than they may stand in the way of those objects."[45] Jefferson might turn in his grave at this appropriation of his view of natural rights, but the rhetorical strategy was clear. Bible reading did more than standardize values; it promoted the "temporal objects" of state building and institutional expansion in a heterogeneous population.

In subsequent cases, a key argument sustaining the use of the Bible for civic purposes held that it could be "religious" without being "sectarian." "Religious" instruction was allowable, indeed necessary as universal moral teaching required for citizenship, but "sectarian" uses of the Bible were discouraged and increasingly prohibited in the legalized secularization of schools through constitutional provisions, statutes, and court decisions.[46] Horace Mann and other Unitarians prominent in the common school movement suggested the existence of universal moral teachings that could be represented with selective passages from the Bible as school text. As the century progressed, school reformers pursued this line of reasoning with ever more secular emphasis on the ethical rather than the devotional character of Scripture. Their strategy paralleled a wider tendency in public policy to incorporate certain legitimating features of Protestant religious culture into the civil religion of statecraft, professionalization, and judicial reasoning. Court cases reflected this secularization of religious text, holding that since the truths of the Bible were universal, the "nonsectarian" use of Christian Scripture was acceptable in civil institutions.[47]

Some typical tests applied in judicial reasoning to distinguish religious from sectarian uses of Scripture were reading without comment, voluntary compliance of students (allowing nonparticipation in school or withdrawal from the exercise with parental permission), local choice on which version of the Bible could be used, and reading excerpts rather than the entire Bible as a school text. These procedural constraints were, at best, sporadic. One must conclude from the legal record that most states continued to view the reading of Scripture as acceptable practice within the discretionary powers vested in local communities and school officials.

This is not to say that any universal pattern existed beyond the fundamental acceptability of ritual indoctrination. The political cultures in which Bible reading took place often differed greatly. The conservative side of the spectrum was apparent in states where the law continued to reflect the religious aims and cultural uniformity so eloquently expressed in the Massachusetts Constitution of 1780. On the other side, a more liberal position was that of New York State, where legal decisions of the state commissioner of public instruction—a power granted to that office under state law—resulted in the following configuration of rules from 1837 to the end of the nineteenth century: prayer in school was acceptable, Bible reading was permitted but not required, the version of the Bible to be used had to be left open for local discretion, and students could not be expelled from school for refusing to participate (the activity was voluntary, not compulsory under law).[48]

Public schools where Bible reading was a part of instruction were not considered places of worship under nineteenth-century American law.[49] Nonpublic schools—increasingly Catholic by the end of the century—were treated as if they were places of worship, sectarian, and therefore ineligible for subsidies under state constitutional and statutory provisions requiring that public funds be used only for nonsectarian instruction. Legal categories thus reinforced the alienation of nonpublic from public forms of school authority, as many Catholics sought protected enclaves for schooling the young, secure against the domination of Protestant values. An insistence in state policy upon nonsectarian but unabashedly pan-Protestant common schooling as the universal norm, accompanied by hostility to Catholic education not only as unacceptably sectarian but as a threatening system of beliefs to be banished from common school subsidies, became a wedge cleaving apart the public and private sectors of education in the United States.[50]

Ironically, while that alienation between public and nonpublic schools was deepening in the latter half of the nineteenth century, the Protestant accord that had shaped the culture of public schools was becoming more fragmented and diffuse. Leading educators were developing a professional culture at odds with the explicitly religious origins of schooling. So successfully were they gaining control of the new professional networks shaping school practice that evangelical Protestants found themselves drifting to the margins of the nation's dominant educational institutions by the end of the century, there to fashion their own strategies of resistance as Catholics had done in the past.[51] Recurrent demands for a unified collective conscience as the supreme aim of public instruction filtered through larger and more interconnected schooling institutions, resembling factories more than churches in the cities by the end of the century. Slowly, not without opposition, the language of control began to shift in discussions of conscience and state schooling. As the process of education became more enmeshed in complex organizations and as the majority of states passed compulsory attendance laws in the latter half of the nineteenth century, educators perceived the glue of social solidarity in administrative and social scientific rather than moral and quasi-religious terms. The rhetoric of civil religion settled into modern-sounding bureaucratic categories on the eve of the twentieth century.

Although pan-Protestant moral instruction remained the dominant paradigm of common schooling through the end of the century, a new direction began to appear in some court challenges after the Civil War. In 1872 the decision on the Cincinnati Bible case affirmed a legal prohibition of Bible reading in public schools because the local jurisdiction had enacted it through legitimate means under democratic majority rule. This was not a substantial advance for individual conscience—the state and local majorities still reigned supreme—but it did represent an important concession to group rights of conscience, if a social group could either constitute itself as a political unit or forge a majority through compromise with other groups that opposed religious indoctrination in public schools.[52]

A more powerful challenge to the pan-Protestant hegemony appeared in *Weiss* v. *District Board,* a case decided by the Wisconsin Supreme Court in 1890. The laws at issue were much the same as in other Bible cases: the power of the legislature (and lower levels of government subject to its laws) to establish and maintain public schools, the state guarantee against infringement of rights of conscience and against use of public funds for religious establishments, and the prohibition against sectarian instruction in the public schools. But in this case the court found the Bible in its entirety to be sectarian and held that its use made public schools religious institutions in violation of rights of conscience. The decision still left the door open for using selections rather than the entire Bible, but it cast aside the procedural guarantee of reading without comment as mere subterfuge, not a protection of rights. Even more harshly, the court rejected the practice of allowing Bible reading if districts also permitted voluntary withdrawal of students when they or their parents objected:

> When, as in this case, a small minority of the pupils in the public school is excluded, for any cause, from a stated school exercise, particularly when such cause is apparent hostility to the Bible, which a majority of the pupils have been taught to revere, from that moment the excluded pupil loses caste with his fellows, and is liable to be regarded with aversion and subjected to reproach and insult. But it is a sufficient refutation of the argument that the practice in question tends to destroy the equality of the pupils which the constitution seeks to establish and protect, and puts a portion of them to serious disadvantage in many ways with respect to the others.[53]

In addition to excluding religious Scripture from secular institutions, this decision is notable for its argument—long before the coverage of the First and Fourteenth amendments to the U.S. Constitution was extended to public policy at the state and local levels—that students in public schools had a right to equal protection of the laws and that this right extended to the formation of conscience. No doubt influenced by the visible effects of immigration on midwestern communities, the court found no merit in the old consensual argument about unified public conscience and Christian nationhood. The concurring opinion of one of the justices noticed the uses to which the Bible was being put in the real world of American education and suggested that the civil and democratic purposes of the schools were quite distinct from the quest for religious indoctrination:

> That version of the Bible is hostile to the belief of many who are taxed to support the common schools, and who have equal rights and privileges in them. It is a source of religious and sectarian strife. That is enough. It violates the letter and spirit of the constitution. . . . The common school is one of the most indispensable, useful, and valuable civil institutions this state has. It is democratic, and free to all alike, in perfect equality, where all the children of our people stand on a common platform and may enjoy the benefits of an equal and common education. An enemy to our common schools is an enemy to our state government.[54]

A few years later the Nebraska Supreme Court, in *State ex rel. Freeman* v. *Scheve* (1902), followed the lead of Wisconsin and held that "if the Bible is used in public schools, if hymns are sung, and if children are compelled to attend school, you compel attendance at a place of worship, which is contrary to the constitution."[55] Although the decision still permitted selective and nonsectarian uses of biblical passages in school, it stated without any ambiguity that the school became a place of worship and therefore unconstitutional if those uses constituted religious instruction.

The most advanced case during that period, in the sense of excluding all religious indoctrination from public schools, held that the Bible, even selected passages used as school text, must be excluded altogether—that is, there could be no such thing as a nonsectarian use of Scripture in any form. "The wrong arises," argued the majority opinion of the Illinois Supreme Court in *People* v. *Board of Education* (1910), "not out of the particular version of the Bible or form of prayer used,—whether that found in the Douay or the King James version,— or the particular songs sung, but out of the compulsion to join in any form of worship. The free enjoyment of religious worship includes freedom not to worship." The court explicitly recognized the rights of non-Christian minorities as protected rights of conscience in public schools, declaring that the Bible "is a sectarian book as to the Jew and every believer in any religion other than the Christian religion and as to those who are heretical or who hold beliefs that are not regarded as orthodox."[56]

These three decisions from 1890 to 1910 appeared during the Populist and Progressive movements in American politics and during a time when an unprecedented flood of new immigrants came to American shores.[57] The decisions represented a vanguard, certainly, but hardly a new consensus on rights of conscience and schooling. It would be decades before a definitive national precedent would be set against prayer and Bible reading in public schools.[58] In the meantime, the current was running the other way during the early decades of the twentieth century, a predictable reaction to the stresses of change. As Jesse K. Flanders demonstrated in his study on the growing legal control of the curriculum after the turn of the century, from 1903 to 1923 the number of states with laws either prohibiting the exclusion of the Bible from public schools or explicitly compelling its use increased from ten to fifteen. The number in the latter category jumped from one to eight.[59] Writing in 1934, nine years after the U.S. Supreme Court widened the application of the First Amendment to the states, a scholar keeping track of the many new court challenges to Bible reading and religious exercises in the public schools concluded that the majority of such cases were still affirming these practices.[60]

Meanwhile, state legislatures were passing new laws defining the Bible as nonsectarian, distinguishing its use from religious worship, requiring minimum amounts to be read each day, even directing that teachers who did not comply be automatically discharged from employment. The trend toward greater severity in majoritarian demands on minority cultures was not limited to religious exercises. Prescriptive legislation on values increased generally after the turn of the century. Temperance reformers, pious patriots, antievolutionists, and assorted nativists and xenophobes mobilized to preserve White Anglo-Saxon Protestant control of collective conscience against rampant diversity and liberal modernism.[61]

Despite judicial decisions in the 1920s that protected nonpublic schools and the reproduction of minority cultures,[62] rights of conscience had been worked into a double bind by the present century. On one side, the school as an implement of positive freedom, interpreted within a pan-Protestant mold of expanding, exclusive, and evangelical nationalism, was still the dominant conception of public instruction in local school districts throughout most of the United States. On the other side, ominous constraints on conscience were appearing in the secular and bureaucratic environment of schooling. Educational planners and social scientists were designing more centralized systems for allocating and evaluating school knowledge in ways thought to be appropriate by secularized professional elites.[63] It remained to be seen whether the shield of American constitutionalism could check the habit of legislative and judicial conformity to the majority in secular as well as religious indoctrination.[64]

Compulsory Attendance and Educational Rights

Moving slowly while the social conditions around them changed precipitously, state courts at the end of the century—a few of them, at any rate—had begun to glimpse the possibility of schooling as a plurality of consciences each with its own rights to freedom of thought and belief. What the legal history does not show clearly is how the entire perspective of public policy on the issue of conscience was beginning to shift by the end of the nineteenth century. To a large degree, as shown by the vanguard cases in state supreme courts from 1890 to 1910, this shift was not yet a major expansion of individual rights per se. It was, though, a growing awareness of the responsibilities that came with greater universality of public authority in an increasingly diverse society. In the realm of law, one can find impulses toward a reconstructed universality in the post–Civil War amendments to the U.S. Constitution, particularly the grossly unrealized possibilities of the Fourteenth Amendment. Some echoes of the idea of equal protection under the law did appear in state cases, but because of the limited interpretation and application of such federal standards, one must look elsewhere for the shift in perspective that yielded bold reversals of prior legal reasoning.

A clue to the shift in perspective can be found in references to compulsory attendance laws. Most states passed such laws in the second half of the nineteenth century.[65] The cases favoring individual rights of conscience acknowledged the growing universality of school attendance as a basis for expanding the protections given to people compelled by the state to be in school. Because of the compulsory attendance requirement, the Nebraska Supreme Court, in its decision mentioned above, found public schools to be unconstitutional places of worship under the law if Bible reading and religious exercises such as prayer and the singing of hymns were permitted. In a striking passage, the court's majority reasoned that parents, public schools, and the state all shared essentially the same interests in this regard:

> If the system of compulsory education is persevered in, and religious worship or sectarian instruction in the public schools is at the same time permitted, parents will be compelled to expose their children to what they deem spiritual contamination, or else, while bearing their share of the burden for the support of public education, provide the means from their own pockets for the training of their offspring elsewhere. It might be reasonably apprehended that such a practice, besides being unjust and oppressive to the person immediately concerned, would, by its tendency to the multiplication of parochial and sectarian schools, tend forcibly to the destruction of one of the most important, if not indispensable, foundation stones of our form of government. It will be an evil day when anything happens to lower the public schools in popular esteem, or to discourage attendance upon them by children of any class.[66]

It is clear from this reasoning that compulsory attendance was placing a greater burden of responsibility upon the state to elaborate rights in the public sphere. Earlier in the previous century, during the common school movement, a strong undercurrent of voluntarism had still accompanied discussions of school reform. A smaller percentage of the population then had attended school, for shorter periods of time, with easier exit to other activities. School reformers saw about them a relatively homogeneous society, despite the signs that Catholic immigration was growing. It was difficult for people to imagine anything but a universalized expansion of familiar sectarian traditions when implementing common schools for a fledgling republic that had, from their point of view, sprung forth from their own most cherished values. But as compulsory attendance requirements became more pervasive, and as attendance became more universal while the population became more diverse, public leaders began to speak of educational rights along with universality of the institution. The California legislation on compulsory attendance made the connection directly, for it was entitled "An Act to Enforce the Educational Rights of Children."[67] In much the same way, one can find a transformed perspective on universality and state responsibility creeping into some of the court decisions by the turn of the century. The duties of the state to make good on the promise of universal schooling, not only as a consensual instrument of democracy but as a guardian of individual and group rights for that purpose, must be more and more scrupulously fulfilled, according to the reasoning of the Nebraska court, as the institution reaches into the lives of more and more citizens in a heterogeneous society.

Compulsory school attendance, along with a progressively more universal institutionalization of schooling throughout society, intensified the quest to define rights "never submitted," in Jefferson's words, to the state. This new level of concern came about in part because the growth of schooling posed threats to those rights, but it was also because—as the Nebraska court surmised—only a truly common schooling, purified of cultural hegemony, could achieve the greatest possibilities for collective freedom in a democratic society. As successive battles took place to reach a consensus on Bible reading and other religious practices in schools, rights of conscience became a contested ground within the expansion of state systems of education, as well as between those systems and the nonpublic organizations they inadvertently helped to create through their maltreatment of religious conscience.

The history of conscience in this nation's schools during the nineteenth century revealed the perils of democratic decision making in matters of conscience, but it also gave voice to the potential. A conception of freedom embodying certain universal obligations necessary to maintain a collective vision of the good, but shaped to allow plural modes of assent and a healthy tolerance for dissenting visions, appears to be the highest wisdom consistent with the small vanguard of Bible-reading cases that sought to strengthen rights of conscience many decades before the application of federal constitutional standards to the problem. In the long run, the institutional perspective of those cases may well stand as a more reliable guide to educational policy than case-by-case elaboration of protected individual rights, though the need for the latter should remain abundantly clear from the record on Bible reading in the past century.

Notes

The Spencer Foundation supported the research for this essay under its Small Grants Program. Thomas Anton, Mark Brilliant, Regina Cortina, Lawrence Cremin, Paul Finkelman, Stephen Gottlieb, Yae Miyake, James Morone, David Tyack, and Tyll van Geel contributed generous help and critical insights to the study.

1. Alexis de Tocqueville, *Democracy in America*, trans. Henry Reeve; translation revised by Francis Bowen; ed. Phillips Bradley (1st French ed. 1835; Reeve trans. 1835–40; rpt. New York: Knopf, 1946), 1:306.
2. For one of the many studies tracing this influence, see Kenneth V. Lottich, *New England Transplanted* (Dallas, Tex.: Royal Publishing Company, 1964); and on the development of those older traditions, the best study is that of Lawrence A. Cremin, *American Education: The Colonial Experience, 1607–1783)* (New York: Harper & Row, 1970). Numerous scholars have noted the prevalence of New Englanders, especially Protestant clergy, at the forefront of the common school movement in the nineteenth century.
3. William G. McLoughlin, *New England Dissent, 1630–1833*, Vol. 1: *The Baptists and the Separation of Church and State* (Cambridge, Mass.: Harvard University Press, 1971), 92–95.
4. In *The Garden and the Wilderness: Religion and Government in American Constitutional History* (Chicago: University of Chicago Press, 1965), Mark DeWolfe Howe develops an illuminating contrast between the ways in which autonomy of religious belief is conceived in the writings of Roger Williams and Thomas Jefferson; for an excellent essay on subsequent

constitutional theory regarding conscience, see Milton R. Konvitz, *Religious Liberty and Conscience: A Constitutional Inquiry* (New York: Viking Press, 1968).

5. Thomas Jefferson, *Notes on Virginia*, in *The Writings of Thomas Jefferson*, Albert Ellery Bergh, ed. (Washington, D.C.: Thomas Jefferson Memorial Association, 1903), 2:220. The statute to which Jefferson refers is "An act for the effectual suppression of vice, and restraint and punishment of blasphemous, wicked, and dissolute persons," *Laws of Virginia*, 1705, chap. 30, §1 in *The Statutes at Large; Being a Collection of All the Laws of Virginia, from the First Session of the Legislature in the Year 1619*, ed. William W. Hening (Philadelphia: Thomas DeSilver, 1823), 3:358.

6. Jefferson, *Notes on Virginia*, 221. Jefferson wrote his celebrated "A Bill for Establishing Religious Freedom" to give this view the force of law; it was passed by the Virginia Assembly in 1786.

7. Reply to Messrs. Nehemiah Dodge, Ephraim Robbins, and Stephen S. Nelson, *A Committee of the Danbury Baptist Association, in the State of Connecticut*, January 1, 1802, in *Statutes at Large*, ed. Hening, 16:281–82. For a useful compendium of Jefferson's views on liberty and education, see *Crusade Against Ignorance: Thomas Jefferson on Education*, ed. Gordon C. Lee (New York: Bureau of Publications, Teachers College, Columbia University, 1961).

8. John Phillip Reid elaborates this argument in his essay "The Irrelevance of the Declaration," in *Law in the American Revolution and the Revolution in the Law*, ed. Hendrik Hartog (New York: New York University Press, 1981), 46–89.

9. The U.S. Supreme Court applied the due process clause to education in *Meyer* v. *Nebraska*, 262 U.S. 390 (1923), and *Pierce* v. *Society of Sisters*, 268 U.S. 510 (1925). It applied the First Amendment to the states in *Gitlow* v. *New York*, 268 U.S. 652 (1925), and *Near* v. *Minnesota*, 283 U.S. 697 (1931). It first applied the religion clauses of the First Amendment to the states in *Cantwell* v. *Connecticut*, 310 U.S. 296 (1940).

10. The same was true for higher education but on a much smaller scale; an interpretation of leading nineteenth-century views of conscience as a moral faculty and its relation to learning can be found in D. H. Meyer, *The Instructed Conscience: The Shaping of the American National Ethic* (Philadelphia: University of Pennsylvania Press, 1972).

11. On the religious strain in educational reform rhetoric, see David B. Tyack, "The Kingdom of God and the Common School: Protestant Ministers and Educational Awakening in the West," *Harvard Educational Review* 36 (1966): 447–69; Timothy Smith, "Protestant Schooling and American Nationality, 1800–1850," *Journal of American History* 53 (1967): 679–95; Lawrence A. Cremin, *American Education: The National*

Experience, 1783–1876 (New York: Harper & Row, 1980); David Tyack and Elisabeth Hansot, *Managers of Virtue: Public School Leadership in America, 1829–1980* (New York: Basic Books, 1982), pt. 1; and Charles Leslie Glenn, Jr., *The Myth of the Common School* (Amherst: University of Massachusetts Press, 1988), chaps. 6 and 7.

12. The use of the school speller as a catechism, blending pietistic teachings with civic culture, is clearly traceable over time from the *New England Primer* (from which the verse for "A" is taken) to *Webster's American Spelling Book* to McGuffey's *First Reader.*

13. Mass. Const. (1780), Declaration of Rights, §3, in *The Federal and State Constitutions, Colonial Charters, and Other Organic Laws of the States, Territories, and Colonies Now or Heretofore Forming the United States of America,* ed. Francis N. Thorpe (Washington, D.C.: U.S. Government Printing Office, 1909), 3:1890.

14. Benjamin Rush, "Thoughts upon the Mode of Education Proper in a Republic," in *Essays on Education in the Early Republic,* ed. Frederick Rudolph (Cambridge, Mass.: Harvard University Press, 1965), 3–23, quotes on 14 and 13.

15. Noah Webster, "On the Education of Youth in America," in *Essays of Education,* ed. Rudolph, 43–77, quote on 77. On Webster's educational views, see Harry Redcay Warfel, *Noah Webster, School Master to America* (New York: Macmillan, 1936).

16. Sanford Levinson offers an insightful reading of civil religion and American constitutionalism in *Constitutional Faith* (Princeton: Princeton University Press, 1988).

17. *Federal and State Constitutions,* ed. Thorpe, 2:961.

18. For a case at the end of the century that reflects earlier arguments and published interchanges on this issue, see *Pfeiffer* v. *Board of Education,* 118 Mich. 560, 565 (1898): "The ordinance of 1787 declared that religion, morality, and knowledge were necessary to good government and the happiness of mankind, and provided that, for these purposes, schools and the means of education should forever be encouraged. It is not to be inferred that, in forming a constitution under the authority of this ordinance, the convention intended to prohibit in the public schools all mention of a subject which the ordinance, in effect, declared that schools were to be established to foster."

19. Federal policy and schooling in new states receives close attention in David Tyack, Thomas James, and Aaron Benavot, *Law and the Shaping of Public Education, 1785–1954* (Madison: University of Wisconsin Press, 1987), 20–42. On the history and politics of the ordinance, see Jack Ericson Eblen, *The First and Second United States Empires: Governors and Territorial Government, 1784–1912* (Pittsburgh: University of Pittsburgh

Press, 1968), 17–47; and Peter S. Onuf, *Statehood and Union: A History of the Northwest Ordinance* (Bloomington: Indiana University Press, 1987).

20. For interpretations of literacy rates and common schooling, see Lee Soltow and Edward Stevens, *The Rise of Literacy and the Common School in the United States* (Chicago: University of Chicago Press, 1981); and Carl F. Kaestle, *Pillars of the Republic: Common Schools and American Society, 1780–1860* (New York: Hill & Wang, 1983). Excellent work has been done on moral instruction in the common schools: for example, see Barbara J. Finkelstein, "The Moral Dimensions of Pedagogy: Teaching Behavior in Popular Primary Schools in Nineteenth-Century America," *American Studies* 15 (Fall 1974): 79–89; and Finkelstein, "Pedagogy as Intrusion: Teaching Values in Popular Primary Schools in Nineteenth Century America," *History of Childhood Quarterly* 2 (1975): 349–78. Charles E. Bidwell analyzes contrasting approaches to defining and enforcing "moral community" at the local level in "The Moral Significance of the Common School: A Sociological Study of Local Patterns of School Control and Moral Education in Massachusetts and New York, 1837–1840," *History of Education Quarterly* 6 (1966): 50–91.

21. The educational provisions of state constitutions are discussed in David Tyack and Thomas James, "State Government and American Public Education: Exploring the 'Primeval Forest,'" *History of Education Quarterly* 26 (1986): 39–69.

22. Daniel P. Resnick and Lauren B. Resnick, "The Nature of Literacy: An Historical Exploration," *Harvard Educational Review* 47 (1977): 370–85; and Michael V. Belok, "The Instructed Citizen: Civic Education in the United States During the Nineteenth Century," *Paedagogica Historica* 18 (1978): 257–74.

23. Kaestle, *Pillars of the Republic,* 153 and passim (on the conflict of "conservative localists" and "cosmopolitan reformers"); see also Lawrence A. Cremin, *The American Common School: An Historic Conception* (New York: Bureau of Publications, Teachers College, Columbia University, 1951), on the program and ideals of the common school movement.

24. Raymond B. Culver, *Horace Mann and Religion in Massachusetts Public Schools* (New Haven: Yale University Press, 1929).

25. The following articles are especially useful in approaching the historical literature on the education of Catholics in the United States: Robert D. Cross, "The Origins of Catholic Parochial Schools in America," *American Benedictine Review* 16 (1965): 194–209; Vincent P. Lannie, "Church and School Triumphant: The Sources of American Catholic Educational Historiography," *History of Education Quarterly* 16 (1976): 131–45; Marvin Lazerson, "Understanding Catholic Educational History," *History of Education Quarterly* 17 (1977): 297–317.

26. Vincent P. Lannie, *Public Money and Parochial Education: Bishop Hughes, Governor Seward, and the New York School Controversy* (Cleveland: Press of Case Western Reserve University, 1968); Carl F. Kaestle, *The Evolution of an Urban School System: New York City, 1750–1850* (Cambridge, Mass.: Harvard University Press, 1973); and Diane Ravitch, *The Great School Wars: New York City, 1805–1973* (New York: Basic Books, 1976). James W. Sanders gives an insightful overview of the research issues in "Roman Catholics and the School Question in New York City: Some Suggestions for Research," in *Educating an Urban People: The New York City Experience,* ed. Diane Ravitch and Ronald F. Goodenow (New York: Teachers College Press, 1981), 116–40.

27. Michael Feldberg, *The Turbulent Era: Riot and Disorder in Jacksonian America* (New York: Oxford University Press, 1980), 9–32.

28. Stanley K. Schultz, *The Culture Factory: Boston Public Schools, 1789–1860* (New York: Oxford University Press, 1973); and James W. Sanders, "Boston Catholics and the School Question, 1825–1907," in *From Common School to Magnet School: Selected Essays in the History of Boston Schools,* ed. James Frazer et al. (Boston: Boston Public Library, 1979).

29. F. Michael Perko, *A Time to Favor Zion: The Ecology of Religion and School Development on the Urban Frontier, Cincinnati, 1830–1870* (Chicago: Educational Studies Press, 1988).

30. James W. Sanders, *The Education of an Urban Minority: Catholics in Chicago, 1833–1965* (New York: Oxford University Press, 1977).

31. Paul Goda, "The Historical Background of California's Constitutional Provisions Prohibiting Aid to Sectarian Schools," *California Historical Society Quarterly* 46 (1967): 149–71; Lee S. Dolson, "The Administration of the San Francisco Public Schools, 1847–1947" (Ph.D. dissertation, University of California, Berkeley, 1964); and Victor L. Shradar, "Ethnic Politics, Religion and the Public Schools of San Francisco, 1849–1933" (Ph.D. dissertation, Stanford University, 1974).

32. Daniel Walker Howe, *The Political Culture of the American Whigs* (Chicago: University of Chicago Press, 1979), 29. On the values of educational leaders, see Cremin, *American Common School* and *American Education: The National Experience,* Tyack and Hansot, *Managers of Virtue,* and Kaestle, *Pillars of the Republic.* As Howe notes, Lee Benson employs the concept of "neopuritans" in *The Concept of Jacksonian Democracy* (Princeton: Princeton University Press, 1961), 89, to contrast the interest of Whigs in transforming the thought and conduct of diverse people in the polity, versus the interest of the Democrats in making sure that those people had equal access and opportunity in the nation's institutions and economic system. In theory, the Whigs sought to conserve a

historical covenant based on character and divine purpose, while the Democrats sought a principled social compact arising from Enlightenment ideals (see Howe, *American Whigs*, 69–70, for a discussion of Horace Bushnell's sermonizing on this point). But in educational practice, reformers in both parties generally endorsed religious teaching in public schools, differing only over the specificity and control of such instruction.

33. Horace Bushnell, "Christianity and Common Schools," *Common School Journal* 2 (February 15, 1840): 58, reprinted from the *Connecticut Common School Journal.*

34. "The Bible in Our Common Schools," *Common School Journal* 14 (January 1, 1852): 9.

35. Howe, *The Garden and the Wilderness*; William G. McLoughlin, "The Role of Religion in the Revolution," in *Essays on the American Revolution*, ed. Stephen G. Kurtz and James H. Hutson (Chapel Hill: University of North Carolina Press, 1973). On positive versus negative freedom, see Isaiah Berlin, "Two Concepts of Liberty," in *Four Essays on Liberty* (New York: Oxford University Press, 1969), 118–72.

36. Charles I. Foster, *An Errand of Mercy: The Evangelical United Front, 1790–1865* (Chapel Hill: University of North Carolina Press, 1960); Clifford S. Griffin, *Their Brothers' Keepers: Moral Stewardship in the United States, 1800–1865* (New Brunswick, N.J.: Rutgers University Press, 1960).

37. Michael Zuckerman, *Peaceable Kingdoms: New England Towns in the Eighteenth Century* (New York: Norton, 1970).

38. *Address of the Catholic Lay Citizens of the City and County of Philadelphia to Their Fellow-Citizens, in Reply to the Presentment of the Grand Jury of the Court of Quarter Sessions of May Term 1844, in Regard to the Causes of the Late Riots in Philadelphia* (Philadelphia: M. Fithian, 1844), 6.

39. As an example of legal sanction given to Catholic control and influence over schooling, *Millard v. Board of Education*, 121 Ill. 29 (1887), permitted a public school to function in the basement of a Catholic church, with a voluntary mass and catechism taking place before school hours, classroom instruction by a Catholic teacher, and the Angelus prayer at the end of the school session. The court was persuaded that the children who attended had done so voluntarily, thus giving credence to an early form of choice as a rationale for private distribution of public goods. The case is reported and discussed in Otto T. Hamilton, *The Courts and the Curriculum* (New York: Bureau of Publications, Teachers College, Columbia University, 1927). Another such case, *Hysong v. School District*, 164 Pa. 629 (1894), approved the presence of Catholic nuns in religious garb as teachers in public schools; for discussion see Hamil-

ton, *Courts*, 103. On the Poughkeepsie Plan in New York, see Lloyd P. Jorgenson, *The State and the Non-Public School, 1825–1925* (Columbia: University of Missouri Press, 1987), 114–15.

40. Perko, *Time to Favor Zion*, 154–206.

41. For an excellent study of Jewish immigrants and public schooling, see Stephan F. Brumberg, *Going to School in America: The Jewish Immigrant Public School Encounter in Turn-of-the-Century New York City* (New York: Praeger, 1986).

42. On the trend toward stricter church rules controlling the education of Catholic children after the Civil War and through the end of the century, see "School Legislation" in James A. Burns, *The Growth and Development of the Catholic School System in the United States* (New York: Benziger Brothers, 1912), 181–96.

43. *Donahoe v. Richards*, 38 Me. 376, 410 (1854).

44. Other salient cases in the nineteenth century repeating this holding include *Spiller* v. *Inhabitants of Woburn*, 94 Mass. 127 (1866), in which the court upheld the expulsion of a student from school for refusing to bow her head during the reading of the Bible and prayer; *McCormick* v. *Burt*, 95 Ill. 263 (1880); *Board of Education of Cincinnati* v. *Minor*, 23 Ohio St. 211 (1872); and *Nessle* v. *Hum*, 1 Ohio N.P. 140 (1894). The Ohio cases are interesting because they play out two permutations of the rule: the 1872 decision upheld a local board decision to prohibit Bible reading in the schools because of the majoritarian consensus to do so; the 1894 case refused, on the same grounds, to prohibit Bible reading elsewhere in the state.

45. *Donahoe v. Richards*, 38 Me. at 412.

46. For a summary of nonsectarian provisions in the law governing schools, see Samuel W. Brown, *The Secularization of American Education as Shown by State Legislation, State Constitutional Provisions and State Supreme Court Decisions* (New York: Bureau of Publications, Teachers College, Columbia University, 1912).

47. *Donahoe v. Richards*, 38 Me. 376 (1854); *Commonwealth v. Cooke* [Police Court of Boston, Massachusetts], 7 Am.L.Reg. 417 (1859); *Spiller v. Inhabitants of Woburn*, 94 Mass. 127 (1866); *McCormick v. Burt*, 95 Ill. 263 (1880); *Moore v. Monroe*, 64 Iowa 367 (1884); *Pfeiffer v. Board of Education*, 118 Mich. 560 (1898); *Stevenson v. Hanyon*, 7 Pa. D. 585 (1898).

48. Decisions of the state superintendent in 1837, 1839, 1866, 1870, 1872, and 1884; see Hamilton, *Courts*, 93–94, for discussion. The source for these cases is Thomas E. Finegan, *Judicial Decisions of the State Superintendent of Public Instruction, State Commissioner of Education, 1822 to 1913* (Albany: University of the State of New York, 1914).

49. *Moore v. Monroe*, 64 Iowa 367 (1884); the rule was summarized clearly

in *State ex rel. Freeman* v. *Scheve*, 65 Neb. 853 (1902), which held that sectarian worship was forbidden but not the use of the Bible as such; thus the test for "worship" was not the presence of Scripture but the use and form of instruction.

50. On the changing categories of public and private in U.S. educational history, see Thomas James, "Questions about Educational Choice: An Argument from History," in *Public Dollars for Private Schools*, ed. Thomas James and Henry M. Levin (Philadelphia: Temple University Press, 1983), 55–70.

51. Patricia M. Lines has written perceptively about this transition in "Treatment of Religion in Public Schools and the Impact on Private Education," in *Comparing Public and Private Schools*, Vol. 1: *Institutions and Organizations*, ed. Thomas James and Henry M. Levin (New York: Falmer Press, 1988), 67–94. The rise of a prevailing bureaucratic and professional culture in American education has been the subject of extensive scholarly inquiry; see, for example, David B. Tyack, *The One Best System: A History of American Urban Education* (Cambridge, Mass.: Harvard University Press, 1974); and Michael B. Katz, *Reconstructing American Education* (Cambridge, Mass.: Harvard University Press, 1987).

52. *Board of Education of Cincinnati* v. *Minor*, 23 Ohio St. 211 (1872); see note 44 above for the later Ohio case showing that such deference to local majority rule also had the effect of ignoring individual or minority conscience in districts where the Protestant majority demanded Bible reading on its own terms. For the entire court proceedings and decision at the lower court level in the Cincinnati case, see *The Bible in the Public Schools: Arguments in the Case of John D. Minor et al. versus the Board of Education of the City of Cincinnati et al., Superior Court of Cincinnati, with the Opinions and Decision of the Court* (1870; rpt. New York: Da Capo Press, 1967).

53. *Weiss* v. *District Board*, 76 Wis. 177 (1890), 199–200.

54. Ibid., 220.

55. *State ex rel. Freeman* v. *Scheve*, 65 Neb. 853 (1902), 863.

56. *People* v. *Board of Educ.*, 245 Ill. 334 (1910), 339–40, 347–48.

57. An important parallel to the Bible-reading cases was resistance to certain compulsory attendance laws that attempted to regulate or suppress religious schools. Two of the most salient examples in the late nineteenth century were in Wisconsin and Illinois, where compulsory education laws were overturned by newly elected Democratic majorities in the state legislatures after years of Republican and nativist hegemony. These states, with their elected judiciaries, also generated landmark cases on conscience and the practice of Bible reading in public schools. For more detailed studies of the political and social conditions that

led to these major shifts in legislative and judicial norms, see Robert J. Ulrich, "The Bennett Law of 1889: Education and Politics in Wisconsin" (Ph.D. dissertation, University of Wisconsin, 1965); and Peter DeBoer, "A History of the Early Compulsory School Attendance Legislation in the State of Illinois" (Ph.D. dissertation, University of Chicago, 1968); see also Jorgenson, *The State and the Non-Public School*, chap. 9.

58. *Engel* v. *Vitale*, 370 U.S. 421 (1962); and *Abington School District* v. *Schempp*, 374 U.S. 203 (1963).

59. Jesse K. Flanders, *Legislative Control of the Elementary Curriculum* (New York: Bureau of Publications, Teachers College, Columbia University, 1925), 155–58. In 1903 the states with laws *permitting* Bible reading in schools were Georgia, Indiana, Iowa, Kansas, Mississippi, New Jersey, North Dakota, Oklahoma, and South Dakota; the only state *mandating* the same in 1903 was Massachusetts. By 1923 the permissive states were Indiana, Iowa, Kansas, Mississippi, North Dakota, Oklahoma, and South Dakota, while those with mandatory provisions in their Bible-reading statutes were Alabama, Delaware, Georgia, Maine, Massachusetts, New Jersey, Rhode Island, and Tennessee (see Flanders, *Legislative Control*, Table 14, 150–51).

60. Alvin W. Johnson, *The Legal Status of Church-State Relationships in the United States* (Minneapolis: University of Minnesota Press, 1934); see also Ward W. Keesecker, *Legal Status of Bible Reading and Religious Instruction in Public Schools*, Bulletin 14, U.S. Office of Education (Washington, D.C.: U.S. Government Printing Office, 1930). In *Cantwell* v. *Connecticut*, 310 U.S. 296 (1940), the U.S. Supreme Court applied the religion clauses of the First Amendment to the states through an expanded interpretation of protections guaranteed by the Fourteenth Amendment. For a review of pertinent cases on schooling in the twentieth century, see William E. Griffiths, *Religion, the Courts, and the Public Schools* (Cincinnati: W. H. Anderson Company, 1966).

61. David Tyack and Thomas James, "Moral Majorities and the School Curriculum: Historical Perspectives on the Legalization of Virtue," *Teachers College Record* 86 (1985): 513–37; see also John Higham, *Strangers in the Land: Patterns of American Nativism, 1860–1925* (New York: Atheneum, 1978).

62. *Meyer* v. *Nebraska*, 262 U.S. 390 (1923); *Pierce* v. *Society of Sisters*, 268 U.S. 510 (1925); and *Farrington* v. *Tokushige*, 273 U.S. 284 (1927).

63. Clarence Karier, "Testing for Order and Control in the Corporate Liberal State," in *Roots of Crisis*, ed. Karier, Paul C. Violas, and Joel Spring (Chicago: Rand McNally, 1973), 108–37; Tyack and Hansot, *Managers of Virtue*, pt. 2.

64. Stephen Arons explores these issues in *Compelling Belief: The Culture of American Schooling* (New York: McGraw-Hill, 1983).

65. For a summary of dates of enactment, see August W. Steinhilber and Carl J. Sokolowski, *State Law on Compulsory Attendance* (Washington, D.C.: U.S. Government Printing Office, 1966), 3.

66. *State ex rel. Freeman* v. *Scheve*, 65 Neb. 853 (1902), 872.

67. *Statutes of California, 1873–1874*, chap. 516, p. 571.

Republican Origins of Constitutionalism

Morton J. Horwitz

I wish to warn against the dangers of a certain kind of lawyer's history, which involves roaming through history looking for one's friends. The problem with the republican revival in American history—the recent effort to reconsider the past in terms of a republican ideology as distinct from, let us say for now, a liberal ideology—has many dangers, and I wish to focus on them.

The discussion of state constitutions is long overdue. American constitutional law in any real functional sense before the Civil War is American state constitutional law. Therefore, to understand constitutional ideology before the Civil War, we must study constitutional law at the state level.

There are some old questions that need to be reexamined. Where did the idea of a written constitution come from? These state documents were the first written constitutions in the world, as Suzanna Sherry points out.[1] What was the ideology behind written constitutions? Did they emerge from a newly formed conception of popular sovereignty? Were they a result of liberal social contract theory or covenant theology? Did they reflect an originally medieval idea of the fundamentality of law and the writing down of previously established fundamental laws? These are questions that can be revived by a renewed focus on state constitutions.

The issue of republicanism has developed significantly in American historiography during the past twenty years.[2] Though it has undergone a number of twists and turns, I believe that the republican revival has by and large been very productive. It has focused historians on factors that have previously not been recognized. We did not understand, for example, why just compensation clauses tended not to appear in early state constitutions.[3] I think the answer can be derived from republican ideas about property and community. We used to believe after studying *Luther* v. *Borden*[4] that by the time of the Rhode Island rebellion, republican ideology had lost its content. Perhaps that was true of the Supreme Court by 1850. But there had once been an entire system of meaning behind the republican form of government clause.

The republican revival in recent years has attempted to capture several missing ingredients in American history. As liberalism has increasingly accepted an interest group pluralist picture of the world, the republican revival has sought to rediscover a communitarian tradition that emphasized notions of public-spiritedness and public interest and also emphasized that there was a normative element to law, not just a neutral framework for managing traffic and facilitating private ordering. As we begin to examine the reasons for the republican revival, we see that the interest group pluralist and individualistic conceptions of political and constitutional theory that have come to dominate constitutional ideology were not present in the thinking that was still prevalent after 1776. The republican revival thus seems to be an important attempt to remedy a distorted picture of American constitutional law.

But the republican revival no longer needs to be justified. One now has to fear instead that it will develop into an unreflective growth industry. There is a danger of a simple-minded search for historical precedent, which becomes increasingly present-minded about the issues of the past and thereby presents an unsubtle, uncomplex, and partial picture of the past that will no longer convince any serious student of the past that there was a "there" there. There is a danger of reification, of making republicanism only one thing when it may be many things. There is clearly a right republicanism and a left republicanism in the constitutional field. But it is also true that the particular elements that constituted republicanism in 1776 or 1789 may be historically contingent and may not always be the true, real, defining reasons for looking at republican ideology in the constitutional period. We should not unselfconsciously propagate the view that republicanism is just one thing. Rather, there were many ambiguities, many complexities, many contradictions in republican ideology in 1789. Indeed, if we trace just two of the many influences on republican ideology in the constitutional period, the eighteenth-century republicanism of the English opposition—what I call right republicanism—and a more radical republicanism sometimes derived from French republicanism, sometimes from a native, radical republicanism with deep religious roots, we can see that there were many contests over the nature of republicanism in the late eighteenth century. We should try to preserve that richness. We should try to recapture those arguments.

I believe there are four particularly important contemporary issues involving republicanism and interpretations of republicanism. The first concerns republicanism and equality. It will not do to maintain that republicanism stands for equality—certainly not social equality in any one-to-one sense—and there is even a debate about political equality, as we see in the essays in this book. It would be a mistake not to see that what James Henretta calls aristocratic-republicanism expresses the hierarchal and paternalistic strands in English republicanism.

Nevertheless, if one keeps all the dangers in mind, there are ways to understand, from the perspective of a contemporary egalitarian, the richness of the republican tradition. There was, at least in another one of its versions, a very powerful republican commitment to political equality. One should note the historical uniqueness of political equality expressed in its left republican version at the time of the framing of the Constitution. Only the seventeenth-century Levellers had gone that far in England. Further, if we look at the forms of social analysis with which left republicans talked about political equality, we will see that one of the important aspects of republicanism, of both left and right, was its commitment to analyzing the social conditions for political stability. Social analysis was lost by the defeat or displacement of republicanism as it had been represented in England from James Harrington through the eighteenth-century English opposition, in the French republican tradition from Montesquieu through Tocqueville, and in the Scottish republican tradition from Adam Smith.[5] Why are there no American Tocquevilles? There are no Tocquevilles in America, not, as Louis Hartz suggested, because there was no feudal tradition, but because the republican tradition was defeated or displaced.[6] The analysis of the social conditions for political equality, which was a standard form of republican analysis, was gradually displaced in the nineteenth century. It is worth recapturing.

But it is not worth recapturing if the conclusion is going to be that republicans favored social equality. Some republicans perhaps converged on that position. Jefferson occasionally did, but only occasionally, with his idealization of the yeoman farmer.[7] This social analysis was also implicit in the Anti-Federalist view that small states are better than large states at preserving freedom because they have a much more egalitarian social base and because there is less envy and less distinction among the populace. Most of these ideas were implicit, not explicit. If we seek to uncover them in their subtlety, we will find much contemporary resonance in republican discourse.

The second idea is about republicanism and democracy, on which there are a number of essays in this book. Anyone who wishes to suggest that there was universal manhood suffrage in 1776 first has to accept some very important qualifications and modifications. Nevertheless, one has to understand in dialectical form the struggle between republicanism and democracy in the constitutional period. For the Federalists, for Madison and Hamilton, republicanism and democracy were opposite conceptions. They reduced the idea of democracy to the totally ridiculous notion of Athenian direct democracy and concluded that republicanism meant representative democracy. Even within the constitutional debates of the time, this constituted a stereotyping of the democratic position. There is room for discussion about what democratic theory really meant at that time. Right republicans arose as much out of fear of democracy as out of anything else. Yet that was not the only available republican tradition. Pennsylvania republicanism, for example, contained a very strong democratic tendency, as did Rhode Island republicanism, with its religious roots. But we should not come to the conclusion that republicanism and democracy are identical. It would be a mistake, it would be unhistorical, it would flatten the historical landscape.

The third point deals with republicanism and pluralism. The most ominous strand in the republican tradition is contained in the widely held view that the only way to have a free society is to have a relatively homogeneous social base. That is good republicanism in both its left and right versions, though the content of the social base may be quite different. Perhaps the right republican tradition with its mixed government founded on a conception of quasi-feudal social orders offers the better model for social diversity and for a conception of social pluralism, though, of course, a hierarchal conception of social pluralism. Hence, it seems to me, the liberal tradition, the pluralist tradition, the interest group pluralist tradition that emerges out of Madison's *Federalist* No. 10 may provide the richer texts for dealing with contemporary problems of diversity and difference. We are going to have to face squarely and directly the very limited version of pluralism that was contained within the republican tradition. I believe that the liberal individualistic tradition produces the ideology for tolerating difference. Here is where we need to rethink the roots of republicanism.

Finally, there is the problem of clarifying the role of rights in the republican tradition. And here, too, we encounter great danger of being present-minded. What the status of individual rights is in republican ideology seems to me to need further understanding. Why the Anti-Federalists, if they more or less reflected a republican ideology, were so passionate about bills of rights is something we need to rethink in a republican context.[8] By and large, republicanism in its late eighteenth-century variety was a theory of powers, not of rights. It did not posit a sharp distinction between public and private realms, which, at least in the liberal tradition, was the way rights discourse emerged. It thus did not posit a sharp conflict between man and the state, which is part of the liberal tradition. It was much more communitarian, organicist, and hostile to the individualist premises on which most modern rights discourse has been built. I am not saying that there is not some version of republicanism and rights that would deeply resonate and be true to late eighteenth-century discourse. I believe there is. But the starting point is to understand in a different way the position of the Anti-Federalists on bills of rights. But I do believe that we should not think of rights and republicanism from the perspective of a card-carrying member of the American Civil Liberties Union. The discourse of eighteenth-century republicanism was not, by and large, a rights discourse. And one of the most striking examples of this is the Jeffersonian arguments against the Alien and Sedition Acts. They were overwhelming arguments from constitutional powers and the absence of such power in the federal government. There are very few formulations that look like modern First Amendment "man against the state" free speech arguments against the Alien and Sedition Acts.[9] It is a different conception.

Notes

1. Suzanna Sherry, "The Early Virginia Tradition of Extratextual Interpretation," in this volume.

2. *The Reinterpretation of the American Revolution, 1763–1789*, ed. Jack P. Greene (New York: Harper & Row, 1968); Gordon Wood, *The Creation of the American Republic, 1776–1787* (Chapel Hill: University of North Carolina Press, 1969); Joyce Appleby, "Republicanism and Ideology," *American Quarterly* 37 (1985): 461–73; Frank Michelman, "Law's Republic," *Yale Law Journal* 97 (1988): 1493–1537; and see generally the text and citations in Peter S. Onuf, "Reflections on the Founding: Constitutional Historiography in Bicentennial Perspective," *William and Mary Quarterly* 3d ser., 46 (1989): 341–75.

3. See, e.g., *Barron v. Baltimore*, 32 U.S. (7 Pet.) 243 (1833) (rejecting federal compensation claim made in absence of state clause).

4. 48 U.S. (7 How.) 1 (1849) and see William Wiecek, *The Guarantee Clause of the U.S. Constitution* (Ithaca: Cornell University Press, 1972). See also Note, "Political Rights as Political Questions: The Paradox of Luther v. Borden," *Harvard Law Review* 100 (1987): 1125.

5. See, e.g., *The English Libertarian Heritage*, ed. David Jacobson (Indianapolis: Bobbs-Merrill, 1965).

6. Louis Hartz, *The Liberal Tradition in America: An Interpretation of American Political Thought Since the Revolution* (New York: Harcourt, Brace, 1955).

7. Stanley N. Katz, "Thomas Jefferson and the Right to Property in Revolutionary America," *Journal of Law and Economics* 19 (1976): 467.

8. See the many Anti-Federalist arguments in *The Complete Anti-Federalist*, ed. Herbert J. Storing (Chicago: University of Chicago Press, 1981).

9. See James Morton Smith, *Freedom's Fetters: The Alien and Sedition Laws and American Civil Liberties* (Ithaca: Cornell University Press, 1956).

Part Two

Interpretive Traditions in State Constitutional Law

The Early Virginia Tradition of Extratextual Interpretation

Suzanna Sherry

As we search for a usable past, it is wise to avoid too "presentist" an approach: one should not necessarily expect a history of state protections of liberty to provide either a familiar or a genteel source from which to work. In the modern world, the search for state protections of liberty generally conjures up an image of state courts using state constitutions to prevent infringement of such core civil liberties as freedom of the press and security from unreasonable searches and seizures. Perusing the reports of judicial decisions from the late eighteenth and early nineteenth centuries, however, will not yield very many (if any) cases of that sort.

But the absence of modern civil liberties cases in those reports does not mean that the past is barren, only that we are looking for the wrong thing. In this essay, I propose to broaden the search in two ways. First, rather than using the modern language of civil liberties, I will discuss state court protection of what judges in the eighteenth and nineteenth centuries labeled natural or inalienable rights, or natural justice.

More important, I want to move from textual to extratextual interpretation. Courts faced with a question of whether a particular positive legislative enactment is consistent with higher or fundamental law can look to two broad types of fundamental law: the written constitution or any of several categories of unwritten law.[1] Textual interpretation focuses on the written constitution (the text) and extratextual interpretation on sources outside the written constitution. Thus modern constitutional law is virtually exclusively textualist, insofar as courts invalidate only statutes that conflict with the written constitution—although interpretation of the written constitution, of course, often involves an examination of many sources of law and tradition not embodied in the text itself. Still, fundamental law must ultimately be tied to the written text. It would, for example, today be considered an anomaly—and a judicial usurpation of legislative authority—for the United States Supreme Court to declare a law unconstitutional on the avowed ground that it conflicted with general principles of natural justice unassociated with the written text.[2]

Judges of the eighteenth and early nineteenth centuries were not so narrowly textualist.[3] Indeed, the earliest state constitutions were largely viewed as merely committing to writing ancient and inalienable unwritten rights. A bill of rights was thought to be the renewed declaration, not the creation, of fundamental law. Only half the states included a bill of rights in their constitutions, although there is no indication that in those states lacking a bill of rights the citizenry ceded any of the inherent rights themselves.[4] One part of these early state constitutions, however, was meant as innovative: the provisions creating the framework of government.

The dual nature of the early written constitutions—as mere declarations of an older tradition of fundamental law and as new social compacts of government—was reflected in the fact that the seven original states with any significant textual protection of rights explicitly separated their constitutions into two distinct parts: a declaration of rights and a frame of government. The first was derived, often explicitly, from unwritten tradition; the second was a written creation of the "new science of politics."

Between 1776 and 1787, state judiciaries carried into practical effect this union of tradition and science. In seven cases during that period, state judges reviewed state statutes for consistency with fundamental law. Five statutes were invalidated, one was upheld, and one was given a questionable interpretation in order to avoid any conflict with higher law. In only two of the cases did the judges rely exclusively on the written constitution. In the others, judges (and lawyers) relied on both the written constitution and unwritten fundamental law, citing such sources as the fundamental laws of England, the law of nations, the Magna Charta, common right and reason, inalienable rights, and natural justice.[5]

Moreover, these cases began to exhibit a pattern. In cases involving individual rights, the natural law component was usually dominant. In cases involving the structure of the government, however, the written constitution was often more decisive. The distinction between natural law and textualism as methods of discovering fundamental law thus followed the dichotomy between tradition and science.

After their establishment in 1789, the federal courts continued the same tradition of measuring positive law against both written and unwritten higher law. The early federal cases also exhibit the same correlation between textualism and governmental powers and between natural law and individual rights. Even within a single case, a judge might rely on the written text to decide a separation of powers question and on unwritten law to decide an individual rights question.

My purpose here is to continue the examination of the role of unwritten fundamental law by looking at state cases after the establishment of the federal republic. In particular, I will focus on Virginia during the last decade of the eighteenth century and the first three decades of the nineteenth. With its long-standing and well-developed court system, its plethora of outstanding judges and lawyers,[6] and its systematic reporting of decisions of the state's highest court, early Virginia offers a wealth of cases through which to investigate the role of unwritten law. Virginia, moreover, had one of the earliest written constitutions, and because it included a substantial bill of rights it affords one of the best opportunities for measuring the relative importance of written and unwritten law.

Two types of cases provide useful ground for testing the hypothesis that Virginia judges had recourse to unwritten as well as written fundamental law. The question is raised directly in cases of judicial review: cases in which the court is reviewing the validity of a positive legislative enactment for its conformity with higher law. In those cases, it is possible to ask whether the judges seemed to measure the enactment against the written constitution (either exclusively or in preference to unwritten law), or whether they seemed indifferent regarding the written or unwritten character of the fundamental law.

The question of the influence of unwritten law is also raised, somewhat less directly, when a court is asked to rule on some statutory or common law dispute that implicates principles of natural law. In early nineteenth-century Virginia, the quintessential example of such a dispute was cases involving slavery. Although few cases directly challenged the institution of slavery as a violation of natural law,[7] any case in which a slave sought a legal declaration of freedom—indeed, perhaps any case governed by the law of slavery—indirectly required the judges to determine the status of the institution. A judicial refusal to free the petitioning slave, and to some extent a refusal to use the case as an opportunity to declare the entire institution in violation of unwritten law, necessarily raises one of two preliminary inferences. Either the institution is not in violation of unwritten fundamental law, or the judge has failed in that instance to invalidate positive law that conflicts with unwritten fundamental law. Thus an examination of the Virginia decisions on the law of freedom provides further illumination of the role of unwritten law in that state.

I turn first to extratextual interpretation in cases of judicial review and then to the role of unwritten law in cases of slaves petitioning for freedom.

Judicial Review of Statutes

To distinguish between textual and extratextual interpretation one must first know what the text says. The Virginia Constitution of 1776 was one of the earliest state constitutions; the drafting process began before the Declaration of Independence was written. The constitution was drafted and adopted by a specially constituted committee of selected members of the Virginia House of Burgesses (the lower chamber of the legislature) without popular ratification. It remained in effect until 1830.

The 1776 Constitution, like those of several other states, included a long and detailed Bill of Rights that appeared primarily to be memorializing unwritten rights rather than creating new ones. This natural law heritage was reflected in the very first section of the Bill of Rights, which began by declaring that "all men are by nature equally free and independent, and have certain inherent rights." Further evidence of the natural law influence on the 1776 Bill of Rights is found in some of its provisions that seem to reflect natural law precepts rather than injunctive limits on the government.[8] For example, section 15 states: "That no government, or the blessings of liberty, can be preserved to any people, but by a firm adherence to justice, moderation, temperance, frugality, and virtue, and by frequent recurrence to fundamental principles." Although the Virginia courts did occasionally refer to the admonition to recur to fundamental principles,[9] the remainder of section 15 does not appear to be directed at any particular governmental action. Similar language, scattered throughout the Virginia Bill of Rights, suggests again that the authors were merely committing to writing familiar ancient principles.

Some of the specific principles included a guarantee of freedom of the press and a right to jury trials, as well as religious toleration. For the purposes of this essay, it is important that the Virginia Bill of Rights included neither a prohibition against ex post facto laws nor a requirement of compensation when private property is taken for public purposes. Nevertheless, Virginia judges in the early republic used unwritten or natural law to protect against both ex post facto laws and uncompensated takings. Judges and lawyers also relied generally on unwritten natural law principles as much as on the written text, occasionally explicitly privileging the former over the latter.

Virginia courts had been reviewing the validity of statutes since at least 1782 and perhaps earlier.[10] The reliance on natural law, however, is first apparent in 1788. In that year, the Virginia legislature passed an act directing sitting judges of the Court of Appeals to take on new duties as district court judges. No additional compensation was provided, and it was argued that requiring additional duties without compensation was equivalent to a diminution of salary and thus unconstitutional. Although no suit was instituted, the Court of Appeals nevertheless made its opinion known to the legislature. Four months after the act was passed, the judges delivered and sent to the legislature "The Respectful Remonstrance of the Court of Appeals."[11] In it, they declared an obligation to favor the written constitution over statutes inconsistent with it and found the 1788 act inconsistent. Rather than invalidate the act, however, they simply refused to execute it and requested the legislature to repeal it.

Despite the overt references to the written constitution, the "Remonstrance" seemed to base its conclusions on both written and unwritten law. The "Remonstrance" first set out the facts and then framed two questions: whether the 1788 act was unconstitutional and, if so, whether "it was their duty to declare that the act must yield to the constitution."[12] The judges began their analysis by noting that in "forming their judgment" on both questions "they had recourse to that article in the declaration of rights, that no free government, or the blessing of liberty can be preserved to any people but (among other things) by frequent recurrence to fundamental principles."[13]

In discussing "fundamental principles" and their relationship to the constitution, the judges relied very clearly on unwritten law. They declared that "the propriety and necessity of the independence of the judges is evident in reason and the nature of their office," explaining that only an independent judiciary can mete out impartial justice to the rich and the poor, the government and the people.[14] Thus the "fundamental principles" to which the constitution directed recurrence were, in fact, the same principles of reason and justice that animated natural law doctrines. Moreover, although the "Remonstrance" later examined and relied upon specific provisions of the written constitution, it discussed fundamental principles first.

One final aspect of the "Remonstrance" might confirm its natural law basis. Immediately after concluding that an independent judiciary is a fundamental principle, the judges considered "whether the people have secured, or departed from [this principle] in the constitution, or form of government."[15] Since the "Remonstrance" ultimately concluded that the constitution did in fact secure the independence of the judiciary, we cannot know what the judges might have done had they decided otherwise. But the very asking of the question tentatively suggests the possibility that the fundamental principles adverted to in the Bill of Rights (which, remember, merely declared ancient principles) were superior even to the written frame of government: it is possible that the judges were prepared to invalidate or ignore any part of the written constitution that directly conflicted with unwritten law.

Four years later, the Virginia court had before it an actual case implicating the constitutionality of a statute. In *Turner* v. *Turner's Executor*,[16] plaintiffs challenged the validity of a legislative enactment changing the law of gifts of slaves, alleging that it was an unconstitutional ex post facto law. Although President[17] Edmund Pendleton ultimately upheld the law as prospective only, he did suggest that a retrospective law would be invalid—despite the absence of any provision in the Virginia Constitution outlawing either ex post facto or retrospective laws.[18]

Pendleton noted that a law retrospectively affecting title to slaves would be "subject to every objection which lies to *ex post facto* laws, as it would destroy rights already acquired."[19] The power to make such laws, he contended, was "oppressive and contrary to the principles of the constitution."[20] Since the constitution did not contain any provision prohibiting retrospective laws, Pendleton's conclusion must rest either directly on unwritten principles of natural justice or on the integration of such principles into the fundamental principles language of the written constitution. The inference of direct reliance on natural law is perhaps stronger for two reasons. Pendleton did not cite the fundamental principles provision in *Turner*, whereas in the "Remonstrance," written only four years earlier (with Pendleton's participation), the judges did cite the fundamental principles provision. Moreover, Pendleton's own opinion in an 1802 ex post facto case directly attributes the invalidity of retrospective laws to "natural justice."[21]

Although both the "Remonstrance" and *Turner* suggest that judges might rely on unwritten higher law in addition to the written law, one 1793 case in the Virginia Court of Chancery provides intriguing evidence of the predominance of unwritten or natural law. Chancellor George Wythe, an eminent Virginia jurist and the holder of the first law chair in the United States, decided in *Page* v. *Pendleton*[22] that the Virginia legislature could not unilaterally discharge debts Virginians owed to British citizens. He did so on the ground that a legislature could not bind one who was not a member of the society because the requisite consent was lacking.

In the course of his opinion, Wythe wrote several long footnotes explaining his holding. Two of these footnotes contain extensive discussions of natural law principles. To support his holding that "the right to money due to an enemy cannot be confiscated," Wythe explained: "If this seem contrary to what is called authority, as perhaps it may seem to some men, the publisher of the opinion will be against the authority, when, in a question depending, like the present, on the law of nature, the authority is against reason, which is affirmed to be the case here."[23] He then proceeded to explain why the "authority" was contrary to reason.

Later, in considering the question of who might be bound by what laws, Wythe dropped an even more interesting footnote. He began: "The position in the sixth article of our bill of rights, namely, that men are not bound by laws to which they have not, by themselves, or by representatives of their election, assented, is not true of unwritten or common law, that is, of the law of nature, called common law, because it is common to all mankind. . . . They are laws which men, who did not ordain them, have not power to abrogate."[24] He then went on to explain how the disfranchised and subsequent generations can nevertheless be held to have consented to the passage of positive laws in which they actually played no part. It is clear from these footnotes that Wythe believed that fundamental law included natural, unwritten law, although his ruling did not depend on much unwritten law. Nor is it important that Wythe was sitting in equity rather than in law, since his dicta were apparently meant more as treatise comments on law in general than as direct authority in the case before him.

In 1797, an enterprising plaintiff's counsel acted on Judge Pendleton's earlier suggestion that ex post facto laws were void and added the idea that government taking of property required compensation. His arguments were to no avail: the court in *Carter* v. *Tyler*[25] upheld a statute that converted all entailed estates into fee simple estates, thus depriving remaindermen of previously acquired contingent rights. Counsel for the plaintiff had argued primarily that the statute should not be construed to dock entails in existence before passage of the act. He also contended, however, although without much elaboration, that any other interpretation would render the act "unconstitutional and void; because it would be *ex post facto* in its operation, taking away private rights without any public necessity, and without making the injured parties any compensation for them."[26] No authority was given for this proposition, nor could any textual support be provided. As noted, the Virginia Bill of Rights contained neither an ex post facto clause nor a just compensation clause.

Judge Pendleton construed the statute as operating retrospectively but did not discuss its constitutionality. This is especially puzzling since Pendleton had remarked during argument that "the defendant's counsel are desired to confine themselves to the question, whether the act is void, as being unconstitutional."[27] Defendant's counsel apparently did not address the question, despite being enjoined to do so by the president. Pendleton never returned to the question. *Carter* therefore affords some support for the notion that lawyers used natural law principles in arguing cases and no evidence at all on how courts received such arguments. In the early nineteenth century, however, and thus at least arguably in 1797, "arguments of counsel were regarded as themselves sources of law."[28] Thus counsel's reliance on natural law in *Carter* provides some evidence that unwritten principles of natural law—whether or not incorporated into the written constitution—were considered dispositive.

Two cases involving fines show that the early Virginia courts subscribed to the related idea that natural rights and written rights were coterminous. In *Jones* v. *Commonwealth*,[29] a 1799 case, the court overturned the imposition of joint fines on several defendants. Judge Spencer Roane noted that the principle against joint fines was "fortified not only by the principles of natural justice . . . but, also, by the clause of the Bill of Rights, prohibiting excessive fines."[30] Judge Paul Carrington held that the fines were invalid, "whether I consider the case upon principle, the doctrines of the common law, or the spirit of the Bill of Rights."[31] Judge Pendleton dissented, distinguishing the common law cases and not mentioning the written constitution. In *Bullock* v. *Goodall*[32] two years later, however, Pendleton revealed his sympathy with his brethren's equivalence of the written and unwritten law. In overturning a fine, he wrote that it was "superlatively excessive, unconstitutional, oppressive, and against conscience."[33]

In 1802, the court revisited the question of retrospective statutes and unwritten law. *Elliott's Executor* v. *Lyell*[34] involved a 1786 statute that changed the law of obligations as it related to joint obligors. The question before the court was whether the statute applied to a contract entered into before enactment of the statute. The court ultimately concluded that the statute could not be read to apply to the contract at issue, but several of the judges apparently reached that conclusion at least partly on the basis of their views about unwritten fundamental law.

Counsel for the appellant argued that a careful reading of the statute showed that the legislature had not intended the statute to apply to existing contracts. He also contended that "perhaps" the legislature could not give the statute retrospective effect because it would then be acting in a judicial capacity by interpreting rather than making law.[35] This mingling of legislative and judicial functions would, he contended, violate the constitutional guarantee that the branches of government be kept distinct. This oblique suggestion was the only argument the appellant made to suggest the invalidity of the statute; he relied primarily on the statutory construction arguments. It is not even clear whether counsel meant that the statute should be construed to make it constitutional, that the legislature could not have intended to enact an unconstitutional statute, or that the statute as enacted was unconstitutional. The statutory question was clearly thought to be of more significance than the constitutional one.

Only Judge Roane followed counsel's lead and confined himself to statutory interpretation, however. Noting that "the question here is not whether the Legislature have power to pass a retrospective law"[36] but rather whether it had done so, he concluded that the statute could not be read to have retrospective effect. The other three judges agreed with his conclusion, but each indicated that the statutory interpretation was compelled by the fundamental principle against retrospective laws.

Judge William Fleming held that the legislature could not be presumed to intend retrospective effect because "retrospective laws [are] odious in their nature."[37] Construing the statute retrospectively, moreover, would "abolish the best established principles of justice."[38] Judge Peter Lyons similarly concluded that the legislature "ought not to be presumed to have willed injustice."[39] He characterized retrospective laws as "unjust and improper" and "necessarily oppressive" and noted that construing the law as retrospective in operation "would destroy the principles of natural justice."[40] Both Fleming and Lyons thus avoided holding the law invalid, but they did so under the canon that statutes should be construed so as to avoid doubts about their constitutionality. Although this does not demonstrate that either judge would have invalidated the statute if he could not construe it consistently with natural justice, it does suggest the strong relationship between unwritten law and judicial review.

Judge Pendleton, who had been hinting since 1782 that judges might strike down unconstitutional laws,[41] and who would write an opinion invalidating a state statute only a year after *Lyell*,[42] took a rather disingenuous approach. He first declared that retrospective laws were "against the principles of natural justice"[43] and then deliberately avoided the consequences of that conclusion. Fleming and Lyons relied on natural law to guide their interpretation of the statute, thus suggesting that fundamental law—written or unwritten—does serve as a constraint on the legislature. After concluding that retrospective laws were invalid, however, Pendleton merely stated that he was "not obliged to give an opinion" on whether the judiciary might void an invalid act and then proceeded to interpret the statute as Fleming and Lyons had, but made his interpretation appear entirely unconstrained by any external principles. He thus again warmed his readers to the idea of judicial review; he virtually announced that he would invalidate a retrospective law; and he made it appear as if his interpretation of the statute as prospective was forced only by the words of the statute itself—thus proclaiming his intentions without having to act on them even to the extent that Lyons and Fleming did. Nevertheless, Pendleton's beliefs are clear: retrospective statutes are against natural justice and thus invalid. Pendleton further confirmed his adherence to the natural law tradition of his time by explaining the relevance of the contract clause of the federal Constitution: "Although that [clause] is subsequent to the present act, I consider it as declaring a principle which always existed."[44]

Pendleton's fidelity to unwritten law as a significant source of higher law enforceable by the court was apparently carried on by his immediate successor, St. George Tucker (although to somewhat different effect). *Turpin* v. *Locket*[45] was argued in 1803, and the decision was to be announced on October 26 of that year. Had events not intervened, the court would have held three to one that a Virginia statute confiscating church glebe lands was unconstitutional. Judge Pendleton had already written an opinion invalidating the law, and Judges Carrington and Lyons agreed with him.[46] But Judge Pendleton died the night before he was to deliver his opinion, and Judge Tucker was appointed to replace him. The case was reargued, and in 1804 Tucker's support of the law led to a tie vote, thus affirming Chancellor Wythe's refusal to enjoin the confiscation.

Judge Roane found that the church had no vested right in the property and voted to affirm. Judges Carrington and Lyons, in a brief joint opinion, found the confiscation law unconstitutional without much elaboration. Judge Tucker, whose vote changed the final outcome, delivered a detailed opinion examining the church's rights in the property. He found both that the church lacked any vested right in the property and that earlier statutes awarding church ministers the monies from glebe lands probably violated various specific sections of the written bill of rights.[47]

He also noted, however, that any *incumbent* ministers (whom he later held did not exist) had acquired "a legal right" and also "a moral right" to the enjoyment of their estates. "So far as any act of the legislature has operated for [the] purpose [of protecting those rights]," he wrote, "it may be considered as pursuing the injunctions of moral justice, and the first article of our bill of rights."[48] This was not an isolated reference to moral rights, moreover. Earlier in his opinion, Judge Tucker set out the procedure for dealing with conflicting state statutes: "If they cannot be reconciled to each other, it will be our duty to pronounce those to be valid, which are most easily reconcilable to the dictates of moral justice, and the principles of the constitution of this commonwealth."[49] Thus Judge Tucker thrice coupled morality with positive law, suggesting either that moral rights were an additional source of fundamental law or that the constitution necessarily reflected moral justice. Despite an apparent setback in the protection of what Pendleton might have considered natural rights, at least some judges continued to adhere to the doctrine of natural rights.

Indeed, the most suggestive endorsement of unwritten law is an 1809 retrospectivity case, *Currie's Administrator* v. *Mutual Assurance Soc.*[50] The legislature had incorporated an insurance company in 1794 and then had changed the charter in 1805. Plaintiff was an insured whose risk had risen as a result of the later act, and he challenged it as unconstitutionally retrospective. The court upheld the 1805 statute: Judge Roane found that the act worked no injustice, and Judge Fleming—in an opinion largely irrelevant to our concerns—held that the original act reserved the right to change the charter. Judge Roane, however, also delivered a stinging refutation of the defendant's attempt to limit the court to a textualist analysis.

John Wickham,[51] counsel for the defendant, had argued that laws may be unjust but still valid: "No doubt every government ought to keep in view the great principles of justice and moral right, but no authority is expressly given to the judiciary by the Constitution of *Virginia*, to declare a law void as being morally wrong or in violation of a contract."[52]

Judge Roane vehemently rejected that limit on the court's authority. He wrote that the legislature's authority is limited "by the constitutions of the general and state governments; and limited also by considerations of *justice.*"[53] He then directly denied the defendant's textualist assumption:

> It was argued by a respectable member of the bar, that the legislature had a right to pass any law, however just, or unjust, reasonable, or unreasonable. This is a position which even the courtly Judge *Blackstone* was scarcely hardy enough to contend for, under the doctrine of the boasted *omnipotence* of parliament. What is this, but to lay prostrate, at the footstool of the legislature, all our rights of person and property, and abandon those great objects, for the protection of which, alone, all free governments have been instituted?[54]

Although he ultimately concluded that the statute did not deprive the plaintiff of any vested rights, Roane's outrage at the suggestion that he was confined to a textualist analysis is palpable.

If the previously noted "Remonstrance" suggests that the Virginia court was influenced by natural law as early as 1788, *Crenshaw* v. *Slate River Co.*[55] demonstrates that the influence was still strong forty years later. Plaintiffs who claimed river rights under a 1726 state grant challenged an 1819 law requiring them to build and maintain locks to make the river navigable. The court unanimously held that the plaintiffs held vested rights in their property and that they could not be deprived of those rights without compensation.

The Virginia Constitution of 1776, which was still in effect in 1828, contained no just compensation clause providing only that persons could not be "deprived of their property for public uses, without their own consent, or that of their representatives so elected." Since the 1819 act was duly passed by the Virginia legislature, that clause was of no avail. Judge John Green, with little elaboration, relied instead on Article 1 of the 1776 Bill of Rights, which protected the rights of "possessing property" and "enjoying liberty." The other judges apparently relied on unwritten law.

Judge Dabney Carr stated that the principle of compensation was "laid down by the writers on Natural Law, Civil Law, Common Law, and the Law of every civilized country."[56] Although he never discussed the written constitution, he concluded that "whether we judge this law by the principles of all Civilized Governments, by the Federal Constitution, or that of our own State, it is unconstitutional and void."[57] Judge John Coalter held that compensation was required, without citing any authority, whether written or unwritten. Judge William Cabell simply stated that he concurred with all the other judges.

In two cases during this period the Virginia court referred to natural law principles governing emigration. In both cases the emigration question was peripheral, but the court's language is nonetheless consistent with the unwritten rights analysis in the cases discussed so far. In 1811 in *Murray* v. *McCarty*[58] the court held, following Grotius, that emigration "is one of those 'inherent rights, of which, when [persons] enter into a state of society, they cannot, by any compact, deprive or devest their posterity.'"[59] The court expanded on this principle in 1829, noting that when a citizen of one state moves to another and subjects himself to the latter's laws, he becomes a citizen of the latter "upon the principles of natural law, and the spirit of our institutions."[60]

As in both the federal cases and the pre-1787 state cases, the Virginia courts did not depend entirely on unwritten natural law. In 1793, in *Kamper* v. *Hawkins*,[61] the court relied exclusively on the written constitution to invalidate a statute giving district court judges equitable jurisdiction and powers. All five judges held that the district judges had not been properly appointed to the chancery court as required by the constitution and thus they could not constitutionally exercise equitable jurisdiction. All of the opinions are conspicuously textualist.

Several judges examined minutely the portion of the written constitution setting out the frame of government. Judge William Nelson and Judge John Tyler discussed judicial review in terms making clear that they envisioned the written constitution as the fundamental law animating judicial review of statutes. Judge Roane defined fundamental principles as "those great principles growing out of the Constitution, by the aid of which, in dubious cases, the Constitution may be explained and preserved inviolate; those landmarks, which it may be necessary to resort to, on account of the impossibility to foresee or provide for cases within the spirit, but not the letter of the Constitution."[62] Judge Tucker distinguished prerevolutionary America from Virginia under its written constitution. In the former, "what the *constitution* of any country *was* or rather *was supposed to be*, could only be collected from what *the government had at any time done*."[63] In these more enlightened times, however, "the constitution is not 'an ideal thing, but a real existence: it can be produced in a visible form:' its principles can be ascertained from the living letter, not from obscure reasoning or deduction only."[64]

Kamper, like the Virginia case of *Commonwealth* v. *Caton*[65] eleven years earlier, raised a pure structure of government question. Individual rights were not at stake. As in *Caton*, the judges in *Kamper* were surely aware of this: except for two offhand references to the Bill of Rights, the only part of the written constitution on which the judges relied was the structural portion, denominated "the constitution or form of government." This failure to import natural law into a decision on the structure of government is consistent with the pattern noted earlier. Unwritten law might define natural rights, but the particular form of government depended primarily or exclusively on the written constitution.[66]

The pattern in early republican Virginia is thus similar to the pattern in the pre-1787 state cases and in the federal cases at least up through the 1820s.[67] Except for some clear decisions regarding governmental powers, judges and lawyers resorted to unwritten law as well as to the written constitution. This provides some confirmation that unwritten law—including principles of natural justice—constituted an important source of the fundamental law by which positive enactments might be measured.

Slavery

During this same period, however, the Virginia courts failed to use principles of natural justice to condemn what might be considered the most flagrant violation of natural rights: the enslavement of the black race. This failure seems inconsistent with the strong natural law reasoning in the cases just discussed. Indeed, many citizens of the early republic—including such Virginia judges as George Wythe, St. George Tucker, and Spencer Roane—were personally convinced that slavery violated principles of natural justice.[68] Several northern states, whose constitutions contained language much like Virginia's to the effect that "all men are by nature equally free and independent," construed that language to prohibit slavery.[69] Abolitionists, especially in the decade preceding the Civil War, stressed the antipathy between the law of nature and slavery.[70]

Why, then, did the Virginia judges fail to enforce unwritten natural law where it might do the most good? Several scholars have suggested one plausible explanation: that the values of natural law and the values of positive law—or results produced by the application of the latter values—tugged southern judges in opposite directions.[71] This thesis rests on the theory that written enactments were held superior to unwritten fundamental law, a theory that is undermined—at least outside the context of slavery—by many of the cases discussed above.

In fact, many of the slave cases in early Virginia reflect an even deeper conflict than that between natural and positive law: a conflict between two unwritten natural rights—the right to liberty and the right to property. In particular, suits by slaves seeking their freedom often tended to put judges in the untenable position of divesting one party of a supposedly "inalienable" right.

An examination of several dozen cases[72] in which slaves petitioned the courts for freedom confirms that the Virginia courts did view the question more as a conflict between natural rights than as a conflict between natural law and positive law. This conflict is reflected in the cases in two ways. First, the result in many of the cases turns on whether the party opposing freedom had what was recognized as an unforfeited vested property right in the slave. Although each case might superficially depend on a particular and isolated rule of law,[73] or peculiarity of facts, taken together the cases suggest a strong pattern: the courts granted petitions for freedom unless doing so would deprive an innocent property owner of vested rights. Second, the language in many of the cases reflects the judges' dilemma when faced with an inherent conflict between two principles of natural justice. I will deal first with the pattern of decisions and then with the language of individual cases.

One common question involved testamentary manumissions. Despite technical and substantive problems with many of the attempted manumissions (some of which were illegal when the will was written or when the testator died), the courts generally upheld such manumissions when no creditors or third-party purchasers were involved.[74]

Moreover, when creditors were involved, the court tried to avoid a conflict between their rights and the rights of the slaves. In *Patty* v. *Colin*,[75] the manumitting testator died in debt, and his creditors sought to satisfy their claims by taking the slaves. The court directed that the slaves be used to satisfy the claims only as a "*last* resort, and after every possible source of redemption should be found to have failed."[76] The court ordered that the testator's lands be sold and the proceeds applied to the debt; if the debt was satisfied, the slaves were to go free. If the sale yielded an insufficient amount, then the slaves were to be "sold for such a term of years as may be sufficient to raise the adequate fund."[77] Only if that too proved insufficient would the slaves' petition for freedom be denied.[78]

Thus heirs, who had no vested property right in the decedent's estate, were distinguished from creditors or purchasers, who did. When the testamentary manumission was opposed by an heir, no conflict between natural rights arose, and the petition for freedom was granted. When creditors could be satisfied with nonslave property, again a conflict was avoided and the petition was granted. At least one judge even held that creditors who failed to press their rights to slaves immediately had forfeited those rights, and again no conflict existed.[79] In general, at least until the 1830s, only when the conflict between a manumitted slave's right to liberty and an innocent creditor's vested right to property was unavoidable did the courts deny a petition based on testamentary manumission.[80]

An analogous pattern is evidenced when a slave claimed manumission by deed, opposed by one who claimed ownership by deed or sale. In *Ben* v. *Peete*,[81] for example, the defendant claimed ownership by virtue of a bill of sale predating the deed of manumission. Because there was insufficient evidence to support the claim of a prior sale, the court did not need to reach the harder question of conflicting natural rights. Ben gained his freedom because Peete could not produce an authenticated bill of sale to prove prior ownership. In *Kitty* v. *Fitzhugh*,[82] by contrast, there was evidence of an attempt by Kitty's original master to commit fraud upon his divorced wife, through whom the defendant claimed. The court thus held the original master's attempt at emancipation—which occurred some ten years after his exwife should have come into possession of the slave—ineffective, in a suit itself brought ten years after the purported emancipation. Similarly, in *Moses* v. *Denigree*,[83] the deed of emancipation under which the slave claimed freedom specified that the slave would become free only fifteen years later. In the meantime, the manumittor died, and his daughter inherited the slave. Shortly after he should have been freed, he was sold to a stranger. He brought suit some twenty years later, and the court denied his petition for freedom.[84] As in the cases involving testamentary manumissions, these cases suggest that the court tried to avoid a conflict between the slaves' right to liberty and third-party rights of property, ruling in favor of the latter only when a conflict was unavoidable.

One case raised an intriguing variation of this situation. In *Thrift* v. *Hannah*,[85] the party opposing the petition for freedom was the husband of the manumittor. Before she married, Hannah's owner executed an *in futuro* deed of manumission. The deed was not proved or recorded, however, and the husband was not aware of it. Hannah stayed with her mistress past the date she should have been emancipated and sued for freedom only after her mistress' death. If one views the rights acquired by the husband upon his marriage as intermediate between the paramount rights of a creditor and the nonvested rights of an heir, this case raises a difficult question. Indeed, the court split three to two against the petition for freedom.

The various opinions indicate that the judges were aware of the peculiar character of a husband's property rights and that their views on his rights were intertwined with their views on Hannah's petition. Judge Green would have upheld Hannah's claim to freedom, and his opinion provides the strongest evidence of such a linkage: "[Allowing Hannah and others like her to sue for freedom so late] could prejudice no stranger to the transaction, if it was not allowed to extend (as I think it ought not) to affect the creditors of or purchasers from either the wife or the husband. But there is none such in this case. A husband is not a purchaser of his wife's property by the marriage."[86] Judge Francis Brooke, by contrast, held that the husband's claim was good: his "marital rights . . . had attached upon the property in her slaves" and thus "his will and not her's was to be consulted."[87] The results—and the opinions—in *Thrift* v. *Hannah* are exactly what might be expected in a case involving a claimant who was in some sense midway between creditor and heir.

Another common fact pattern allowed judges to conclude in essence that there was no conflict between natural rights because the slaveowner had somehow forfeited his property right. The court held as early as 1811 that though legislatures may not deprive citizens of an "inherent" right, "they may regulate the manner . . . of its exercise."[88] One such regulation was a 1792 law requiring anyone bringing slaves into the state to swear an oath that the slaves were not brought in for the purpose of sale. Moreover, only citizens of other states were permitted even this grace; others were absolutely prohibited from importing slaves. Slaves brought into Virginia in derogation of the 1792 act, and remaining there for a year, were legally entitled to freedom. Between 1805 and 1829, the Virginia court freed slaves in six cases involving transportation into or out of Virginia. In only two cases during this period, both in 1821, did the court deny petitions for freedom in this context.

In several cases, the slaveowner's failure to comply with the law in every technical particular led the court to grant petitions for freedom. In *Murray* v. *M'Carty*[89] a Virginian resettled in Maryland, purchased a slave there, and eventually returned permanently to Virginia (with the slave) and took the prescribed oath. The court nevertheless granted the slave's petition for freedom. The court reasoned that importation was permitted only by citizens of other states and that the defendant had never sufficiently renounced his Virginia citizenship to qualify.[90] In *M'Michen* v. *Amos*[91] a Maryland citizen brought his slaves with him to Virginia. He, however, failed to take the oath: his wife took it instead. The court held that insufficient and granted the slaves' petitions.[92] In *Garnett* v. *Sam*[93] the court freed two slaves because their erstwhile owner could not prove that he had taken the oath when he had brought them into the state almost thirty years earlier. Although in none of these cases did the court frame the issue as a forfeiture of otherwise vested property rights, an argument can be made that that potential characterization colored their views and allowed them to free the slaves without depriving their owners of any vested property rights.

A similar argument can be made about two cases involving slaves purchased in or taken to free states. An owner who attempted to take his property into a state that had put him on notice that if he did so the property would be confiscated can be said to have forfeited any rights in the property. Thus in *Hunter* v. *Fulcher*[94] the Virginia court freed a slave who had been taken by his Virginia master to reside in Maryland for twelve years and then returned with him to Virginia. Maryland law at the time freed all imported slaves. Judge Green noted that the master had "voluntarily becom[e] a permanent member of [the Maryland] community, and submitt[ed] himself and his property to the full force of the laws of Maryland."[95] He thus concluded that freeing the slave would give effect "to those laws, operating on the rights of persons, who were to all intents and purposes justly subjected to them, and touching the rights of no others."[96] The law of Maryland had operated to deprive the defendant of his property rights in the slave, and no conflict of natural rights remained. In *Griffith* v. *Fanny*,[97] the forfeiture of rights was even more apparent: an Ohio citizen had attempted to evade the Ohio prohibition against slavery by having the bill of sale for his purchase of a slave drawn up in Griffith's name, Griffith being a citizen of Virginia. The court affirmed the grant of Fanny's petition for freedom without opinion. Counsel for Fanny, however, had argued that "the residence of Fanny in Ohio, by the consent and connivance of Griffith, dissolved the connection of master and slave, and Fanny is free."[98] Again, the slaveowner had forfeited his rights.

In other cases, the facts did not so conveniently allow the court to evade a conflict of natural rights by implicitly finding a forfeiture. As in the cases involving truly unsatisfied creditors, in these cases the court denied the petitions for freedom. In *Lewis* v. *Fullerton*[99] (later distinguished in *Hunter*), petitioner claimed his freedom partly on the ground that before his birth his mother had become free by spending part of one day in the free state of Ohio. The court rejected this argument on the ground that she had been there "in the absence of her master, and without any evidence that it was with his permission."[100] Thus the court implicitly held that the owner had not forfeited his rights. *Barnett* v. *Sam*[101] entailed a double problem of innocent property rights. Sam's original owner took him from Virginia to North Carolina and brought him back after 1792 without complying with the statute. The statute, however, specifically exempted slaves owned by Virginians at the time of enactment, and thus the original owner had not violated any provision of the statute. Moreover, Sam remained her slave in Virginia for another eighteen years and was then sold to Barnett. Several years later, Sam brought suit. Thus the original owner had not forfeited her rights, and even if she had, Barnett was an innocent third party. The court denied Sam's petition on the ground that the 1792 statute did not apply to his original owner.

Thus a careful examination of the cases involving petitions for freedom suggests that a solicitude for property rights had a significant influence on the court, counteracting the tendency to favor liberty. Moreover, as is common when two fundamental principles collide, the court tried whenever possible to avoid a direct conflict.[102]

Many of the cases also contain language directly reflecting a judicial awareness that petitions for freedom raised a conflict between two natural rights. That liberty was itself a natural right of persons had long been recognized and was reflected in the much repeated phrase that "liberty is to be favored."[103] As counsel for defendants frequently reminded the court, however, "although it may be true that liberty is to be favored, the rights of property are as sacred as those of liberty."[104] In one case, counsel for the petitioning slave noted that "we all agree" that a claim for freedom "must stand on precisely the same ground with any question of property."[105] Judge Roane, despite his discomfort with slavery, was careful to note the validity of the opposing right: "The spirit of the decisions of the Court in relation to suits for freedom, while it neither abandons the rules of evidence, nor the rules of law as applying to *property*, with a becoming liberality respects the *merit* of the claim, and the general imbecility of the claimants."[106] Judge Cabell wrote in 1829 that "the right to emancipate slaves is subordinate to the obligation to pay debts previously contracted."[107] Perhaps the most succinct articulation of the conflict came in an 1824 case denying a petition for freedom: "Emancipation is an utter destruction of the right of property."[108]

The judges also frequently reminded the public that a decision to free a particular slave did not trample on property rights. Sometimes they noted explicitly that no individual's vested rights were at stake: "The question has nothing to do with the rights of Mr. *Whiting,* her former master,"[109] or "the . . . question . . . as to the power of the State of Pennsylvania to confiscate the property of a citizen of Virginia, does not directly occur."[110] In *Pleasants* v. *Pleasants*[111] the court upheld a testamentary manumission despite the fact that manumission became legal only after the death of the testator. Judge Roane deliberately began his analysis in *Pleasants* by considering the claim to freedom "only, as that of ordinary remaindermen, claiming property in them[selves], and endeavor[ed] to test it by the rules of the common law, relative to ordinary cases of limitation of personal chattels."[112] In one case not involving freedom, the court emphasized that the rights of slave and master were in fact congruent: "It is as important for the interest of the [master] as for the safety of the [slave], that a *stranger* should not be permitted to exercise an unrestrained and lawless authority over him."[113]

Nor did the court neglect to assuage the fears of those who foresaw the end of slavery as an institution—and thus of judicial protection for property—with each decision to grant a petition for freedom. Judge Tucker noted in *Hudgins* that his decision to free the petitioners did "not by a side wind . . . overturn the rights of property."[114] Judge Roane explained that he had freed petitioners in *Pleasants* "upon such grounds . . . of strict legal right, and not upon such grounds, as, if sanctioned by the decision of this Court, might agitate and convulse the Commonwealth to its centre."[115] The Virginia judges were not only aware that petitions for freedom potentially raised a conflict between inherent unwritten rights, they knew the political consequences of leaning too much in favor of the right to liberty.

Thus both the decisions and the judges' opinions reflect a tension between two of the most venerable rights in the natural law pantheon. It is no wonder that the judiciary could not resolve the issue of slavery, nor that in the decades just preceding the Civil War southern judges ultimately took refuge in a narrow formalism that eliminated questions of unwritten law or stressed the property aspects of fundamental rights.[116]

Conclusion

Like their state predecessors and their federal counterparts, Virginia judges between 1790 and 1830 looked to unwritten, as well as written, sources of law. Drawing on a rich tradition of natural rights, they combined reason, history, and judgment to grapple with the issues that came before them. Though their resolution of those issues would not be ours, their commitment to doing justice might be worth emulating.

Recourse to unwritten fundamental law is not a panacea for social injustice. Extratextual interpretation, like textual interpretation, depends on the judges who engage in it. It yields more or less just results depending on the commitments and the consciences of judges and lawyers, the receptivity of the citizenry, and the bounds of the legal imagination.

Notes

I would like to thank Daniel A. Farber, Paul Finkelman, and Leslie F. Goldstein for their helpful suggestions on earlier drafts of this essay.

1. The categories include the laws of God, the common law (largely derived incrementally from custom and tradition), the law of nature, and natural law. The latter two were distinct, at least during the period of the early republic: the law of nature was grounded in observation and human sentiment, while natural law was founded on abstract reason. I am grateful to Donald Lutz for suggesting to me the niceties of these distinctions. For the purposes of this essay, however, I need not distinguish between these categories because my aim is to contrast written with unwritten sources of law. Thus I will use *unwritten law, natural law,* and *law of nature* interchangeably and will group together cases and judges who may have been referring to different unwritten sources of law. I will also use *natural rights* to refer to unwritten individual rights, although there was also subtle distinction between natural rights and natural law. See G. Edward White, *Oliver Wendell Holmes Devise: History of the Supreme Court of the United States: The Marshall Court and Cultural Change, 1815–35* (New York: Macmillan, 1988), 676–77.

2. It should be obvious from this discussion that by *textualist* I mean something far broader than the most common jurisprudential meaning of one who focuses on the constitutional text to the exclusion of such things as history or intention. See Lawrence C. Marshall, "Fighting the Words of the Eleventh Amendment," *Harvard Law Review* 102 (1989):

1342–45, n. 9. I use the term simply to indicate the tradition that judicial decisions must be anchored by the text, in contrast to the extratextualist tradition of ignoring the text.

3. This section is a brief summary of my earlier work on state uses of natural law up to 1787 and federal uses of natural law up to 1820. Suzanna Sherry, "The Founders' Unwritten Constitution," *University of Chicago Law Review* 54 (1987): 1127. For a similar and more detailed description of the multifarious sources of law used by the Supreme Court between 1815 and 1835, but reaching a somewhat different conclusion about the relative importance of textualism, see White, *History of the Supreme Court*, 76–156, 595–740.

4. Seven of the original thirteen states enacted separate bills or declarations of rights. By 1800, only eight of sixteen states had them.

5. See *Rutgers* v. *Waddington* (N.Y. City Mayor's Ct. 1784), in Julius Goebel, Jr., ed., *The Law Practice of Alexander Hamilton: Documents and Commentary* (New York: Columbia University Press, 1964), 1:393–419; *Trevett* v. *Weeden*, described in James Mitchell Varnum, *The Case, Trevett Against Weeden: On Information and Complaint, for Refusing Paper Bills in Payment for Butcher's Meat, in Market, at Par with Specie* (Providence: Printed by John Carter, 1787); *Holmes* v. *Walton*, described in Austin Scott, "Holmes v. Walton: The New Jersey Precedent," *American History Review* 4 (1899): 456–60; *Symsbury Case*, 1 Kirby 444 (Conn. Super. Ct. 1785); and the "Ten-Pound Act" cases in New Hampshire, described in William Winslow Crosskey, *Politics and the Constitution in the History of the United States* (Chicago: University of Chicago Press, 1953), 2:969–71.

6. These included George Wythe, Spencer Roane, Edmund Pendleton, and St. George Tucker on the bench, as well as Edmund Randolph and John Marshall at the bar.

7. Probably the only case that did so was Chancellor Wythe's opinion in *Hudgins* v. *Wrights*, 11 Va. (1 Hen. & M.) 133 (1806), which was disapproved by the Virginia Supreme Court of Appeals. Wythe's opinion, which has not been preserved, apparently freed the petitioning slaves on two alternative grounds: that they were not Negroes but Indians and thus were illegally enslaved, and that "freedom is the birthright of every human being." Id. at 134. Although the Supreme Court of Appeals upheld Wythe's decree on the first ground, both appellate opinions (by Judge Tucker and President Lyons) explicitly disapproved of the second ground. Id. at 144.

8. Robert Palmer has made a similar observation about the 1776 Pennsylvania Declaration of Rights in "Liberties as Constitutional Provisions, 1776–1791," in *Constitution and Rights in the Early American Republic* (Williamsburg: Institution of Bill of Rights Law, 1987), 55, 65–66.

9. See, e.g., *The Case of the Judges*, 8 Va. (4 Call) 135, 143 (1788). All cases

cited in this essay are from the Virginia Supreme Court of Appeals (sometimes called simply the Court of Appeals) unless otherwise noted.

10. See *Commonwealth* v. *Caton*, 8 Va. (4 Call) 5 (1782). There have been persistent rumors of an earlier case, purportedly described by Thomas Jefferson in his reports of general court decisions prior to independence. *Robin* v. *Hardaway* (1772), in Thomas Jefferson, *Reports of Cases Determined in the General Court of Virginia* (Charlottesville: F. Carr, 1829), 109; see also Helen T. Catterall, *Judicial Cases Concerning American Slavery and the Negro* (1926; rpt. New York: Octagon Books, 1968), 1:91–92; Robert M. Cover, *Justice Accused: Antislavery and the Judicial Process* (New Haven: Yale University Press, 1975), 19. No other record of this case exists, and Jefferson's report may be inaccurate. Moreover, although the plaintiffs, according to Jefferson, did contend that the statute at issue was void (as "contrary to natural right"), Jefferson's description suggests that the primary argument was that the statute had been repealed. *Robin* v. *Hardaway*, in Jefferson, *General Court of Virginia*, 109, 113–18. Later Virginia cases dealing with the same pair of statutes generally failed to cite *Robin*, suggesting that Jefferson's report may have been inaccurate. See, e.g., *Butt* v. *Rachel*, 18 Va. (4 Munf.) 209 (1813); *Pallas* v. *Hill*, 12 Va. (2 Hen. & M.) 149 (1807); *Hudgins* v. *Wrights*, 11 Va. (1 Hen. & M.) 133 (1806). The one case I am aware of that did cite *Robin* used it only to support the proposition that the earlier statute had been repealed. *Gregory* v. *Baugh*, 29 Va. (2 Leigh) 665, 681 (1831).

11. *The Case of the Judges*, 8 Va. (4 Call) 135, 141 (1788).

12. Id. at 142.

13. Id. at 142–43.

14. Id. at 143.

15. Id.

16. 8 Va. (4 Call) 234 (1792).

17. In Virginia, president was the equivalent of chief justice.

18. There was some debate during that time about the meaning of the term *ex post facto*. Some thought it referred only to retrospective criminal laws, and some believed that it encompassed retrospective civil laws as well. Compare James Madison, *Notes of Debates in the Federal Convention of 1787*, ed. Adrienne Koch (Athens: Ohio University Press, 1966) (Dickinson, August 29) 547, with id. (Mason, September 14), 640; see also *Calder* v. *Bull*, 3 U.S. (3 Dall.) 386 (1798). That dispute, however, is irrelevant to the discussion in the text; Virginia's written constitution contained no bar to any type of retrospective law.

19. 8 Va. at 237.

20. Id.

21. *Elliott's Executor* v. *Lyell,* 7 Va. (3 Call) 268 (1802), discussed below, text at notes 34–44.
22. Chancery 1793, reported in George Wythe, *Decisions of Cases in Virginia by the High Court of Chancery,* ed. B. B. Minor (Richmond: J. W. Randolph, 1852), 211.
23. Id. at 212 n.(b).
24. Id. at 214 n.(e).
25. 5 Va. (1 Call) 165 (1797).
26. Id. at 171.
27. Id. at 174.
28. White, *History of the Supreme Court,* 291.
29. 5 Va. (1 Call) 554 (1799).
30. Id. at 556.
31. Id. at 558.
32. 7 Va. (3 Call) 44 (1801).
33. Id. at 49.
34. 7 Va. (3 Call) 268 (1802).
35. Chancellor Kent of New York relied on the same argument a few years later to deny the validity of a retrospective law in *Dash* v. *Van Kleeck,* 7 Johns. 477 (N.Y. Sup. Ct. 1811).
36. 7 Va. at 277.
37. Id. at 281.
38. Id.
39. Id. at 284.
40. Id. at 283.
41. See *Commonwealth* v. *Caton,* 8 Va. (4 Call) 5, 17–18 (1782).
42. Pendleton wrote an opinion in *Turpin* v. *Locket,* 10 Va. (6 Call) 113 (1804), invalidating a Virginia statute requiring the sale of church lands, but he died the day before it was to be delivered. See 10 Va. at 187; David J. Mays, *Edmund Pendleton, 1721–1803: A Biography* (Cambridge, Mass.: Harvard University Press, 1952), 2:345.
43. 7 Va. at 285.
44. Id.
45. 10 Va. (6 Call) 113 (1804).
46. See above, note 42.
47. Tucker held that a grant of state monies to a specific denomination violated Article 4 of the Virginia Bill of Rights, which provided "that no man, or set of men, are entitled to exclusive or separate emoluments or privileges from the community, but in consideration of public service." According to Tucker, after the Revolution "the promulgation of doctrines of any religious sect ceased to be a common benefit to the community" and thus ministers were not entitled to community

payment. *Turpin* v. *Locket,* 10 Va. (6 Call) at 152.

48. Id. at 152.

49. Id. at 150.

50. 14 Va. (4 Hen. & M.) 315 (1809).

51. John Wickham was a prominent Virginia lawyer who often collaborated with Edmund Randolph. In addition to the case in the text, Wickham and Randolph were co-counsel for the church parties in *Turpin* v. *Locket,* 10 Va. (6 Call) 113 (1804), discussed above at note 47, and represented the slaveowners in *Pleasants* v. *Pleasants,* 6 Va. (2 Call) 319 (1799), discussed below at note 73. Their most famous collaborative effort was defending Aaron Burr. See John J. Reardon, *Edmund Randolph: A Biography* (New York: Macmillan, 1974), 350–52, 357–58; Dumas Malone, *Jefferson the President: Second Term, 1805–1809* (Boston: Little, Brown, 1974), 296, 310–11; Charles Warren, *A History of the American Bar* (1911; rpt. New York: Howard Fertig, 1966), 267–68.

52. *Currie's Administrator,* 14 Va. at 341.

53. Id. at 346.

54. Id. at 346–47.

55. 27 Va. (6 Rand.) 245 (1828).

56. Id. at 265.

57. Id.

58. 16 Va. (2 Munf.) 394 (1811).

59. Id. at 397. See also id. at 405 (right of emigration is "of *paramount* authority, bestowed on us by the God of Nature").

60. *Hunter* v. *Fulcher,* 28 Va. (1 Leigh) 172, 181 (1829).

61. 3 Va. (1 Va. Cas.) 20 (Va. Gen. Ct. 1793).

62. Id. at 40.

63. Id. at 78.

64. Id.

65. 8 Va. (4 Call) 5 (1782). For a discussion of the use of the written constitution primarily to resolve structure of government questions, see Sherry, "The Founders' Unwritten Constitution," 1143–45, 1169, 1173–74.

66. See also *Case of the County Levy,* 9 Va. (5 Call) 139 (date unknown) (Judge Pendleton interpreted the written text to allow courts as well as legislatures to assess levies to support courthouses, prisons, and the like).

67. It is also similar to the pattern between 1789 and 1830 in several other states, including New York, Massachusetts, and South Carolina. See Suzanna Sherry, "Courts of Justice and Courts of Law" (forthcoming).

68. See, e.g., Imogene E. Brown, *American Aristedes: A Biography of George Wythe* (Rutherford, N.J.: Fairleigh Dickinson University Press, 1981),

266–67; Cover, *Justice Accused*, 205–6; A. E. Keir Nash, "Reason of Slavery: Understanding the Judicial Role in the Peculiar Institution," *Vanderbilt Law Review* 32 (1979): 127–28; White, *History of the Supreme Court*, 683.

69. Vermont did so explicitly in its 1777 Constitution, immediately following the general language of natural equality. 1777 Vt. Const. ch. 1, § 1, in *The Federal and State Constitutions, Colonial Charters, and other Organic Laws of the States, Territories, and Colonies Now or Heretofore Forming the United States of America*, ed. Francis N. Thorpe (Washington, D.C.: U.S. Government Printing Office, 1909), 6:3739–40. Massachusetts did so through judicial construction of the general language. See Paul Finkelman, *An Imperfect Union: Slavery, Federalism, and Comity* (Chapel Hill: University of North Carolina Press, 1981), 41; William M. Wiecek, *The Sources of Antislavery Constitutionalism in America, 1760–1848* (Ithaca: Cornell University Press, 1977), 45–48. With the Massachusetts example, contrast *Aldridge* v. *Commonwealth*, 4 Va. (2 Va. Cas.) 447, 449 (1824).

70. See, e.g., Daniel A. Farber and Suzanna Sherry, *A History of the American Constitution* (St. Paul: West, 1989), chap. 9; Wiecek, *Antislavery Constitutionalism*, 249–60; Cover, *Justice Accused*, 154–58; William E. Nelson, "The Impact of the Antislavery Movement upon Styles of Judicial Reasoning in Nineteenth Century America," *Harvard Law Review* 87 (1974): 528–38.

71. Different scholars describe the attraction of the positive law in different ways, but all share the idea that natural rights could be "trumped" by some other value. Cover describes judges as torn between the substantive antislavery value and "fidelity to the formal system." *Justice Accused*, 197. Finkelman concludes that judges were committed to "preserving the integrity of the law." *An Imperfect Union*, 182. A. E. Keir Nash explains that the Virginia court in particular was caught between "procedural self-restraint and pro-freedom results." "Reasons of Slavery: Understanding the Judicial Role in the Peculiar Institution," *Vanderbilt Law Review* 32 (1979): 158. See also White, *History of the Supreme Court*, 674–703 (making similar argument about Supreme Court treatment of natural law, positive law, and slavery). For Virginia cases making explicit the conflict between natural rights and proslavery positive law, see *Commonwealth* v. *Turner*, 26 Va. (5 Rand.) 678 (Va. Gen. Ct. 1827); *Butt* v. *Rachel*, 18 Va. (4 Munf.) 209, 212–13 (1813) (argument of counsel).

These theories illustrate the modern tendency to draw what Morton Horwitz has identified as a "stark jurisprudential dichotomy between natural law and positive law." "History and Theory," *Yale Law Journal* 96 (1987): 1834. Indeed, Cover has gone even further and suggested that at least where positive law governing procedure is at issue, it *ought* to triumph over remedying even the most blatant violations of natural rights. See Robert M. Cover, "For James Wm. Moore: Some Reflections on a Reading of the Rules," *Yale Law Journal* 84 (1975): 722–23.

72. I have tried to locate and examine every published case between 1787 and 1831 in which the Virginia Court of Appeals ruled on a slave's petition for freedom. I am sure I have missed a few, but I believe the cases discussed in the text are a representative sample, if not the bulk, of the cases actually decided.

73. Some of the rules involved were statutory, and some were common law. In all the cases, however, the rule was either ambiguous or commonly interpreted in a way that would have defeated the slave's claim. Occasionally, judges explicitly refused to apply a general rule of law in slave cases if it would defeat the slave's claim to freedom. For example, Judge Carrington held that the rule against perpetuities was specifically inapplicable to testamentary provisions conferring freedom on slaves. *Pleasants* v. *Pleasants*, 6 Va. (2 Call) 319, 347 (1799). More often, however, the court simply interpreted an ambiguous rule; my contention is that in doing so, the judges were influenced by the conflict between two natural rights.

74. See, e.g., *Isaac* v. *West's Executor*, 27 Va. (6 Rand.) 652 (1828); *Spotts* v. *Gillaspie*, 27 Va. (6 Rand.) 566 (1828); *President and Professors of William and Mary College* v. *Hodgson*, 20 Va. (6 Munf.) 163 (1818); *Charles* v. *Hunnicutt*, 9 Va. (5 Call) 311 (1804); *Pleasants* v. *Pleasants*, 6 Va. (2 Call) 319 (1799); cf. *Talbert* v. *Jenny*, 27 Va. (6 Rand.) 159 (1828) (manumission by deed upheld against manumittor's son, who claimed under earlier deed).

75. 11 Va. (1 Hen. & M.) 519 (1807).

76. Id. at 529 (Judge Roane, concurring).

77. Id. at 528 (Judge Tucker, writing for a unanimous court).

78. *Accord, Dunn* v. *Amey*, 28 Va. (1 Leigh) 465 (1829); *Woodley* v. *Abby*, 9 Va. (5 Call) 336 (1805).

79. See *Woodley* v. *Abby*, 9 Va. (5 Call) 336, 349 (1805) (Carrington, dissenting).

80. In several fairly late cases, the court refused to implement a testamentary manumission even in the absence of creditors. *Winn* v. *Bob*, 30 Va. (3 Leigh) 140 (1831); *Rucker's Administrator* v. *Gilbert*, 30 Va. (3 Leigh) 8 (1831); *Walthall's Executor* v. *Robertson*, 29 Va. (2 Leigh) 189 (1830); *Maria* v. *Surbaugh*, 23 Va. (2 Rand.) 229 (1824). Several scholars have noted that by the early 1830s the courts were becoming less willing to uphold slaves' right to freedom, and these cases may exemplify that trend. See Cover, *Justice Accused*, 74–75; Finkelman, *An Imperfect Union*,

181–82; see also *Gregory* v. *Baugh*, 29 Va. (2 Leigh) 665, 680 (1831) (ruling against slave, with the following comment: "But all who have examined the earlier cases in our books, must admit, that our judges (from the purest motives, I am sure) did, *in favorem libertatis*, sometimes relax, rather too much, the rules of law").

Moreover, in both *Maria* v. *Surbaugh* and *Rucker's Administrator* v. *Gilbert*, the testator's intentions were unclear; it is possible to read both wills as not intended to free the petitioning slaves. In *Walthall's Executor* v. *Robertson*, Judge Carr dissented, and Judge Cabell—who had often voted in favor of freedom—was absent. Thus these few cases do not significantly undermine the thesis in the text.

81. 23 Va. (2 Rand.) 539 (1824).
82. 25 Va. (6 Rand.) 600 (1827).
83. 27 Va. (6 Rand.) 561 (1828).
84. The court relied on the invalidity of the emancipation deed under positive law. The overall pattern of the cases, however, suggests that the court was influenced by the presence of an innocent third party. See above, note 73. See also *Peggy* v. *Legg*, 20 Va. (6 Munf.) 229 (1818) (petition denied when slave conditionally manumitted by will had already been sold by heir to third party); *Givens* v. *Manns*, 20 Va. (6 Munf.) 191 (1818) (facts not clear, but slaves claiming manumission by former master subsequent to purchase by another not freed when by the time of suit they were held by an apparently uninvolved third master). One case appears to break this pattern. In *Whiting* v. *Daniel*, 11 Va. (1 Hen. & M.) 390 (1807), the testator's nephew (Whiting) claimed that his aunt had deeded him the slaves several years before she wrote a will emancipating them. No other parties were involved. The court, in a brief and uninformative opinion, nevertheless upheld Whiting's claim to the slaves. Whiting's counsel, however, suggested that Whiting had sustained considerable hardship in acquiring the slaves, perhaps to make him look more like an innocent creditor. Whiting had agreed to support and take care of his aunt in her waning years. Counsel stressed both that the aunt had given him the slaves for this valuable consideration and that she was an exceptionally difficult woman to live with (one relative had turned her out, and no others would take her in).
85. 29 Va. (2 Leigh) 326 (1830).
86. Id. at 316.
87. Id. at 320. See also id. at 318 (Judge Cabell): "By the marriage of Rachel Magruder, in this case, she ceased to be the owner of the slaves, which thereby became the property of her husband."
88. *Murray* v. *M'Carty*, 16 Va. (2 Munf.) 394 (1811).
89. 16 Va. (2 Munf.) 394 (1811).

90. Similarly, in *Wilson* v. *Isbell,* 9 Va. (5 Call) 425 (1805), a Virginian who moved to Maryland there sold a slave (who had come with him from Virginia) to another Virginian; the latter took her back to his home in Virginia. The court granted the slave's petition for freedom because the new owner was not a citizen of another state. Ironically, the original owner also returned to Virginia. As the court noted, had he not sold Isbell to Wilson, he would have been entitled to bring her back with him. The statute explicitly exempted slaves who were owned by Virginians at the time of enactment, allowing those owners to remove them from the state and then bring them back.

91. 25 Va. (4 Rand.) 134 (1826).

92. The court considered this a very easy question. The jury had found the facts as described in the text but had left to the judge to determine whether "the law be for the defendant," and if so "then they find for the defendant." *M'Michen* v. *Amos,* 25 Va. (4 Rand.) at 135. Counsel for the defendant on appeal had suggested that the jury could not possibly be suggesting that the wife's taking the oath might be legally sufficient: "This question is so plain that [the court] cannot presume the parties intended to submit it: that no lawyer would have made it, nor would the Judge have suffered it to be put on the record." Id. at 138–39. The court responded that "if the records of this Court be searched, it would be found that questions as plain (plainer there could not be) have been often made, and in some instances, incorrectly decided, in the Inferior Courts." Id. at 139.

93. 19 Va. (5 Munf.) 542 (1817).

94. 28 Va. (1 Leigh) 172 (1829).

95. Id. at 198–99. Judge Carr similarly noted that the defendant had "voluntarily submitt[ed] himself and the slave to the operation of [Maryland's] laws." Id. at 200. The last judge, Judge Cabell, concurred in the judgment without opinion.

96. Id. at 199.

97. 21 Va. (Gilmer) 143 (1820).

98. Id. at 144–45.

99. 22 Va. (1 Rand.) 15 (1821).

100. Id. at 22. The *Lewis* case is something of an anomaly. The plaintiff also claimed that his mother had been freed by court order in Ohio and by a deed of manumission executed in Ohio by her Virginia owner. Neither ground was sufficient, according to the court. The court's rejection of the Ohio court's power to free a Virginia slave rested on a fear of the consequences of any other ruling: "The right of our citizens under the constitution to reclaim their fugitive slaves from other states, would be nearly a nullity, if that claim was permitted to be intercepted by a pro-

ceeding like the one in question; a proceeding of so extremely summary a character, that it affords no fair opportunity to a master deliberately to support his right of property in his slave." Id. at 23. The deed was apparently executed as the only way of persuading the slave—newly freed by the Ohio court—to return voluntarily to Virginia. I suspect that *Lewis* may have involved either a fugitive slave or an Ohio court that did not respect the generally accepted doctrine that mere transit through a free state, with no intent to become a resident, did not deprive an owner of his slaves. For the northern acceptance of that doctrine in this period, see Finkelman, *An Imperfect Union*, 46–70.

101. 21 Va. (Gilmer) 232 (1821).

102. For an example of this in the context of the conflict between two sorts of property rights, see White, *History of the Supreme Court*, 628–48.

103. *Pleasants v. Pleasants*, 6 Va. (2 Call) 319, 324 (1799) (argument of counsel); see also id. at 335–36 (Judge Roane: ordinary legal arguments in favor of petitioners "hold, with increased force, when the case is considered in its true point of view, as one which involves human liberty"); *Isaac v. West's Executor*, 27 Va. (6 Rand.) 652, 657 (1828); *President and Professors of William and Mary College v. Hodgson*, 20 Va. (6 Munf.) 163, 165 (1818); *Charles v. Hunnicutt*, 9 Va. (5 Call) 311, 322–23, 330 (1804). See generally Finkelman, *An Imperfect Union*, 187–234.

104. *Pleasants v. Pleasants*, 6 Va. (2 Call) 319, 324 (1799) (argument of counsel); see also *Whiting v. Daniel*, 11 Va. (1 Hen. & M.) 390, 400 (1806) (argument of counsel) ("In this Court, the case now under consideration, will be decided not as a case of freedom, but in the same manner as if [the manumittor] had given her property to others, or had died intestate"); *Hudgins v. Wrights*, 11 Va. (1 Hen. & M.) 133, 136 (1806) (argument of counsel) ("In deciding upon the rights of *property*, those rules which have been established are not to be departed from, because *freedom* is in question").

105. *Talbert v. Jenny*, 27 Va. (6 Rand.) 159, 161 (1828) (argument of counsel). The court affirmed the chancellor's granting of Jenny's petition for freedom.

106. *Patty v. Colin*, 11 Va. (1 Hen. & M.) 519, 529 (1807).

107. *Dunn v. Amey*, 28 Va. (1 Leigh) 465, 472 (1829).

108. *Maria v. Surbaugh*, 23 Va. (2 Rand.) 228, 231 (1824).

109. *Wilson v. Isbell*, 9 Va. (5 Call) 425, 429 (1805).

110. *Spotts v. Gillaspie*, 27 Va. (6 Rand.) 566, 572 (1828).

111. 6 Va. (2 Call) 319 (1799).

112. Id., 335–36.

113. *Commonwealth v. Carver*, 5 Rand. 660, 665 (Va. Gen. Ct. 1827).

114. *Hudgins v. Wrights*, 11 Va. (1 Hen. & M.) 133, 141 (1806).

115. *Pleasants* v. *Pleasants*, 6 Va. (2 Call) 319, 344 (1799).
116. See Cover, *Justice Accused*, 232–36. But see Nelson, "The Impact of the Antislavery Movement upon Styles of Judicial Reasoning," 528–38 (formalism was an antislavery response to the perceived relationship between instrumentalism and proslavery jurisprudence).

Common Law Antecedents of Constitutional Law in Connecticut

Ellen A. Peters

There has been renewed interest in the last decade in the role properly to be assigned to the intent of the framers of the Constitution when courts are confronted with new constitutional issues or with old issues arising in new circumstances. This debate has focused on contemporaneous secondary materials, principally the *Federalist Papers*, that illuminate the jurisprudential scene at the time of the enactment of the Constitution of the United States. When we turn our attention to state constitutions, such detailed jurisprudential exegeses are virtually nonexistent. If we were to hypothesize that the intent of the framers, though not dispositive, is at least worthy of examination in conjunction with textual analysis of constitutional provisions, where does that leave us with regard to the interpretation of state constitutions?

Those of us on state courts who have become committed to assigning independent constitutional weight to our state constitutions, particularly with regard to the protection of civil rights and liberties, have urged counsel and the academy to search for historical data to illuminate state constitutional texts.[1] In the absence of local equivalents to the *Federalist Papers*, what kind of search is it appropriate to undertake?

Two fruitful avenues of exploration are an inquiry into comparative analytic techniques in the nineteenth and twentieth centuries by such outstanding jurists as Chancellor James Kent and Judge

Benjamin Cardozo and an inquiry into the early nineteenth-century persistence of natural law despite the emergence of written constitutions. I would suggest a third approach as well.

Let me briefly set the stage for Connecticut constitutional history in the eighteenth and nineteenth centuries. We call our state the Constitution State, not because of our contribution to the crafting of the federal Constitution, but because, as early as 1638, we had promulgated an organic document of constitutional principles called the Fundamental Orders. Our first functionally operative constitution was, however, the Constitution of 1818, which has continued to furnish the framework for our subsequent state constitutions. The principal purpose and achievement of the Constitution of 1818 was to establish the division of the powers of government into three distinct departments: legislative, executive, and judicial. Until that time, Connecticut had operated on what we would now call a parliamentary model. Undoubtedly, the 1818 constitutional adoption of a system of government incorporating the doctrine of separation of powers had implications for the protection of individual constitutional rights. Furthermore, the Constitution of 1818 contained a bill of rights that has survived until the present time. It is my impression, however, that safeguarding individual rights was not a central part of the constitutional agenda in 1818.[2]

The question posed by this Connecticut history is what to conclude from the absence of any authoritative exegesis of early constitutional principles relating to human rights. On the one hand, it may be that constitutional issues did not engage sustained judicial interest during a period of economic growth and consolidation in a community that was relatively homogeneous in its composition and outlook. As Professor Donald Lutz reminds us, "Bills of rights [in eighteenth-century America] were viewed as providing the statement of broad principles rather than a set of legally enforceable rights."[3] On the other hand, it may be that issues that we now label constitutional were formerly subsumed under different, common law rubrics. Lutz reports, in accordance with what I take to be the generally accepted wisdom, that, as a corollary to a less rights-oriented view of constitutional provisions, eighteenth-century state courts "did not worry . . . much about protecting [constitutional] rights in any substantive sense." Professor Suzanna Sherry suggests, however, that constitutional principles were indeed being protected by invocation of natural law principles.[4]

In Connecticut, at least, the latter view seems closer to the mark, particularly if one includes common law developments as an aspect of the eighteenth century's reliance on natural law. If the Connecticut experience is any guide, we should cast a wider net to discover the variety of ways in which substantive rights were protected in state courts in our early years.

In Connecticut constitutional law, it is well established that several rights now denominated as constitutional had well-recognized common law antecedents. For example, Connecticut has had a common law right to protection against double jeopardy since at least 1807. In the case of *State* v. *Woodruff*,[5] the court assumed that no criminal defendant could be twice put into jeopardy but held that the right to be tried by a single jury did not, despite the defendant's objection, preclude a retrial after a hung jury. It is only in the latter half of this century that we have come to call this a right of due process.[6] Similarly, Connecticut in the late eighteenth century, a century and a half before *Gideon* v. *Wainwright*,[7] had established by custom a criminal defendant's right to assigned legal counsel.[8]

This multifaceted constitutional heritage led me to wonder about other areas in which common law cases might presage the protection of individual rights that we now associate with constitutional law. The opinions of the Connecticut Supreme Court have been reported since 1785. What would an examination of these reports for the years 1785 to 1818 reveal about substantive protection of other "constitutional" rights in the period before the adoption of our state bill of rights? Even a cursory examination of these state reports lends considerable support to the proposition that constitutional principles were indeed being vindicated regularly, in a substantive sense, in our early years.

What issues came to the court? On free speech, in *Beers* v. *Strong*,[9] the court held, in an action on the case for libel, that a verdict for the plaintiff should be sustained, the accusation of having suborned perjury being actionable because the verdict had ascertained that the words "were spoken maliciously, and with intent to defame."[10] To avoid censorship, the court, in *Knowles* v. *The State*,[11] construed a sign statute narrowly so as to avoid criminal sanctions for "the mere exhibition of a work of art." On freedom of religion, in *The Ecclesiastical Society of South-Farms* v. *Beckwith*,[12] the court declared insufficient an action on covenant seeking to resolve a dispute between a church and its duly designated minister. Counsel for the defendant minister premised a demurrer in part on the proposition that "the whole matter is merely spiritual. It is only whether the defendant has taught the best scripture doctrine; which is a matter the court can never take cognizance of." [13] The court agreed, construing the defendant's undertaking as overall performance of his pastoral obligations, whose particular content the court declared to be "too general" to be "traversable." Perhaps because of the dominance of the common law forms of pleading, these cases reached "constitutional" results by reference to ordinary common law explication.

Another "constitutional" issue with which the common law courts dealt repeatedly was the legality of searches and seizures. In *Frisbie* v. *Butler*,[14] a justice of the peace had issued a warrant "to search all suspected places and persons that the complainant thinks proper, to find his lost port, and to cause the same, and the person with whom it shall be found, or suspected to have taken the same, and have him to appear before some proper authority, to be examined according to law." [15] By virtue of this warrant, the defendant Frisbie was arrested and eventually ordered to pay "eighteen shillings as treble damages, to the complainant, and a fine of six shillings to the town treasurer." [16] The court overturned this judgment, both because of defective averments in the complaint and because of the terms of the warrant. "The warrant in the present case, being general, to search all places, and arrest all persons, the complainant should suspect, is clearly illegal." [17] Because of the defects in the complaint, the court found error in the judgment, while reserving for another day the question of how far the illegality of the warrant "vitiates the proceedings upon the arraignment." [18] A few years later, in *Grumon* v. *Raymond and Betts*,[19] a similarly overly broad warrant was held to sustain a damages action in trespass, for unlawful arrest and imprisonment, both against the issuing magistrate and the officer who had executed the illegal warrant.

Many cases explored aspects of what we now encompass within due process: the limits of personal jurisdiction;[20] the division of responsibility between judge and jury;[21] and the right to unprejudiced jurors.[22] The court limited the classes of those who could legally make arrests without written warrants[23] and defined the process required for criminal arraignments.[24] In *Palmer* v. *Allen*,[25] the court held that even body attachment in an action of debt did not allow a defendant to be arrested and committed without a mittimus: "In Connecticut, such is her Constitution, and such her laws, and system of jurisprudence, from her infancy, that no man's person shall be imprisoned, unless by judgment of court, or the direction and order of a magistrate."[26] *Mumford* v. *Wright*[27] expressed doubt about "how far an *ex post facto* law can operate, to impair contracts."

The court's concern with protection from self-incrimination led it repeatedly to enforce the right of a criminal prisoner to exclude from evidence a confidential statement given to the state's attorney.[28] In the case of witnesses, though the court recognized a similar right against self-incrimination, it left room for judicial authority to define the scope of this right.[29]

My examination of this thirty-year record of judicial protection of individual rights does not purport to be exhaustive. I suspect that a closer look at all the cases would unearth further support for common law enforcement of "constitutional" rights. Notably, few of the relevant holdings occur in appeals from judgments in criminal cases, even though such appeals were undoubtedly available. The typical context is a tort action for misuse of process, or false imprisonment, or even trespass. The common law trappings of the cases undoubtedly explain why the court's opinions resonate in common law terms. Nonetheless, the case law demonstrates a striking resemblance between some of the "constitutional" issues with which we struggle now and some of the "common law" issues with which the court struggled two hundred years ago.

On reflection, it is not surprising that constitutional principles and common law rules should share a common history. In defining and enacting constitutional bills of rights, state and national constituencies would naturally have drawn upon the experience of the common law—where else could they have turned? The natural law aspects of the common law may have come under siege in the early part of the nineteenth century, but we know that the common law retained its capacity for flexibility and adaptation to changing societal needs.

In modern terms, appellate courts develop bright lines to distinguish between rights that are constitutional and those that are "merely" statutory, evidentiary, or otherwise rooted in the common law. We do this principally to limit the scope of our review and to add finality to trial court determinations. In pursuit of these entirely salutary purposes, courts must guard against allowing nomenclature to obscure the role that common law courts and principles have played in the history of the development of constitutional principles. Just as the precepts of the common law influence the style of constitutional adjudication in common law courts,[30] so common law case law itself is part of our usable past.

Notes

1. *See State* v. *Jewett,* 146 Vt. 221, 222, 500 A.2d 233 (1985); Ellen A. Peters, "State Constitutional Law: Federalism in the Common Law Tradition," *Michigan Law Review* 84 (1986): 583–86.
2. Although Connecticut ratified the United States Constitution on January 9, 1788, the fifth state to do so, ratification of the federal Bill of Rights did not occur until 1939.
3. See Lutz's essay in this volume.
4. See Sherry's essay in this volume.
5. 2 Day 504, 507 (1807).
6. *Kohlfuss* v. *Warden,* 149 Conn. 692, 695, 183 A.2d 626, 627 (1962), *cert. denied,* 371 U.S. 928 (1962).
7. 372 U.S. 335 (1962).
8. Zephariah Swift, *A System of Laws of the State of Connecticut* (Windham, Conn.: Printed by J. Byrne, 1795–96), 392, 398–99; *State* v. *Stoddard,* 206 Conn. 157, 164–66, 537 A.2d 446, 451–52 (1988).
9. 1 Kirby 12 (1786).
10. Id., at 13.
11. 3 Day 103, 107 (1808).
12. 1 Kirby 91 (1786).
13. Id., at 95.
14. 1 Kirby 213 (1787).
15. Id., at 213–14.
16. Id., at 214.
17. Id., at 215.
18. Id.
19. 1 Conn. 40 (1814).
20. See, e.g., *Whiting & Frisbie* v. *Jewel,* 1 Kirby 1 (1786); *Brinley* v. *Avery,* 1 Kirby 25 (1786); *Bulkley* v. *Starr,* 2 Day 552 (1807); *Stoyel* v. *Westcott,* 3 Day 349 (1809).
21. *State* v. *Green,* 1 Kirby 87 (1786).
22. *Tweedy* v. *Brush,* 1 Kirby 13 (1786); *Smith* v. *Ward,* 2 Root 302 (1795).
23. *Knot* v. *Gay,* 1 Root 66 (1774); *Wrexford* v. *Smith,* 2 Root 171 (1795).
24. *Meacham* v. *Austin,* 5 Day 233 (1811).
25. 5 Day 193, 196 (1811), *rev'd,* 11 U.S. 550 (1813).

26. Although body execution was legal, concerns about involuntary servitude implicitly led the court to take every opportunity to narrow the boundaries of the statute permitting this practice. See, e.g., *Huntington* v. *Jones,* 1 Kirby 33 (1786); *Smith* v. *Huntington,* 2 Day 562 (1807).
27. 1 Kirby 297, 298 (1787).
28. *State* v. *Phelps,* 1 Kirby 282 (1787); *State* v. *Thomson,* 1 Kirby 345 (1787).
29. *Grannis* v. *Branden,* 5 Day 260, 272–73 (1812).
30. Peters, "State Constitutional Law," 592–93.

The Uses of State
Constitutional History
A Case Note

H. Jefferson Powell

 The study of state constitutional history clearly is an orphan child. Students of our constitutional past generally have concentrated their attention on the federal Constitution and even more narrowly on the United States Supreme Court. State constitutional case law has been especially neglected, except for the occasional decision[1] that appears to be a precursor to a federal case or doctrine. The consequence of this disinterest in the history of state constitutional cases has been the impoverishment both of our understanding of American legal history and of the fundamental issues raised by the enterprise of defining and limiting government power by written constitutions. In this essay I suggest that both legal history and constitutional jurisprudence would benefit from enhanced attention to those traditions of argument and interpretation that center on the fundamental law of the several states rather than on the federal Constitution. State constitutional history, in short, is "usable," at least in the sense of being intellectually enlightening. The essay makes this argument by way of a brief case study, but before doing so I need to enter a couple of cautionary warnings about the general thesis.

First, history is to be used, but its proper use depends on careful attention to the demands—and the limits—of responsible historical scholarship.[2] Ransacking the past for isolated "good quotes" is bad history and bad law (although, of course, at times politically effective).

My second caution is related: we cannot assume, as a matter of a priori truth, that there is a unitary tradition of constitutional law across the several states or even within a single state. That there is a meaningful tradition is an assertion to be proven rather than a premise to be assumed. This is a point of more than mere methodological significance. One of the most common sources of misunderstanding and anachronism in constitutional history stems from the desire to identify a common set of ideas and arguments shared by groups labeled "the founders," "framers," "traditional" constitutional lawyers, and so on. This desire easily leads one to find more agreement and intelligibility in the past than was in fact there. We must take seriously the possibilities of radical disagreement among, say, judges interpreting a state constitution as well as of internal contradictions within particular people's thinking. One good example of this sort of disagreement can be found in the debates in the 1780s over the Pennsylvania Constitution. Everyone involved in the discussion agreed that Pennsylvania ought to have a "republican" form of government, but the supporters of the 1776 Constitution and its critics held radically different views of what republicanism might be.

Another example of deep—and deeply interesting—disagreement over state constitutional law is to be found in the case *Kamper* v. *Hawkins*,[3] on which the rest of this essay is focused. *Kamper*, decided in 1794 by the Virginia General Court, raised some nice questions about the Virginia Constitution's distribution of judicial power; even more interestingly, the case prompted the judges of the General Court to engage in a lively debate over the nature of judicial review. *Kamper* sheds important light on the development of American thinking about the relationship between judges and constitutions in the decade and a half between the drafting of the United States Constitution and *Marbury* v. *Madison*. An understanding of the divergent views of judicial review expressed by the *Kamper* judges, furthermore, is of more than antiquarian interest: *Kamper* raises the central jurisprudential question of what judges are doing when they decline to obey a statute for constitutional reasons. Are they "striking down" an offending action of the legislature and thereby fulfilling a unique role as the guardians of the constitution? Or are they simply refusing to participate in what they perceive as unconstitutional governmental action without denying that for other actors and other viewpoints the challenged statute may be legal and binding? Or, as John Marshall seems to have said in *Marbury,* is judicial review nothing more than a corollary of the ordinary judicial role: the court must decide which of a set of conflicting legal rules is the authoritative one, and between an act of the legislature and an act of the people the latter must prevail? Twentieth-century American constitutional theory tends to assume that the latter is the basic and legitimate rationale for judicial review. Such an assumption suggests that judicial review should be an occasional and extraordinary event akin to a judicial decision that a subsequent statute has repealed an earlier law *sub silentio.* If two statutes are in irreconcilable conflict, a court must decide which to follow, but that necessity does not imply that the court should look for such conflict or view itself as the chosen defender of the later (or the earlier) law. The *Marbury* vision of judicial review implies that judicial review, rather than exemplifying some special function of courts in the American constitutional order, is almost mundane, nothing more than a necessary part of the judge's ordinary job of declaring what the law is. A great deal of recent constitutional scholarship from every political corner has concerned itself with the project of easing or resolving the paradox of courts exercising great political power on the basis of a narrow and even technical understanding of the act of judging. Perhaps light may be shed on the problem if we look at a time and an American political system that had not canonized *Marbury.*

The Setting of Kamper *v.* Hawkins

The court structure of prerevolutionary Virginia essentially consisted of two separate layers. On one hand were the local county and corporation courts, exercising jurisdiction over a variety of petty civil matters, the day-to-day criminal law supervision of misconduct by free persons, and the social control of slaves.[4] In the capital the governor and council sat as a General Court with original and appellate jurisdiction and both legal and equitable powers. A variety of problems emerged in the colonial period from the oligarchal and unprofessional nature of the local courts and from the General Court's inaccessibility and inadequacy for an increasingly legalistic society.[5] The Revolution provided "occasion and opportunity" to address those problems, and "court reform was a perennial theme of politics during the early years of the new state."[6] The Virginia Constitution of 1776 directed the General Assembly to "appoint judges of the supreme court of appeals, and general court, judges in chancery, judges of admiralty."[7] Between 1776 and 1779 the state legislature, acting under this constitutional mandate, restructured the central judicial system but left the local courts basically unchanged. The General Court, the High Court of Chancery, and the Court of Admiralty were each established as multimember panels; for reasons of economy, the General Assembly directed that the Court of Appeals be made up of the entire body of central court judges, a pattern familiar from English legal history.[8] Continued dissatisfaction with the administration of justice on the local level led within a decade to the passage of a district court act establishing a system of professionalized trial courts staffed by ordering the central court judges to ride circuit in addition to their other duties. The judiciary collectively refused to act under the statute, complaining in a "Remonstrance" to the legislature that it unconstitutionally interfered with their salaries and independence.[9] In response, the legislature remodeled the central judicial system. The new scheme established a Court of Appeals with its own membership, but it staffed the district courts by imposing double duty on the judges of an expanded General Court.[10]

The Virginia judges accepted commissions under the new act, but problems immediately emerged. Cases in which most or all members of the new Court of Appeals had a personal financial interest were sufficiently common to lead the General Assembly, in November 1789, to direct the General Court judges to sit as substitute appeals judges in such cases, an expedient that reproduced the same practical and constitutional difficulties the judges' 1788 "Remonstrance" had found unacceptable. For the moment, however, the judges acquiesced in the arrangement, and this alternative appeals court met on several occasions between 1789 and 1794. The reduction of the High Court of Chancery to a single judge also caused problems by exacerbating the difficulty of obtaining timely equitable relief in appropriate cases. In response, in December 1792, the General Assembly enacted a statute granting the district courts certain equitable powers. The following May, Mary Hawkins prayed for an injunction against enforcement of a judgment obtained by Peter Kamper in the Dumfries district court.

The General Court judge sitting on circuit, Spencer Roane, was inclined (as he later explained) to obey the statute and consider the motion for the injunction, but because of his concern over the statute's constitutionality he referred that issue to the entire General Court. In November 1793, the judges of the General Court present in Richmond unanimously concluded that the statute violated the state constitution and that as a consequence the district court ought not exercise powers under it.

The Kamper *Debate over the Nature of Judicial Review*

There were a variety of arguments against the constitutionality of the 1792 act. One was purely textual: section 14 of the state constitution directed the General Assembly "by joint ballot [to] appoint judges of the supreme court of appeals, and general court, judges in chancery, judges of admiralty." As Judge William Nelson pointed out, "the insertion of the word *judges* between the general *court* and chancery" arguably "evinced an intention that the judges of the general court and those in chancery should be distinct persons," although Nelson conceded that this was "so critical a construction" of the text that by itself it was not persuasive.[11] A second line of argument, accepted by the entire court, relied on the Virginia Constitution's definition of the means (legislative election by joint ballot of the two houses sitting together followed by commissioning by the governor) by which state judges were to be appointed. The extension of equity powers to the district courts could be seen as purporting to make the judges of the latter chancery judges as well by passage of an ordinary statute and without executive commission. Two judges (Nelson and St. George Tucker) found the constitutional arrangements for judicial impeachment contravened by the 1792 act: the constitution placed trials of chancery judges before the General Court and trials of General Court judges before the Court of Appeals in an arguable effort to avoid requiring judges to sit on the trial of a colleague. The hybrid chancery-district judge, at least for matters arising out of his exercise of equity jurisdiction, seemingly would be tried before his brethren in violation of this constitutional purpose.[12]

The unanimity of the General Court judges in finding the 1792 act unconstitutional and in therefore refusing to obey it was accompanied by striking disagreement over why they were entitled so to act and, indeed, over what exactly it was they were doing. The *Kamper* judges recognized (what modern lawyers sometimes forget) that there is no single, relatively clear and uncontroversial notion of judicial review for which there are differing rationales. There are, instead, a variety of ways to understand the place of judges in an American constitutional order, each of which includes at least an implicit account of what "the Constitution" itself is and what power judges can and should wield when they review legislative acts for their constitutionality.

At one end of the *Kamper* spectrum of opinion was James Henry. Henry, originally an admiralty judge, sat on the old Court of Appeals under the pre-1788 scheme as well as on the special Court of Appeals the General Assembly cobbled together for judicial conflict-of-interest situations. Having decided that without a special election and commission he would not wield equity powers, Henry found the apparent "inconsistency in my conduct"[13] somewhat uncomfortable. Although his actions as an admiralty judge were in his view justified by the general understanding and positive law of the pre-1788 period, he conceded that after 1789 "I consider this special court, with respect to me, who have been neither appointed nor commissioned since the passing of that law as unconstitutional." Henry nevertheless insisted that he had acted properly in serving on the special court: "The case cannot often happen; it is exceedingly disagreeable to be faulting the legislature; and, perhaps one particular mischief had better be submitted to, than a public inconvenience."[14] A judge's personal conclusion[15] that a legislative act transgressed the constitution, in Henry's view, did not render the legislation unconstitutional in any strong sense, for Henry did not regard judicial interpretations as privileged as over against legislative constructions of the constitution. The repeated encounters between the judges and the General Assembly over the structure of the courts were "unhappy differences of opinion between . . . the different departments of government." They were appropriately to be handled in the case of limited or "temporary"[16] issues by judicial acquiescence and in the event of a major disagreement resolvable finally only "by calling a convention of the people."[17] Judicial review for Henry seems to have been an expedient for a particular situation, one in which he was being called upon to exercise jurisdiction "of a permanent nature" not conferred upon him by the forms prescribed in the constitution. Henry's decision not to obey the 1792 law was a purely self-defensive act, a refusal to act beyond his "duly authorized" powers and nothing more.[18]

Judges William Nelson and John Tyler articulated views of judicial review similar to each other's—and to John Marshall's a decade later in *Marbury*. Both understood judicial review as one form of the general judicial activity of determining what law applied in particular cases. As Nelson observed, with reference to statutory repeals by implication of earlier legislation, it was no "novelty" for courts "to declare, whether an act of the legislative *be in force* or *not in force,* or in other words, whether it be a *law* or *not."* [19] When the constitution and statute both appear relevant to a case before a court and appear furthermore to conflict, it is the court's judicial obligation to decide which law governs by comparing the two.[20] Since the constitution "is to the *governors,* or rather to the departments of *government,* what a law is to individuals," [21] a statute conflicting with it simply is not a law: "the prior *fundamental law* has prevented its *coming into existence* as *a law."* [22] A judicial decision against a law's constitutionality, for Nelson and Tyler, thus was not (as Henry argued) merely a declaration by the judges that they personally would not overstep their own view of the constitution's forms, but a "judicial act" declaring the law "void" [23] and "of no obligation." [24] Judicial review, in short, derived both its significance (courts have the power to declare a statute to be "no law") and its limitations (a court's only function is to decide which law applies in a particular case) from its definition as a straightforward part of the ordinary judicial business of comparing legal rules. Nelson stated that "I do not consider the judiciary as the champions of the people, or of the Constitution, bound to sound the alarm, and to excite an opposition to the legislature. But, when the cases of individuals are brought before them judicially, they are bound to decide." [25] (This position amounted to an anticipatory repudiation of the views of Nelson's colleague Spencer Roane, who would argue in his dissent that the judiciary was the special guardian of the constitution.) Tyler emphasized the existence of substantive limits on judicial review: "the violation [of the constitution] must be plain and clear" and the courts "cannot supply defects [or] reconcile absurdities, if any there be" in the constitution.[26]

Nelson and Tyler presented early versions of what has become the canonical view of judicial review now associated with *Marbury* v. *Madison.* But there were yet other views of the matter (which, as has been suggested, Nelson at least explicitly rejected), put forward by Spencer Roane and St. George Tucker. Both Roane and Tucker understood judicial review as more than a mere corollary of the duty to decide cases, indeed as a particular and unique function of the courts in an American constitutional order.

Tucker's account of judicial review took off from a point close to that of Nelson and Tyler. Before the American Revolution, the "constitution" of a country was nothing more than the collection of those acts and procedures the government previously had done and followed. "The judiciary, having no *written constitution* to refer to, were obliged to *receive* whatever *exposition* of it the legislature might think proper to make." The American creation of written constitutions, however, gave those constitutions "a real existence" and gave courts a written letter on the basis of which to judge the legitimacy of the legislature's acts.[27] For Tucker, unlike Nelson and Tyler, this implied that the judiciary enjoyed a unique place in the constitutional scheme: "This exposition [of the constitution] it is the duty and office of the judiciary to make. . . . Now since it is the province of the legislature to make, and of the executive to enforce obedience to the laws, the duty of expounding must be exclusively vested in the judiciary."[28] The exclusive interpretive role of the courts Tucker thus asserted he then used to support his arguments against legislative interference with the constitution's distribution of jurisdiction among the various courts. A vigorous protection of judicial independence was necessary to preserve "the principles of our government" that appoint "the judiciary as a barrier against the possible usurpation, or abuse of power in the other departments."[29] The logic of Tucker's argument also led him to identify the state Court of Appeals, the highest court in the commonwealth, as possessing a unique function: its decisions, he said, "are to be resorted to by all other courts, as expounding, in their truest sense, the laws of the land."[30] The idea of a judicial monopoly over interpretation combined with a hierarchical judicial system to identify a single judicial body as the source of authentic ("truest") constitutional thought.

Roane articulated a similarly aggressive vision of judicial review, although in different terms. He had initially doubted whether any form of judicial review was "authorized," but "on mature consideration . . . I now think that the judiciary may and ought not only to refuse to execute a law expressly repugnant to the Constitution; but also one which is, by a plain and natural construction, in opposition to the fundamental principles thereof."[31] Like Tucker, Roane viewed the courts as the proper and exclusive interpreter of the laws, including the constitution. "It is the province of the judiciary to expound the laws."[32] Roane described the case in which a constitutional issue about a statute is raised as a "controversy . . . between the legislature on one hand, and the whole people of Virginia (through the medium of an individual) on the other." In such a struggle between the people and the governors the courts constituted the "proper" decision maker, even if (as in *Kamper*) the judges' own personal interests were involved. The exercise of judicial review for Roane was not simply a necessary part of the judicial task of deciding which law to apply in individual cases: courts exercising the power act as the people's champions; "they are bound to decide, and they do actually decide on behalf of the people."[33]

The different accounts of judicial review offered by the General Court judges in *Kamper* v. *Hawkins* raised a variety of issues that remain of theoretical and practical importance. Do judges properly enjoy a monopoly on authoritative constitutional interpretation, as Roane and Tucker believed, or is the legislature equally entitled to its opinion, as seems to have been Henry's opinion? Is the power of judicial review based on the judges' general obligation to decide cases (Nelson and Tyler thought so), or do courts have a special role in defending the people and the constitution against unconstitutional and oppressive actions? Should the power be wielded with restraint and only in clear cases of unconstitutionality, or should judges seek to uphold not only the constitution's letter but also its spirit? *Kamper* reveals that these questions are not merely modern concerns but were the subject of dispute at the very beginning of the American constitutional order.

The Significance of Kamper *v.* Hawkins

The Virginia General Court's decision in *Kamper* v. *Hawkins* to hold unconstitutional a long forgotten state statute holds important lessons for American constitutional historians. On the most basic level, *Kamper* raises questions about the origins of American judicial review. Nine years before *Marbury* v. *Madison,* in a setting fraught with political significance, the Virginia court unanimously asserted the power to disregard statutory law the judges thought unconstitutional. *Marbury*, perhaps rightly, often is seen as a remarkably clever ploy by Marshall and his colleagues: the case afforded Marshall the opportunity to read President Jefferson a lesson on the rule of law while by holding unconstitutional the Judiciary Act's apparent grant of original jurisdiction in the case the Supreme Court was able to avoid a direct confrontation with the executive. *Kamper,* in contrast, exacerbated friction between the state legislature and the judiciary by forcing the politically hot issue of the local administration of justice back onto the legislature's agenda. It did so, furthermore, in the almost immediate aftermath of the legislature's wholesale overhaul of the judicial system. In that context, *Kamper* was no mere potshot from the bench but a direct "warning to the legislature to keep hands off the judiciary."[34] The judges' boldness in doing so, and their success in a practical sense (the General Assembly eventually responded by establishing a separate system of superior courts of chancery), suggest that some form of judicial review was widely accepted as an element of American constitutionalism by the mid-1790s.[35] Further investigation of state constitutional history will strengthen the conclusion that *Marbury*'s exercise of judicial review took place against a background of state discussion and activity that rendered that part of Marshall's opinion rather uncontroversial. Only the eclipse of state constitutional law has led to *Marbury*'s enthronement as the case that "established" judicial review.[36]

Marbury's post hoc stature has played a major role in modern constitutional theory. At least since James Bradley Thayer's famous article "The Origin and Scope of the American Doctrine of Constitutional Law,"[37] constitutional lawyers have treated the exercise of judicial review as the extraordinary exercise of a power requiring special justification in a representative democracy. Even theorists supportive of an active role for the judiciary often concede that they are arguing *against* a historical expectation of judicial "restraint."[38] *Kamper* suggests that, at least in the earliest period, Americans held divergent views about the scope and justification of judicial review. Judges Nelson and Tyler, for example, understood the power as a necessary corollary of their obligation to decide cases according to law, and their implicit understanding of their role in the constitutional order was correspondingly limited (and similar to John Marshall's in *Marbury*). Tucker and Roane, however, viewed judicial review in a different light. For Tucker, "the duty of expounding" the state constitution "must be exclusively vested in the judiciary"; judicial review is the normal and essential function of the courts under a written constitution. When a statute is challenged as repugnant to the constitution, Roane asserted, "the controversy is between the legislature on one hand and the whole people of Virginia . . . on the other." Roane and Tucker held correspondingly broad understandings of the grounds on which judges might wield their authority as tribunes of the people. In Roane's terms, the court should consult not only "the letter of the Constitution" but also its "fundamental principles" and "spirit."[39] Further study of state constitutional history will show that *Kamper* was not a fluke and that founding-era Americans held a much broader range of views on the methods of constitutional interpretation and the role of the judiciary than many modern constitutional lawyers acknowledge. This is a point of more than antiquarian interest. In an era in which the federal judiciary's constitutional activity is increasingly shaped by a particular and purportedly historical vision of American constitutionalism, it is incumbent on lawyers and state judges to examine the extent to which that vision is appropriate or historically justified in the individual states. Recent developments in state constitutional law are sometimes criticized as merely responsive to the politics of the federal Supreme Court. As *Kamper* illustrates, state constitutional history is a rich source of reflection and precedent for the creation of a genuinely independent state constitutional jurisprudence.

Notes

I am extremely grateful to Carol Barry for her many contributions to my thinking on this subject.

1. An example of the rare exception is *Wynehamer v. People*, 13 N.Y. 378 (1856), which usually receives a citation as a state forerunner of federal substantive due process. See, e.g., Laurence Tribe, *American Constitutional Law*, 2d ed. (Mineola, N.Y.: Foundation Press, 1988), 562 n. 15.
2. I have explored these issues more thoroughly in Powell, "Rules for Originalists," *Virginia Law Review* 73 (1987): 659.
3. 3 Va. (1 Va. Cas.) 20 (Gen. Ct. 1794).
4. For a contemporaneous account of the activities of a colonial county court see *Criminal Proceedings in Colonial Virginia*, ed. Peter C. Hoffer

and William B. Scott (Athens: Published for the American Historical Association, Washington, D.C., by the University of Georgia
Press, 1984).

5. See A. G. Roeber, *Faithful Magistrates and Republican Lawyers* (Chapel
Hill: University of North Carolina Press, 1981).

6. *The Papers of John Marshall*, ed. Charles Hobson et al. (Chapel Hill: University of North Carolina Press, 1987), 5:xxviii. The introductory essay
to this volume, which covers Marshall's law practice from 1784 to 1800,
is a brief but superb description of the legal system of Virginia in the
period of *Kamper.*

7. Va. Const. Art. 14 (1776), in *Sources and Documents of United States Constitutions,* ed. William Swindler (Dobbs Ferry, N.Y.: Oceana Publications, 1973–78), 10:54.

8. As Virginian readers of Lord Coke would have known, Exchequer
Chamber, which from 1585 exercised appellate review jurisdiction over
King's Bench, was made up of the Common Pleas justices and the bar-
ons of the Exchequer. John Hamilton Baker, *An Introduction to English
Legal History,* 2d ed. (London: Butterworths, 1979), 119.

9. See *Cases of the Judges of the Court of Appeals,* 8 Va. (4 Call) 135 (Va. 1788).

10. The judicial reorganization statute attempted to balance the concerns of
the judges that led to their refusal to act under the earlier district court
statute with the legislature's concern for frugality. Even though the new
act established a separate Court of Appeals and doubled the General
Court's membership to ten, it required the appointment of only four
new judges to the previous eleven-judge system (three chancellors,
three admiralty judges, and five General Court judges): the members of
the admiralty court, now superseded by the new federal district court,
were transferred to the General Court, and two of the chancellors were
moved to the new Court of Appeals.

11. 3 Va. (1 Va. Cas.) 20, 33 (Gen. Ct. 1794).

12. Id. at 33–34 (Nelson), 89–90 (Tucker). Tucker, alone of the *Kamper*
judges, accepted two additional arguments: that the separation of law
and equity was constitutionally mandated and that the previous appeals court's refusal to obey the initial reorganization statute was an
authoritative precedent. Id. at 88–89, 94–97.

13. Id. at 53.

14. Id. at 55.

15. Cf. id. at 51 ("Where I am not bound by regular adjudications of the
superior court, I cannot rest on other men's opinions. I must and will
think for myself").

16. Id. at 55.

17. Id. at 50.

18. Id. at 53.
19. Id. at 31.
20. Tyler stated that "I will not in an extra-judicial manner assume the right negative a law . . . but if by any legal means I have jurisdiction of a cause, in which it is made a question how far the law be a violation of the constitution . . . I shall not shrink from a comparison of the two, and pronounce sentence as my mind may receive conviction." Id. at 61.
21. Id. at 24.
22. Id. at 32.
23. Id. at 32 (Nelson).
24. Id. at 61 (Tyler).
25. Id. at 30.
26. Id. at 61, 62.
27. Id. at 77–78.
28. Id. at 79.
29. Id. at 87.
30. Id. at 93.
31. Id. at 35–36. Roane later described these "fundamental principles" broadly and extratextually: "From the above premises I conclude that the judiciary may and ought to adjudge a law unconstitutional and avoid, if it be plainly repugnant to the letter of the Constitution, or the fundamental principles thereof. By fundamental principles I under- stand, those great principles growing out of the Constitution, by the aid of which, in dubious cases, the Constitution may be explained and preserved inviolate; those land-marks, which it may be necessary to resort to, on account of the impossibility to foresee or provide for cases within the spirit, but without the letter of the Constitution." Id. at 40.
32. Id. at 38.
33. Id. at 39.
34. Roeber, *Faithful Magistrates*, 225.
35. Some form of judicial review was endorsed by Republicans (Roane and Tucker were active Anti-Federalists) as well as Federalists, see, e.g., James Kent, *An Introductory Lecture to a Course of Law Lectures* (1794), in *American Political Writing During the Founding Era, 1760–1815*, ed. Charles S. Hyneman and Donald S. Lutz (Indianapolis: Liberty Press, 1983), 2:936, 942–44 (asserting the power of the judiciary "of determin- ing the constitutionality of Laws"). By the end of the decade a Republi- can attorney defending a journalist charged under the 1798 Sedition Act could state that "it seems to be admitted on all hands, that, when the legislature exercises a power not given them by the constitution, the judiciary will disregard their acts." *United States* v. *Callender*, 25 F. Cas. 239, 253 (C.C.D. Va. 1800) (argument of counsel); see also id. at 255

(Chase, J.) (by the Constitution the power "to declare a statute void" "is expressly granted to the judicial power of the United States").

36. It is possible that *Kamper*'s relationship to *Marbury* was even more direct. John Marshall practiced before the General Court and conceivably could have been present when the judges announced their opinions.

37. James B. Thayer, "The Origin and Scope of the American Doctrine of Constitutional Law," *Harvard Law Review* 7 (1893): 129.

38. See, e.g., Michael Perry, *The Constitution, the Courts, and Human Rights* (New Haven: Yale University Press, 1982).

39. Tucker's discussion of the appropriate method of interpreting the United States Constitution in his edition of Blackstone makes it clear that he agreed with Roane on the necessity of going beyond the letter of the instrument. See Tucker, Appendix to 1 *Blackstone's Commentaries, with Notes of Reference to the Constitution and Laws of the Federal Government of the United States and of the Commonwealth of Virginia*, ed. St. George Tucker (1803; rpt. New York: Augustus M. Kelley, 1969), note D, at 154 (invoking a "maxim of political law" and international law views of treaties to justify strict construction of federal powers).

Part Three

Interdependence of State and Federal Constitutional Law

Before Plessy, Before Brown

The Development of the Law
of Racial Integration in
Louisiana and Kansas

J. Morgan Kousser

Robert H. Isabelle faced a complicated legal situation when he tried to get his son William admitted to a school in his ward of New Orleans in 1870.[1] Under articles 13 and 135 of the Louisiana Constitution of 1868, every public facility, specifically including schools, was declared open to every person regardless of race.[2] Fearing that courts might rule the constitutional guarantee not self-executing, the Radical Republican legislature of 1869, of which Isabelle was a leading member, wrote the integration provision into the state education law.[3] Still, the Democratic-dominated Orleans Parish school board refused to grant "colored" children—Isabelle was lighter in complexion than many people who were considered "white" —the permits necessary to admit them to the "white" schools.[4] The legislature in 1870 therefore acted to circumvent the board by authorizing the state superintendent of schools, Thomas W. Conway, a white Radical carpetbagger, to appoint new school boards for each ward of Orleans Parish, which would supersede the parish board.[5] When Conway packed the ward boards with integrationists, as the legislators had no doubt intended,[6] the teachers still refused to admit Isabelle's child, preferring to obey the parish board segregationists rather than the ward board integrationists.[7] Isabelle sued.

The petty legal point immediately at issue in Judge Henry C. Dibble's Eighth District court on November 21, 1870, was which boards had legal control of the money that the state had allocated to schools. Behind this, however, lay the question of integration. Isabelle's lawyer could have argued the case purely on the basis of the 1870 law, the grounds on which the wily Judge Dibble decided it, or he could have relied on the nondiscrimination section of the 1869 law, or he could have harkened back to section 135 of the state constitution, or he could have pled the equal protection clause of the Fourteenth Amendment, or like the usual risk-averse attorney, he could have argued all of these. But in his brief, the lawyer, John B. Howard, did not cite any specific provisions of state or national law. Instead he appealed to the general nature of "republican government." "That universal consent, so essential to the safety of a republic," Howard proclaimed, "requires—1st. That the laws of a public character should be universal in their application; 2nd. That such laws should be framed and enacted so as to recognize, enforce and maintain the duties and rights of all inhabitants—in government, in property, in person, in society, in morals and in education, and in whatever satisfies the wants of everyone, without injury or trespass on the domain of any other."[8]

Howard's short extant brief in this unreported state district court case was extreme in its refusal even to go through the formal mechanics of citing constitutional or statutory provisions, but it was typical of nineteenth-century briefs and judicial opinions on school segregation in its lack of distinction between "legal" issues, on one hand, and "legislative" or "policy" issues, on the other, as well as in its explicit grounding in the fundamental questions of what was "reasonable" for legislators or administrators to do and what rights each citizen had. Howard's two natural law arguments amounted, after all, to equality and protection—just the phrase that his fellow Republican John A. Bingham had recently written into the Fourteenth Amendment.[9] But since the *Isabelle* case was never appealed—there was a substantial degree of school integration in New Orleans from 1870 to 1877, no doubt including William R. Isabelle, Robert's son, among its beneficiaries—and since Judge Dibble, an integration sympathizer who later became president of the reorganized Orleans Parish school board, decided the issue narrowly, the *Isabelle* case did not become an integrationist, equal rights precedent in the state that two decades later produced *Plessy* v. *Ferguson.*[10]

For a second, somewhat less obscure factual prelude to the discussion of school segregation law in the nineteenth century, let us take the Mississippi River and its tributaries north to Kansas, as many black folks from Louisiana did at the end of the 1870s. In his opinion for the Kansas Supreme Court in the 1881 case of *Board of Education of Ottawa, Kansas* v. *Leslie Tinnon,* Justice Daniel M. Valentine[11] used sonorous language about equal rights similar to that of John Howard several hundred miles down the Mississippi River in 1870.[12] Since some legal commentators, such as Herbert Hovenkamp and Raoul Berger, have alleged that "the Radical Republicans did not want racial integration any more than southern whites did,"[13] it is worth quoting Valentine's words at length:

> The tendency of the times is, and has been for several years, to abolish all distinctions on account of race, or color, or previous condition of servitude, and to make all persons absolutely equal before the law. . . .
>
> Is it not better for the grand aggregate of human society, as well as for individuals, that all children should mingle together and learn to know each other? At the common schools, where both sexes and all kinds of children mingle together, we have the great world in miniature; there they may learn human nature in all its phases, with all its emotions, passions and feelings, its loves and hates, its hopes and fears, its impulses and sensibilities; there they may learn the secret springs of human actions, and the attractions and repulsions, which lead with irresistible force to particular lines of conduct.[14] But on the other hand, persons by isolation may become strangers even in their own country; and by being strangers, will be of but little benefit either to themselves or to society. As a rule, people cannot afford to be ignorant of the society which surrounds them; and as all kinds of people must live together in the same society, it would seem to be better that all should be taught in the same schools. . . .
>
> And what good reason can exist for separating two children, living in the same house, equally intelligent, and equally advanced in their studies, and sending one, because he or she is black, to a school house in a remote part of the city, past several school houses nearer his or her home, while the other child is permitted, because he or she is white, to go to a school within the distance of a block? No good reason can be given for such a thing. . . . If the board has the power, because of race,

to establish separate schools for children of African descent, then the board has the power to establish separate schools for persons of Irish descent or German descent; and if it has the power, because of color, to establish separate schools for black children, then it has the power to establish separate schools for red-headed children and blondes.[15]

Like Judge Dibble in New Orleans, Valentine rested his opinion, representing also the views of Chief Justice Albert H. Horton of the three-man state supreme court, formally on the narrowest possible grounds. He assumed, "for the purposes of this case," that neither the Fourteenth Amendment nor the Kansas Constitution prohibited a school board from classifying students by race and inquired only whether the Kansas legislature had authorized such a classification and, if not, whether the board's general mandate to regulate schools included an inherent power to segregate.[16]

In a larger sense, however, Valentine's consideration of this last question opened up all the issues related to the reasonableness of segregation that courts discussed throughout the nineteenth century whenever they decided school or public accommodations segregation cases. From *Roberts* v. *Boston* to *Plessy* v. *Ferguson* and beyond, courts asked two fundamental questions: First, was treating people of different races differently "reasonable" or merely "arbitrary"? Second, if racial distinctions were unreasonable, did judges, under the Fourteenth Amendment, state laws or constitutions, or natural law, have the power to disallow such actions or were they bound to defer to legislative or administrative bodies?[17] That contemporaries understood that Valentine's soaring rhetoric had these wider implications is shown by the vigorous dissent of future U.S. Supreme Court Justice David J. Brewer in the *Tinnon* case.[18] Brewer, who earlier had presided as school superintendent and school board member over the segregated schools of Leavenworth, found a "suggestion" in Valentine's opinion that the Fourteenth Amendment prohibited segregation, and he "dissent[ed] entirely" from that position. Moreover, even though he conceded that racial segregation "may be unreasonable," Brewer, whose career on the nation's highest court constituted a continual quest for judicial supremacy, insisted in *Tinnon* that the Kansas courts had to defer to the local board because the board was "elected by the community."[19]

Since Justice Henry Billings Brown in *Plessy* tested the reasonableness of segregation under the Fourteenth Amendment by citing laws and state and lower federal court opinions on the subject, it should have been incumbent on him to distinguish or at least mention the majority opinion in *Tinnon*.[20] Ironically, Brown's finesse—he did not directly refer to *Tinnon*, other pro-integration cases, or the numerous northern laws mandating integration in schools and public accommodations—would have been even more blatant had Valentine merely followed the opinion of Kansas district court judge Nelson T. Stephens in the first stage of the *Tinnon* case.[21] Quoting plentifully from both the U.S. Supreme Court majority and minority opinions in *Slaughter-House*, as well as from Justice William Strong's 1880 opinion in *Strauder* v. *West Virginia* and Justice David Davis's opinion in the 1873 case of *Railroad Co.* v. *Brown*, Stephens concluded that "it is evident to every mind" that the Fourteenth Amendment prohibited segregation.[22]

Nineteenth-Century Lessons for the New States' Rights

Why bother about obscure cases, over a century old, one of them not even publicly printed? What possible relevance can they have to contemporary efforts to reinvigorate state courts as protectors of individual rights in the face of the Nixon-Reagan counterrevolution against the Warren Court?[23] Their relevance, and that of the other cases from those two states that I will discuss in this essay, is three-fold. First, in each the lawyers, and, in *Tinnon*, the judges, discussed the broadest issues, exactly the same issues that judges always considered when they asked baldly whether the Fourteenth Amendment or natural law prohibited some regulation or classification. There was (and *is*) no escaping such issues, and to phrase the inquiry in terms of *state* constitutions, laws, or traditions, instead of more abstractly or nationally, strikes me as artificial and disingenuous.[24] Second, in their laudable effort to follow the best judicial practice, racially egalitarian nineteenth-century judges crafted their final opinions in formally narrow terms of state law, which greatly reduced the value of the decisions as precedents, even in their own states. When the state laws or constitutions changed, or when the issues were framed in formally larger terms, later lawyers and judges could more easily ignore, dismiss, or distinguish these rulings. By contrast, opinions in cases that upheld segregation logically *had* to consider the more abstract, national questions of whether racial classifications were against the Fourteenth Amendment or fundamental notions of equal rights. Thus these latter, pro-segregation opinions, interpreted under the usual legal shorthand convention that cases "stand for" pithy principles, inevitably played a larger role in shaping equal protection law than the state-based, closely focused, pro-integration decisions. Analogous dangers may lurk in the *sauve qui peut* stance of current liberal states' righters. Third, even the clearest of state constitutional guarantees and the most expansive egalitarian judicial rhetoric provided fragile support for civil rights in the face of the violent counterrevolution in Louisiana and the subtler pressure-group machinations in the Kansas legislature. James Madison's commendation of national diversity as a protection of minority rights in *Federalist* No. 10 is forgotten at our peril.[25] As a citizen of the state that recalled Rose Bird and two other liberal justices of the state supreme court, I cannot ignore the comparative ease with which policy in the states can be reversed.

In addition to seeking to avoid some unintended consequences of contemporary legal tactics, there are other, more historical reasons for recounting these tales. First, they refute or at least greatly complicate the pessimistic view, shared by some on the left and nearly everyone of an opposite policy orientation who has written on the subject, that white racial opinion in nineteenth-century America was uniformly and deeply racist.[26] Second, the analysis that proves this point expands the usual boundaries of constitutional history, which has been slow to follow the examples of J. Willard Hurst, Morton Horwitz, and others into social, economic, and non-"legal" political history and to venture beyond the covers of printed books of cases.[27] Third, many published accounts of the history of school integration in these two states during the nineteenth century are either incomplete or incorrect and need revision.[28] Finally, many of the brave, idealistic men and women who fought for racial justice then have been forgotten or unjustly maligned, while their opponents have often been celebrated or at least insufficiently pilloried.[29] Both groups deserve more fitting notice.

The Legal Framework

The laws, administrative acts, and state constitutional provisions on school integration in Louisiana and Kansas were more complex than historians have sometimes realized, and one cannot understand the judicial actions on the subject without first reviewing the actions of these (other) political bodies.

From Exclusion to Integration to Segregation in Louisiana

Blacks were taxed to support public schools in antebellum Louisiana—which were well organized only in New Orleans—but prohibited from entering them. The relatively affluent community of *gens de couleur* in New Orleans was permitted to establish private academies and schools for black indigents, however, and Paul Trévigne, who later figured prominently in the school integration struggle, was a longtime teacher in an antebellum indigent school.[30] The first system of publicly supported schools for blacks in the state was established by the occupying Union army during the Civil War. Because its control was limited, the system it established was temporary and failed to reach many of the "country" parishes. Even so, New Orleans blacks made an attempt to integrate the existing schools, an effort that failed in the wartime confusion.[31]

In a move to restore state control of education, the 1864 constitutional convention, called by moderate white Unionists under Lincoln's wartime "10 percent" plan, first adopted a "conservative" plan providing that segregated public schools would be supported by racially segregated taxes—the taxes paid by whites would be used for white schools, and the relatively tiny amount of taxes paid by blacks for black schools. Reasoning that the numerous group of predominantly white Afro-Americans "could not be distinguished from the whites by facial features or color," some delegates (none of whom was "colored" under any such rule) proposed to define people with three-fourths or more white ancestry as "white" for school purposes. The convention rejected this "quadroon bill," 47 to 23, and also voted down a proposal to integrate all persons indiscriminately in the schools, 66 to 15.[32] Under pressure from Radicals outside the convention, the 1864 delegates three weeks later removed all mention of race from the constitution (55 to 29), leaving the legislature to structure a public education system now open to all children between the ages of six and eighteen.[33]

With the collapse of the Confederacy, a radically racist Democratic government replaced the Unionists. Its state superintendent of schools, Robert M. Lusher, simply disregarded the state constitution, refusing to authorize any funds to be spent on what he termed "the mental training of an inferior race."[34] The congressional refusal to recognize this government of former rebels, the landslide Republican victory in the 1866 national elections, and the calling of a new constitutional convention in Louisiana, with the delegates to be elected by black as well as white voters, gave blacks a chance to reverse Lusher's patently unconstitutional policies. Presciently fearing that once established, a segregated system would be impossible to change, a group of black activists grouped around the radical *New Orleans Tribune* pushed simultaneously for an end to exclusion and for completely nonsegregated institutions.[35] In the 1868 constitutional convention, half of the delegates to which were considered black, the integrationists attained their goal. Among the whites voting in favor of integrated schools and public accommodations was Louisiana-born Simeon Belden, later state attorney general and subsequently a lawyer for blacks in three school integration suits.[36]

Despite the explicit ban on segregated schools in the 1868 Constitution and in the 1869 state law, schools in parishes outside New Orleans seem to have been almost entirely segregated.[37] The key was enforcement, which depended on the views of local school administrators, who were appointed by the state superintendent of schools, and on white public opinion, which was virtually a unit against school integration. Indeed, upper-class whites were none too favorable toward any publicly financed schooling.[38] When Democrats violently "redeemed" the state in 1876, they did not explicitly require segregation by state law, though they did repeal the 1869 legal guarantee of no racial discrimination.[39] Similarly, fearing intervention by the federal government, the 1879 state constitutional convention delegates repealed Article 135 of the 1868 Constitution but did not make school segregation mandatory.[40] Instead, they authorized the new state superintendent of education, Robert M. Lusher (again), to appoint new school boards that would carry out the discriminatory will of the legislature less formally.[41] In New Orleans, the board resolved on July 9, 1877 to segregate students beginning in the fall term.[42]

From Exclusion to Segregation to Integration to Confusion in Kansas

In the 1850s, Kansas was the national focal point of the slavery controversy. Ever since, Kansans have clashed over issues of race relations.

Proslavery Missourians exploded into the territory after 1854, to be met with "Beecher's Bibles" from New England. "Bleeding Kansas" became not only a potent symbol of slave state aggression but also an important ingredient in Kansans' creation myth. Its sanguinary epitome was John Brown, whose "Pottawatomie Massacre" took place in the same county as the later *Tinnon* case. In the 1870s, Kansas became the goal of the black "Exodusters." Even before the organized exodus, Kansas had the highest percentage of blacks outside the former slave states. Overwhelmingly Republican from the late 1850s until the Populist revolt of the 1890s, the state followed a zigzag course on racial legislation that no doubt perplexed contemporaries. It has certainly confused scholars since. Indeed, the shifts in the legal status of blacks in public education in the Jayhawk State were so frequent and dramatic that they can be followed only with a tabular guide, as given in Table 1.

In 1855, the first territorial legislature, fraudulently elected by proslavery Missourians, banned the territory's few free blacks from the public schools and voted to prohibit further black immigration. Even the nascent Free State party initially endorsed an all-white Kansas.[43] By 1858, however, the power of the antislavery forces was secure enough that the legislature omitted a black exclusion clause in its education law.[44] The next year, delegates to the convention that framed the constitution that Kansans would enjoy throughout the nineteenth century avoided all mention of race in the section on education, as Louisiana Unionists did in 1864. Although Democrats warned the Kansas convention's dominant free-state forces that the section would enable blacks to sue for admission into white schools, the majority refused to change it, and the delegates explicitly rejected attempts to exclude blacks from all schools and to require segregation.[45] As Maine-born Republican Dr. J. J. Blunt of Anderson County prophesied: "We don't know what will be the peculiar views of the people of Kansas upon this subject before there will be a change of the organic law. There may be a progress made by which the prejudices which involve and surround this question of negroes or mulattoes to our common schools may be laid aside; and then the Legislature could provide for the education of persons of color."[46]

During the Civil War, the legislature first mandated separate but equal across the state, then allowed the town of Marysville and the city of Leavenworth (the state's only "first-class city"[47] at the time) to

Table 1. Kansas Legislative and Constitutional Convention Actions on Black School Rights

Session	Nature of bill or amendment	Action on bill (journal reference)*	Session law reference
1855	Exclude blacks	Passed	Ch. 144, art. 1, §1
1858	End exclusion	Passed	Ch. 8, §71
1859†	Exclude blacks	Lost, 26–25, 29–20, 33–17, 34-16	Debates, 91, 106–9
1861	Separate but equal	Passed	Ch. 76, art. 3, §1
	Segregate taxes, schools, in Marysville	Passed	Private, Ch. 43, §5
1862	Segregate taxes, schools, in first-class cities	Passed	Ch. 46, art. 4, §18
1865	Equal tax, possibly segregate schools	Passed	Ch. 46, §1
1867	Separate but equal in second-class cities	Passed	Ch. 69, §7
	Separate but equal (reenacted 1861 law)	Passed	Ch. 123, §1
	Fines if blacks not offered education	Passed	Ch. 125, §1
1868	Separate but equal in first-class cities (no segregated taxes)	(H.B. 131) House 66–0 (HJ, 535–36) Senate 23–0 (SJ, 399)	
1870	Require segregated schools	(H.B. 219) no vote (HJ, 661)	
1872	Separate but equal in second-class cities	(H.B. 478) House 56–0 (HJ, 910) Senate 17–0 (SJ, 588)	Ch. 100, §105
1873	No segregation in second-class cities	(H.B. 39) House 67–2 (HJ, 642) Senate 22–1 (SJ, 436–37)	
	No racial discrimination in schools	(H.B. 247) House 57–7 (HJ, 980–81)	Ch. 65, §5

Year	Description	Bill / Vote	Citation
1874	No exclusion from any school	(H.B. 1) House 64–17 (HJ, 662–63) Senate 24–2 (SJ, 313)	Ch. 49, §1
1876	No exclusion from any school	(S.B. 202) House 56–30 (HJ, 1386–89) Senate 27–4 (SJ, 698–701)	Ch. 122, art. 5, §3
	Reenacted 1867, Ch. 125, §1		
	No authority for segregation in first-class cities	Part of S.B. 202	Ch. 122, art. 5, §4
	Banned segregation in second-class cities		Ch. 122, art. 11
1879	Separate but equal in first-class cities	(S.B. 35) Senate 30–0 (SJ, 430) House 96–4 (HJ, 1069–70)	Ch. 81, §1
1881	Repeal 1879 law, Ch. 81, §1	(S.B. 238) Senate 25–3 (SJ, 533)	
1889	Allow segregation in first-class cities only if two-thirds of each race favor, neighborhood schools	(S.B. 197) no floor action	
	Ban segregation in Wichita	(S.B. 351) House 78–0 (HJ, 897–98)	Ch. 227, §4
	Ban segregation in first-class cities	(S.B. 108) Senate 29–0 (SJ, 474)	
	Ban segregation everywhere (part of general school law revision)	(H.B. 42) Senate 10–24 (SJ, 922, 970) House 93–0 (HJ, 442–43)	
1905	Segregated high schools all right in Kansas City	Passed	Ch. 414
1911	Segregated high schools all right in first-class cities	House 119–0 Senate (no action)	

*HJ = House Journal, relevant year; SJ = Senate Journal, relevant year
† Constitutional Convention

allocate all taxes paid by whites to white schools, leaving only the pittance paid by refugee freedmen for black schools.[48] At the close of the conflict, the legislature authorized localities that had too few blacks to make segregation feasible to admit them into the common schools. It is difficult to determine the effect of these laws. Leavenworth County, which contained 47 percent of the state's black population in 1860, certainly had a separate black school by 1864, but many other black children probably went without public schooling, and others presumably entered the common schools.

Under pressure from the state teachers' association, which had endorsed integration in 1866, and the Radical Republican state school superintendent, Peter McVicar, the 1867 legislature moved to guarantee blacks access to schooling, allowing localities to exercise their option on whether it would be segregated.[49] After reenacting the 1861 equal advantage law, perhaps as a reminder to school boards, the legislature explicitly authorized segregation in second-class cities. On the session's last day, the members rushed through a bill levying a mandatory $100 a month fine on any district board that refused admission to "any children into the common schools," the fines to be allocated to a special fund to be spent by each county school superintendent for the education of the locked-out children. In small towns or rural areas, such a sum would pay for two teachers and a rented schoolroom—a quite adequate school for blacks or whites by the standards of the time.[50]

Despite annual pleas for integration from Superintendent McVicar, the legislature from 1868 to 1872 merely reaffirmed earlier laws permitting first- and second-class cities to establish segregated schools.[51] In 1873, however, the congressional struggle for a civil rights law spun off movements in several states (New York, California, and Pennsylvania, as well as Kansas) to pass state guarantees of nondiscrimination in admissions to schools and other places of public accommodation.[52] Black Kansans from throughout the state lobbied the legislature and succeeded in getting a nearly unanimous repeal of segregation in second-class cities and in convincing the lower house to mandate nondiscrimination everywhere.[53] The state senate failed to act on the statewide nondistinction bill.

The next year, the black lobby succeeded. H.B. 1, a slightly rearranged version of the 1873 H.B. 247, passed both houses overwhelmingly. Prohibiting school officials, as well as those in charge of businesses that served the public, from making "any distinction on account of race, color or previous condition of servitude," and repealing all contrary laws or parts of laws, it clearly made it illegal to deny any Kansan entry into a common school because of race.[54] The parallel to articles 13 and 135 of the 1868 Louisiana Constitution and the subsequent statutes is clear and striking. Kansas followed Louisiana, chronologically at least, on issues of civil rights. If litigation and practices in other states are a guide, then under such a law districts could still maintain one or more "colored" schools.[55] This issue was apparently not litigated in Kansas. What they could not do was to exclude a black student who met the age, achievement, and neighborhood qualifications from any white school, nor could they force students into segregated schools by maintaining different, overlapping attendance zones for children of each race. This was, in effect, the practical definition of de jure school segregation in the nineteenth century, and it underlines the connection between nonexclusion and integration— a connection that has sometimes confused historians.[56]

When it codified the school laws in 1876, the legislature deleted all authority to operate segregated schools in Kansas cities. Far from an "error . . . of oversight," as one historian alleged, or an event that occurred "for reasons that are not stated," as the lawyer who represented the state in *Brown* v. *Board of Education* before the U.S. Supreme Court concluded, the 1876 codification merely reaffirmed the doctrine in the state's 1874 civil rights law.[57] In fact, the Senate Education Committee's draft of S.B. 202 had explicitly allowed segregation, but the Republicans on the floor, chastised by Samuel N. Wood, a reformer who supported every cause from abolition, through black and female suffrage, to the Greenback and Populist parties, amended the bill to omit all authorization of segregation.[58] The small minority of Democrats in the legislature race-baited in classic fashion a representative from Coffeyville declaiming, for instance, that he "would not insult nor misrepresent his intelligent and respectable constituents by voting such an outrageous proposition as to have 'niggers' and white children educated together. . . . He was glad that the [R]epublicans were going to put themselves on record in favor of 'nigger' equality. The white people were paying all the taxes and they should be permitted to say how their children should be educated."[59]

Three years later, the legislature reversed course again, authorizing racial separation in first-class cities in a bill passed near the two-month session's end. Why the still overwhelmingly Republican body took this action is unclear, but two suggestions may be offered. First, such bills were generally drafted by and sent to committees composed of the representatives of the cities involved, and the legislature usually followed their lead.[60] Second, legislative deference to local delegations was encouraged by the utter confusion that prevailed at the end of each fifty-day session. As a reporter for the *Topeka Commonwealth* noted, "It is almost impossible at the closing hours of the session to give a clear and succinct account of the proceedings. Bills pass in one house, are considered in the other, conference committees are appointed and so on. Hardly one of the members can tell you just the condition of a given bill."[61] During the last days of the 1889 session, the house resembled "a bear garden" (according to the correspondent of the *Leavenworth Times*), with twenty or more members simultaneously bellowing for recognition and shouting at each other.[62]

And as blacks learned when they tried to repeal the 1879 act two years later, bedlam could kill a bill as well as pass it. Very late in the 1881 session S.B. 238, which would have negated the 1879 law, passed the senate but was not considered in the house.[63] The same fate awaited them when in 1889 blacks launched a more thoroughgoing campaign, spearheaded by the state's first black legislator, Alfred Fairfax, and complete with a petition drive and an active lobbying effort.[64] In that year, several bills providing for integration in first-class cities were proposed and then abandoned in favor of an amendment to a more general education bill. That bill, however, was defeated at the last moment, apparently because of a disagreement not over integration but over tax rates.[65] From then until the mid-twentieth century, the best Kansas Afro-Americans could do was to block all attempts to expand segregation, except for a 1905 act allowing segregated high schools in Kansas City.[66]

The Interdependence of Nationally and State-Based Rights and the Failure of State Protection

Louisiana: Judicial Farces

Within two weeks of the ratification of the Radical state constitution, blacks filed the first New Orleans school integration case.[67] Alderman Blanc Joubert, whose given name announced the tone of his skin, entered his daughter Cecile in a private school for white girls at the Convent of the Sacred Heart in January 1868.[68] In February the school expelled her on grounds of "color." Retaining Alexander P. Field, a Kentucky-born white Unionist politician who had previously flirted with various factions of the Republican party and who became the state attorney general in 1873, Joubert charged that, as a publicly licensed corporation, Sacred Heart could not discriminate between patrons on the ground of race.[69] The defendants responded not by disputing the constitutional argument but by denying that the three-teacher school had any legal affiliation with the convent. Sixth district judge Guy Duplantier, a native white Republican who was later associated with Simeon Belden as counsel in Paul Trévigne's integration suit, accepted the teachers' contention and dismissed Joubert's suit, which was not appealed, presumably because their control of the new government gave people of color other means of attaining their goals.[70] With an administration friendly to integration, at least in New Orleans, there was no need for suits between 1870 and 1876.

Faced with widespread Democratic violence and intimidation in the last years of the Reconstruction regime, Louisiana Republicans sought the best deals they could get for themselves and their constituencies.[71] Most expected that the Grant and Hayes administrations (the latter seated with disputed Louisiana electoral votes) would preserve law and order. As that hope failed, some, such as former lieutenant governor P. B. S. Pinchback, who was the son of a white Mississippi planter and his former slave common-law wife and the principal framer of the state's civil rights laws, had little choice but to accept the Democrats' public assurances that they would abide by the postwar national constitutional amendments.[72] When it became clear that trusting in the vaunted honor of the southern upper class was futile, blacks turned to the courts, only to see the same honorable men brazenly disregard laws they initially feared to repeal and then, when northern pressure receded further, renege on even separate but equal.[73]

The first of the post-Reconstruction Louisiana cases was filed by Paul Trévigne, teacher, editor, and bilingual poet, who served on the Orleans Parish school board from 1876 until the Redeemers replaced almost all the Republicans with White Leaguers in 1877.[74] In September of that year, Trévigne, through his lawyers Belden and Duplantier, sought in the state district court to enjoin the parish school board from putting its July segregation resolution and the accompanying

enabling regulations into effect when the schools opened, thereby barring Trévigne's son, also called Paul, from the common school that he
had previously attended.[75] Belden and Duplantier claimed that segregation doubly violated Trévigne's privileges or immunities under
the Fourteenth Amendment—as a citizen of the United States and of
the state.[76] As a national citizen, Trévigne had a fundamental right
to be free of discrimination in public services on account of race. As
a citizen of Louisiana, he was guaranteed by article 2 of the 1868
state constitution enjoyment of "the same civil, political, and public
rights" as any other Louisianian, and by article 135, access to public
schools without racial distinction.[77] Egalitarian provisions of the state
constitution, then, strengthened as well as complemented the federal
guarantee, Trévigne's counsel asserted, and the two were intrinsically
intertwined.[78] The injury that gave Trévigne standing to sue, furthermore, expressed at the same time the fundamental national and state
right that had been infringed: segregation by law, in the words of his
petition, "tends to and does degrade . . . petitioner and his son Paul
Trévigne and the entire colored population of this city.[79] . . . However
meritorious they may be, a distinction thus made detracts from their
status as citizens and consigns them to the contempt of their fellow
men and citizens of this community and elsewhere."[80]

    With state constitutional provisions so clearly against them, city
attorney Benjamin F. Jonas[81] and volunteer counsel Edgar H. Farrar[82]
quibbled over questions of remedy and standing.[83] The segregation
resolution had already passed, so how could it be enjoined? But since
it had not yet been put into effect, Trévigne had suffered no real but
only a prospective injury.[84] Further, even if Trévigne had been injured,
others might approve segregation, and enjoining it might trample on
their rights. What gave Trévigne the right to speak for all people of
color? As for the national and state constitutions, Jonas and Farrar
paid them no more attention than their fellow White Leaguer, Sixth
District Judge Nicholas H. Rightor, did to Belden and Duplantier's
precise and detailed answer to the board lawyers' pettifoggery.[85]

    Trévigne, Judge Rightor ruled, "cannot assume either the tasks
or the prerogatives of a public functionary nor constitute himself the
champion of any right but his own." Even if the remedy the former
school board member requested were applied to the subdistrict in
which he resided, his petition would fail, for it did not specify that
subdistrict. If the law was as clear as Belden and Duplantier claimed,

should the court presume that administrators would defy it by denying young Trévigne access to his neighborhood school? Adding insult to disingenuousness, Rightor closed his opinion with a rhetorical
flourish: "Courts have a sufficiently difficult task in the effort to redress 'real and actual' rights, without multiplying their duties in the
rectification of prospective injuries which may never be suffered and
the vindication of future rights which may never be born." [86]

Trévigne appealed to the state supreme court, which delayed the
case and finally issued an opinion, which it did not deign to publish,
on January 20, 1879.[87] Justice Alcibiades DeBlanc's opinion was brief
and cynical.[88] Judge Rightor said Trévigne had come to court too early,
before his son had been excluded. DeBlanc said he came too late. Since
segregation was now an accomplished fact, a mandamus directing the
board to admit the boy, not an injunction restraining it from refusing
to admit him, was the proper remedy, and Belden and Duplantier had
not asked for a mandamus. Like Rightor, DeBlanc ignored the fact,
strongly pressed by Trévigne's lawyers, that the wrong continued,
just as he paid no attention to the increasing merger of notions of injunction and mandamus in nineteenth-century law.[89] No doubt as a
prophylactic against such frivolous lawsuits, he assessed costs to the
plaintiff.

Three weeks after Judge Rightor's decision in *Trévigne,* but before
the appeal to the state supreme court was entered, Belden filed two
more state cases in the Sixth District court, one of which, *Harper* v.
Wickes, was subsequently dropped for unstated reasons.[90] When Judge
Rightor dismissed the other case, *Ursin Dellande* v. *George H. Gordon,*
on the grounds that Gordon, then a school principal, was a functionary who was merely acting on the orders of the school board,
Belden sued the school board in Dellande's name.[91] In his briefs at
the local and state supreme court levels, Belden referred to the same
provisions of the 1868 Louisiana Constitution as he had in *Trévigne,*
but this time he invoked the Fourteenth Amendment generally, rather
than singling out the privileges or immunities clause. The Fourteenth
Amendment made all people "equal before the law," which, Belden
claimed, meant the same thing as did article 135, the explicit school
integration provision of the 1868 state constitution. Citing two Louisiana and one U.S. Supreme Court public accommodations cases that
had ruled separate but equal unlawful, Belden again grounded his
case on the confluence of state and federal constitutional provisions.[92]

In his May 20, 1878, district opinion, Judge Rightor wrote as if an 1877 Democratic law had not merely repealed the Radical 1869 school integration statute but had blotted the earlier act out of memory—as, indeed, it was no doubt meant to do. Article 135 was not self-executing but "a mere general declaration addressed to the legislative department," unenforceable by the judiciary. Even the Radicals in the legislature, the impartial jurist announced, had failed to implement an integrationist policy "which upsets the whole order of society, tramples upon the usages of centuries and contains the germ of social war . . . so much do men shrink in action from what their madness may proclaim in theory."[93] Rather than respond directly to this revisionism in his appellate brief, perhaps because it would have forced him to admit that the 1869 law had been overturned, Belden rested his case on natural rights constitutional theory: "No enabling act is ever necessary to carry into effect a constitutional declaration of a personal right or liberty. It [the declaration] is simply the enunciation of a pre-existing right and carries the force of recognition in the declaration made."[94]

The Louisiana Supreme Court delayed justice in order to deny it. Although Rightor made his decision in May 1878, the supreme court waited three years to issue its judgment, which it reported in a mere one-sentence summary.[95] In the meantime, the 1879 Redeemer state constitutional convention expunged articles 2, 13, and 135 from the constitution, leaving the rights of blacks to the mercies of Democratic legislators and administrators.[96] Justice Felix Poché might have stopped after recognizing that the articles' repeal mooted the state-based part of the case. (He ignored the Fourteenth Amendment entirely.) But the justice, a plantation-born Louisianian, whose college oration was a panegyric of John C. Calhoun, and a Democratic activist who had been a key member of the education committee at the 1879 constitutional convention, went on to deny that the now moribund article 135 had been meant to prohibit segregation.[97] The Radicals, according to Poché, had not even clearly intended to establish separate but equal but only to ban "public schools for the *exclusive* benefit of any race," which would "*entirely* deprive other races of school facilities or privileges."[98] The court did not print its egregiously unhistorical opinion, perhaps to discourage an appeal, perhaps out of a momentary sense of shame.

In an earlier editorial, the *New Orleans Daily Picayune* condemned

the Republicans who had recently been unseated from the state supreme court. "Many of these [Republicans'] decisions bear evidences
of a strong political bias, and of the influence of the partisan and sectional prejudices and passions of the times. The present [Democratic]
tribunal is composed of men who have too exalted an idea of the
responsibility and dignity of their position to yield to any such influence, or to be swerved from the straight path of jurisprudential truth,
logic and authority by any political considerations or sentiments. It is
a great blessing to our people to have this confidence in the purity of
this tribunal of last resort to receive from so pure a source, the true
doctrines and interpretations of their legal rights and duties."[99]

Shortly after *Dellande* was initially filed in 1878 (before the 1879
Redeemer state constitutional convention), New Orleans blacks prosecuted a fourth antisegregation case, this time in the federal district
court of William B. Woods.[100] Through his skillful lawyer John Ray,[101]
Arnold Bertonneau charged that by excluding his sons John and Henry
from the school nearest his residence, the board of education had
denied them nationally guaranteed privileges or immunities, as well
as the equal protection of the laws.[102] Like Belden, Ray based his case
not only on the Fourteenth Amendment but on article 135 of the 1868
state constitution.[103] Article 135 gave Bertonneau the right as a state
citizen to a nonsegregated education. To deny that right was an abro-
gation of his Fourteenth Amendment right to the equal protection of
state laws, even if integration were not guaranteed by the Fourteenth
Amendment per se (which Ray did not admit). For the "degradation
placed on" Bertonneau and his family by the act of segregation, Ray
asked $10,000 damages and an order requiring school officials to admit
Bertonneau's sons to their neighborhood school.[104]

Jonas and Farrar, who again represented the school board, ignored Ray's elaborate statements on the federal laws and the state and
national constitutions and denied that the court ever had jurisdiction
over any controversy between a state and a citizen of the same state.[105]
Under this constitutional theory, the state could prohibit black education entirely, reinstitute the post–Civil War black codes that had so
inflamed northern public opinion, or even reestablish slavery. True,
article 3 of the 1868 state constitution prohibited slavery, and other
provisions guaranteed education for all children and sought to prohibit legal discrimination by race. But if the state courts refused to
vindicate a black's equally clear right to be admitted into a common

school under section 135 and federal courts were powerless to intervene, what legal remedy would a slave have unless, like Dred Scott,
he happened to be owned by a resident of another state?[106] Perhaps
like Judge Rightor and Justice DeBlanc, Jonas and Farrar wished to
revise history—in their case, to deny that the Civil War took place.

Judge Woods did not go quite that far.[107] A "doughface" Democrat
(a "northern man with southern principles") in Ohio before the Civil
War, Woods as Speaker of the Ohio House had continued to lambaste
the Lincoln administration and oppose all efforts to prepare for war
until the day Fort Sumter was fired upon. He then became a patriot
and a soldier, being breveted to the rank of major general before his
decommissioning. Though a nominal Republican when he settled in
Alabama after the Civil War, he was always sufficiently conciliatory
to white southerners to avoid being treated as a stereotypical carpetbagger, and when he was nominated for the U.S. Supreme Court in
1880, there was an outpouring of support from southern bar association meetings. His three-page opinion in *Bertonneau*, the first printed
opinion by a federal district judge on the constitutionality of segregated schools, was undoubtedly a major reason for the support that
white southerners gave him.[108]

Without giving any consideration whatsoever to the argument
that excluding a person from a public school because of race degraded
him and denied him the "equal benefit" of the laws, guaranteed in
the national 1866 Civil Rights Act, Woods merely asserted that under
segregation "both races are treated precisely alike. White children and
colored children are compelled to attend different schools. That is all.
The state, while conceding equal privileges and advantages to both
races, has the right to manage its schools in the manner which, in
its judgment, will best promote the interest of all."[109] Ignoring cases
from Michigan and Iowa that had ruled segregation unlawful, Woods
lifted one phrase from a prosegregation case from his native Ohio
and another from U.S. Supreme Court Justice Nathan Clifford's one-
man attempt to revivify the doughface tradition in *Hall* v. *DeCuir*.[110]
"Any classification which preserves *substantially equal* school advantages," Judge Woods disingenuously asserted, "does not impair any
rights and is not prohibited by the constitution of the United States.
Equality of rights does not necessarily imply identity of rights."[111] Moreover, if segregation did no damage to any federal right, that was the
end of the inquiry. Even if article 135 gave blacks rights to nonexclu-

sion as Louisianians, the federal court lacked "authority to inquire into every violation of a state law or state constitution by officers of the state." [112] This striking extension of Justice Samuel Miller's view in *Slaughter-House* that the privileges or immunities clause protected only the rights Americans held as national citizens lacked even Miller's crucial linguistic evidence in its favor, for the equal protection clause applied to all "persons," not just to "citizens of the United States." [113]

In its triumphant editorial commending Woods's rebuff to what it called "political and social theorizers," the *New Orleans Daily Picayune* lamented that Woods had not gone further and ruled that the Fourteenth Amendment could not "be invoked to set aside any regulations of the subject of education that the State may choose to make." [114] Even so, Woods's blank check gave Democrats the ability to slash expenditures for the education of blacks and poor whites with no fear of effective judicial intervention. In 1900, Louisiana had the highest rate of black illiteracy among adult males in the South, as well as the second highest rate for whites. [115]

Bertonneau filed a bond for an appeal to the U.S. Supreme Court —he was the second black plaintiff in a school segregation case to do so—but the appeal was abandoned for unstated reasons. [116]

Kansas—Of Floors and Ceilings

In Louisiana, the contrasts between pro- and anti-integration forces were clear and stark, the stakes high, and the constitutional issues broadly drawn. In Kansas, divisions were blurred, struggles often inconclusive, and legal questions narrow. At the mouth of the Mississippi, statutory guarantees proved worthless when administered by unfriendly hands. Along the same river system, but further north, blacks could usually invoke the state civil rights law successfully but could not extend it to the larger cities, and they often had to go to court to obtain their rights. In consequence, there were at least fourteen court cases on school integration in Kansas from 1880 to 1910 (see Table 2), and though the blacks won at least eight of them, the legal doctrines enunciated did not expand on *Tinnon.*

During the 1870s, the black proportion of the population in Topeka rose to 31 percent, which exceeded that of Orleans Parish, Louisiana (27 percent). [117] Most of the black immigrants probably came from the South (one section of Topeka became known as Tennesseetown)

Table 2. *Currently Known Kansas School Integration Cases, 1880–1910*

Plaintiff	Defendant school board	Date	Level*	Outcome†	Reported
Eveline Phillips	Topeka	1880	L	?	N
Leslie Tinnon	Ottawa	1881	L	B	N
			S	B	Y
Columbus Daniel	South Topeka	1886	L	W	Y
Daisy James	Tonganoxie	1889	L	B	N
Georgianna Reeves	Fort Scott	1888	L	W	N
Buford Crawford	Fort Scott	1889	S	W	N
Luella Johnson	Olathe	1890	L	B	N
Jordan Knox	Independence	1891	S	B	Y
George Jones	Oskaloosa	1901	S	W	Y
William Reynolds	Topeka	1903	S	W	Y
Bud Cartwright	Coffeville	1906	S	B	Y
Mamie Richardson	Kansas City	1906	S	W	Y
Sallie Rowles	Wichita	1907	S	B	Y
D. A. Williams	Parsons	1908	S	B	Y

*L = local court; S = state supreme court.
†? = unknown; B = black victory; W = school board victory.

during the black "exodus" late in the decade. Almost immediately after arriving from the South, where schools, if available at all to blacks, were usually very poor and, outside Louisiana, always strictly segregated, Topeka blacks began political and legal actions to bring about integration. There may have been a test case as early as 1878, and the 1880 *Phillips* suit illustrates both the porous quality of segregation in Kansas and the sort of incident that typically set off northern school integration cases.[118]

At the opening of school in October 1880, Eveline and Lilly Phillips were refused admission to the mostly white Clay Street school, which they had attended during the preceding year, and sent instead to an all-black school much farther from their house—a school named, ironically, for the deceased national leader of the school integration struggle, Charles Sumner. After personally appealing to the teacher, the superintendent of schools, and various board members, their father, James Phillips, sued, charging a violation of the state civil rights law. Conceding that Topeka had recently attained the population requisite to qualify as a first-class city, which would allow it, under the 1879 statute, to maintain segregated schools, Phillips's counsel pointed out that the mayor had not yet completed the requirements to bring the city under the shelter of the first-class city law.[119] While the litigation was continued, apparently because both sides expected the 1881 legislature to repeal the 1879 law allowing segregation in first-class cities, some blacks seem to have boycotted Sumner school.[120] The suit was later dismissed on what one historian calls a "technicality."[121]

Had it reached the state supreme court, *Phillips* might have set a useful precedent for integrationists because the judges would presumably have had to face the question of whether the Fourteenth Amendment prohibited segregation, and Valentine's opinion in *Tinnon* seemed to promise a majority for an affirmative answer. At least one contemporary legal observer even believed that the U.S. Supreme Court would decide the question that way, and, indeed, there is little in the language and specific findings in *Slaughter-House, Strauder* v. *West Virginia,* and the *Civil Rights Cases* to indicate otherwise.[122]

However powerfully and clearly stated an appellate court opinion, there is, in the American system, little besides fear of embarrassment to force lower or appellate court judges to follow precedents. South Topeka, a second-class city in the mid-1880s, had no attendance zones but assigned all black students to one school and all whites to another. Each school served the same grades, allegedly had the same seating capacity and equally competent teachers, and was approximately equally convenient to the homes of plaintiffs Columbus Daniel and Violet Jordan in *Daniel* v. *South Topeka.* But when on September 20, 1886, Daniel and Jordan attempted to register at the white Walnut Grove school, they were told that the room in which grades three through six were taught was full, fifty-seven white students having enrolled, and that they should go to the black Quincy Street school, which had only twenty-five students in the room for these grades.[123]

Despite an extensive argument by future congressman, senator, and vice-president Charles Curtis[124] applying the clearly governing *Tinnon* precedent to the case, district court judge John Guthrie,[125] recognizing that the law was against him, decided the case on "the facts." The white teacher could not effectively minister to more than fifty-seven students in four grades—how the judge knew that fifty-seven and not fifty-nine was the tipping point, he did not say. To force the school board to transfer some whites to Quincy Street to allow Daniel to attend Walnut Grove, moreover, would mean that "the colored boy would have advantages that would be denied to the white boy." How racial assignment in a second-class city could be legal under *Tinnon* or the 1874 Kansas civil rights bill, Guthrie did not bother to explain.[126]

Twenty-five miles northeast and some years later, blacks in the hamlet of Oskaloosa tried to enter the high school, which, under Kansas law, they had a right to attend. Yet the Kansas Supreme Court, in a one-paragraph *per curiam* decision, brushed aside their contention, ruling that the racially separate schools were equal even though whites, but not blacks, could continue past the ninth grade.[127] And without so much as a printed word, the state's highest court dismissed a case challenging segregation in the second-class city of Fort Scott.[128] Local blacks were so angry at the Republican-dominated Fort Scott administration's maintenance of school segregation that they temporarily and successfully coalesced with Democrats to expel the GOP officeholders. Even though a black minister, C. C. Goins, became president of the school board, integration of the schools did not take place.[129]

Yet in two other small towns in eastern Kansas, Toganoxie and Olathe, Republican[130] and Democratic[131] district court judges, relying only on *Tinnon*, ordered the schools integrated in cases in which the facts were very similar to those in *Daniel*.[132] And in a case from Independence, Kansas Supreme Court justice Albert H. Horton curtly ruled that blacks could not be excluded from the only school in the ward in which they lived. *Tinnon*, he held, was determinative.[133] The only novelty in the *Independence* case was that it was the first school integration case at the state supreme court level in which all the plaintiffs' attorneys were black. One of the lawyers, William A. Price, had been born a slave, and the other, younger man, Albert M. Thomas, had been one of the first black graduates of the University of Michigan Law School.[134] The state supreme court ruled similarly in a 1906 case from Coffeyville[135] and a 1907 case from Wichita,[136] and in a 1908 Parsons case, it went further in examining the facts, declaring that integration was a fitting remedy for extreme inequalities even in first-class cities.[137]

Having avoided the issue of whether school segregation was contrary to the Kansas Constitution and the Fourteenth Amendment in *Tinnon* in 1881, *Crawford* in 1889, and *Jones* in 1900, the Kansas Supreme Court finally faced it in 1903.[138] Lowman Hill, then on Topeka's outskirts, had had racially mixed elementary schools and continued to do so after being annexed to the city. In 1900, however, the school accidentally burned down, but before a new brick school opened in 1902 at a less swampy location than the old one, white patrons petitioned the school board to segregate schools in the area. The board secretly agreed, left nearly half the rooms in the brick building unfinished, and dragged to the old site an abandoned frame school building from central Topeka.[139] Unaccustomed segregation and resentment at the contrast between the up-to-date white building on the hill and the secondhand one for blacks down in the hollow touched off a black protest, a boycott (100 percent successful for four months) and, when the Republican-dominated board refused any compromise, a suit.[140]

The participants in the suit were particularly notable. Tennessee-born William Reynolds was a young tailor and political activist who had been a captain in the Spanish-American War during the 1890s.[141] His chief lawyer was one of the town characters, Gaspar Christopher Clemens, born poor in Xenia, Ohio, orphaned and left to fend for himself at age thirteen, open agnostic, public defender of the Haymarket anarchists, leading adviser to Populist governor L. D. Lewelling, and later Socialist gubernatorial candidate himself, a prolific newspaper controversialist, pamphleteer, and legal treatise writer.[142] The lead opposing counsel was James Wilson Gleed, Vermont-born grandson of a pioneer abolitionist minister, scion of a family wealthy enough to provide him with a European tour, railroad lawyer, ten-year school board veteran, president of the state temperance alliance, and legal defender (against Clemens) of compulsory prayer and Bible reading in the schools.[143] Clemens, who claimed to be a cousin of Mark Twain, loved to taunt people whom he considered pharisaical hypocrites, and he no doubt relished the chance to spar with Gleed.[144]

Clemens charged that segregation violated the Thirteenth as well as the Fourteenth Amendment because it placed on blacks "the badge of a servile race, and holds them up to public gaze as unfit to associate, even in a public institution of the State, with other races and nationalities."[145] He also cited the 1859 state constitution's "equal protection and benefit" and "uniform system of common schools" clauses,[146] as well as making technical arguments about what laws, in the confusing welter of Kansas statues, were legally in force.[147]

The Kansas electorate in 1900 expanded the state supreme court from three to seven members and gave Republican governor William E. Stanley the right to nominate the four new ones.[148] Valentine,

Horton, and Brewer were now gone, and into their places and the new seats moved men almost all of whom were too young to have participated in the abolition movement, the Civil War, or even Reconstruction. The average justice in *Reynolds* was born in 1853, the year before the passage of the Kansas-Nebraska Act, and at the time of the passage of the Kansas Civil Rights Act in 1874, he had barely reached manhood.[149] For many in the earlier generation, the Republican party was "the party of great moral ideals" forged in the struggle against slavery, secession, and racism. For most in the *Reynolds* era, it was the convenient choice of aspiring railroad lawyers, the haven of the satisfied bourgeois, the party, to use a phrase common in the state of the time, of "stand pat."

Justice Rosseau Burch did not distinguish between the state and national equal protection clauses or a similar guarantee in the 1780 Massachusetts Constitution, and he seemed to view the "uniformity" and "common schools" clauses as more specific applications of the concept of equality to schools.[150] The uniformity and common schools phrases of the 1851 Indiana Constitution, on which the 1859 Kansas constitution makers no doubt drew, had been construed by the supreme court in Burch's home state as allowing segregation.[151] Uniformity, Burch held, did not prevent school boards from establishing different types of schools in city and rural areas or in different subdistricts, and they could make any classification of scholars that they judged best.[152] Whereas Justice Valentine in *Tinnon* had scornfully dismissed the defendant's reliance on the 1850 Massachusetts case of *Roberts v. Boston* as a "very old" decision that was "rendered before the war," Burch padded his pages with quotations from its segregationist dogma.[153] State supreme court decisions from Ohio, New York, and California ruling school segregation in accord with the Fourteenth Amendment largely disposed of that question,[154] Burch averred, and if this were not enough, he invented a novel reading of the argument from silence: the fact that no school segregation case had ever reached the U.S. Supreme Court proved "a remarkable consensus of opinion on the part of the bar of the country as to the result of such an appeal."[155] Moreover, U.S. Supreme Court Justice Brown's decision in *Plessy*, in an aside, had cited the same state cases as Burch had upholding the validity of school segregation.[156] The patent inequality of the school facilities Burch dismissed as a mere "incidental matter," and the Thirteenth Amendment argument, he entirely ignored.[157] There was, as usual in the Kansas Supreme Court, no dissent.[158]

Implications for Contemporary Tactics in the Protection of Constitutional Rights

It was a long way, figuratively speaking, from Ottawa to Topeka, and an even longer and bloodier one from John Howard's optimistic, egalitarian argument in *Isabelle* to Judge Felix Poché's desecration of the moribund 1868 Louisiana Constitution's integration clause, but both journeys reaffirm the old aphorism that constitutions are what the judges say they are. The protections offered by laws and the state and federal constitutions were not useless. Blacks did win nearly half the cases sketched in this essay, and in other instances, they no doubt used the laws and decisions as levers to wedge the school door open or at least to obtain physical and other improvements in racially isolated schools. In Kansas, the state supreme court might well have ruled all school segregation unconstitutional, and legislators did outlaw it from 1874 to 1879 and only barely failed in another repeal attempt in 1889. After 1874, Kansas blacks outside the larger cities never lost the nominal right to attend racially mixed schools. The political careers of judges, legislators, and lawyers who fought for equal rights did not suffer, as might be expected if white racism had been omnipresent. But in the end in both states, blacks lost out because a new set of racist judges took office and emasculated constitutional guarantees.

To assess the adequacy of judicial protection of rights at the state level, it is obviously necessary to go beyond printed cases. Only half of the twenty cases treated here appear in casebooks, and the briefs, which especially in Louisiana contain much more theoretically interesting arguments than the judges' opinions, must be ferreted out in archives. Furthermore, the judge-centered constitutional history that still dominates the field should be broadened to include pressure groups, legislators, and those who bring and argue cases. Although judges are by no means the passive seers of convenient myth, they and the framers are not the only relevant shapers of the Constitution, either. It is those nonjudicial figures who struggled for constitutional rights—and mostly lost—who impress me most in the dramas from these two states, and it is they, not those who passed upon and denied their pleas, whose memory deserves to last: Belden, Bertonneau, Isabelle, Ray, and Trévigne of Louisiana; Clemens, Curtis, Daniel, Reynolds, and Tinnon of Kansas.

In the briefs and opinions in these cases, state and national laws and constitutional provisions were intermixed not simply because nineteenth-century jurisprudents were confused or imprecise, but because the motives of those who passed the enactments and the basic issues involved really were the same, regardless of distinctions of form. Proponents of equality might appeal to state law, as in *Knox;* to natural law, as in *Isabelle* and *Tinnon;* to the state constitution, as in *Trévigne;* to a combination of the state and national constitutions, as in *Bertonneau;* or to all of these, as in *Reynolds.* But, to paraphrase Judge Woods, there was no "substantial" distinction between the contentions, whatever their formal bases.

More recent claims of "separate state grounds" are not only often patently disingenuous, they are potentially destructive of constitutional rights. In his most recent pronouncement on the subject—ironically in lectures named for James Madison, who more than anyone else understood how size and diversity protect civil rights—Justice William J. Brennan, Jr., repeatedly promised his audience that "federal preservation of civil liberties is a minimum, which the states may surpass." [159] Nineteenth-century school segregation cases suggest that this view is both too optimistic and too simple. It is too optimistic because state judicial interpretations of laws, constitutions, and written understandings do not stand apart but help to shape the ultimate readings of national rights by the Supreme Court. State and lower federal court judges and state legislators as well can raise the ceiling or undermine the floor of those rights. It is too simple because, as John Ray and Simeon Belden understood, all the guarantees—of natural law, national and state laws, and national and state constitutions—form part of the same structure. To rest the foundation of rights on state laws or constitutions alone is to hazard a collapse of the whole building later. It is better, as the experiences of nineteenth-century Louisiana and Kansas show, for judges to declare openly and honestly that their opinions rest on their fundamental views of liberty, equality, and reasonableness drawn from their study not only of the constitutions of their state governments but also of the national government and of moral philosophy and their own practical experience in policy making. That was what Justice Daniel Valentine actually *did* in *Tinnon,* and if he had just said so openly, we might not have had to wait seventy-three more years for *Brown.*

Notes

I thank Bob Cottrol, Bob Dykstra, and Doug Flamming for helpful comments on an earlier draft of this essay.

1. *Louisiana ex rel. Isabelle* v. *Board of Public School Directors of Orleans Parish* was not reported in any official document. The sketchy case records, hereafter referred to as Isabelle Case File (Case No. 153, 8th D. Ct., Orleans Parish, 1870), are in the Orleans Parish Public Library. The opinion of the court, some background information, and editorial responses are in *New Orleans Daily Picayune,* November 22, 1870, pp. 2, 4; November 24, 1870, pp. 1, 4; *New Orleans Times,* May 1, 1870, p. 4; August 20, 1870, p. 4; November 22, 1870, p. 5; November 23, 1870, p. 4; *New Orleans Republican,* November 22, 1870, p. 5. I discovered this case while perusing the *San Francisco Elevator,* March 14, 1874, p. 2.
2. The relevant sentences of article 135 stated: "All children of this state between the ages of six and twenty-one shall be admitted to the public schools or other institutions of learning sustained or established by the State in common, without distinction of race, color, or previous condition. There shall be no separate schools or institutions of learning established exclusively for any race by the State of Louisiana." *The Federal and State Constitutions, Colonial Charters, and Other Organic Laws of the States, Territories, and Colonies Now or Heretofore Forming the United States of America,* ed. Francis N. Thorpe (Washington, D.C.: U.S. Government Printing Office, 1909), 3:1465.
3. Act 121 of 1869, 81, La. Laws. On Isabelle's role in the 1869 and 1870 legislative sessions, see Charles Vincent, *Black Legislators in Louisiana during Reconstruction* (Baton Rouge: Louisiana State University Press, 1976), 89–97.
4. The background of this struggle may be followed in Roger Fischer, *The Segregation Struggle in Louisiana* (Urbana: University of Illinois Press, 1974), 113–14. See also the classic article by Louis R. Harlan, "Desegregation in New Orleans Public Schools during Reconstruction," *American Historical Review* 67 (1962): 663–75.
5. Act 6 of 1870, 12–29, La. Laws. In the usual calm, measured phrases of Louisiana Democrats of the era, the *New Orleans Times,* November 23, 1870, p. 4, denounced Conway as "that malignant, ignorant and vulgar

demagogue and insatiate enemy of this people" whose only purpose was "with diabolical activity, to kindle bitter hostilities between the white and colored people." It denounced the legislature as "that body of unparalleled ignorance, dishonesty and corruption." Blacks, the paper felt sure, preferred segregation, but Conway and "a few pestulent [sic] white demagogues" forced integration on them.

6. The house voted 44 to 11 to require integrated schools in New Orleans. This explicit amendment was later shelved and the matter disposed of in a general education bill, but the action clearly indicates the legislature's intent. See *New Orleans Daily Republican,* February 12, 1869, p. 3.

7. During the debate over the integrated schools provision of the U.S. Civil Rights Bill in 1874, Conway claimed in a public letter that school integration had worked in New Orleans and asserted, in a touchingly idealistic statement that echoes many similar remarks of the 1950s, "All that is wanted in this matter of civil rights is to let the foes of the measure simply understand that we mean it." *Washington* (D.C.) *New National Era,* June 4, 1874, p. 2.

8. Isabelle Case File.

9. A convenient introduction to the vast historiography of the Fourteenth Amendment is Eric Foner, *Reconstruction: America's Unfinished Revolution, 1863–1877* (New York: Harper & Row, 1988), 251–61.

10. Born in Indiana in 1844 of an old but not particularly prosperous New England family, Dibble enlisted in the Civil War in 1862 and lost a leg in the battle of Port Hudson. During his recuperation in Louisiana, he read law and was admitted to the bar before he was twenty-one. By the age of twenty-three, he was the de facto head of the Republican organization in New Orleans. President of the school board for all six integrationist years, he was twice nominated for Congress but was defeated by Democrats. He was acting state attorney general in 1875. In 1881, he moved to Arizona, where he became the law partner of former Nevada Supreme Court Judge James F. Lewis, who had sat in the school integration case of *State ex rel. Stoutmeyer* v. *Duffy,* 7 Nev. 342 (1872). In 1883, Dibble moved to San Francisco, where he was still residing in 1905. Very successful there, he served for several terms in the California legislature as a Republican. He was an excellent orator and also published at least one romantic western novel. See Leigh H. Irvine, *A History of the New California* (New York: Lewis, 1905), 2:718–20; Dale Somers, "Black and White in New Orleans: A Study in Urban Race Relations, 1865–1900," *Journal of Southern History* 40 (1974): 27; *New Orleans Republican,* December 19, 1874, p. 2.

11. Born in Ohio in 1830 of New York forebears, Valentine moved to

Kansas in 1859 and lived in Ottawa from 1860 to 1875. Son of a rest-
less farmer, Valentine had only a common school education. A staunch
Republican, he served in the state house, 1862; the senate, 1863; on
the district court bench, 1865–69; and the supreme court, 1869–93.
Henry Inman, "The Supreme Court of Kansas," *Green Bag* 4 (1892): 338;
Howard D. Berrett, *Who's Who in Topeka* (Topeka: Adams Bros., 1905),
124; Anonymous, "Current Topics," *Kansas Law Journal* 3 (1886): 353.
The other member of the majority in *Tinnon*, Chief Justice Albert H.
Horton, was born in Brookfield, New York, in 1837, and came to Atchison, Kansas, in 1859. Like Valentine, he sat in both houses of the legislature and on the district bench before being appointed to the high
court in 1877. Son of a physician, he attended the University of Michigan. Horton was much more deeply involved in partisan politics than
Valentine was, editing a newspaper during the Civil War, serving as a
presidential elector for Grant in 1868, becoming federal district attorney
from 1869 to 1873, and almost being elected to the U.S. Senate in 1885.
Inman, "Supreme Court of Kansas," *Green Bag* 4 (1892): 333–35; *Topeka
Daily Capital*, September 3, 1902, pp. 1–2; September 4, 1902, p. 4.

12. *Tinnon*, 26 Kan. 1 (1881).

13. Herbert Hovenkamp, "Social Science and Segregation before Brown,"
    Duke Law Journal (1985): 641–42. Similarly, in *Government by Judiciary:
    The Transformation of the Fourteenth Amendment* (Cambridge, Mass.: Har-
    vard University Press, 1977), 10, Raoul Berger states: "The key to an
    understanding of the Fourteenth Amendment is that the North was
    shot through with Negrophobia, that the Republicans, except for a
    minority of extremists, were swayed by the racism that gripped their
    constituents rather than by abolitionist ideology."

14. That Radical Republicans, white and black, northern and southern,
    shared a common ideology is suggested by the parallel sentiments
    of Robert H. Isabelle in the Louisiana legislature in 1870: "I want to
    see the children of the state educated together. I want to see them
    play together; to be amalgamated (laughter). I want to see them play
    together, to study together and when they grow up to be men they
    will love each other, and be ready, if any force comes against the flag of
    the United States, to take up arms and defend it together." Quoted in
    John W. Blassingame, *Black New Orleans, 1860–1880* (Chicago: Univer-
    sity of Chicago Press, 1973), 112.

15. *Tinnon*, 26 Kan. 1, 18–19, 21–23.

16. Id. at 18–19, 21–23.

17. *Roberts* v. *Boston*, 5 Cush. 198 (1849); *Plessy* v. *Ferguson*, 163 U.S. 537
    (1896). On these and other cases on segregation in the nineteenth
    century see J. Morgan Kousser, *Dead End: The Development of Nineteenth-*

Century Litigation on Racial Discrimination in Schools (Fair Lawn, N.J.: Oxford University Press, 1986); Kousser, " 'The Supremacy of Equal Rights': The Struggle Against Racial Discrimination in Antebellum Massachusetts and the Foundations of the Fourteenth Amendment," *Northwestern University Law Review* 82 (1988): 941.

18. *Tinnon*, 26 Kan. 1, 24 (1881).

19. Id. The judges of the supreme court, of course, were elected by voters throughout the state. On Brewer, see Arnold Paul, "David J. Brewer," in *The Justices of the U.S. Supreme Court, 1789–1969: Their Lives and Major Opinions*, ed. Leon Friedman and Fred Israel (New York: Chelsea House, 1969), 2:1516. John Semonche, *Charting the Future—The Supreme Court Responds to a Changing Society, 1890–1920* (Westport, Conn.: Greenwood Press, 1978), 15, 21; Albert H. Horton, "Brewer, David Josiah," *Green Bag* 2 (1890): 1; Morton Keller, *Affairs of State: Public Life in Late Nineteenth Century America* (Cambridge, Mass.: Harvard University Press, 1977), 366; *Leavenworth Times*, August 22, 1865, p. 3; August 29, 1866, p. 2. Paul terms Brewer "an outspoken and doctrinaire conservative, who made little pretense of 'judicial self-restraint.' " *Tinnon* was the only one of 130 cases in 26 Kan. in which there was a dissent.

20. *Plessy* v. *Ferguson*, 163 U.S. at 537–52. On this finesse, see Kousser, *Dead End*, 26–27, 54.

21. Interestingly, a Radical Republican school board had voted to integrate the Ottawa schools in 1870, claiming that separate schools were too expensive and that black children made much quicker progress if integrated with white children. "There is little room now to doubt," a board committee wrote, "that by virtue of the [Thirteenth and Fourteenth] constitutional amendments, the laws of Kansas, and the decisions of the courts, the black man has equal rights with the white man in schools which he is taxed alike to support. . . . The cry of 'negro equality' is a bug-bear only calculated to frighten timorous aristocrats." Judge Stephens's judicial position was merely the party line of the Radicals. *Washington* (D.C.) *New National Era*, October 20, 1870, p. 1; March 2, 1871, p. 3.

22. *Slaughter-House Cases*, 83 U.S. (16 Wall.) 36 (1873); *Strauder* v. *West Virginia*, 100 U.S. 303 (1880); *Washington, Alexandria, and Georgetown R.R. Co.* v. *Brown*, 84 U.S. (17 Howard) 445 (1872). Stephens's opinion is in *Ottawa Daily Republican*, January 19, 1881, p. 2. Rejecting the disingenuous contention that the school board's action was racially neutral because whites were barred from black schools, as well as the reverse, Stephens read the discriminatory motive of the school board's action

on the face of its policy. "It is evident as to the purpose of the rule," he announced, without extended consideration.

23. William J. Brennan, Jr., "The Bill of Rights and the States: The Revival of State Constitutions as Guardians of Individual Rights," in *The Evolving Constitution: Essays on the Bill of Rights and the U.S. Supreme Court,* ed. Norman Dorsen (Middletown, Conn.: Wesleyan University Press, 1987), 254; see generally *Developments in State Constitutional Law,* ed. Bradley D. McGraw (St. Paul: West, 1983).

24. Perhaps this feeling reflects only my lack of training as a lawyer. If I were properly socialized, I might better appreciate, for instance, the profound differences between state and federal equal rights clauses, instead of seeing such distinctions as fundamentally trivial.

25. James Madison, *Federalist* No. 10 in Alexander Hamilton, James Madison, and John Jay, *The Federalist,* ed. Jacob E. Cooke (Middletown, Conn.: Wesleyan University Press, 1961), 56–65.

26. The foremost pessimists about race relations on the left are Joel Williamson, *The Crucible of Race* (New York: Oxford University Press, 1985); and Leon F. Litwack, *North of Slavery: The Negro in the Free States, 1790–1860* (Chicago: University of Chicago Press, 1961), and Litwack, *Been in the Storm So Long: The Emergence of Black Freedom in the South* (New York: Knopf, 1979). Sharing their pessimism and drawing on Litwack's scholarship, but deducing much less liberal policy conclusions, is Berger, *Government by Judiciary.* The classic expression of this viewpoint is Ulrich B. Phillips, "The Central Theme of Southern History," *American Historical Review* 34 (1928): 30–43. For a different opinion, and one much closer to my own, see Paul Finkelman, "Prelude to the Fourteenth Amendment: Black Legal Rights in the Antebellum North," *Rutgers Law Journal* 17 (1985–86): 415.

27. J. Willard Hurst, *Law and the Conditions of Freedom in the Nineteenth Century United States* (Madison: University of Wisconsin Press, 1960); Morton Horwitz, *The Transformation of American Law, 1790–1860* (Cambridge, Mass.: Harvard University Press, 1977). Although there are exceptions, scholarship in constitutional history continues to be predominantly "internalist," to borrow a phrase from the history of science.

28. Thus none of the numerous books and articles on Louisiana history during this period mentions the unpublished *Joubert* or *Dellande* cases or the Louisiana Supreme Court's opinion in *Trévigne,* and no one has treated the *Isabelle* or *Bertonneau* cases in any depth. Published discussions of the Kansas case are fragmentary at best, and Thomas C. Cox, *Blacks in Topeka, Kansas, 1865–1915: A Social History* (Princeton: Princeton University Press, 1982), 113, misses the date of the Reynolds case by

thirteen years. The lawyer who appeared for the state before the U.S. Supreme Court in *Brown* v. *Board of Education,* 347 U.S. 483 (1954), seriously misunderstood the succession of laws on school segregation in the 1860s and 1870s. See Paul E. Wilson, "Brown v. Board of Education Revisited," *University of Kansas Law Review* 12 (1963–64): 509–13.

29. When, as a member of the 1868 Louisiana legislature, John Ray, a "scalawag" who later represented Arnold Bertonneau in his attempt to prevent the segregation of the New Orleans schools, voted for a public accommodations statute, he was marked for death by the *New Orleans Daily Picayune*—no empty threat in a state where, according to *House Misc. Docs.,* 41st Cong., 2d sess., no. 154, pt. 1, pp. 161–62, more than one thousand Republicans, white as well as black, were assassinated during 1868 alone. "DOOM FOR THE TRAITOR," the widely circulated paper titled its editorial. Ray was "this degenerate white man . . . a great social criminal" because he had voted against "God's eternal decree of separation of the white and black races." *Picayune,* September 20, 1868, quoted in Frank J. Wetta, "The Louisiana Scalawags" (Ph.D. dissertation, Louisiana State University, 1977), 336–37.

T. H. Harris, the state superintendent of education in Louisiana from 1908 to 1940, asserted in his Orwellian history that school integration never took place in New Orleans. See Harris, *The Story of Public Education in Louisiana* (New Orleans: The author, 1924), 30–31. Similarly, the Democratic *New Orleans Times,* October 3, 1877, p. 4, misremembered recent events: "In the darkest hours of the Radical regime there never were mixed schools except in theory." Evidently an 1874 riot against such schools had been a chimera. On the riot, see *New Orleans Weekly Louisianian,* February 13, 1875, p. 1.

Two men who were involved on the other side of segregation cases, Robert H. Marr and Benjamin F. Jonas, who were among the leaders of the violent White League revolution against the legally constituted government of the state in 1874, were rewarded with places on the state supreme court and in the U.S. Senate, respectively, and receive celebratory treatment in older state histories. See, e.g., *Biographical and Historical Memoirs of Louisiana* (Chicago: Goodspeed Publishing Co., 1892), 201–2, hereafter referred to as *Biographical Memoirs.*

30. Fischer, *Segregation Struggle,* 13–14. Interestingly, the state legislature in 1854 allocated $2,000 to the school in which Trévigne taught. H. E. Sterkx, *The Free Negro in Antebellum Louisiana* (Rutherford, N.J.: Fairleigh Dickinson University Press, 1972), 269.

31. Peyton McCrary, *Abraham Lincoln and Reconstruction: The Louisiana Experiment* (Princeton: Princeton University Press, 1978), 264–65; Fischer, *Segregation Struggle,* 28–30.

32. Donald Everett, "Free Persons of Color in New Orleans, 1803–1865" (Ph.D. dissertation, Tulane University, 1952), 348–49; William F. Messner, "Black Education in Louisiana, 1863–1865," *Civil War History* 22 (1976): 54–55; *Debates in the Convention* (New Orleans: W. R. Fish, 1864), 476, 499–502, 547–48.
33. Fischer, *Segregation Struggle*, 25–26; *Debates in the Convention*, 575, 601; Messner, "Black Education," 54–55. Article 141 of the 1864 Constitution stated simply: "The legislature shall provide for the education of all children of the State, between the ages of six and eighteen years, by maintenance of free public schools by taxation or otherwise." *Federal and State Constitutions*, ed. Thorpe, 3: 1446.
34. Fischer, *Segregation Struggle*, 27.
35. Ibid., 43. Paul Trévigne and Arnold Bertonneau were among the editors of the *Tribune* and its predecessor, *L'Union*. In this case, as well as in many places in the North that had relatively sparse black populations, the struggle for an end to exclusion and an end to segregation largely coincided. The different pattern that Howard N. Rabinowitz, *Race Relations in the Urban South, 1865–1890* (New York: Oxford University Press, 1978), 331–32 and passim, found in five other southern cities was by no means universal.
36. On the struggle for the provision, see Fischer, *Segregation Struggle*, 43–52. Article 135, quoted above, note 2, was adopted by a vote of 61 to 12. This vote, in which Belden joined with Bertonneau and Isabelle, is given in *Official Journal of the Proceedings of the Louisiana Constitutional Convention of 1867–68* (New Orleans: J. B. Roudanez, 1868), 201. The same three men joined fifty-five others in adopting article 13, which banned segregation in public accommodations. There were only sixteen dissenters on this article. Ibid., 121–25. A Unionist during the war, Belden was Speaker of the state House of Representatives in 1864. A native of New Orleans, he taught in the black Straight University law school (from which Robert Isabelle graduated) during Reconstruction. Ted Tunnell, *Crucible of Reconstruction: War, Radicalism, and Race in Louisiana, 1862–1877* (Baton Rouge: Louisiana State University Press, 1984), 21, 27, 98, 115, has Belden being born in both Massachusetts and "the South" and for unstated reasons calls him a "conservative," but the 1880 census and Belden's obituary notice in the *New Orleans Daily Picayune*, December 4, 1906, put his birth in Louisiana. Other facts are from Blassingame, *Black New Orleans*, 127.
37. Act 121 of 1869, 81, La. Laws. Fischer, *Segregation Struggle*, 91–109, contains the best discussion of segregation outside New Orleans, finding evidence of scattered integration. See also *Washington* (D.C.) *New National Era*, June 11, 1874, p. 3. Earlier histories, in ministry of truth

fashion, denied that whites in the rural parishes had ever attended integrated schools. See Edwin Whitfield Fay, *The History of Education in Louisiana* (Washington, D.C.: U.S. Government Printing Office, 1898), 101.

38. See, e.g., Leon Odom Beasley, "A History of Education in Louisiana during the Reconstruction Period, 1862–1877" (Ph.D. dissertation, Louisiana State University, 1957), 90–91.

39. Act 23 of 1877, 28–39, La. Laws; Act 70 of 1882, 90–93, La. Laws; Act 81 of 1888, 91–109, La. Laws.

40. On the reasons for their actions, see Harris, *Story of Public Education*, 52; Fischer, *Segregation Struggle*, 144–45.

41. Act 23 of 1877, 28–39, La. Laws; Harris, *Story of Public Education*, 52.

42. *New Orleans Times*, July 4, 1877, pp. 1, 8; *New Orleans Picayune*, July 4, 1877, p. 8; *New Orleans Democrat*, September 27, 1877, p. 8. About three hundred people of (light) color reportedly entered "white" schools in New Orleans that fall, forcing officials to examine many pedigrees. By December, all but two of the schools had been segregated. In those two, authorities knew that some students were "colored," while others were "white," but were unable on the basis of appearance to tell members of one group from the other. Records of the Orleans Parish School Board, vol. 9 (1877–78), 186, unpublished, in offices of Orleans Parish School Board. This was not the first such difficulty at the Bayou Road school. In 1868, before the Radical constitution went into effect, twenty-eight "colored" girls who appeared white were admitted to the "white" school, unbeknownst to the teacher, a Mrs. Bigot. Fischer, *Segregation Struggle*, 111, 138–39; *Hartford* (Conn.) *Courant*, May 29, 1868, p. 3. Similarly, during the 1874 anti-integration riots, the white mob ejected as "colored" one female student whose father was a leading member of the White League. *New Orleans Weekly Louisianian*, February 13, 1875, p. 1.

43. Eugene H. Berwanger, *The Frontier Against Slavery: Western Anti-Negro Prejudice and the Slavery Extension Controversy* (Urbana: University of Illinois Press, 1967), 97–118; Wilson, "Brown v. Board," 509.

44. Wilson, "Brown v. Board," 509–13. Berwanger, who lavished attention on antiblack sentiment in 1854 and 1855, in his *Frontier Against Slavery*, 97–115, spends but three pages on its apparent rapid waning, which he does not attempt to explain.

45. *Proceedings and Debates in the Kansas Constitutional Convention of 1859* (1859; rpt. Topeka: Kansas State Printing Plant, 1920), 170–82, 191–95, 465, hereafter referred to as *Debates* (1859).

46. *Debates* (1859), 14, 176–77.

47. Cities in Kansas were divided into classes by population size, the mini-
    mum for first-class cities being fifteen thousand during this period.

48. The pertinent clause of the 1861 law (Act of 1861, ch. 76, § 1, cl. 10,
    1861 Kan. Laws 261) gave school district meetings the power "to make
    such order as they deem proper for the separate education of white
    and colored children, securing to them equal educational advantages."
    Article 4, section 6, p. 266, of chapter 76 bears the marks of an appar-
    ent compromise on its face. District schools, the law stated, were to be
    "equally free and accessible to all the children resident therein" (which
    might be read to prohibit excluding pupils from nearby schools because
    of race), but then added an escape clause, "subject to such regulations
    as the district board in each may prescribe" (which obviously allowed
    segregation by race, sex, and perhaps ethnicity). Art. 4, § 6, ch. 76,
    Kan. Laws 266. Unfortunately for the historian, the 1861–65 legisla-
    tive journals are not indexed, nor are bill titles informative, making
    following a bill's course or locating roll calls on it exceptionally difficult.

49. On the teachers' actions, see Wilson, "Brown v. Board," 509–13. Peter
    McVicar, *Report of Kansas Superintendent of Public Instruction* (1867), 49–
    51.

50. Act of 1867, ch. 123, § 1. cl. 10, 1867 Kan. Laws 207; Act of 1867, ch.
    125, § 1, 1867 Kan. Laws 211. Clyde Lyndon King, "The Kansas School
    System—Its History and Tendencies," *Kansas State Historical Society
    Collections* 11 (1909–10): 427–28, misreads chapter 125 as a pure integra-
    tion law.

51. Thus in 1869, McVicar, a minister and temperance crusader, remarked:
    "Separate schools in nearly every case are bad economy, as well as a
    disgrace to republican institutions. If colored persons are human, treat
    them as humanity deserves. Why close the school room against a child
    because he is of darker hue than his fellows? Why waste funds in sup-
    porting a separate school for a handful of colored children? The time
    will come when such a course will be looked on as both foolishness and
    barbaric injustice combined." McVicar, *Report of Kansas Superintendent
    of Public Instruction* (1870), 2–3. Similarly, see McVicar, *Report of Kansas
    Superintendent of Public Instruction* (1869), 3–4.

52. H.B. 247 reads: "Section 1. That the owners, agents, trustees or man-
    agers in charge of any public inn, hotel or boarding house, or any place
    of amusement or entertainment for which a license is required by any
    of the municipal authorities, or the owners or persons in charge of any
    stagecoach, railroad or other means of public carriage for passengers
    or freight; or the members of any school board, or the directors, clerk
    or trustees of, or other persons in charge of any of the public schools

within this state, who shall make any distinction on account of race, color, or previous condition of servitude, he or they shall be deemed guilty of a misdemeanor, and upon conviction thereof shall be fined in any sum not more than $500, and shall be liable for damages in any court of competent jurisdiction to the person injured thereby.

"Sec. 2. That any acts or parts of acts that conflict with this act the same be and are hereby repealed."

The (Republican) *Topeka Daily Commonwealth*, February 19, 1873, p. 2, remarked of the bill that "it is only simple justice [a phrase used repeatedly in the nineteenth century in similar contexts, long before Richard Kluger's book of that name on the *Brown* case] that is asked for. The freedmen are citizens now, and voters; and there is neither right nor logic in longer denying them the ordinary privileges of citizens merely because of their color. This proposed law covers the whole ground, and its adoption will but redeem a pledge of the [R]epublican party of Kansas to these people, and place the state on the high ground of equal and exact justice to all citizens. Let no [R]epublican vote against it."

53. *Topeka Daily Commonwealth*, February 18, 1873, p. 4; February 20, 1873, p. 4. The repeal of the segregative power of second-class cities was accomplished by omitting the clause of the 1872 law that had provided the segregation power. This repeal was not accomplished by subterfuge, for the bill had been referred in the senate to a special committee of all the senators whose districts contained second-class cities, who amended the bill to drop the power to make racial distinctions. After the amended bill passed the senate, it went to a joint conference committee (as many bills did) before final passage by both houses. The point is that representatives from Wichita, Fort Scott, and other small cities approved the changes. The story may be pieced together in the *Kansas House Journal* (1873), 99, 105, 508, 614, 642, 952–53; *Kansas Senate Journal* (1873), 406, 434, 436–37. Unfortunately, reports on the legislature in the *Topeka Daily Commonwealth* were uninformative about H.B. 39 and H.B. 247, explaining neither why the legislature almost unanimously reversed its 1872 stand on segregation in second-class cities nor why the senate apparently did not consider H.B. 247. For consideration of H.B. 247 in the house, see *Kansas House Journal* (1873), 385, 387–88, 548, 941, 980–81.

54. The bill raised the maximum fine from $500 to $1,000 and, more important, set a minimum fine of $10. It was not unusual in the nineteenth century for a jury to convict a white of a state civil rights law violation but then to fine him one cent or some similarly nominal amount. The progress of the bill and a companion, S.B. 34, which appears to have

been consolidated with H.B. 1, may be followed in *Kansas House Journal* (1874), 58, 107–8, 280, 411, 662–63; *Kansas Senate Journal* (1874), 30, 43, 123, 163, 165, 172, 174, 198–99, 204, 313, 331. Scholars such as Wilson, "Brown v. Board," and Daniel Glenn Neuenswander, "A Legal History of Segregation in the Kansas Public Schools from Statehood to 1970" (Ed.D. thesis, University of Kansas, 1973), appear to have overlooked this bill entirely.

55. See Kousser, *Dead End*, 42–43, n. 41.

56. Charles Lofgren, *The Plessy Case: A Legal-Historical Interpretation* (New York: Oxford University Press, 1987), 133; Alexander M. Bickel and Benno C. Schmidt, Jr., *The Judiciary and Responsible Government, 1910– 1921* (New York: Macmillan, 1984), 757.

57. Neuenswander, "Legal History," 35; Wilson, "Brown v. Board," 513. Similarly, see Mary L. Dudziak, "The Limits of Good Faith: Desegregation in Topeka, Kansas, 1950–1956," *Law and History Review* 5 (1987): 357–58.

58. *Kansas House Journal* (1876), 1058, 1386–89; *Kansas Senate Journal* (1876), 100, 307, 312, 335, 567, 694, 698–701, 822. Born in Mt. Gilead, Ohio, in 1825 of abolitionist Quaker parents whose home was a recognized station on the underground railroad, Sam Wood became chairman of the county's Liberty party at the age of nineteen and a delegate to the 1848 national Free Soil Convention at twenty-three. When Kansas became the chief battleground in the slavery conflict, Wood moved to Lawrence to take part in the battles. A delegate to the Republican National Convention in 1856 and an editor of a series of Kansas newspapers from 1855 on, he served in the legislature repeatedly and was Speaker of the house in 1877. After he was shot and killed in 1891 as a result of a feud over the location of the county seat of Stevens County, his obituary notice called him "an extremist in everything he did," and a black newspaper called him a "staunch friend of the negro," whose death would be mourned by all "Afro-American citizens of Kansas." *Baxter Springs Southern Argus,* July 2, 1891, pp. 7, 8; Margaret L. Wood, *Memorial of Samuel N. Wood* (Kansas City: Hudson-Kimberly Publishing Co., 1892), 10–115.

59. *Topeka Daily Commonwealth,* February 17, 1876, p. 2. A black statewide meeting to push for school integration was held in the legislative chamber. Ibid., February 19, 1876, p. 1. For other legislative actions, see ibid., February 23, 1876, p. 1; February 27, 1876, p. 2; March 3, 1876, p. 2.

60. It seems probable that differences of opinion in the more numerous second-class cities prevented them from imposing segregation suc-

cessfully. Lawrence and Atchison, for instance, always allowed blacks to attend common schools, and Wichita and Fort Scott wavered. See *Leavenworth Times*, April 5, 1890, p. 2; February 21, 1891, p. 2.

61. *Topeka Daily Commonwealth*, March 3, 1876, p. 1; similarly, see *Topeka Capital Commonwealth*, February 24, 1889, p. 3; *Topeka Daily Commonwealth*, March 1, 1889, p. 3.

62. *Leavenworth Times*, March 1, 1889, p. 1.

63. *Topeka Tribune*, December 25, 1880, p. 3; *Topeka Daily Commonwealth*, March 2, 1881, p. 3; *Ottawa Daily Republican*, March 4, 1881, p. 1.

64. *Topeka American Citizen*, January 25, 1889, p. 4; February 1, 1889, pp. 1, 4; February 8, 1889, p. 4; February 15, 1889, p. 4; February 22, 1889, p. 4; *Kansas House Journal* (1889), 442–43, 713, 1187; *Kansas Senate Journal* (1889), 99, 153, 179, 221, 243, 263, 388, 452, 474, 475, 528, 922, 970; Cox, *Blacks in Topeka*, 123; *Leavenworth Advocate*, May 11, 1889, p. 2.

65. *Topeka American Citizen*, February 22, 1889, p. 4, said the Topeka Board of Education had threatened to fire every black teacher if the integration bill passed. One prominent black teacher in Topeka lobbied the legislative to preserve segregation (and his job, since teacher integration was much more controversial among whites than student integration was). See *Leavenworth Advocate*, February 7, 1891, pp. 2, 3; February 14, 1891, p. 3; February 21, 1891, p. 2. *Topeka American Citizen*, March 15, 1889, p. 1, charged that the general education bill was torpedoed not over taxes but through covert action by men from Topeka and Leavenworth, who acted out of antipathy to integration.

66. Cox, *Blacks in Topeka*, 167.

67. *Joubert v. Sacred Heart Academy* No. 21761 (6th D. Orleans Parish), in Orleans Parish Public Library. I happened on a reference to this case, heretofore unmentioned by Louisiana historians, in the *Hartford* (Conn.) *Times*, May 2, 1868, p. 3. The 1868 state constitution was ratified April 17. Joe Gray Taylor, *Louisiana Reconstructed, 1863–1877* (Baton Rouge: Louisiana State University Press, 1974), 158. The Fourteenth Amendment to the federal Constitution went into effect on July 28. Alfred H. Kelly and Winfred A. Harbison, *The American Constitution: Its Origins and Development*, 5th ed. (New York: Norton, 1976), 1066.

68. Joubert was a member of the Republican state central committee from at least 1878 through 1880 and probably earlier. See *New Orleans Republican*, October 2, 1878, p. 1; *New Orleans Louisianian*, October 25, 1879, p. 2; March 20, 1880, p. 3. Educated in France, Joubert was a member of the New Orleans Common Council during the Civil War, the first man of color to hold a judicial position in the South, presidential elector on the Grant ticket in 1868, and a federal officeholder. *San Francisco Elevator*, May 7, 1869, p. 1. Born free, he was a "gentleman of hand-

some fortune . . . so nearly white that one could scarcely take him to be colored" and, allegedly, a slaveholder before the war. *Cleveland Gazette,* September 22, 1883.

69. Article 13 of the Radical constitution, adopted March 13, 1868, stated: "All persons shall enjoy equal rights and privileges upon any conveyance of a public character; and all places of business, or of public resort, or for which a license is required by either State, parish, or municipal authority, shall be deemed places of public character, and shall be opened to the accommodation and patronage of all persons, without distinction or discrimination on account of race or color." *Federal and State Constitutions,* ed. Thorpe, 3:1450. Joubert's petition was filed on an unspecified date in April. The judgment was rendered on April 28. On Field, see Taylor, *Louisiana Reconstructed,* 55; *New Orleans Republican,* August 20, 1876, p. 5.

70. Duplantier was vice-president of the parish Republican central committee in 1867. See *Buffalo* (N.Y.) *Commercial Advertiser,* January 12, 1867, p. 1. Other than that his family had been in Louisiana for at least two generations, I have been able to learn very little about Duplantier.

71. Among the tactics blacks used against the 1875 movement to desegregate the schools was a threat to expose the "mixed" ancestry of older citizens who were now considered "white." See *New Orleans Louisianian,* September 18, 1875, p. 2. In Armistead L. Robinson, "Beyond the Realm of Social Consensus: New Meanings of Reconstruction for American History," *Journal of American History* 68 (1981): 294, Robinson elevates evanescent tactical differences into enduring class-based factional alignments within the New Orleans black community. The closer one looks, however, the less clear any such divisions seem. The partisan course of the leading black politician in New Orleans, P. B. S. Pinchback, for instance, shifted repeatedly, but he remained committed to integration. He and other members of the so-called "colored aristocracy" correctly predicted how the Democrats would treat Jim Crow schools, and they did everything they could to prevent it. Their struggle deserves more respect, and divisions within the black community, less attention than they sometimes get.

72. On Redemption, see Taylor, *Louisiana Reconstructed,* 480–505. On Pinchback, see Charles Vincent, "Louisiana's Black Governor: Aspects of His National Significance," *Negro History Bulletin* 42 (1979): 34; Emma Lou Thornbrough, "Pickney Benton Stewart Pinchback," *Dictionary of American Negro Biography,* ed. Rayford W. Logan and Michael R. Winston (New York: Norton, 1982), 493; William Simmons, *Men of Mark: Eminent, Progressive and Rising* (1887; rpt. New York: Arno Press, 1968), 759–75. On the failure of black efforts to sustain integration by tactical

compromises with the Redeemers, see Harris, *Story of Public Education,* 58; Rodolphe Lucien Desdunes, *Our People and Our History,* trans. and ed. Sister Dorothea O. McCants (1911; rpt. Baton Rouge: Louisiana State University Press, 1973), 135–38; *New Orleans Louisianian,* September 29, 1877, p. 2; *New Orleans Daily Picayune,* June 27, 1877; July 4, 1877, p. 8.

73. When blacks held a meeting to collect contributions to finance the Trévigne case—Pinchback contributed the sizable sum of $50—the *New Orleans Daily Picayune,* September 28, 1877, p. 1, accused them of a desire "to make a political issue out of the question." Of course, the Democrats never considered turning the school integration issue to political purposes.

74. Born free in 1824, son of a veteran of the battle of New Orleans, Trévigne was an active politician, serving on the Republican state committee in 1867 and in a steady federal patronage job from at least 1880 through 1884. Author of the first historical sketch of blacks in Louisiana, he wrote for four successive black newspapers in New Orleans and was very active in the struggle to overturn the Jim Crow railroad law in the 1890s, a six-year campaign doomed to lead to *Plessy.* The ever temperate *New Orleans Democrat,* September 28, 1877, p. 4, termed Trévigne's suit an effort to gain "cheap notoriety" by a "haughty descendent of Ham," whose attempt to substitute "African supremacy" for "civilization and christianity" endangered any white support for the education of "African ignorance and savagery." The constitution, this organ of "conservatism" asserted, "is not binding." On Trévigne, see Edward Larocque Tinker, *Les écrits de langue française en Louisiane aux XIX siècle* (Paris: Librarie Ancienne Honoré Champion, 1932), 475; William P. O'Connor, "Reconstruction Rebels: The New Orleans Tribune in Post-War Louisiana," *Louisiana History* 21 (1980): 159; Vincent, *Black Legislators,* 24; Sister Dorothea Olga McCants, "Paul Trévigne," *American Negro Biography,* ed. Logan and Winston, 601–2; Everett, "Free Persons of Color," 241, 330, 362, 364; Records of the Orleans Parish School Board, vol. 8 (1876–77), 151, 159, in Orleans Parish School Board offices; Otto H. Olsen, ed., *The Thin Disguise: Turning Point in Negro History, Plessy v. Ferguson, A Documentary Presentation, 1864–1896* (New York: Humanities Press, 1967), 47–67; Jean-Charles Houzeau, *My Passage at the New Orleans Tribune,* ed. David C. Rankin (Baton Rouge: Louisiana State University Press, 1984), 71 n. 6. On the replacement of Republicans with Democrats, see *New Orleans Daily Picayune,* April 6, 1877, p. 8.

75. *Trévigne* v. *Board of Educ. of Orleans Parish,* No. 9545, in Orleans Parish Public Library, hereafter referred to as Trévigne Case File. A briefer

form of the petition appeared in *New Orleans Democrat*, September 27, 1877, p. 8. Among the three men who guaranteed the $1,000 bond that had to be filed to bring the case was Blanc F. Joubert.

76. Trévigne's counsel did not raise equal protection or due process claims, presumably because they believed that even after the Supreme Court's decision in *Slaughter-House* 83 U.S. (16 Wall.) 36 (1873), the privileges or immunities clause retained considerable vigor. Of course, raising issues of the national Constitution before a state court in which they must have known that they would probably lose indicates an intention to appeal an adverse judgment to the federal courts.

77. Obviously patterned partly on the Fourteenth Amendment, Article 2 stated: "All persons, without regard to race, color, or previous condition, born or naturalized in the United States, and subject to the jurisdiction thereof, and residents of this state for one year, are citizens of this state. . . . They shall enjoy the same civil, political, and public rights and privileges, and be subject to the same pains and penalties." *Federal and State Constitutions*, ed. Thorpe, 3:1449.

78. Belden was surely aware of the U.S. Supreme Court's decision in *Slaughter-House*, for as state attorney general he had argued one of the three cases later consolidated under the name *Slaughter House* in the state court. Charles Fairman, *Reconstruction and Reunion, 1864–88* (New York: Macmillan, 1971), 1326. Perhaps he ignored Justice Samuel Miller's ruling that the rights Americans claimed as national citizens were ludicrously limited, whereas those they enjoyed as state citizens were not protected under the privileges or immunities clause because he hoped that five-to-four decision might be reversed by the time it considered Trévigne, if the case was appealed that far. Or perhaps he hoped that the Court might give the clause a more expansive reading if black rights were involved, as Miller's "one pervading purpose" language might lead one to believe. *Slaughter-House Cases*, 83 U.S. (16 Wall.) at 74.

79. Blacks used the same argument in less formal contexts. Trévigne and the *Tribune* editors declared that they favored the 1869 state civil rights bill not so much because they wished to attend the opera or saloon with whites, or even because they wanted to be able to ride on streetcars, boats, and trains freely, but because "under the present order of things our manhood is sacrificed . . . the broad stamp of inferiority is put upon us." *New Orleans Tribune*, February 7, 1869, quoted in Philip M. Mabe, "Racial Ideology in the New Orleans Press, 1862–1877" (Ph.D. dissertation, University of Southwestern Louisiana, 1977), 131–32.

80. Trévigne's lawyers also speculated that segregation would cause the school board to violate article 118 of the 1868 Constitution, which pro-

vided that "taxation shall be equal and uniform throughout the State." *Federal and State Constitutions,* ed. Thorpe, 3:1464. Their reasoning was that segregated schools would cost more and therefore require either unequal tax rates from parish to parish or "the closing of the avenues of Education to Petitioner's Son and the entire colored population." Unwieldy as a legal argument, it was all too accurate as a factual prediction. Trévigne Case File.

81. Born in Kentucky and raised in Quincy, Illinois, Jonas moved to Louisiana in 1853. Like his father, who had served in the legislatures of both Kentucky and Illinois, B. F. Jonas became a Whig politician. Although a prominent Unionist in 1860, he went with the Confederacy, serving throughout the Civil War as a lowly private. Unlike his fellow Whig John Ray, Jonas became a Democrat in 1865, serving in the legislature, 1865–68, and being nominated by the Democrats for lieutenant governor in 1872. The city attorney of New Orleans, 1874–78, he was simultaneously the Democratic floor leader in the legislature in 1877. After a term in the U.S. Senate, he was appointed collector of the Port of New Orleans. A longtime member of the Democratic state committee, he was a prominent leader of the White League revolt in September 1874. He became law partner of E. H. Farrar in 1887. *Biographical Memoirs,* 201–2, 495–98; Alcee Fortier, *Louisiana* (Atlanta: Southern Historical Association, 1909), 627–28. Long actively involved in the school segregation campaign, Jonas had at a white mass meeting in 1870 promised violence if school integration took place. See *New Orleans Daily Picayune,* February 13, 1870, p. 1.

82. A native Louisianian born in 1849, Farrar graduated from the University of Virginia and practiced law in Louisiana from 1872 on. He was elected New Orleans city attorney in 1880 and subsequently served as president of the American Bar Association. An antilottery, Gold Democratic "reformer," he framed the article on taxation in the 1913 state constitutional convention. *Biographical Memoirs,* 481–82; *New Orleans Times,* January 7, 1922, p. 1; *New Orleans Daily Picayune,* January 7, 1922, p. 3.

83. Trévigne Case File. Farrar tendered his services free to the cause of white supremacy. Records of the Orleans Parish School Board, vol. 9 (1876–77), 110, 113, in Orleans Parish School Board offices.

84. Because of infighting on the Orleans Parish School Board, the public schools did not open for the fall until October 22, 1877. *New Orleans Daily Picayune,* October 23, 1877, p. 1.

85. Born in Louisiana, Rightor, though a Catholic, attended Wesleyan College in Connecticut before returning south to practice law. A colonel in the Confederacy, Rightor, in the biased phrases of the *New Orleans Daily*

Picayune, August 12, 1900, "was among the first to take up arms for the liberation of the state from radical rule, and was in command of one of the companies of the White League on the memorable 14th of September [1874]." On that date, the White Leaguers' attempted coup d'état against the state government had to be put down by federal troops. For his efforts, he was appointed judge in 1877. See also *New Orleans Daily States*, August 12, 1900; *New Orleans Times-Democrat*, August 12, 1900.

86. Rightor's opinion is printed in full in the *New Orleans Daily Picayune*, October 24, 1877, p. 2.

87. The opinion of the court, in manuscript, is in the files of the Louisiana Supreme Court in New Orleans. *Trévigne* v. *School Board and William O. Rogers*, No. 6832 (1879). It appears to have escaped the attention of previous historians.

88. DeBlanc, a native Louisianian, was a Confederate officer and "one of the leading spirits in the organization of the White League." Fortier, *Louisiana*, 339. The other justices were Thomas Courtland Manning, a member of the state secession convention and Confederate general and "the highest type of the lordly Anglo-Saxon"; Robert H. Marr, another leading White Leaguer; William B. Spencer, a plantation-born Confederate captain and Democratic congressman; and William B. Egan. Ibid., 93, 487; Lamar C. Quintero, "The Supreme Court of Louisiana," *Green Bag* 3 (1891): 113; *National Cyclopedia of American Biography* (New York: James T. White & Co., 1897), 4:344; *Biographical Directory of the American Congress, 1789–1971* (Washington, D.C.: U.S. Government Printing Office, 1971), 1736.

89. On the merging of the two "extraordinary remedies," see J. Morgan Kousser, "Separate but Not Equal: The Supreme Court's First Decision on Racial Discrimination in Schools," *Journal of Southern History* 46 (1980): 29–30.

90. *State of Louisiana ex rel. Josephine Harper* v. *Mrs. M. A. Wickes, Principal of the Live Oak School* (6th D. Orleans Parish), case file in Orleans Parish Public Library, asked for a mandamus to compel Mrs. Wickes to admit Frances and Mary Ardene Harper and Josephine Harper's niece Ida Sawler, who lived with them. The girls had been admitted to the school, then ejected solely on account of color. Although a hearing was set for later in November 1877 before Judge Rightor, there is no evidence in the case file or the newspapers that the case went any farther. The petition, which is summarized in *New Orleans Daily Picayune*, November 11, 1877, p. 2, does not mention the constitutional or statutory grounds of the suit.

91. These developments may be followed in *New Orleans Daily Picayune*, November 11, 1877, p. 1; November 13, 1877, p. 2; January 15, 1878,

p. 2; January 29, 1878, p. 3; February 19, 1878, p. 3. The case files are in the Louisiana Supreme Court, New Orleans, No. 7500 (1881), hereafter referred to as Dellande Case File. Less prominent than Isabelle, Joubert, Trévigne, or Bertonneau, Dellande was a cigar manufacturer who owned $9,000 worth of property in 1879, according to the New Orleans city directories for the period and No. 10763 (6th D. Orleans Parish, 1879) in Orleans Parish Public Library. I find no mention of him or of Mrs. Harper in the newspapers of the time, except in connection with their court cases.

92. *DeCuir* v. *Benson*, 27 La. Ann. 1 (1875); *Sauvinet* v. *Walker*, 27 La. Ann. 14 (1875); *Washington, Alexandria, & Georgetown R. R. Co.* v. *Brown*, 17 How. 445 (1873). In the lower court, Judge Henry Dibble awarded black sheriff C. S. Sauvinet $1,000 damages under the state's 1869 civil rights law and articles 2 and 13 of the 1868 Constitution. Fischer, *Segregation Struggle*, 69–70. Mrs. DeCuir was awarded a like sum when the owner of a steamboat denied her first-class accommodations as she was traveling from New Orleans to her up-country plantation. The then Republican-dominated state supreme court upheld both verdicts, though the U.S. Supreme Court overturned *DeCuir* on interstate commerce grounds a month before *Dellande* was filed. *Hall* v. *DeCuir*, 95 U.S. 485 (1877). The fact that Jonas and Farrar did not even bother to mention this reversal or to cite Justice Nathan Clifford's concurrence, in which this last Buchanan appointee on the Court argued that segregation was constitutional, indicates how little attention they paid to constitutional issues. The *Brown* case ruled that separate but equal violated the federal charter granted to the railroad, but Justice David Davis's language was more expansive than the bare ruling implies.

93. The local court decision was printed in full in *New Orleans Daily Picayune*, May 21, 1878, p. 1.

94. Dellande Case File. In an attempt to demonstrate the arbitrariness of the caste system in Louisiana, Belden asked Dellande during the trial whether it could "be ascertained that your children are colored, by their appearance, without being told?" Dellande replied: "No. The children are as white in color as anybody." In his lower court opinion, Rightor briefly toyed with the idea of denying Dellande standing to sue because, the judge remarked, he "does not belong exclusively to any separate race." It would have been interesting to watch the judge's contortions if he had ruled that Dellande was "colored" for the purposes of the schools but not for the purposes of the courts.

95. *State ex rel. Dellande* v. *New Orleans School Bd.*, 13 La. Ann. 1469 (1881).

96. *Federal and State Constitutions*, ed. Thorpe, 3:1508, art. 224. It was not until the disfranchising convention of 1898 that the state constitution mentioned school segregation. Ibid., 1575, art. 248.

97. *Biographical Memoirs,* 314–16. His "one object" during Reconstruction, this biographical sketch asserts, was to "starve out" the Republicans in his home parish, and he also attended all the state and national Democratic conventions during the era and canvassed southwestern Louisiana extensively. Poché was one of the founders of the American Bar Association. Other justices were Edward E. Bermudez, a "cooperationist" member of the Louisiana secession convention and Confederate soldier who was removed from local office in 1867 as "an impediment to Reconstruction"; Charles E. Fenner, another active secessionist, a Confederate major, and leader in the effort to unseat the state's Republican governor in 1876–77; William M. Levy, a native of Virginia, Confederate, and congressman; and Robert B. Todd. Fortier, *Louisiana,* 65, 84; Quintero, "The Supreme Court of Louisiana," 113–38; *Dictionary of American Biography,* ed. Dumas Malone (New York: Charles Scribner's Sons, 1929), 2:220, 323.

98. Emphasis added. The handwritten opinion is in Dellande Case File.

99. *New Orleans Daily Picayune,* December 23, 1877, p. 4.

100. Bertonneau's children were denied entry to the Fillmore school (the same school to which Dellande applied) on November 13, 1878, three days after the Dellande case was filed. Bertonneau's case was filed on November 28. See the case file of *Bertonneau* v. *Board of Directors of the City Schools,* case No. 8306, Fifth Cir. and D. of La., in Federal Records Center, Fort Worth, Texas, R.G. 21, Eastern District, Louisiana, New Orleans Division, General Records, Case Files, 1837–1911, hereafter referred to as Bertonneau Case File.

101. A member of both houses of the Louisiana legislature in the prewar era, twice Whig nominee for lieutenant governor during the 1850s, elected to the U.S. House in 1865 and the Senate in 1873 (though not seated by Congress), the man who single-handedly codified the laws of the state during Reconstruction, Ray deserves more favorable mention than he has gotten from the state's historians. For instance, the leading historian of Louisiana Reconstruction, Joe Gray Taylor, omits Ray, as well as the other Louisiana- and border-state-born white Republican lawyers in the other school segregation cases, from a list of the only three whites in the state at the time "who seem honestly to have believed that all men were created equal." Taylor does not enunciate a criterion for determining subjective honesty, and he mistakenly lists Paul Trévigne as one of the three whites. See Joe Gray Taylor, "Louisiana—An Impossible Task," in *Reconstruction and Redemption in the South,* ed. Otto H. Olsen (Baton Rouge: Louisiana State University Press, 1980), 222. A Unionist during the Civil War, Ray attracted national attention as counsel to the Republican state returning board in 1876–77, the actions of which allowed Rutherford B. Hayes to become president.

Although allegedly involved in certain shady deals himself, he served as a competent special prosecutor in the Whiskey Ring cases, which involved corrupt actions by government officials. Assessed for $70,000 worth of property in 1870 and said to have a "thriving law practice" in New Orleans after 1877, Ray almost certainly did not take on *Bertonneau* because he needed the fee. In view of the facts that as state senator in 1868, he had been the floor manager of the Fourteenth Amendment and had voted for state integration laws, and that during the 1870s, he was a member of the Louisiana Club, a largely black social and political group, it seems likely that Ray represented Bertonneau because he believed in racial equality. Biographical sources on Ray include *Appleton's Cyclopedia of American Biography*, ed. James G. Wilson and John Fiske (New York: D. Appleton, 1888), 5:192; Wetta, "Louisiana Scalawags," 80–82, 354–55; Wetta, " 'Bulldozing the Scalawags': Some Examples of the Persecution of Southern White Republicans in Louisiana During Reconstruction," *Louisiana History* 21 (1980): 53–54; *Louisiana Senate Journal* (1868), 13, 21, 183–84; *Louisiana Senate Journal* (1869), 98; *Louisiana Senate Journal* (1870), 290; Taylor, "Louisiana," 194, 197–98; *New York Herald*, February 14, 1873, p. 5; March 27, 1873, p. 7; *New Orleans Daily Picayune*, August 2, 1877; January 23, 1878, p. 1; January 27, 28, 1878; February 8, 1878, p. 3; Thomas William Herringshaw, *Herringshaw's Encyclopedia of American Biography in the Nineteenth Century* (Chicago: American Publishers' Association, 1898), 773; *New Orleans Louisianian*, November 12, 1872, p. 1; January 30, 1875, p. 3. The *Topeka Daily Commonwealth*, January 23, 1873, p. 2, called Ray "a prudent and able legislator" whose "private character is irreproachable."

102. Son of a French-born father and a Cuban mother, Bertonneau was light enough to have been termed "white" in the 1880 census and on his death certificate in Pasadena, California, where he moved and "passed" sometime between 1890 and 1912. Owner of $1,800 worth of real estate in the 1879 city tax records, he worked at a variety of jobs: wine merchant, cigar store owner, dry-goods store owner, and U.S. customs employee. An officer in the Native Guards during the Civil War, he carried a petition for black suffrage to President Lincoln in 1864 and was afterward feted in Boston at a public dinner hosted by Massachusetts governor John A. Andrew and attended by William Lloyd Garrison, Wendell Phillips, and Frederick Douglass. Responding to a toast at that meeting, Bertonneau promised to carry the message that Boston blacks enjoyed integration in streetcars and schools back to Louisiana, which he did as a member of the 1868 state constitutional convention. David Rankin, "The Impact of the Civil War on the Free Colored Community of New Orleans," *Perspectives in American History* 11 (1977–78):

400; McCrary, *Lincoln and Reconstruction,* 256; James M. McPherson, *The Negro's Civil War* (New York: Vintage Books, 1965), 278–80; *New Orleans Louisianian,* October 25, 1879, pp. 1, 4; March 20, 1880, p. 3; Desdunes, *Our People,* 131; Everett, "Free Persons of Color," 362, 364, 379; *Washington* (D.C.) *People's Advocate,* February 18, 1882, p. 1. I thank David C. Rankin for sending me a copy of Bertonneau's death certificate.

103. Ray also charged a violation of section 1979, U.S. Revised Statutes, which read in pertinent part: "Every person who under color of any statute, ordinance, regulation, custom, or usage of any state or territory, subjects or causes to be subjected any citizen of the United States or other person within the jurisdiction thereof to the deprivation of any rights, privileges, or immunities secured by the Constitution and laws, shall be liable to the party injured in an action at law, suit in chancery, or other proper proceeding for redress." He also contended that the action violated section 1977 (the 1866 Civil Rights Bill, reenacted in 1870, after the passage of the Fourteenth Amendment, to clear up any doubts about its constitutionality): "All persons within the jurisdiction of the United States shall have the same right in every state and Territory . . . to the full and equal benefit of all laws and provisions for the security of persons and property as is enjoyed by white citizens." Quoted in original complaint and supplementary briefs, Bertonneau Case File.

104. Ibid.

105. Ibid. They even failed to point out the "good faith" that the school board had so ostentatiously paraded in its segregation resolution: "Whereas this Board in the performance of its paramount duty which is to give the best education possible within the means at its disposal to the whole population without regard to race color or previous condition is assured that this end can be best attained by educating the different races in separate schools."

106. *Scott v. Sandford,* 60 U.S. (19 How.) 393 (1857). Ray replied to the jurisdictional point by citing Act of March 3, 1875, ch. 137, 18 Stat. 470, which provided for federal court jurisdiction, "concurrent with the courts of the several states, of all suits of a civil nature at common law or in equity when the matter in dispute exceeds, exclusive of costs, the sum or value of $500, and arising under the Constitution or laws of the United States." Supplementary briefs in Bertonneau Case File.

107. *Bertonneau v. New Orleans,* 3 F. Cas. 294 (1878), hereafter referred to as *Bertonneau.*

108. Louis Filler, "William B. Woods," in *Justices of the U.S. Supreme Court,* ed. Friedman and Israel, 2:1327; Harold Chase et al., *Biographical Dic-*

tionary of the Federal Judiciary (Detroit: Gale Research Co., 1976), 309; Whitelaw Reid, *Ohio in the War* (Cincinnati: Moore, Wilstach, & Baldwin, 1868), 1:863–64; *Cincinnati Commercial,* December 23, 1880, p. 5; December 24, 1880, p. 1; December 31, 1880, p. 4.

109. *Bertonneau,* 296.

110. *Workman v. Detroit,* 18 Mich. 400 (1869); *Clark v. Muscatine,* 24 Iowa 266 (1868); *Garnes v. McCann,* 21 Ohio St. 198 (1871); *Hall v. DeCuir,* 95 U.S. 485 (1878). Woods also cited *Stoutmeyer v. Duffy,* 7 Nev. 342 (1872), in which, as in *Garnes* and *Hall,* judges had gone well out of their way to declare segregation constitutional under the Fourteenth Amendment. A strict construction of each opinion would have treated the approbations of segregation as dicta. On Clifford, see the excellent sketch by William Gillette, in *Justices of the U.S. Supreme Court,* ed. Friedman and Israel, 2:963–75.

111. The phrases that I italicized and that subsequent legal commentaries quoted endlessly, derive from *Garnes,* 21 Ohio State at 207; and *Hall,* 95 U.S. at 503.

112. *Bertonneau,* 296.

113. In *Slaughter-House,* 83 U.S. (16 Wall.) 36, 73–77 (1873), Justice Miller distinguished the broad rights that a person enjoyed as a "state citizen" and what he asserted were the very limited ones that he held as a "national citizen." He put heavy emphasis on the fact that the privileges or immunities clause referred explicitly to rights held as "citizens of the United States," but did not mention, and therefore, he asserted, offered no national protection for, the rights people held as state citizens.

114. *New Orleans Daily Picayune,* February 21, 1879, p. 1.

115. J. Morgan Kousser, *The Shaping of Southern Politics: Suffrage Restriction and the Establishment of the One-Party South, 1880–1910* (New Haven: Yale University Press, 1974), 55. In 1887, according to the *New Orleans Pelican,* January 8, 1887, p. 2, and January 15, 1887, p. 2, there were so few schools provided for blacks in New Orleans that ten thousand children were unable to enroll. The vice-president of a committee established to agitate for more schools was Homer A. Plessy, and the president was a son of Blanc Joubert.

116. Bond for Appeal, in Bertonneau Case File. The first such case, so far as I know, in which plaintiffs instituted an appeal, which was dropped for financial reasons, was *Cory v. Carter,* 48 Ind. 327 (1874). The large and relatively affluent black community of New Orleans probably could have supported an appeal to the U.S. Supreme Court, as they later did in *Plessy v. Ferguson.*

117. F. W. Giles, *Thirty Years in Topeka: A Historical Sketch* (Topeka: George W. Crane & Co., 1886), 371.

118. *Topeka Colored Citizen,* September 20, 1878, p. 4; Randall Bennett Woods, *A Black Odyssey: John Lewis Waller and the Promise of American Life, 1878–1900* (Lawrence: University of Kansas Press, 1981), 56–57. The *Ottawa Daily Republican,* October 30, 1880, p. 1, reported that Judge Stephens of the district court had delayed his decision in *Tinnon* because another school segregation case "was known to be pending in the supreme court," which all the Ottawa parties hoped would settle the question. No such decision was ever reported.

119. *Topeka State Journal,* October 28, 1880, p. 4; *Ottawa Daily Republican,* November 1, 1880, p. 4; *Topeka Daily Commonwealth,* November 2, 1880, p. 4; November 9, 1880, p. 4. Ignoring *Phillips,* Nell Irvin Painter, *Exodusters* (New York: Knopf, 1977), 50, presents Topeka blacks as reluctantly accepting school segregation in the fall of 1880.

120. *Topeka Daily Commonwealth,* January 4, 1881, p. 4; *Topeka State Journal,* October 9, 1880, p. 4; *Topeka Tribune,* December 25, 1880, p. 3.

121. Woods, *Black Odyssey,* 57 n. 48. Woods's source for this conclusion is unclear, and it is uncertain whether Phillips's lawyers, one of whom, John H. Stuart, was black, challenged segregation as contrary to the Fourteenth Amendment. The case does not seem to have been appealed to the Kansas Supreme Court, and the local court no longer holds any records on the case. In the fall of 1881, Topeka blacks were again said to be "greatly exercised because their children were refused admission to the white schools." *Ottawa Daily Republican,* October 24, 1881, p. 3.

122. D. S. Spear, "The Law of Extradition," *Independent,* May 11, 1882. Discussing *Tinnon,* Spear hoped that a similar case would be appealed to the U.S. Supreme Court and declared that "there cannot be much doubt," in light of its past decisions, that it would strike down exclusion from any particular school because of race. *Slaughter-House* emasculated the privileges or immunities clause but left equal protection unscathed and highlighted the concentration of the framers on the reform of race relations. Justice William Strong's opinion in *Strauder* seemed to offer broad protection against statutory or administrative discrimination on account of race. And though the *Civil Rights Cases* overturned a congressional ban on discrimination by "private" citizens, it did not limit the protection of the Fourteenth Amendment against official state discrimination.

123. *Columbus Daniel et al.* v. *Board of Education of South Topeka et al.,* 4 Kan. L. J. 329 (1886–87).

124. Born in Topeka in 1860, Curtis was one-eighth to one-fourth Indian. He was orphaned early and raised by his grandmother. His minority-group heritage and underprivileged boyhood may have given him

a special feeling for those who suffered discrimination. Unable to afford college, he read law with Aderial Hebard Case, with whom he formed the partnership that represented Columbus Daniel. As Shawnee County attorney, he might have been expected to have represented the school board, but he did not. The picture of an aspiring politician, he apparently did not believe that being associated with school integration would hurt his career, and it did not. Beginning in 1893, he served in the U.S. House of Representatives for seven terms, moving to the Senate in 1907. Well respected in Congress, he was party whip from 1915 to 1924 and majority leader from 1924 until he descended to the vice-presidency in 1929. Case, his law partner and senior by thirty-two years, was born in Pennsylvania and moved to Topeka the year Curtis was born. A Republican officeholder during the Civil War, he became a Democrat thereafter and specialized in murder trials. It seems likely that Curtis carried most of the burden in *Daniel*. *History of Shawnee County, Kansas and Representative Citizens*, ed. James L. King (Chicago: Richmond & Arnold, 1905), 279–80; Berrett, *Who's Who in Topeka*, 18, 27; *Kansas, a Cyclopedia*, ed. Frank Blackmar (Chicago: Standard Publishing Co., 1912), 3:20–22; *The United States Biographical Dictionary: Kansas Volume* (Chicago and Kansas City: S. Lewis & Co., 1879), 641–42; *History of the State of Kansas* (Chicago: A. T. Andreas, 1883), 557, 559; *Topeka Daily Capital*, September 14, 1902, p. 11; *Biographical Directory of Congress*, 814–15.

125. Born and raised in Logansport, Indiana, Guthrie had been a member of the first Topeka school board in 1867, a board that continued the segregated black school, which had been established in 1865. He was elected to the board in 1879 and may have served continuously. A captain in the Civil War and later Kansas state commander of the Grand Army of the Republic, Guthrie was a prominent Republican. After serving in the state house, 1868–70, he was a presidential elector in 1872, chairman of the Republican state committee in 1872 and 1876, a prominent candidate for his party's nomination for governor in 1876, district court judge from 1884 to 1892, and postmaster of Topeka from 1898 through at least 1905. Oxymoronically, he was an antitemperance Presbyterian whose father had been born in Scotland. *History of Kansas*, 545, 564; *U.S. Biographical Dictionary*, 333–34; Berrett, *Who's Who in Topeka*, 50; *Topeka Colored Citizen*, April 5, 1879; *Topeka Daily Commonwealth*, July 19, 1881, p. 4.

126. *Daniel* v. *Board of Educ.*, 4 Kan. L.J. 392 (1886–87). A similar district court decision was much less fully reported in the *Fort Scott Weekly Monitor*, October 13, 1887, p. 6, in the case of *Reeves* v. *Board of Educ. of Fort Scott*.

127. *Jones* v. *McProud*, 62 Kan. 870, 64 P. 602 (1901). Blacks had been trying
to enter the white schools in Oskaloosa off and on for nineteen years
before they brought a case. See *Topeka Colored Citizen*, October 12, 1898,
p. 1; September 21, 1900, p. 1; Plaintiff's Brief and Depositions, case
file, case No. 11921, in Kansas Historical Society, Topeka. As the case
file makes clear, the *Jones* case was more complex than the printed
opinion makes it appear. The white "high school" was a room in the
white school building; all the black children in grammar school were
taught by a single black teacher. Before August 1900, the black school
only went up to the eighth grade, and the (white) high school began
in the ninth grade. Learning that some black children meant to apply
to the ninth grade, the school board ordered the black teacher to add a
ninth grade curriculum and changed the grade designations at the high
school from nine to twelve to ten to thirteen. This allowed the board's
attorneys to argue that Gracie and Mabel Jones had not been excluded
because of race but because they were not qualified to enter the tenth
grade, a rationale that allowed the three-man supreme court, none of
whom had been serving in 1881 at the time of the *Tinnon* case, to side-
step precedent. The supreme court used its discretion to refuse to allow
the plaintiffs to amend their brief to bring the issue of racial exclusion
in all grades more clearly before the court.

128. *Crawford* v. *Board of Educ. of Fort Scott*, was an original action for a
mandamus in the Kansas Supreme Court. Unreported, the case was
merely noted as dismissed in the *Topeka Daily Capital-Commonwealth*,
March 6, 1889, p. 4, and the *Fort Scott Daily Monitor*, March 11, 1889,
p. 4. In the *Reeves* case, counsel had applied for an injunction, over
which district courts had original jurisdiction. Instead of appealing
Reeves, the lawyers for the blacks sought a quicker decision by the
Kansas Supreme Court by applying for a mandamus. See *Fort Scott
Weekly Monitor*, November 4, 1887, p. 3. It is unclear why Justices
Horton, Valentine, and William A. Johnston (who had replaced Brewer
when Brewer was appointed to the U.S. Circuit Court in 1884) held up
the decision for sixteen months, during which time the booming Fort
Scott gained enough population to become a first-class city and therefore undermined the chief argument—*Tinnon*—made in the plaintiff's
brief. Nor is it evident why the justices did not ask for supplementary briefs in light of the changed legal status of the city. Perhaps they
hoped that the attempt to repeal the authorization for segregation in
first-class cities would succeed in the 1889 legislature. The plaintiff's
brief is summarized in *Fort Scott Weekly Monitor*, November 4, 1887,
p. 3. Fort Scott was proclaimed a first-class city on May 30. *Fort Scott
Weekly Monitor*, May 31, 1888, p. 1.

129. *New York Age*, May 4, 1889, p. 2; *Fort Scott Weekly Monitor*, August 16, 1888, p. 8; August 23, 1888, p. 7; *Fort Scott Daily Monitor*, March 19, 1888, p. 4; March 21, 1889, p. 2; April 6, 1889, p. 4; April 9, 1889, p. 2; James C. Malin, *Doctors, Devils, and the Woman Question: Fort Scott, Kansas, 1870–1890* (Lawrence, Kan.: Coronado Press, 1975), 120.

130. Robert Crozier, the judge who decided in favor of the black students in Tonganoxie, a small town near Leavenworth, was born in Cadiz, Ohio, in 1827 and came to Leavenworth in 1856, where he established and was editor of the *Times*. A member of the territorial legislatures in 1857 and 1858, he served as U.S. district attorney from 1861 to 1864 and chief justice of the Kansas Supreme Court for a few months during 1873–74. From 1877 to 1893, he was judge of the district court in Leavenworth. Despite that city's Democratic majority, Judge Crozier was a consistent Republican. Henry Miles Moore, *Early History of Leavenworth* (Leavenworth, Kan.: Samuel Dodsworth Book Co., 1906), 306; *Biographical Directory of Congress*, 807–8.

131. Born in Butler County, Ohio, in 1828, Judge John T. Burris had switched parties often. In 1890 he was a Democrat. Raised in Ohio, Kentucky, and Iowa, he came to Olathe, Kansas, in 1858 after serving in the Mexican War. Up to that time, he had been a Whig, but he shifted to become an anti-Lecompton Democrat and won a seat in the 1859 state constitutional convention, where, on all but one roll call, he backed the compromise that allowed later legislatures and school boards to decide whether or not to segregate blacks in schools. Appointed U.S. district attorney for Kansas by Lincoln in 1861, he shortly resigned to become a lieutenant colonel in state troops during the Civil War. By 1865, when he was Speaker of the state house, he had become a Republican. County attorney of Johnson County from 1866 to 1869 and for a few years during the 1870s, he was judge of the district court from 1869 to 1870 and again from 1879 through at least 1890. He became a Democrat again, in either 1872 or 1878, depending on which source one believes. *Leavenworth Advocate*, May 3, 1890, p. 2; *Topeka Capital-Commonwealth*, January 8, 1889, p. 3; Ed Blair, *History of Johnson County, Kans.* (Lawrence, Kan.: Standard Publishing Co., 1915), 113–14, 229–32; William E. Connelley, *A Standard History of Kansas and Kansans* (Chicago: Lewis Publishing Co., 1918), 3:1303; *Debates* (1859), 192–95.

132. *James v. Henry Metz*, quoted in *Leavenworth Times*, November 10, 1889, p. 5; *Johnson v. Olathe School Bd.*, quoted in *Leavenworth Advocate*, April 26, 1890, p. 2.

133. *Knox v. Independence School Board*, 45 Kan. 152, 25 P. 616 (1891). Horton did stress that Independence had attendance zones and that the

"white" school in the ward had empty seats. Although he did not cite *Daniel*, he must have been aware of it and may have been seeking to distinguish it.

134. Price was manumitted and "adopted" by a white man, J. C. Price (perhaps his father), in 1861. Trained by a tutor in Cairo, Illinois, he migrated to Texas, where he taught school, edited three newspapers, two of which were "white," and served as county attorney and county judge during Reconstruction. Moving to Kansas in 1877, he succes- sively became a law partner of several leading black figures and wrote the pro-integration speech that Alfred Fairfax, the first black state legis- lator in Kansas, delivered in the Kansas house in 1889. *Topeka American Citizen*, March 1, 1889, p. 1; Woods, *Black Odyssey*, 58. Thomas was born in Boone County, Missouri, apparently of free black parents, in 1860. A graduate of Lincoln Institute, in Jefferson City, Missouri, and of the University of Michigan Law School, he practiced in Topeka from 1887 through at least 1905. *Cleveland Gazette*, November 5, 1887; Berrett, *Who's Who in Topeka*, 120; *Topeka Kansas State Ledger*, January 20, 1903.

135. *Cartwright* v. *Board of Educ. of Coffeyville*, 73 Kan. 32, 84 P. 382 (1906). *Cartwright* involved segregated classrooms within the same school building. The court banned them.

136. *Rowles* v. *Board of Educ. of Wichita*, 76 Kan. 361, 91 P. 88 (1907). As noted above, the Kansas legislature passed a special act in 1889 banning seg- regation in Wichita, a first-class city. The legal question in *Rowles* was whether a subsequent 1905 act authorizing segregation in first-class cities generally was meant to overturn the specific Wichita act. Up- holding the *Tinnon* line, the supreme court ruled that any exceptions to the integrationist state policy must be explicit. For the background of *Rowles*, see Sondra Van Meeter, "Black Resistance to Segregation in the Wichita Public Schools, 1870–1912," *Midwest Quarterly* 20 (1978): 64–77.

137. *Williams* v. *Board of Educ. of Parsons*, 76 Kan. 202, 99 P. 217 (1908). When his four children were transferred from the common school in his ward and assigned to a segregated school a mile and a half and one railroad switching yard with sixteen constantly used tracks away, Williams pro- tested, then sued. The court agreed that this was a breach of the school board's admitted discretion. It is instructive to note that the supreme court's unanimous opinion was penned by Alfred W. Benson, who had been mayor of Ottawa during the *Tinnon* case and who as a state senator in 1881 had voted to end the exclusion of blacks from common schools in first-class cities. Born in Chautauqua County, New York, of New England Congregationalist parents, Benson was a leading prohibi- tionist politician who filled numerous county and state offices and was

appointed to the U.S. Senate in 1906–7. *Kansas*, ed. Blackmar, 1:59–61; *Ottawa Daily Republican*, February 17, 1881, p. 2; March 4, 1881, p. 2; *Ottawa Journal and Triumph*, November 29, 1877, p. 3.

138. *Reynolds* v. *Board of Educ. of Topeka*, 66 Kan. 672, 72 P. 274 (1903), hereafter referred to as *Reynolds*. Materials in the case file for *Reynolds*, in the Kansas State Historical Society, will be referred to as Reynolds Case File.

139. School board brief, depositions of Clarence Long, A. T. Allen, William Reynolds, all in Reynolds Case File. *Topeka Daily Capital*, February 6, 1902, p. 6; February 13, 1902, p. 5; February 15, 1902, p. 5; March 4, 1902, p. 6; March 7, 1902, p. 4.

140. *Topeka Daily Capital*, February 2, 1902, p. 9; February 5, 1902, p. 5; February 25, 1902, p. 2; March 5, 1902, pp. 1, 2; March 6, 1902, p. 5; March 7, 1902, p. 6; March 15, 1902, pp. 3, 8; March 27, 1902, p. 6; September 11, 1902, p. 8; October 11, 1902, p. 5; April 12, 1903, p. 9.

141. *Topeka Colored Citizen*, June 15, 1900, p. 1; August 31, 1900, p. 4; *Topeka Kansas State Ledger*, March 20, 1900, p. 1.

142. King, *History of Shawnee County*, 626–27; Walter T. K. Nugent, *The Tolerant Populists: Kansas Populism and Nativism* (Chicago: University of Chicago Press, 1963), 135–36; *Topeka Daily Capital*, February 9, 1902, p. 6; February 11, 1902, p. 6; March 9, 1902, p. 7; March 11, 1902, p. 6; May 27, 1902, p. 2; August 23, 1902, p. 6; October 14, 1902, p. 4; October 22, 1902, p. 8.

143. *Kansas*, ed. Blackmar, 3:670–72; Berrett, *Who's Who in Topeka*, 45–46; *Topeka Colored Citizen*, February 10, 1898, p. 3. Gleed was so often disloyal to the Republican party that the *Topeka Daily Capital*, October 29, 1902, p. 3, reported that when he asked a party loyalist for his support, claiming to have voted Republican before the worker had been born, the worker refused, replying, "That may be true, but the trouble is that you have never voted it since."

144. Contrasting the Ministerial Union's activism in favor of coerced Bible reading with its actions on segregation, Clemens asked rhetorically, "Has the Ministerial union passed any resolutions about this attempt to exclude part of God's children from the best schools because God was so thoughtless as to give them dark skins? . . . It is so much easier and safer to denounce saloons than to run counter to a strong popular prejudice . . . I rebel against this entire spirit. The Pharisees must go." *Topeka Daily Capital*, March 5, 1902, pp. 1, 2.

145. Reynolds deposition, in Reynolds Case File.

146. The first sentence of section 2 of the Bill of Rights read: "All political power is inherent in the people, and all free governments are founded on their authority, and are instituted for their equal protection and

benefit." Article 6, section 2, commanded the legislature to "encourage the promotion of intellectual, moral, scientific and agricultural improvement, by establishing a uniform system of common schools, and schools of a higher grade, embracing normal, preparatory, collegiate and university departments." *Federal and State Constitutions,* ed. Thorpe, 2:1242, 1252.

147. These technical issues are treated in *Reynolds,* 66 Kan. at 673–77, 72 P. at 275–76.

148. *Topeka Daily Capital,* May 25, 1902, p. 8. The expansion, which had long been sought by the justices and the bar, was a response to the increased work load of the court since it had been established in 1859.

149. The seven justices, all Republicans, who sat in *Reynolds* were Rosseau A. Burch, born in rural Indiana in 1862 and a graduate of the University of Michigan Law School; Edwin W. Cunningham, born in 1842 in rural north-central Ohio and a longtime resident of Emporia, Kansas; Adrian L. Greene, born in the tiny Mississippi river town of Canton, Missouri, in 1848, who practiced in the metropolis of Newton, Kansas, for thirty-one years before his appointment to the supreme court; William A. Johnston, Canadian-born of Scotch-Irish immigrant parents, a member of the Kansas house and then senate in 1876 to 1880, state attorney general from 1880 to 1884, and justice of the supreme court since then; Henry F. Mason, born in Racine, Wisconsin, in 1860, a newspaper editor, lawyer, county attorney, and state legislator who happened to be chairman of the judiciary committee when four vacancies on the supreme court opened up; John C. Pollock, born in eastern Ohio near Wheeling, West Virginia, in 1857, who moved successively to Iowa, Missouri, and Kansas and primarily represented railroads, banks, and other corporations; and William R. Smith, born in rural northern Illinois in 1853, another Michigan Law School graduate who practiced in Atchison. See *Topeka Daily Capital,* May 25, 1902, p. 8; Inman, "Supreme Court of Kansas," 321–42; Berrett, *Who's Who in Topeka,* 15, 48, 64, 82; *Kansas,* ed. Blackmar, 2:36; In Memoriam, 76 Kans. vi–x (1908).

150. After first construing "common schools" to be merely elementary schools, he allowed for the purpose of argument that the phrase might be interpreted as "equally open to all." *Reynolds,* 66 Kan. at 680, 72 P. at 277.

151. Burch quoted extensively from *Cory v. Carter,* 48 Ind. 327 (1874). The extremely racist 1851 Indiana document, which banned blacks from further entry into the state, required the legislature "to encourage, by all suitable means, moral, intellectual, scientific, and agricultural improvement, and to provide by law for a general and uniform system of

common schools, wherein tuition shall be without charge, and equally
open to all." *Federal and State Constitutions,* ed. Thorpe, 3:1086. (Art. 7
§ 1). Compare the 1859 Kan. Const., Art. 6, § 2, ibid., 3:1252.

152. *Reynolds,* 66 Kan. at 681, 72 P. at 277.

153. *Tinnon,* 26 Kan. at 23; *Reynolds,* 66 Kan. at 684–86, 72 P. at 278–79,
quoting from *Roberts* v. *Boston,* 5 Cush. 198 (1849).

154. *Reynolds,* 66 Kan. at 687–88, 72 P. at 279–80, quoting from *State ex rel.
Garnes* v. *McCann,* 21 Ohio St. 198 (1871); *People ex rel. King* v. *Gallagher,*
93 N.Y. 438 (1883); *Ward* v. *Flood,* 48 Cal. 36 (1874).

155. On arguments from silence, see my "Expert Witnesses, Rational Choice,
and the Search for Intent," *Constitutional Commentary* 5 (1988): 351, and
references cited therein. In at least three instances—*Cory* v. *Carter,
Bertonneau,* and *Gazaway* v. *Springfield, Oh.* (C.C.S.D. Ohio, 1882, case
no. 3200, unpublished)—blacks began efforts to appeal to the U.S.
Supreme Court but abandoned them. In *Gazaway,* the explicit reason for
abandonment was financial. See my *Dead End,* 50 n. 70.

156. *Reynolds,* 66 Kan. at 691–92, 72 P. at 281, quoting *Plessy* v. *Ferguson,* 163
U.S. 544.

157. *Reynolds,* 66 Kan. at 692, 72 P. at 281.

158. This was hardly the end of the struggle in Kansas. Besides the cases
cited in Table 2, blacks won *Woolridge* v. *Galena,* 98 Kan. 397, 157 P. 1184
(1916), and *Graham* v. *Board of Educ.,* 153 Kan. 840, 114 P.2d 313 (1941).
The lead lawyer in *Graham,* J. L. Hunt, had assisted Gleed in *Reynolds*
nearly forty years earlier. There were no doubt other cases that I have
missed or that were not reported.

159. Brennan, "Bill of Rights and the States," 266.

State Constitutions and Criminal Justice in the Late Nineteenth Century

Lawrence M. Friedman

In recent years, interest in state constitutions, and what state supreme courts make out of them, has noticeably increased. At one time, of course, state constitutional law, at least if one aggregates all of the states, seemed to matter a great deal indeed. Many of the most famous (and infamous) doctrines of constitutional law in the period after the Civil War were hatched in the states—including that cluster of doctrines usually referred to as substantive due process.[1] But imperial Washington—the Washington of the New Deal, the Great Society, and the Warren Court—buried localism and states' rights in obscurity and deep disgrace. State constitutional law became a fading star; as a subject of scholarship and debate, it went into what appeared to be a terminal decline.

To a certain extent, the decline was more apparent than real. State constitutions continued to function; state supreme courts continued to grind out thousands of decisions. These decisions, many of them on constitutional issues, made an impact on litigants and on thousands of other citizens. But the panjandrums of constitutional law paid no attention. Among political scientists, the subject evoked a flicker or two of interest, but law schools ignored the whole affair. Law schools were generally concerned with "legal science"; their prestige depended on their national rather than local status; state constitutional law was irrelevant to their central concerns.

In recent years, state constitutional law has made a minor comeback. The doctrine of independent state grounds, which has recently received a "tremendous burst of energy," has been partly responsible.[2] It is too early—and too difficult—to assess what, if anything, the comeback means to our constitutional system. But it has rekindled at least a modest interest in historical aspects of state constitutions, state constitutional law, and state high courts.

This essay will look at one fragment of that history, or rather a fragment of a fragment: the constitutional activity of the states with respect to crime and criminal justice in the late nineteenth century.

The Dog That Did Not Bark

In the nineteenth century, almost every state expended tremendous political energy on making, unmaking, and remaking constitutions. Between the Civil War and the end of the century, many states molted constitutions, some more than once—notably most of the southern states. In addition, a flock of newly minted western states—Colorado, Utah, Montana, the Dakotas, Wyoming—crowded into the Union, each with its own fresh constitution.

Surprisingly little of this organic energy went into issues of criminal justice. Each state constitution, of course, had a bill of rights; and each bill of rights, like the federal model, contained a healthy dose of material on criminal justice. But in the typical constitution, the bill of rights was a copycat version of the bill of rights of some other state or some earlier constitution. The provisions were carried over without much thought or debate. There were minor variations of language but not much novelty or evolution.

The Pennsylvania Constitution of 1873 is a typical instance. It was graced with a declaration of rights, some twenty-six sections long. This declaration was essentially drawn from the comparable text of the Constitution of 1838, also twenty-six sections long. The federal Bill of Rights, of course, was the ultimate source of most state provisions (except for a few of the original states). The language was simply accepted as boilerplate. Often, to be sure, the variations in style, the additions, or the subtractions are not uninteresting. The Mississippi Constitution of 1890, for example, specifically authorized trial judges, in cases of rape, fornication, adultery, or sodomy, to clear the courtroom of everyone except those persons "necessary in the conduct of the trial" (Art. I, sec. 26). But in general, there was little change and little thought of change. Among the thousands of pages of debates on new state constitutions or amendments to old ones, the amount of talk or effort devoted to criminal provisions or the bill of rights is amazingly meager.[3]

Other provisions of state constitutions, of course, did bear on the criminal justice system. Judiciary articles had direct or indirect relevance. States often revamped their judicial systems, and this had consequences for criminal justice. There were also, in many cases, new substantive provisions—on such burning issues as railroad regulation or corporate charters—which had a criminal coda attached to them.[4] In a few instances, the constitution directed state legislatures to prohibit this or outlaw that: Utah, for example, in its Constitution of 1895, instructed its legislature to outlaw the labor of women and children in mines. And a ban on polygamy was part of the price Utah had to pay for admission to the Union. North Dakota's Constitution of 1889 included a separate prohibition article, to be submitted to the voters (they approved of it). Yet even after these concessions and observations, the record remains unusually barren.

Constitutional litigation on criminal justice was in its own way meager as well, though not quite as meager as litigation on freedom of speech or the press. Indeed, certain subjects generated a healthy load of cases—dozens of opinions on whether confessions were voluntary or not, many dozens on double jeopardy. These are, of course, important issues. They test the boundaries of known concepts. What is rarer are cases in which plaintiffs attack the *structure* of criminal justice on the basis of constitutional provisions or in which such issues are even discussed. This was a far cry from the key decisions of the Warren Court; in *Miranda, Gideon,* and other leading decisions on criminal justice of the 1950s and 1960s the issue was not whether the particular facts of a case did or did not bring the defendant within some known rule but whether a statute or institution violated the constitutional scheme. Constitutional litigation in the nineteenth century, by contrast, was static, not dynamic.

The double jeopardy cases illustrate the point. In *Commonwealth* v. *Arner,*[5] the defendant was indicted for fornication and bastardy; the victim, Elsie L. Weller, was under age sixteen at the time. The defendant was also charged with rape, on the same facts; after the fornication-bastardy case went to the jury, but before the verdict, the defendant was forced to plead to the rape charge. He was convicted of all the offenses. He appealed only from the rape conviction, which carried a "jolt" in the state penitentiary. The appellate court reversed that conviction. Arner had been indicted and convicted for one offense and he could not be tried, on the same facts, for a serious crime that would logically include the lesser offense—for example, an acquittal for assault would bar trial for manslaughter arising out of the same blow of the fist.

All this was, of course, a serious matter for Arner and his victim, if nobody else. Many pages in the digests and abridgments cover points like the point in *Arner*. Yet on the whole, they do not seriously derange the existing order of criminal justice. In most of the cases, constitutional points seem raised almost as an afterthought and rejected cavalierly, almost with a yawn. Serious discussion is rare. Few courts ever struck down criminal statutes and practices as offensive to constitutional right. The cumulative number of cases is not insubstantial, but there is no comparison between the role constitutional issues play in criminal jurisprudence today and in, say, the 1870s.

A few empirical studies have touched on the subject. Robert Kagan and associates studied the work load of sixteen state supreme courts between 1870 and 1970; they found relatively few constitutional cases in the late nineteenth century, and few of these touched on criminal justice issues. By contrast, in the period 1965–70, of the vastly greater number of criminal appeals to state supreme courts, almost half raised constitutional issues.[6] On the trial court level, too, constitutional issues were rare in the nineteenth century. At least this is suggested by the findings of Lawrence M. Friedman and Robert V. Percival in their study of Alameda County.[7]

Somewhat inconsistently, some appellate cases on criminal justice showed a degree of mindless legalism, a finicky attachment to tiny points of law; Roscoe Pound indignantly called this phenomenon "hypertrophy" of procedure.[8] The *Arner* case, arguably, falls into this category. I will return to this point.

On the surface, then, our subject is a nonsubject; it allows at best some negative inferences, like the famous dog that did not bark in the Sherlock Holmes story. It contrasts sharply with the contemporary situation in which criminal justice has been highly constitutionalized. The Warren Court in the 1950s was extremely active in creating new constitutional doctrine out of the words of the Bill of Rights. Much of this doctrine has been bold and imaginative; some has generated intense controversy. Many cases attacked entrenched police practices. The states, at first reluctantly, then with a certain zeal, have followed the same path.[9]

The nineteenth century can also be contrasted with the late eighteenth century. The rights of man were at the center of political discussion and debate in the age of the drafting of the federal Constitution and the framing of the Bill of Rights. The issue of fairness in criminal trials was central to the discussion. Out of this period of creativity came the famous guarantees of the Bill of Rights, state and federal—prohibitions against unlawful searches and seizures, excessive bail, cruel and unusual punishment, double jeopardy, and self-incrimination, among others.

We tend, of course, to look at the past through the lenses of today. It is natural, then, to ask why this or that was missing in the nineteenth century. The nineteenth century had its own viewpoint. To understand the period, we have to look at civil rights and civil liberties as contemporaries saw them. (This does not mean accepting the dominant norms of the past—on race or sex or crime—but analyzing them in their setting.) The issue is one of legal culture—popular attitudes toward law and expectations with regard to law—in the nineteenth century.[10] Paradoxically, if we understand nineteenth-century constitutionalism, it helps us understand the amazing constitutional developments of our own century as well.

Modern legal culture is remarkably imperial. At its root is an attitude I have called the general expectation of justice.[11] This is the notion that every instance of wrong or injustice must have some remedy in law. This trait, I have argued, helps explain the major developments of our century: the amazing efflorescence of "private law" rights (tort liability, for example), the vast expansion of public law entitlements, and the civil rights movement itself.

The nineteenth century had its own expectations about law and the legal system. These were considerably more limited than twentieth-century expectations. Legal rights occupied a definite, bounded domain; its narrow limits were clearly marked off from other social space. Indeed, another way to describe the general expectation of justice—the modern legal culture—is precisely in terms of the blurring and breakdown of boundaries, the erosion of zones of immunity from law. These zones of immunity were the domain of authority—

teachers, the state, prison wardens, husbands, fathers, employers—
and although they were, in contrast to the earlier past, rather weakened (and in some regards—churches, the aristocracy—extremely
so), they were very strong in comparison to the 1980s.

Another trait of modern legal culture, clearly linked to the general
expectation of justice, is what I have called plural equality.[12] Equality,
of course, is an old and respected concept, vital to American political theory and to popular culture as well. But the inner sense of the
concept has changed greatly between then and now. Older concepts
of equality presupposed a more hierarchical arrangement of society.
Equality was primarily a political concept, and it meant that, within a
society with a clear top and a clear bottom and a clear understanding
of which norms were dominant, everyone, whether top or bottom,
possessed certain basic political rights. These included rights to a fair
criminal trial. Such rights were part of the social definition of toleration—along with freedom of speech and religion. But none of these
involved equality in the modern sense; they were consistent with
moral and social stratification and clear recognition that the country
belonged to the dominant group, white Protestant men. The modern
concept is more plural, as it were. Equality carries with it today an implication of something more than formal rights, something more than
toleration; it implies an equality of dignity, a sharing of social ownership, a widening of the band of accepted habits, customs, norms, and
styles.

Nineteenth-century legal culture, then, militated against vigorous testing of boundaries in criminal justice as in other areas of legal
life. Constitutional law—the litigating part of it—is nothing but the
testing of boundaries. The state of litigation, the state of controversy,
is an indicator of legal culture; it tells us where the ragged edges are,
the points at issue. In (say) 1850, there was no problem seeing conflict
over slavery or over the limits of federal power. In (say) 1880, there
was no problem finding conflict over railroad regulation, public utility
rates, monopoly, strikes and boycotts, and the limits of police power.
But criminal justice, on the whole, slept a hegemonic sleep.

From Leviathan to the Dangerous Classes

Case law, as I said, is more interesting for what it is not than for what it is. Case law in its constitutional aspects reflects a shift in under-lying goals of criminal procedure. Fear of leviathan—the despotic, overbearing state—was a pervasive influence on the original Bill of Rights in the eighteenth century. This theme weakened and wore out in the course of the nineteenth century. Theoreticians of the late nine-teenth century would have no part of it. "I do not think there can be much doubt," wrote Christopher Tiedeman in 1890, "that the danger of official tyranny has been successfully dissipated in the American constitutional system."[13]

Not everyone would have agreed, of course, and the old themes still produced at least minor echoes. But on the whole, a new set of fears replaced fears of tyranny: fears of the criminal. To the dominant segments of society, the organs of state posed no threat to Ameri-can legal order; that came rather from defendants—the "dangerous classes," which included deviants of all sorts, tramps, hoboes, juve-nile delinquents, gangs.[14] Accordingly, emphasis shifted from what Herbert Packer has called the "due process" theme of criminal justice to the competing theme of "crime control."[15]

This shift drained away constitutional interest in criminal justice. The dangerous classes lacked spokesmen, and plural equality was an idea whose time had not yet come. The shift had consequences in the criminal justice system itself; some of these took constitutional form. The search for reform in criminal justice focused on ways to control and eliminate crime, rather than on ways to protect the accused. Any recounting of major developments in nineteenth-century criminal jus-tice would have to list the development of police forces, the rise of the penitentiary, and the codification of criminal justice. Of these, only the last had anything remotely to do with themes of due process.

Crime control crops up, too, as an element in a few constitutional changes—for example, reform or replacement of the grand jury. The Indiana Constitution of 1851 provided that "the General Assembly may modify or abolish the Grand Jury system" (Art. VII, sec. 17). In debates over this clause, both sides invoked the spirit of freedom and the usual catchwords about tyranny and liberty, but there was an unmistakable undercurrent of concern about "efficiency" and other code words for crime control.[16] Amasa Eaton, writing in 1892, spoke of the grand jury as an "archaic survival" and criticized constitutions in Mississippi, Kentucky, Idaho, and Wyoming which held on to the institution. Eaton preferred the system of "information": after all, "in a democracy, where the prosecuting officer is elected by the people, there is no danger of abuse of the power of proceeding by information."[17]

California, "progressive" on this point, made the grand jury optional. Its constitution, adopted in 1879, provided in Article I, section 8, that "offenses heretofore required to be prosecuted by indictment shall be prosecuted by information, after examination and commitment by a magistrate, or by indictment . . . as may be prescribed by law." In *Hurtado* v. *California* (1884),[18] the Supreme Court of the United States upheld the California statute that carried out this clause. Federal doctrine would not stand in the way of "progressive developments" in "legal ideas and institutions." The old methods had been "guards against executive usurpation and tyranny," but now they "might prove obstructive and injurious when imposed on the just and necessary discretion of legislative power."[19]

Popular opinion—middle class and up—in the nineteenth century tended to be complacent and self-satisfied about American democracy. Visitors as different as Alexis de Tocqueville and Frances Trollope commented on American superpatriotism, on the pride and bumptiousness of the public, on the smug sense that America was truly egalitarian, truly democratic.[20] It would have been hard to sell the idea—and not just to Tiedeman and Eaton—that the elites now sat on the vacant throne of George III and were themselves repressive.

A Dual System

The tension between the two themes—due process and crime control—has never been resolved and perhaps never can be. A balance must always be struck. The word *balance* may be unfortunate; it implies stability. Sometimes the balance is a house of cards. The history of criminal justice suggests a tilt of the scales toward crime control in the nineteenth century. State supreme courts were constitutionally active on issues of taxing power, labor legislation, and the like but supine with regard to "progressive" legislation in criminal justice. It was a period of many innovations; but the innovations sailed through the courts unchallenged or with challenges that failed to prevail. For example, the United States Supreme Court upheld Massachusetts' habitual criminal statute of 1887 against attack on the grounds of double jeopardy, denial of equal protection, cruel and unusual punishment, ex post facto, and the right of trial by jury in a three-page opinion that was remarkably snappy and offhand even for its day.[21]

One reason for the reticence has already been mentioned. Due process was a major constitutional concept, yet the definition of a fair trial and a fair correctional system was relatively narrow (in hindsight). Today, the concept of due process permeates the legal system. There is an unspoken norm that large power centers—governmental or otherwise—should act fairly, insofar as they make major impacts on people's lives. The nineteenth century had no such concept and no such body of doctrine. Due process related, to be sure, to criminal trials; but even there it was carefully bounded, and it showed little propensity to expand. Outside the courtroom, too, were the zones of power and immunity: the army, schools, factories, prisons, poorhouses, institutions of all sizes and sorts.

Consider, for example, a Pennsylvania case on what we would now call prisoners' rights (1912).[22] The plaintiff, in jail, refused to go to religious services on Sunday. He was punished by the keeper, who put him "in the dungeon"; afterward, a deputy warden forced him to "attend . . . religious exercises." The court derisively rejected any claim that rights had been violated. The court looked at the prison as the locus of a private sphere of authority; the judge compared the warden's power to a parent's control over children. Modern cases, of course, tend to treat prisoners like everybody else, in terms of rights, or almost so, except for the small detail of iron bars. The standards applied to organs of state reach into the prison. The presumption today is that due process covers everybody, everywhere, of every condition of life, whenever subject to state power. There was no such presumption in 1912, let alone 1870.

This is not to say that criminal justice and corrections were completely uncontrolled, that crime control elements completely replaced due process elements. (This would be as inaccurate as to assume that prisoners today actually enjoy all the rights they have on paper or in published opinions.) The system operated under an umbrella of norms, constitutional and otherwise. The tilt toward crime control was simply that: a tilt. There was an equilibrium, and there were expectations about fairness in criminal justice, which, though more rubbery and plastic than they are today, still had definite limits.

One way of expressing an equilibrium is through a system of criminal justice that operates on two inconsistent levels. The nineteenth-century system was dual with a vengeance. There was a formal, official system on top, crowned with a wreath of constitutional rights; it was, indeed, operational in uncommon but important instances—murder trials, for example. For the average, ordinary case, there was a very different operating system—more routine, less finicky about rights and procedures. And the mode of dealing with petty cases—the thousands of daily cases on drunkenness, disturbing the peace, and vagrancy—was even more summary and slapdash.

Another form of duality is to be seen in the extravagant outbursts of lawlessness that disfigured the century—lynch law and vigilantism and, on a more covert and regular basis, police brutality. At night, on the streets, and in the darker corners of station houses, lawlessness was more of a reality than constitutional delicacy. Lynch law was southern, vigilantism western, police brutality eastern and urban, but these regional emanations, though they had their own inner natures, shared an impatience with due process and a strong belief that society could not afford the luxury of legal niceties.

The vigilante movement, often misunderstood, and the focus of a large literature,[23] was not always the angry work of an unruly mob, or, contrariwise, a public expression of outrage against desperadoes. It was at times a revolt of elites against an all-too-popular justice—juries too prone to acquit. Lynching was on the whole a more serious deformation. Its function was to enforce a vicious code against southern blacks with more violence and cruelty than the law would or could officially permit. White mobs found judges and court officials too lax with regard to the southern "code." The vigilante movement and lynching must be understood as revolts *against* the constitutional system, *against* the Bill of Rights; and a history of state constitutionalism (and federal constitutionalism, for that matter) would be incomplete if it did not take these revolts into account, along with the silence, apathy, and approval of broad segments of the public.

Dualism was not, on the whole, ever formally recognized as a constitutional issue. The South Carolina Constitution of 1895, to be sure, took a stand against lynching and imposed (in theory) damages of "not less than two thousand dollars" against any county in which a lynching took place (Art. VI, sec. 6). This was exceptional. Lynching in the South was the very obverse of a constitutional issue. The thrust of the bills of rights had been to protect defendants against the tyranny of the state; under the dual system, popular justice stepped into the tyrant's vacant throne and wrapped itself in the mantle of law and order. The defendant was still victimized; but the oppressor was diffuse: not a clique of courtiers but a middle-class and upper-class mass. It was not King George, or the president in Washington who dragged blacks from jail cells and burned them alive; it was crowds of southern whites who thought of themselves as decent, respectable citizens—and as democrats.

There were people who spoke out against lynch mobs, against vigilantes, against police brutality and the third degree. Some protectors and defenders of rights were themselves among the elite—perhaps more there than among "the people."[24] Even today, at least in the white community, the average citizen probably thinks a Bernard Goetz is justified in shooting "hoodlums" who act menacingly in the New York subway; the average citizen prefers law and order to the rarefied positions of the American Civil Liberties Union (ACLU). George Bush, campaigning successfully for president in 1988, made a campaign issue of denouncing the ACLU. He won heavily, especially in the South.[25]

Dualism takes many forms in criminal justice. Plea bargaining is a variety of dualism. It is by no means a contemporary invention; it goes back at least to the nineteenth century.[26] Routine, hurried, summary forms of criminal justice go back even further. Routinization seems, often enough, a simple necessity. The system would otherwise be swamped by sheer numbers of cases. But this is not the source of routine. The true source of summary justice is the sense that long, drawn-out trials, bristling with safeguards, are a pointless waste of time and money for the typical defendant—the pickpocket of the nineteenth century or the man in a ski mask who knocks off a 7-11 store and gets caught. These people neither need nor deserve a slow, careful process—let alone the possibility that they will slip through some loophole and go free. When elaborate "rights" have no firm support in public opinion, shortcuts are bound to flourish; when the public is unable or unwilling to pay for an elaborate, carefully crafted working system of criminal justice, no such system will be in place. Thus dualism is perhaps a social necessity—or at least a tough, deep-rooted problem. This is not to say that plea bargaining is a good idea or that it cannot be replaced but only that the problem of routine has to be honestly faced and almost never is.

Plea bargaining at least has some overt defenders. Police brutality does not. Today, the nineteenth-century attitude toward such matters looks like pure hypocrisy; but a label is not the same as an explanation. Underlying dual systems are popular theories of social control.[27] These are notions that formalism produces more and better criminal justice in combination with an informal, even lawless system, than either would produce alone. Whether the theory is true or false does not concern us. Some such theory is implicit in the working system of criminal justice. This was true in the nineteenth century and is still true today.

The implicit theory helps us understand the persistent dualism of law: between high-flown bills of rights and the working system of criminal justice. These dualisms were most obviously at work in the vice laws. Legislators drank like fish and passed laws against liquor; they gambled and patronized brothels, then voted to outlaw gambling and prostitution. Like the noble rights set out in state constitutions, these vice laws were not intended to be futile. They were passed as control devices—just as legislators today enact speed limits, which they fully intend to violate themselves and which all of us in fact violate, yet at the same time believe in and defend.

The constitutional regime had a genuine function. The expression of formal rights was intended to affect behavior. The texts were meant to express social ideals; but beyond this, the goal was to limit and control deviant behavior and, perhaps most important, to force it underground. Police brutality, for example, was against the law and was not as common as in a regime—there have been many of them—that accepts brutality openly and embraces it. Police brutality was subterranean, and it was used mostly against "criminals," against those who deserved no better—and against unpopular and unpowerful people. Most compromises, for obvious reasons, are made at the expense of such people.

Hypertrophy

Hypertrophy is another aspect of dualism. Roscoe Pound used the term to mean legalism, sticklerism, meticulous attention to (empty) forms. Occasional excesses of proceduralism, including constitutional proceduralism, strengthen the impression of meticulous care—a pleasant and useful fiction. Most cases, of course, do not get such kid-gloves treatment.

How common was hypertrophy? It is not easy to say. There are, to my knowledge, no systematic studies of the subject. It is not hard, however, to find examples. The disease seemed to be especially virulent in late nineteenth-century Texas. Strict scrutiny (as it were) was the Texas habit for indictments. In *Haun* v. *State* (1883),[28] an emanation from that state, an indictment concluded with these words: "Against the peace and dignity of the State, this the third day of November, 1882." According to the Court of Appeals of Texas, the Texas Constitution required the words "against the peace and dignity of the State," but the court went on to declare that the extra words were worse than unnecessary—they destroyed the value of the indictment. In an 1882 case, the same court struck down a statute that dared to provide a simple, nonlegalistic form for indictments for theft.[29]

What are we to make of hypertrophy? It can be looked at as a pathology, an aberration; but again, this is a label, not an explanation. Hypertrophy had the same effect in the nineteenth century as it does today: it made some lawyers, and no doubt many citizens, angry. Decisions like *Haun,* a lawyer from Indiana wrote in 1884, were "in flagrant violation of a common-sense view of law and justice."[30] Cases of "palpable guilt and heinous atrocity" create a desire for "speedy justice without the formalities of law." Yet people must be taught, the writer continued—a bit inconsistently—"to believe in stern justice."[31]

To find a function for hypertrophy, the best place to look is in the rubble of ideology. Douglas Hay has described such functions for eighteenth-century England: "The punctilious attention to forms, the dispassionate and legalistic exchanges . . . argued that those administering and using the laws submitted to its rules. The law thereby became something more than the creature of a ruling class—it became a power with its own claims." The "very inefficiency" of law, its "absurd formalism," was "part of its strength as ideology."[32] Conditions in the United States, of course, were not exactly the same. But there were, as always, deficiencies of justice, and the deficiencies were strongly correlated with income and class. Justice appeared to be blind only to people who did not see too well themselves. But hypertrophy seemed classless and totally neutral. Cases like *Haun* gave out a message of absolute justice in criminal affairs: no amount of care, no measure of attention to form was too great if it could save one man— or even one out of ten—from unlawful conviction.

To whom was this message addressed? In *Haun,* it was no doubt directed to the legal profession, itself in a period of transition and doubt, and to the judges, always anxious about their role. The general public, of course, was not normally in the habit of reading the Texas reports. But the public had its own source of information about criminal justice, including its hypertrophies. The public today "learns" about criminal justice from television; and the public of the late nineteenth century "learned" from popular culture too—from the show trials and murder cases that were headline news in newspapers and mass magazines.[33]

The lesson was a double one, however—inconsistent and most probably false. One lesson was that the law took amazing care of the rights of defendants. At the same time, people saw a jungle of absurd technicality, and it fed their anger as well as their pride. Both aspects of the system had an ideological function. The attention to rights legitimated the fairness of the system as a whole. At the same time, "the popular feeling that the administration of the law is uncertain and dilatory" kept alive, as one writer remarked, "the tendency in many sections to lynch law."[34]

A Final Word

These pages, as I look back on them, seem to put heavy emphasis on ideology. The concept was used to account for the way state constitutional law intersected with criminal justice. I did not intend, however, to advance a general proposition about the nature of law or even about its ideological functions. All legal systems have more than one function. They are both instrumental and ideological. They express moral values, and at the same time, they try to mold conduct through punishments and rewards.[35] Constitutional law, for obvious reasons, has a heavy ideological component.

But the various state constitutions and their bills of rights were never "mere" ideology, mere symbols and empty forms. It is certainly worthwhile to talk about shortcomings in criminal justice. On such matters as lynching, it is imperative to do so. But most people, in most times and places, were probably satisfied with the system. After all, few of them ran personally afoul of criminal justice. Many aspects of nineteenth-century trials were indeed fair, according to nineteenth-century lights and local understanding.

What do we learn from looking at the way state constitutions and state courts dealt with criminal justice? One lesson—it may still be valuable—is a warning not to draw too sharp a line between state and national behavior. Each state, to be sure, had its own history, tradition, and habits. But everywhere courts were part of a single social system, they were exposed to the same dominant strands of legal culture, and they reacted to the great trends and events in the world around them. A close study of state constitutional history can be, and often is, a way to see the country as a whole.

Notes

1. See, for example, Peter J. Galie, "State Courts and Economic Rights," *Annals* 496 (1988): 76; Arnold Paul, *Conservative Crisis and the Rule of Law: Attitudes of Bar and Bench* (Gloucester, Mass.: Peter Smith, 1976).
2. Lawrence M. Friedman, "State Constitutions in Historical Perspective," *Annals* 496 (1988): 33, 41; see *Pruneyard Shopping Center* v. *Rubins*, 447 U.S. 74 (1980).
3. See Gordon M. Bakken, *Rocky Mountain Constitution Making, 1850–1912* (New York: Greenwood Press, 1987), 23–25, 102–3.
4. Thus Idaho and Wyoming had provisions against monopolies, which took the form of forbidding and outlawing—criminalization, in short.
5. 149 Pa. 35, 24 A. 83 (1892).
6. Robert Kagan et al., "The Business of State Supreme Courts, 1870–1970," *Stanford Law Review* 30 (1977): 121. The Kagan study was focused, of course, on state courts, and one might wonder whether constitu-

tional issues were common in the nineteenth century in federal courts. But before the full development of the incorporation doctrine, defendants in state cases could not often make effective use of federal courts. Federal crimes were few and insignificant. The federal government did not even have a prison before the 1890s; it farmed out its few prisoners to state penitentiaries.

7. Lawrence M. Friedman and Robert V. Percival, *The Roots of Justice: Crime and Punishment in Alameda County, California, 1870–1910* (Chapel Hill: University of North Carolina Press, 1981), 283.

8. Roscoe Pound, *Criminal Justice in America* (New York: H. Holt, 1930), 161. Pound also spoke of "record worship," that is, "excessive regard for the formal record at the expense of the case," and "strict scrutiny of the record for 'errors of law' at the expense of scrutiny of the case to insure the consonance of the result to the demands of the substantive law." Ibid.

9. See Kagan et al., "Business of State Supreme Courts"; for a case study of the reaction of four states to the Warren revolution, see G. Alan Tarr and Mary C. A. Porter, *State Supreme Courts in State and Nation* (New Haven: Yale University Press, 1988).

10. For the concept of legal culture, see Lawrence M. Friedman, *The Legal System: A Social Science Perspective* (New York: Russell Sage Foundation, 1975), 15–16.

11. Lawrence M. Friedman, *Total Justice* (New York: Russell Sage Foundation, 1985).

12. Ibid.

13. Christopher G. Tiedeman, *The Unwritten Constitution of the United States* (1890; rpt. New York: Putnam Books, 1974), 162. Tiedeman went on to add his opinion that the danger of "tyranny" in his period came from "a popular majority" and officials who were "too ready to obey every popular caprice." He was thinking, of course, of social legislation. The written constitution "is not needed for the protection of the people against the tyranny of the officials; its only value is to serve as a check upon the popular will in the interest of the minority." Ibid., 163.

14. See Eric H. Monkkonen, *The Dangerous Class: Crime and Poverty in Columbus, Ohio, 1860–1885* (Cambridge, Mass.: Harvard University Press, 1975). American laborers and union organizers had, to be sure, good grounds to fear the tyranny of the state, but the respectable majority did not hear those voices. See, in general, William E. Forbash, "The Shaping of the American Labor Movement," *Harvard Law Review* 102 (1989): 1109.

15. Herbert Packer, *The Limits of the Criminal Sanction* (Stanford: Stanford University Press, 1968), 149ff.

16. On the debates in Indiana, see David J. Bodenhamer, *The Pursuit of Justice: Crime and Law in Antebellum Indiana* (New York: Garland, 1986), chap. 3.
17. Amasa M. Eaton, "Recent State Constitutions," *Harvard Law Review* 6 (1892): 53, 64.
18. 110 U.S. 516 (1884). Justice Matthews wrote the opinion; Justice Harlan dissented.
19. Id. at 529, 532.
20. "Nothing is more annoying," Tocqueville wrote, than the "irritable patriotism" of Americans. A foreigner "will gladly agree to praise much in their country, but he would like to be allowed to criticize something, and that he is absolutely refused." Alexis de Tocqueville, *Democracy in America,* ed. J. P. Mayer, trans. George Lawrence (Garden City, N.Y.: Doubleday, 1969), 237. Trollope also noted that Americans did not tolerate a "single word indicative of doubt, that any thing, or every thing, in that country is not the very best in the world." Frances Trollope, *Domestic Manners of the Americans,* 5th ed. (1839; rpt. Oxford: Oxford University Press, 1984), 362.
21. *McDonald* v. *Mass.,* 180 U.S. 311 (1901). The Court dismissed some of the constitutional points without giving a reason. State courts also upheld these statutes, effortlessly it seems. See, for example, *Blackburn* v. *State,* 50 Ohio St. 428, 36 N.E. 18 (1893).
22. *Merrick* v. *Lewis,* 22 Pa. D. 55 (1912).
23. On vigilantism, see Richard Maxwell Brown, *Strain of Violence* (New York: Oxford University Press, 1975), pt. III.
24. See, for a similar point with regard to modern attitudes, Herbert McClosky and Alida Brill, *Dimensions of Tolerance: What Americans Believe About Civil Liberties* (New York: Russell Sage Foundation, 1983).
25. Of course, no one dares to run for office against the Constitution or the Bill of Rights, which are revered as symbols if as nothing else.
26. See Lawrence M. Friedman, "Plea Bargaining in Historical Perspective," *Law and Society Review* 13 (1979): 247.
27. This is the system described for eighteenth-century England, in the famous essay by Douglas Hay, "Property, Authority and the Criminal Law," in *Albion's Fatal Tree: Crime and Society in Eighteenth-Century England,* ed. Douglas Hay et al. (New York: Pantheon Books, 1971). Here the duality consisted of a mixture of harsh, punitive laws, with a generous dose of mercy. The combination of the two resulted in a tougher system than either alone would have engendered.
28. 13 Tex. Crim. 383 (1883). The logic of the case, if it can be called that, was that nothing could be added to the proper, constitutional conclusion of an indictment. The ordinary person might think it was pretty

harmless to throw in the date; one could safely ignore or exclude this. But the court solemnly intoned that "if the words with which this indictment concludes are no part of it, and can be rejected as surplusage, then any other words or allegations with which the pleader may choose to conclude his indictment may be so treated"; this would render the "constitutional requirement" nugatory and of "no imaginable efficacy." What that efficacy might have been in the first place is hard to imagine.

29. *Williams* v. *State*, 12 Tex. Crim. 395 (1882). The statute (Tex. Laws, ch. 57, p. 60 [1881]) made it acceptable for an indictment to state, simply, that "A.B. did steal a horse from C.D." But, said the court, the Texas Constitution talks about an *indictment*, and the word "had a well-known legal signification." It must "charge explicitly all that is essential to constitute the defense." Commonsense language would not do. The indictment, presumably, had to allege that the defendant—charged with stealing four hogs from H. L. Williams—took the property from the owner, without his consent, and "with the intent to deprive the owner of the value" of the hogs and "appropriate" them to himself. The legislation had no power to dispense with this rigamarole.

30. J. Kopelke, "Criminal Law Reform," *Albany Law Journal* 29 (1884): 148–49.

31. Ibid., 148.

32. Hay, "Property, Authority and the Criminal Law."

33. See Friedman and Percival, *Roots of Justice*, chap. 7.

34. Anonymous, "Current Events," *Central Law Journal* 23 (1886): 529.

35. Lawrence M. Friedman, "Two Faces of Law," *Wisconsin Law Review* (1984): 13.

Part Four

Risks

The Search for a Usable Present

Burt Neuborne

I would like to focus not so much on a "search for a usable past" as, from the perspective of a civil liberties lawyer, on the search for a usable present in state constitutional law and the possibilities of using state courts as enforcement mechanisms for a broad conception of individual rights.

If we focus on a basic problem in constitutionalism, worldwide, about how one interprets constitutions and what the purposes of constitutions are, we are immediately driven into what is often called the formalism/reality dichotomy.

If aliens dropped down from Mars and were given a copy of the various constitutions that exist in the polities around the world, the place that they would probably single out as among the freest on earth would be Poland. After Poland, they would say the Soviet Union and after the Soviet Union, they would say the People's Republic of China, because totalitarian societies tend to have extraordinarily lyrical constitutional descriptions of the rights that exist in those societies. The Western democracies' constitutions tend to be much flatter. They lack style and lyricism. The United States Constitution and the various state constitutions would never be confused with models of clarity or of style.

What is missing from the lyrical totalitarian constitutions and what we have been fortunate enough in recent years to have enjoyed in our own constitutional experience is an enforcement mechanism—the structural mechanism that translates formal rights on a piece of paper into real-world considerations that individuals living in a society can actually enjoy.

The dilemma of how to avoid constitutional formalism and move to an enjoyment of constitutional realism is the task that I have spent a good deal of my professional life attempting to address. As an ACLU lawyer, I have always considered myself a law enforcement official. I simply enforce a different kind of law against a different kind of law-breaker. The structural mechanisms that determine whether or not law will be enforced are the same in virtually all areas of law enforcement. If you eliminate the enforcer and simply leave the law, with no enforcement mechanism, law will always revert to an empty formalism. We know that as a truism in almost every other area of law enforcement, and it should not surprise us if the same thing is true in constitutional law as well. If the antitrust laws are not enforced, they do not mean anything. If the securities laws are not enforced, they do not mean anything, and if the Constitution is not enforced, it does not mean very much either.

In this essay I focus on what the preconditions are for an effective structural enforcement mechanism in the area of constitutional law; whether those preconditions can be said to exist in state courts today; and how those structural mechanisms can be used to open up a second market or a second front in the enforcement of individual rights. It is no secret that the goal I pursue as a law enforcement official in the civil liberties–civil rights area is to reach an end in which a broad conception of individual liberty is efficiently and effectively enforced by a series of mechanisms and a series of structures in the society.

Preconditions

There are, I believe, three indispensable enforcement components that come to us out of common sense and are reinforced by history. The very helpful essays in this volume reinforce the fact that, in the absence of these structural components, the constitutional dog will never bark. What are those three components?

First, there has to be some articulable, nonmajoritarian norm to repair to.[1] It does not necessarily have to be a written constitution. Just recently the law lords in Britain finally ended the tragic/comic litigation over whether the book *Spycatcher* could be published in Great Britain.[2] They finally ruled that the Thatcher government could not obtain a prior restraint on the publication of the book.[3] Their reference was to an unwritten set of norms that limit what a democratically elected government wishes to do in particularly important areas.

We are blessed in our legal system with a set of written norms that make it a little easier to deal with the problem; but as we know, the written norms are norms of such generality that any realistic assessment of them has to recognize that we often pour into them what we wish to see there and not what is intrinsically there. It is a myth that when we enforce a written constitution, we enforce something that is reified, that is "a thing" that is there for all times and always was and always will be. In Frederic William Maitland's pithy phrase, the only way that we can worship words is to be able to misunderstand them.[4] Words become venerable precisely because they are capable of misunderstanding and reconstruction in different periods of a society's history. But there must be formally in place somewhere in the structure a nonmajoritarian norm to which we can repair in an attempt to enforce individual rights. We have two possibilities: the federal and the state constitutions. So the first prerequisite is in place everywhere in the United States.

The second prerequisite is very important and obvious, and I have written a good deal about it.[5] We need some form of insulated and sympathetic oracle to interpret those norms because the norms are open-ended and are not self-executing. In the absence of a sympathetic and insulated interpreter that will give real bite and meaning to the norms, the norms will remain formalisms. They will be on paper but would not translate into reality.

In our system, historically, there has been an important structural divide between state and federal courts. It is a structural divide that is narrowing and that may well not exist very much longer. But it has existed in our history. The structural divide is that the founders created the Article III judiciary as an insulated body expecting it to be drawn from an elite social class with a particular set of values that resonated with traditional eighteenth-century philosophy. Those values resonate well with the notion of individual rights. That group as a body was particularly well suited to enunciate a powerful vision of nonmajoritarian individual rights. We must not confuse this the way the Bush campaign did with "liberal" and "conservative" because at some points in the nation's history, federal judges enunciated a powerful antimajoritarian set of values that were very conservative, in the sense that conservative means that wealthy people like it and poor people do not. The earliest example of powerful conservative constitutional adjudication was the enforcement of the fugitive slave clause to knock out attempts by abolitionists in the North to shelter slaves who had escaped from the South. That was a powerful enforcement tool. A key component of the Compromise of 1850 was the Fugitive Slave Law. The 1850 act was the creation of a core of commissioners who would be insulated from local majority will and who could be trusted to enforce the fugitive slave clause rigorously because the elected state judges in the North would not.[6] That pattern in American history has repeated itself at least four times.

The attempt by the bar that tended to represent southern slaveowners to use the federal courts as an insulated nonmajoritarian forum to enforce the fugitive slave clause is the first success story in the use of the Constitution to protect individual rights. It is a story we do not like to think about anymore because those are rights that we do not like to think that we ever took seriously in this society. But we did and we used the federal courts to enforce them.[7]

Immediately after the Civil War there was an attempt to replicate exactly the same setting. During Reconstruction, civil rights lawyers learned from the experience of abolitionist lawyers who had lost the earlier cases in which they tried to block the enforcement of the fugitive slave acts. These civil rights lawyers borrowed the mechanism that had defeated the abolitionists and attempted to replicate it as the mechanism to enforce the Reconstruction amendments in the South.[8] The tragic failure of that attempt to use the federal courts as an antimajoritarian forum to enforce the fundamental rights of an oppressed group is one of the burdens that we bear in twentieth-century America.[9] We are still trying to cope as a society with the collapse of that law enforcement effort.

When that law enforcement effort collapsed, another one grew up out of its ashes, on behalf of a different social class. It was the brilliant use by corporate lawyers of the federal courts, beginning in about the 1870s and ranging all the way until the middle of the 1930s, to ward off Progressive regulation of corporations.[10] When that movement collapsed in 1937 and 1938 because the substantive law in the Supreme Court shifted, all civil rights lawyers did was crawl into the shell that had been left vacant when the corporate lawyers vacated it. Civil rights lawyers since then have used exactly the same model— the attempt to use the federal courts as a countermajoritarian forum significantly insulated from the popular will, or at least as insulated an institution can be, as the mechanism to enforce a broad set of individual rights.

So we have two preconditions: first, the need for a nonmajoritarian norm to which we can repair; and second, the existence of an insulated forum calculated to enunciate antimajoritarian doctrine in a sustained way over time. By putting those two things together, we have the beginnings of a structural enforcement mechanism for a broad set of individual liberties.

The third precondition has also been referred to in this volume: a powerful bar systematically able to provide the bench with a set of sympathetic fact patterns wrapped up in a set of powerful legal arguments that will lead the bench to move in a particular way. We all know that law grows by accretion. It does not grow by any single dramatic bound. It grows slowly and over time and through the exertion of constant pressure by forces in the society. If the dog is not barking for certain of those forces, the law will not grow in that direction; if the lawyers are not there to present the fact patterns in a sustained and steady diet, even a sympathetic bench will not have the raw material from which to forge sustained antimajoritarian norms.

So that as a structural matter, and I do not care what the system is—it can be our system or Mikhail Gorbachev's attempt to bring glasnost to fruition in the Soviet Union—in the absence of those three preconditions, the norm, the enforcement arm, and the lawyers or some sort of input mechanism, there will be no sustained antimajoritarian set of norms and consequently no effective, realistic enjoyment of individual liberties. For the last thirty years, and sometimes even before, we have enjoyed the combination of those three factors.

This, of course, is a volume on state constitutions, and I have spent a fair amount of time in the last ten to fifteen years in the care and feeding of this state constitutional forum. But from the standpoint of both structuralism and efficiency, there is no substitute, I believe, for a strategy of first choice, which is federal court enforcement of federal constitutional norms. It offers the most insulated forum possible and it provides efficient national coverage very quickly so it serves the most people through what looks to be the best structurally suited forum.

But conditions beyond the control of even the ACLU are forcing a rethinking, and I confess that it is a rethinking that is strategic. Left to myself, I would not be thinking a good deal about state constitutional law. I would continue to push the button that we pushed effectively in the 1950s, the 1960s, and the 1970s, in the hope of getting a powerful, countermajoritarian enunciation from the federal courts.

But if the federal courts go sour, the question then is whether to move somewhere else. And from the strategic standpoint of a law enforcement official, the answer is "of course." Rather than banging away in a system that is enunciating undesirable norms, one looks for alternative fora, and that search leads to an obvious but often ignored phenomenon in American law—state courts and state constitutions. Certainly, the first precondition is there. The raw material for judgment is there in every single state constitution. In fact, it is even richer than the raw material that exists in the federal Constitution. The textual language of the state constitutions lends itself to an extraordinarily rich development of a broad vision of individual liberty. For example, many state constitutions do not have a state action problem. They are designed to act directly on the people. And so one of the great doctrinal dilemmas that civil rights lawyers have struggled with for years would be eliminated. In many state constitutions there is no doctrinal problem about enforcing constitutional norms against powerful entities that are not state entities. And so the opportunity is quite extraordinary.

State Courts

What is changing a little bit, and it is a very important structural event to recognize, is the state bench. The state bench is changing in three ways which give me hope. Although I think there has been a fair amount of hyperbole about how far state courts have actually gone, I am hopeful that they can be moved effectively into the forefront of the protection of individual liberty.

There has been a complete generational turnover in the membership of the state courts. When I started litigating cases in court, the hardest thing that I had to do either in federal or state court was to persuade the judge that the law had changed from when that judge was in law school. Judges in those days had gone to law school under a different conception of the role of courts and the role of individual liberties in the society. They were educated in a different legal culture. When arguing before these judges, it was necessary to educate them on changes in legal culture while at the same time presenting a traditional legal argument. One reason why it was so much easier to win in federal court in those days than in state court was that there was a competence gap. The federal judges were smarter, by and large. They were chosen from a smaller pool. They were much more elite. If a civil rights lawyer had to persuade somebody that the law that he—in those days it was always he—remembered from law school had changed, and the judge was very smart, the lawyer could make that argument and make it stick. If the judge never really understood the law in law school to begin with, it was impossible to explain to him why it changed, and the lawyer would lose. Since civil rights lawyers generally have the inertial disadvantage, they are moving against the status quo; if they could not persuade the judge they should win, the status quo would remain in place and they would lose. So that, in the early days—twenty years ago—it really did make a big difference in terms of competence and generation whether one was arguing in a federal or state court.

That situation has changed dramatically in the last twenty years. Obviously, the generational situation has changed completely. Most current state judges went to law school since the beginning of the Warren Court and have internalized its norms. It does not surprise them to find protection for individual rights in the law. They understand that it is their responsibility to work cases through logically and to come out with some lawyerlike resolution, using the Warren norms as the raw material. That makes a tremendous difference in a lawyer's being able to argue effectively about civil rights so that the generational turnover, and I think it fair to say, the dramatic increase in competence that has taken place at the state level in a number of states, makes the state courts potentially favorable arenas in which to litigate.

Second, there are significant geographical and political differences in the society now that we are beginning to see in the breakdown of legislative elections and presidential elections. There are pockets in the society that are much more receptive to individual norms than others, and it is possible to mine that difference. It is possible to use the powerful current running in a particular area that is sympathetic to the notion of civil rights, even though the nation as a whole may be much more skeptical about it, and essentially to gear down and make a litigation effort in the fora where there is the best chance to win. Oregon is an example. There is a libertarian heritage in Oregon that is not necessarily shared on the federal level anymore. Picking and choosing state courts can be very important, therefore, because even as the society moves away from an embrace of a libertarian tradition, geographical pockets continue to adhere to it. From our standpoint, it is a shame not to take advantage of those pockets by moving into the state fora and litigating as aggressively as possible.

Then, finally, there is the very existence of the pump-priming effect of the Warren years. Even if the Supreme Court fails to press the Warren Court precedents vigorously, there is no way to erase the Warren Court years from the consciousness of the legal culture. Those pump-priming years have an effect, not just on people who know the norms, but on people who think about what judges should do. The role of judges has been irrevocably altered in this society. Although we can articulate a verbal notion of going back to a much more re-strained judiciary, the expectations of the populace for justice from the courts are so great and the courts have generated such an enor-mous demand for their services that for the courts to attempt to step away would create enormous tension. My sense is that the prevailing expectations for justice can be mined effectively at the state level.

The issue that cuts against using state courts has been raised in several of these essays. State courts still, by and large, are majori-tarian institutions. They are less majoritarian than they used to be. The movement toward the appointment of the highest courts of some states has reached the level now where close to three-quarters of the highest courts of the states are appointed or serve with a formal elec-tion process that is not particularly threatening to the judges. So that there is a movement toward a more insulated state judiciary which ought to translate itself over time into sustained countermajoritarian norms, if the rest of the equation stays constant. But that movement has not taken place at perhaps the single most important area, the trial level. At the trial level, where the facts are found, where the twig is bent and the case is essentially determined, those fora, all over the country, continue to be elected. Not only do they continue to be elected, but they are chosen by political machines that are intensely attuned to popular will, and they are extremely unlikely to generate a group of judges who will over time enunciate countermajoritarian norms. The Achilles' heel of the state constitutional movement is at the state trial level because unless those state trial courts can be beefed up both with respect to competence and insularity, they are not fora, I think, that over time can be expected to bear the weight of powerful majoritarian anger at a particular set of rules.

The promise and the dangers of state constitutional adjudication, it seems to me, are illustrated by two factors. First, two Pacific states, side by side, operate with different cultures, but nevertheless operate in very similar legal norms. One is Oregon, where Hans Linde and an extraordinary group of judges on the supreme court have enunciated a vision of broad individual rights that has gone beyond the United States Supreme Court in a number of settings.[11] The Oregon Supreme Court has come closer to putting into practice the Black-Douglas absolutist view of the First Amendment than any other institution in American life, based on Article 1, section 8, of the Oregon Constitution, which is its free speech clause. One of the interesting things to see is whether we can use the federalism laboratory that we like to talk about so much and take a look and see what a society is like over time that is going to be living under the vision of the First Amendment that libertarians have sought for years but have never been able to put into practice anywhere.

By contrast, across the border is the spectacle of a supreme court that attempted to enunciate countermajoritarian norms in a sustained way and was turned out of office by an angry populace in an election—the California Supreme Court. The possibility of Oregon and the dangers of California show that the use of state constitutions for protection of individual liberty can go either way—there is great promise, but there is also great danger.

Opportunity

There is also great opportunity—an opportunity that has not been mentioned yet, which goes even beyond what this volume is about. This volume is about the use of state constitutions to enforce state constitutional norms in the states. There is a very real possibility, which the founders thought about, that state courts will be important fora enforcing federal constitutional norms as well. They already are in the sense that section 1983 damage claims for constitutional torts are more and more being brought in state court for a number of procedural and substantive reasons. The state courts are already acting in many states as important primary enforcement mechanisms for federal constitutional rights, and if state courts really do start becoming sympathetic fora, there will be a massive shift of enforcement attention into the state courts, using section 1983 as the mechanism to bring federal claims in state court. Of course, they will still be reviewed by the United States Supreme Court, but the United States Supreme Court can review only a very small percentage of the cases sent to it, and the state courts will have the final say in 92 percent of the cases because the Supreme Court reviews only about 8 percent of the cases that are sent to it.[12]

The possibility is enhanced by something that happened in the 1987 term in the Supreme Court, and has not really been mentioned very much, and that is an extraordinary shift in the conception of federalism. Nineteenth-century conceptions of federalism in the area of immunity talked of dual sovereignty and created powerful federalism-based immunities that prevented state courts from effectively dealing with federal officials. For example, under the nineteenth-century concept, federal officials were immune from state tort law as long as they were acting within the outer scope of their professional responsibilities. That doctrine was overturned by the Supreme Court in 1988, when the justices said that if a federal official is engaged in a ministerial act, he is subject to state tort law, litigated in state court.[13] Similarly, they overturned the intergovernmental tax immunity doctrine, which was also based on the conception of dual sovereignty.[14] With the demise of the notion of dual sovereignty, intergovernmental federalism, my sense is that *Tarbles Case*[15] goes as well. *Tarbles Case* is the nineteenth-century case that said that state judges have no equitable power over federal officials, that a state judge cannot enjoin a federal official who is acting in violation of the federal Constitution or some other federal norm. *Tarbles Case* is based on a conception of dual sovereignty that says a state judge cannot jump the federalism gap and enjoin somebody in the other sovereignty. Once the immunity for tort and the intergovernmental immunity go down, and they both went down this past term, the reasoning underlying *Tarbles Case* is significantly weakened as well. I suspect that we will see *Tarbles Case* reversed in a very short time by the Supreme Court, opening the way for state judges not just to be enforcement mechanisms for their own constitutions but to assume the role that the founders thought they would assume—to be the primary enforcement mechanism of fundamental rights in the society. It is no coincidence that the Constitution does not provide for lower federal courts; it permits but does not guarantee them. It is no coincidence that there was no federal question of jurisdiction in the federal courts until 1875. For the first one hundred years of our existence, we relied on state courts as the primary enforcement fora for federal rights. The day may be coming when it is time to go back to that well. Going back to that well is concededly strategic, though it is a strategy of second choice. I would rather have stayed in the federal courts, but to the extent that federal courts are closed or unpromising fora for the enunciation of a powerful vision of individual rights, a usable present may be found in the state courts.

Notes

1. Not all that courts do in the name of the Constitution is countermajoritarian. For example, it is not countermajoritarian for a federal judge who has been appointed by the president and confirmed by the Senate to tell a local police officer who has not been elected by anybody to stop beating up a group of black demonstrators. That enforces a majority consensus. If, however, a judge sets aside the considered act of a legitimately elected legislature, it seems that it is necessary to explain why, what the source of power is, and what the structural justification is. See Charles Black, Jr., *Structure and Relationship in Constitutional Law* (Baton Rouge: Louisiana State University Press, 1969), 67–98.

    Democracy is not a sufficient answer to every abuse. History does not show consistent majority respect for minority rights over sustained periods of time. The genius of our political structure is that we have worked into it a mechanism that respects democratic judgment in the vast majority of situations and frustrates democratic judgment when that judgment infringes a small category of fundamental rights drawn from a document that we call a Constitution.

    The debate over the confirmation of Robert Bork was essentially a debate over exactly how to identify those instances. Bork's appeals to literalism and history are not satisfactory in most situations because of the complexity of both, to say nothing about the wisdom and utility of locking us into a vision of the world that is two hundred years old. Justice Marshall reminded us that the Constitution was born in racism, in sexism, and in classism and that to look back and venerate those days, as though they are simply days that we want to reinvent today, is an exercise in absurdity. Thurgood Marshall, "Reflections on the Bicentennial of the United States Constitution," *Harvard Law Review* 101 (1987): 1 (text of Remarks of Thurgood Marshall at the Annual Seminar of the San Francisco Patent and Trademark Law Association, Maui, Hawaii, May 6, 1987).

2. Peter Wright, *Spycatcher: The Candid Autobiography of a Senior Intelligence Officer* (New York: Viking Press, 1987).

3. "Court Overturns British Ban on Spy Memoirs," *New York Times*, October 14, 1988, p. A5.

4. Quoted in *The Roots of the Bill of Rights*, ed. Bernard Schwartz (New York: Chelsea House, 1980), 1:7. I am grateful to Professor Peter Preiser for bringing attention to Maitland's remark at the conference for which these papers were originally prepared.

5. Burt Neuborne, "The Myth of Parity," *Harvard Law Review* 80 (1977): 1105; Neuborne, "Toward Procedural Parity in Constitutional Litigation," *William and Mary Law Review* 22 (1981): 725.

6. On local nonenforcement, see Paul Finkelman, "*Prigg v. Pennsylvania* and Northern State Courts: Anti-Slavery Use of a Proslavery Decision," *Civil War History* 25 (1979): 5.

7. See *Prigg v. Pennsylvania*, 47 U.S. (16 Pet.) 536 (1842); *Jones v. Van Zandt*, 46 U.S. (5 How.) 215 (1847); *Moore v. Illinois*, 55 U.S. (14 How.) 13 (1852); *Ableman v. Booth*, 62 U.S. (21 How.) 506 (1859); Robert M. Cover, *Justice Accused: Antislavery and the Judicial Process* (New Haven: Yale University Press, 1975), 159–91. Contemporary writings bearing on these cases are discussed in Paul Finkelman, *Slavery in the Courtroom* (Washington, D.C.: Library of Congress, 1985), 59–138. Efforts by slaveowners to use federal courts to recover fugitive slaves (and to protect their own ability to travel with their slaves outside of the slave states) are discussed in Paul Finkelman, *An Imperfect Union: Slavery, Federalism, and Comity* (Chapel Hill: University of North Carolina Press, 1981), 236–84.

8. But see Donald G. Nieman, *To Set the Law in Motion: The Freedman's Bureau and the Legal Rights of Blacks, 1865–1868* (Millwood, N.Y.: KTO Press, 1979), 135–50; Harold M. Hyman and William M. Wiecek, *Equal Justice Under Law: Constitutional Development, 1835–1875* (New York: Harper & Row, 1982), 425–29, 488–89.

9. See, for example, *United States v. Reese*, 92 U.S. 214 (1876); *Virginia v. Rives*, 100 U.S. 313 (1880); and *Plessy v. Ferguson*, 163 U.S. 537 (1896).

10. See Kermit L. Hall, *The Magic Mirror* (New York: Oxford University Press, 1989), 226–46; Lawrence M. Friedman, *A History of American Law*, 2d ed. (New York: Simon & Schuster, 1985), 553–63.

11. On freedom of speech, see *Lewis v. Oregon Beauty Supply Co.*, 302 Or. 616, 733 P.2d 430 (1987) (punitive damages excluded in defamation

cases); *State* v. *Robertson,* 293 Or. 402, 416–17, 649 P.2d 569, 579 (1982) ("laws must focus on proscribing the pursuit or accomplishment of forbidden results rather than on the suppression of speech or writing either as an end in itself or as a means to a legislative end"); *State* v. *Harrington,* 67 Or. App. 608, 614, 680 P.2d 666, 671 (1984) (Oregon Constitution "precludes the state legislature or the courts from balancing away the right to free expression"). On equal protection, see Hans A. Linde, "E Pluribus—Constitutional Theory and State Courts," *Georgia Law Review* 18 (1984): 183–84.

12. Lawrence Baum, *The Supreme Court* (Washington, D.C.: CQ Press, 1989), 90; Stephen L. Wasby, *The Supreme Court in the Federal Judicial System* (New York: Holt, Rinehart and Winston, 1984), 155.
13. *Westfall* v. *Erwin,* 484 U.S. 292, 296–98 (1988).
14. *South Carolina* v. *Baker,* 485 U.S. 505, 515–27 (1988).
15. 80 U.S. 397 (1871).

Just Say No

Birth Control in the Connecticut Supreme Court before Griswold *v.* Connecticut

Mary L. Dudziak

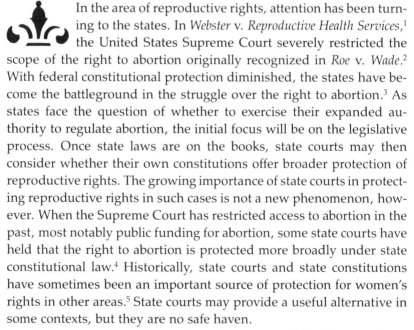 In the area of reproductive rights, attention has been turning to the states. In *Webster* v. *Reproductive Health Services*,[1] the United States Supreme Court severely restricted the scope of the right to abortion originally recognized in *Roe* v. *Wade*.[2] With federal constitutional protection diminished, the states have become the battleground in the struggle over the right to abortion.[3] As states face the question of whether to exercise their expanded authority to regulate abortion, the initial focus will be on the legislative process. Once state laws are on the books, state courts may then consider whether their own constitutions offer broader protection of reproductive rights. The growing importance of state courts in protecting reproductive rights in such cases is not a new phenomenon, however. When the Supreme Court has restricted access to abortion in the past, most notably public funding for abortion, some state courts have held that the right to abortion is protected more broadly under state constitutional law.[4] Historically, state courts and state constitutions have sometimes been an important source of protection for women's rights in other areas.[5] State courts may provide a useful alternative in some contexts, but they are no safe haven.

This essay will explore an important aspect of the history of protection of reproductive rights under state constitutional law: the Connecticut Supreme Court's treatment of the right to use contraceptives. Until 1965, the United States Supreme Court largely kept its hand out of cases involving reproductive rights. The notable exception was sterilization; the Court in 1927 upheld eugenical sterilization,[6] and in 1942, the Court overturned punitive sterilization of persons considered to be "habitual criminals."[7] Cases involving birth control were confined to the state courts[8] and, on questions of federal law, to the lower federal courts.[9] Appeals to the Supreme Court in cases involving constitutional challenges to state restrictions on contraceptives were regularly dismissed for want of a substantial federal question[10] or due to lack of standing.[11] Because the Supreme Court would not hear these cases, the right to use birth control was determined by state law until 1965, when the Court decided *Griswold* v. *Connecticut*.[12] Consequently, an examination of this area of law enables us to see the independent treatment of constitutional rights by one state court without meaningful input from the U.S. Supreme Court.

This essay will examine the right to use birth control in Connecticut before *Griswold*. The cases challenging Connecticut birth control restrictions have been derided by some scholars as irrelevant.[13] The assumption often held is that the Connecticut laws were not enforced and consequently did not affect access to birth control in the state. Accordingly, the cases challenging the state statutes are thought of as not real cases or controversies deserving of court attention.[14] As a result, Robert Bork has argued that *Griswold* was "framed by Yale professors" simply "because they like this type of litigation."[15] Such a view of the Connecticut birth control cases is erroneous. Connecticut law was enforced against the personnel of birth control clinics for aiding and abetting the use of contraceptives. Enforcement of the statute against those working in clinics kept birth control clinics closed in Connecticut for twenty-five years. The lack of birth control clinics may not have greatly affected middle-class and wealthy people who could afford private medical care because doctors would often break the laws.[16] The lack of clinics primarily harmed lower-income women who needed the free or low-cost services birth control clinics provided. As historian Thomas Dienes has argued, the effect of the Connecticut restrictions was that "while birth control services were generally available, the poor, dependent on free medical services, were effectively denied assistance."[17]

Restrictions on Birth Control

Reproductive freedom is at the heart of women's rights because having control over reproduction is critical to women's autonomy.[18] Throughout history women have tried different strategies to control when, whether, and how often they had babies.[19]

Searching for a way to have some control over how often they gave birth, many women in the 1920s wrote to birth control activist Margaret Sanger for answers. Some women had health problems associated with pregnancy. One woman wrote, "The doctor said at last birth we must be 'more careful,' as I could not stand having so many children." But how could she be "more careful"? She asked Sanger for answers her doctor would not or could not give her. The constant fear of pregnancy made sexuality a burden for many women, yet some longed for a day when they could again find pleasure in marital sex. One woman wrote, "For two years I have not allowed my husband a natural embrace for fear of another pregnancy which I feel I can never live through. You can readily guess that keeping my husband away from me thus is having its effect on the ideally happy home which was ours before. . . . So can you help me and tell me how to bring back the happiness to our home? Or at least give me a hint?"[20]

Margaret Sanger did her best to distribute information about birth control to women like these.[21] But every time she placed a birth control pamphlet in an envelope and sent it through the mail, Sanger committed a federal crime. The Comstock Law, passed by Congress in 1873, made it a crime to send through the mails any contraceptives, any information about contraceptives, or any information about how to find out about contraceptives. The penalty was a fine and/or one to ten years at hard labor.[22] Following the passage of the Comstock Law, many states enacted their own restrictions, barring the distribution of contraceptives or the dissemination of information about contraceptives.[23]

Eventually the courts eased most restrictions on birth control. Notwithstanding the blanket prohibition on contraceptives suggested by the language of the Comstock Law, the federal courts read into the law a limitation that it only forbade transmission of contraceptives for "illegal contraception" but not for "proper medical use," freeing pharmacists to market contraceptives when ordered by a doctor.[24]

State laws generally met a similar fate in the state courts. For example, in *People* v. *Sanger*,[25] decided in 1918, the New York Court of Appeals upheld the prosecution of Margaret Sanger for distributing contraceptives and copies of her article on birth control, "What Every Girl Should Know." In doing so, however, the court narrowly construed the permissible scope of the statute. New York law prohibited the sale of contraceptives, but the law allowed doctors to prescribe articles for the cure and prevention of disease.[26] The court broadly construed the word *disease* to include any illness[27] so that doctors could prescribe contraceptives to prevent diseases associated with pregnancy and childbirth. The exception to the New York law essentially swallowed the rule so that, after *People* v. *Sanger*, the sale of contraceptives to married persons was legal in New York as long as they were prescribed by a physician.[28]

During the 1940s and 1950s, many areas of the country adopted a more permissive approach to birth control.[29] Until 1923, there were no birth control clinics. In 1944, there were at least eight hundred.[30] In 1938, a *Ladies' Home Journal* survey found that 79 percent of American women were in favor of birth control.[31] Meanwhile, the birth control movement lost its radical edge. Margaret Sanger and other reformers couched their rhetoric in conventional terms. They no longer argued, as they had in the 1910s and 1920s, that birth control was important because it would liberate women.[32] Rather, they argued that birth control would bring scientific rationality to the traditional family. It would allow families to use scientific expertise to bring order to the otherwise uncontrollable process of childbearing. In 1942, when the American Birth Control League changed its name to Planned Parenthood, the new title reflected the organization's focus on planning within the context of the traditional family structure.[33]

Contraception enabled couples to separate sex from reproduction. That gave rise to fears of rampant sexual immorality and a focus on what Elaine Tyler May has called "sexual containment," the containment of sex within marriage.[34] But marital sex took on a new significance, at least in the eyes of psychologists and marriage counselors. According to John D'Emilio and Estelle Freedman, during the 1940s and 1950s the middle class embraced "sexual liberalism," sex for its own sake, as an important part of marriage. Many marriage counselors considered sexual fulfillment to be the measure of a happy and successful marriage. At the same time, during these baby boom years, women and men were marrying at younger ages and having children earlier. Contraceptives gave couples some control over when they had children and enabled them to be sexually active with less fear of pregnancy once they had the number of children they desired. Accordingly, as May points out, "contraceptive technology actually reinforced existing mores and further encouraged a drop in the marriage age." Increased use of contraceptives was therefore highly consistent with the postwar version of the ideology of domesticity.[35]

Although birth control was increasingly available and increasingly used in most parts of the country, the states of Connecticut and Massachusetts lagged behind in the area of law reform. Largely because of the influence of the Catholic church on state politics, those states retained very restrictive birth control statutes until the 1960s.[36]

Birth Control in Connecticut

In 1879, the Connecticut state legislature passed a statute that would prove to be the most restrictive birth control law in the country.[37] Whereas most states with birth control statutes regulated sales and advertising, Connecticut forbade the use of contraceptives.[38] Standing alone, a statute restricting the use of birth control would obviously be difficult to enforce. But Connecticut had another statute that would prove to be crucial in its effort to restrict birth control usage: a general accessory statute. Under Connecticut law "any person who assists, abets, counsels, causes, hires or commands another to commit any offense may be prosecuted and punished as if he were the principal offender."[39]

State v. Nelson

The role of religion in the battle over birth control in Connecticut was evident early on. The first prosecution under the Connecticut statutes would be at the instigation of Catholic priests in Waterbury. In 1938, the Connecticut Birth Control League opened a clinic in that heavily Catholic community. The clinic was to serve married women who could not afford private medical care. Before opening the clinic, Connecticut birth control activists sought advice about the legality of a clinic under Connecticut law. They were told by a local attorney that, in light of recent federal court rulings, Connecticut law would be interpreted to have an implied medical exception. The part-time clinic operated openly in the heart of town, serving an average of ten to twelve patients each week.[40]

Initially, the Waterbury Police Department left the clinic alone. Then, according to the *New Republic,* in June 1939 the Catholic Clergy Association of Waterbury "passed a resolution condemning birth control and demanding that the Waterbury Maternal Health Center be investigated and prosecuted 'to the fullest extent of the law.'" On June 11, the resolution "was read at mass in every Roman Catholic Church in Waterbury."[41] A priest at the Church of the Immaculate Conception pointed out to town officials "that the clinic was operating in wanton disregard, not only of the laws of God, but of the State of Connecticut also." The next day, the state obtained a warrant and raided the clinic. Doctors Roger B. Nelson and William B. Goodrich, the clinic's medical directors, and Clara McTernan, its nurse, were arrested and charged with aiding and abetting the use of contraceptives. Nelson and Goodrich were "panic stricken" after their arrest. "They were young, newly in practice, had very little money, and had families to support. If convicted they faced possible loss of their licenses, since the crime was one involving moral turpitude."[42]

Nelson, Goodrich, and McTernan filed a demurrer to the charges, arguing that unless state law was construed as having an exception for prescription of contraceptives by doctors, the ban on contraceptives violated the state and federal constitutions by depriving citizens of liberty without due process of law. The superior court sustained the demurrer, finding that the statute could not be construed as having a medical exception and, consequently, it was unconstitutional.[43]

The state appealed, and in a three-to-two ruling, the Connecticut Supreme Court of Errors reversed the lower court and upheld the state law. The court first considered the question of whether the statute could be construed to have an implied medical exception. The court noted that the proper interpretation of a statute was "controlled by the intention of the Legislature." An implied exception could be made only "in recognition of long existing and generally accepted rights . . . or to avoid consequences so absurd or unreasonable that the Legislature must be presumed not to have intended them." Religious beliefs and "sociological and psychological views" could not enter into the determination. The court found that the possibility that the legislature had intended a medical exception "was negatived not only by the absolute language used originally and preserved ever since but also, signally, by its repeated and recent refusals to inject an exception." At every legislative session from 1921 through 1935, bills were introduced to amend the birth control law. No amendments to the statute were enacted. Accordingly, the court believed that "we may not now attribute to the Legislature an accidental or unintentional omission to include the exception. . . . Rejection by the Legislature of a specific provision is most persuasive that the act should not be construed to include it."[44]

The court then turned to the question of whether the statute, without an implied exception, was a constitutional exercise of the state's police power. The court invoked the "familiar principles that the exercise by states of the police power to conserve the public safety and welfare, including health and morals, may not be interfered with if it has a real and substantial relation to these objects; and that the Legislature is primarily the judge of the regulations required to that end and its police statutes may only be declared unconstitutional when they are arbitrary or unreasonable attempts to exercise its authority in the public interest." The police power could be employed "in aid of what is . . . held by the prevailing morality to be necessary to the public welfare." The defendants had argued that people have a "natural right" to make decisions about childbearing and, consequently, a right to use contraceptives if they wished to avoid pregnancy. But "the civil liberty and natural rights of the individual under the federal and state constitutions are subject to the limitation that he may not use them so as to injure his fellow citizens or endanger the vital interest of society." As to the harm the Connecticut law redressed, the court found:

> Whatever may be our own opinion regarding the general subject, it is not for us to say that the Legislature might not reasonably hold that the artificial limitation of even legitimate child-bearing would be inimical to the public welfare and, as well, that use of contraceptives, and assistance therein or tending thereto, would be injurious to public morals, indeed, it is not precluded from considering that not all married people are immune from temptation or inclination to extra-marital indulgence, as to which risk of illegitimate pregnancy is a recognized deterrent deemed desirable in the interests of morality.

The court dismissed the contention that the statute interfered with "the free exercise of conscience and the pursuit of happiness," noting that "a like claim could be made, with no more force, as to statutes prohibiting adultery, or fornication, or any one of many other crimes."[45]

Regarding the purpose underlying the Connecticut statute, the court did not delve into legislative history. Instead, the court believed that it was "reasonable to assume" that the legislature's motives were similar to those found by the Massachusetts Supreme Court to have motivated the Massachusetts legislature in passing its laws. The Connecticut court quoted with approval a statement in *Commonwealth* v. *Allison*[46] that the "plain purpose" behind restrictions on birth control was "to protect purity, to preserve chastity, to encourage continence and self restraint, to defend the sanctity of the home, and thus to engender . . . a virile and virtuous race of men and women." If a purpose was to increase or maintain the population, that would not be improper. Finally, "if all that can be said is that it is unwise or unreasonably comprehensive, appeal must be made to the Legislature, not the judiciary."[47]

The court in *Nelson* left birth control activists with an opening, however. Though not finding a general medical exception in the statute, the court reserved judgment on the question of "whether an implied exception might be recognized when 'pregnancy would jeopardize life.' "[48]

After the Supreme Court of Errors upheld the Connecticut statute in *State* v. *Nelson,* the prosecuting attorney offered to *nolle prosequi* the case if the defendants would keep the clinic closed. The prosecutor believed that the defendants had acted in good faith upon the opinion of counsel that the state law had an implied medical exception. Further, the state's real interest was not in punishing the defendants but in closing down the clinic and in establishing the constitutionality of the statute as enforced against medical personnel. In arguing in support of the motion to dismiss the prosecutions, the state prosecutor told the trial court that the purpose of prosecution was "the establishment of the constitutional validity and efficacy of the statutes under which these accused are informed against. Henceforth any person, whether a physician or layman, who violates the provisions of these statutes, must expect to be prosecuted and punished in accordance with the literal provisions of the law." The defendants accepted the state's offer to drop the case, circumventing a potential United States Supreme Court appeal in *Nelson.*[49]

Following the *Nelson* ruling, the other birth control clinics operating in the state also closed their doors.[50] Doctors in the state were unwilling to violate the law openly. Consequently, birth control advocates turned to declaratory judgment actions as a way of challenging the validity of the state law without placing doctors and nurses at risk.[51]

Tileston *v.* Ullman

Two years after the conclusion of the *Nelson* litigation, Dr. Wilder Tileston, a professor at the Yale Medical School, brought a declaratory judgment action to determine the questions left open in *Nelson:* first, whether the state statute had an implied exception when pregnancy would endanger a woman's life or health, and second, if there was no exception, whether the statute was constitutional. Tileston filed a complaint describing the case histories of three of his patients whose health would be dramatically impaired by pregnancy. The patients were all married women. One had high blood pressure so that, in the words of the Connecticut Supreme Court, "if pregnancy occurred there would be imminent danger of toxemia of pregnancy which would have a 25 per cent chance of killing her." The second woman had "an arrested case of tuberculosis of the lungs of an acute and treacherous type, so that if she should become pregnant such condition would be likely to light up the disease and set back her recovery for several years, and might result in her death." The third woman was in good health except that she had been "weakened by having had three pregnancies in about twenty-seven months and a new pregnancy would probably have a serious effect upon her general health and might result in permanent disability."[52]

The New Haven Superior Court reserved the questions in the case for the Supreme Court of Errors. The Supreme Court first considered the argument that the statute had an implied medical exception when pregnancy threatened a woman's life or health. The court referred to its discussion of the statute's legislative history in *Nelson* and noted that another attempt to amend the law had failed since that case was decided. The court found the failed attempts to amend the statute to be significant, "for in the consideration of these bills year after year there was ample opportunity for the legislature to accept a compromise measure. It might have adopted a partial exception, as for instance, in cases where life might be in jeopardy if pregnancy occurred." Because the legislature had not availed itself of its many opportunities to amend the statute, the court concluded that it was "the manifest intention of the legislature" to have an "all-out prohibition" on contraceptives. "For us now to construe these plainly worded statutes as inapplicable to physicians, even under the limited circumstances of this case, would be to write into the statutes what is not there and what the legislature has thus far refused to place there."[53]

According to the court, "an implied limitation upon the operation of the statute may only be made in recognition of long existing rights or to avoid consequences so absurd or unreasonable that the legislature must be presumed not to have intended them."[54] Accordingly, the court implicitly found no "long existing rights" at stake in the case and found nothing absurd or unreasonable about the prohibition on birth control and recommendation of abstinence for married women for whom pregnancy posed serious risks.

Having construed the statute to ban all uses of contraceptives, even when pregnancy endangered a woman's life, the court then turned to the question of whether such a statute violated the state and federal constitutions. The court noted that the state argued that contraceptives were "not the only method open to the physician for preventing conception." The consensus of medical opinion was that the safest way for doctors to aid patients for whom pregnancy was life-threatening was to prescribe contraceptives. However, "the state claims that there is another method, positive and certain in result. It is abstention from intercourse in the broadest sense—that is, absolute abstention. If there is one remedy, reasonable, efficacious and practicable, it cannot fairly be said that the failure of the legislature to include another reasonable remedy is so absurd or unreasonable that it must be presumed to have intended the other remedy also."[55] The case came down to the question of "whether abstinence from intercourse is a reasonable and practicable method of preventing the unfortunate consequences. . . . Do the frailties of human nature and the uncertainties of human passions render it impracticable?" The court believed that "that is a question for the legislature, and we cannot say it could not believe that the husband and wife would and should refrain when they both knew that intercourse would very likely result in a pregnancy which might bring about the death of the wife."[56] In framing the issue this way, the court implied that the unreasonable behavior was on the part of married couples who had sex when pregnancy would be harmful to the woman, rather than on the part of the state legislature. A result of the court's ruling was that Connecticut law on contraceptives was more restrictive than Connecticut law on abortion, which allowed abortion when it was necessary to preserve a woman's life.[57]

Justices Christopher Avery and Newell Jennings dissented from the court's ruling. Justice Avery wrote:

> It is argued that in all cases it is possible for a married woman to avoid conception by a policy of continence and abstention from marital intercourse. Even if it be conceded that such a course of conduct is reasonably practicable, taking into consideration the propensities of human nature, the resort to such a practice would frustrate a fundamental of the marriage state. The alternative suggested . . . would tend in many cases to cause unhappiness and discontent between parties lawfully married, would stimulate unlawful intercourse, promote prostitution, and increase divorce.

The dissenters believed that "a proper respect for the legislature forbids an interpretation [of the statute] which would . . . be so contrary to human nature."[58]

Tileston appealed to the United States Supreme Court, but the case was dismissed on standing grounds. Tileston had not alleged that his own liberty or property rights were infringed by the statutes. "The sole constitutional attack . . . is confined to their deprivation of life—obviously not appellant's but his patients'." The doctor's patients were not parties to the suit, however, and there was "no basis on which we can say that he has standing to secure an adjudication of his patients' constitutional right to life, which they do not assert in their own behalf."[59]

With the Supreme Court's dismissal of *Tileston*, the Connecticut court's interpretation of the state law remained in force. This did not mean that all uses of birth control in Connecticut were halted. The effects of the ban were more subtle but still pernicious. Some forms of contraceptives were easy to purchase in drugstores. If sold "for the prevention of disease" or for "feminine hygiene," and not for contraceptive purposes, condoms, douches, suppositories, and spermicides were not illegal.[60] Condoms could be used to prevent venereal disease, but diaphragms, which were more effective for contraception, could not, so the restrictions meant that only less effective forms of birth control were readily available. As Planned Parenthood General

Counsel Harriet Pilpel put it, "The chief result of the most restrictive laws has been to put a premium on the use of inferior methods free from the supervision of the medical profession."[61] In addition, birth control restrictions had an effect on the quality of these products. A *Fortune* magazine report on the contraceptive industry found that "the industry harbors hundreds of scoundrels who make small fortunes out of ignorance."[62] According to Pilpel, states having "the most rigid laws are least able to cope with the problem of wholesale trafficking in inadequate contraceptives."[63] The more effective forms of birth control, such as the diaphragm, and instructions in the proper use of contraceptives could be obtained from some physicians who would break the laws.[64] But not all women could afford private medical care. Consequently, the law's greatest impact was on the poor.[65] As Pilpel remembers, "The only way we could provide public access to contraception in those years was to have an underground railroad, transporting women in station wagons to Rhode Island or New York to get contraceptive materials."[66] For many women, the practical result was no birth control and unwanted pregnancy.[67]

The Catholic Church and Birth Control Politics

The dissenters in *Tileston* assumed that the Connecticut legislature could not be so unreasonable as to enact a law that would forbid married persons access to birth control when pregnancy was life-threatening. In the years after *Tileston*, the state legislature would prove itself undeserving of such charitable thoughts. In every legislative session after *Tileston*, a bill to amend the birth control statute was introduced and, like clockwork, defeated.[68] The proposed changes were modest: they either authorized doctors to prescribe contraceptives or, more narrowly, authorized doctors to do so only when pregnancy was life-threatening. At times, the legislation died in committee. Often, it would pass the Connecticut house and be defeated in the senate.[69]

The central reason for the repeated inability of the Connecticut legislature to modify its birth control statutes was the role of religion in state politics. Thomas Dienes has found that the Catholic church was the "primary obstacle" to birth control reform in Connecticut and that "Catholic opposition constituted an effective impediment to change."[70]

The influence of the Catholic church was felt even without the church's overt involvement in the birth control controversy. During an unsuccessful attempt to modify birth control statutes in 1931, a commentator noted that "the Catholic Church did not openly enter this controversy, but it was not obliged to; the legislators were fully aware of its position." Their "reluctance to incur its disfavor and eagerness to win its approval were perhaps the chief factors in determining the outcome."[71] In later years, Catholic priests became heavily involved in the effort to defeat legislative attempts to ease birth control restrictions. Their efforts were not confined to anti-birth-control sermons on Sundays. They engaged in voter registration drives, they encouraged parishioners to support anti-birth-control candidates for the legislature, and they actively campaigned to defeat any changes in the birth control laws.

In 1947, as *Time* magazine put it, "Connecticut medicine was shaken by one of its biggest rows in years." The fight began when Connecticut doctors formed a Committee of 100 to back a birth control reform bill that would enable doctors to give information on contraceptives to patients whose lives or health would be endangered by pregnancy. This time Catholic opposition was direct: "Roman Catholic spokesmen promptly opposed it."[72] Appropriately enough in the postwar period, during the 1947 legislative battle, the Catholic War Veterans figured prominently in the opposition to the legislation. At first, the controversy was confined to speeches and letters to newspapers. Ultimately, however, "professional blood began to flow. Six angry doctors, members of the Committee of 100, announced that they had been kicked off the staff by the Roman Catholic hospitals in Waterbury, Stamford and Bridgeport" for refusing to remove their names from the petition.[73] Dr. Oliver Stringfield of Stamford testified in favor of the bill and then was removed from the staff of a Catholic hospital. He protested that the church forced him to choose dismissal or "with gross hypocrisy to conceal my sincere beliefs from disclosure to the public, so as to escape [its] disapproval."[74] Father Lawrence E. Skelly, director of hospitals for the Hartford diocese, explained: "The [hospital's] action was self-defensive. . . . You gave your name publicly to the support of a movement which is directly opposed to the code under which the hospital operates."[75]

Catholic priests used the pulpit to try to influence the outcome of state legislative races in Connecticut in 1948. On October 31, the

Sunday before election day, the pastors of all Catholic churches in the Hartford diocese called their parishioners' attention to an anti-birth-control editorial in the diocesan newsletter. The *New York Times* reported that "the editorial said it was the 'duty of every voter' to learn before casting his vote what 'commitments' had been made on the birth control issue by candidates for the General Assembly." The Reverend John J. Kennedy, rector of St. Peter's Church in Danbury, said that "no Catholic person in conscience [sic] can support any candidate favoring such legislation." The Reverend Austin B. Digman of Saint Mary's Church in Bethel told his parishioners that support for a candidate who favored reform of birth control laws "would be a violation of the natural moral law which Catholics and the Catholic Church are duty bound to uphold and would be a direct violation of God's Sixth Commandment."[76]

The heavy involvement of the Catholic church in birth control politics was very effective in Connecticut. During the many unsuccessful attempts to amend the birth control law, proponents of the measure would sometimes succeed in the Connecticut house, but the senate would then defeat the legislation. The reason given for differential treatment of birth control by the house and senate was that house members were elected by a primarily Protestant constituency, whereas senators tended to represent areas with a more heavily Catholic constituency.[77] According to a report on the 1957 legislative session by the Legislative Committee of the Planned Parenthood League of Connecticut,

> the makeup of the Senate is from 36 districts and that many of its members come from the central city or town in these districts, where our opposition is strongest. These centers represent the more Roman Catholic segment of the State population, which at the time of our action was about 43% of the total population. House members, on the other hand, come from the smaller towns and rural areas, generally Protestant, and are, in the main, less influenced by party pressures and are closer to their constituents.[78]

Notwithstanding its biannual failures, the Planned Parenthood League of Connecticut continued its legislative efforts.

Although religion was a critical factor in the legislative process, the religious backgrounds of the Connecticut Supreme Court justices did not determine the outcome of the birth control cases. All five members of the court during the years the *Nelson* and *Tileston* cases were decided were Protestants.[79] Of greater importance was the close tie between the court and the legislature. Judges in Connecticut were nominated by the governor and elected by the General Assembly.[80] At least until the late 1940s, the custom was to appoint state politicians to the bench.[81] Another tradition until the late 1970s was that Connecticut governors almost always nominated to vacancies on the supreme court the state superior court judge with the most seniority.[82]

In 1947, the *Connecticut Bar Journal* questioned the state tradition of appointing politicians to the state courts. According to a *Bar Journal* editorial, when studying the backgrounds of the judges sitting at that time, "rare indeed will be the case in which the background of appointment has not been a narrative of political activity." The editorial questioned whether "politicians really make the best judges." The *Bar Journal* editors felt that "surely there are enough patronage jobs to be dealt out" to satisfy political needs so that judicial positions need not be among them.[83]

The tradition of selecting politicians for judicial appointments may have contributed to the state supreme court's deferential posture. Many members of the court had previously served in the state legislature.[84] In ruling on state legislation, the justices were reviewing the handiwork of a political body they had close connections with. In upholding state laws, they affirmed the validity of a process they had previously participated in and the integrity of a group of people they knew. Accordingly, the customary judicial selection process operating in Connecticut during the time the birth control cases came before the court contributed to the likelihood that the Connecticut Supreme Court would be particularly deferential to the state legislature. Consequently, though religion may not have had a direct influence on the court, it had an indirect influence; the court's deferential posture meant that the confluence of religion and state politics in the legislature would be codified in Connecticut constitutional law.

Buxton *v.* Ullman

Fifteen years after *Tileston,* after their long series of unsuccessful attempts in the legislature, birth control advocates again turned to the courts. This time one of the plaintiffs was Dr. C. Lee Buxton, chair of Yale Medical School's Department of Obstetrics and Gynecology.[85] Buxton became involved in efforts to challenge the Connecticut birth control ban because he considered it to be a "travesty."[86] He said that the statutes were "actually preventing us from giving birth control advice to ward patients in the hospital"[87] and so kept doctors from giving birth control information to people who "desperately needed help." The consequences, in Buxton's view, were "tragic": "Within a few months in 1955, several of our obstetrical patients suffering from severe medical complications of pregnancy either died or suffered vascular accidents which were permanently incapacitating. These patients should never have become pregnant in the first place but they had never been able to obtain contraceptive advice." One case involved a twenty-eight-year-old woman with "severe mitral stenosis," a form of heart disease. "She had sought contraceptive advice in our clinic in vain at the time of her marriage. She died in the sixth month of pregnancy as a result of the added heart strain imposed by this condition, and in spite of several months of heroic efforts on the part of the medical and nursing staff to save her." Buxton considered the Connecticut statutes to be "largely responsible for the death of two individuals, the mother and the unborn baby." For him, "the irony of this situation . . . [was] that following cardiac surgery she would have been able in all probability to have several children."[88]

In part because Yale was the only medical school in the state, Buxton, as chair of obstetrics and gynecology, felt that it was his personal responsibility to do something about the situation.[89] In 1958, Buxton, along with Fowler Harper, a Yale Law School professor and president of the Planned Parenthood League of Connecticut, Estelle Griswold, the executive director of the league, and Catherine Roraback, a Connecticut attorney, began to plan a legal challenge to the birth control statutes.[90] They filed a series of lawsuits in New Haven Superior Court.

Buxton found individuals willing to bring suit anonymously.[91] Three were women with medical conditions that made pregnancy dangerous or unadvisable. Jane Doe had nearly died during a previous pregnancy, and "another pregnancy would be exceedingly dangerous to her life." Pauline Poe, who sued with her husband, had "borne three abnormal children, no one of whom lived more than ten weeks," making "another pregnancy extremely disturbing to both Mr. and Mrs. Poe." Hanna Hoe had given birth to four children, all of whom died. Mr. and Mrs. Hoe had incompatible Rh blood factors so that it was unlikely that they could bear a healthy child.[92] A fourth was a graduate student who wanted to avoid pregnancy for economic reasons.[93] Catherine Roraback acted as counsel in the cases, and Estelle Griswold and the Planned Parenthood League of Connecticut provided support.[94]

Abraham Ullman, the state's attorney, was named as defendant in these cases. Ullman demurrered to the complaints, arguing that the declaratory judgment actions were improper because the issues in the cases had already been conclusively determined and that the passage of time and changes in court personnel did not justify reconsideration of the issues. The demurrers were sustained by the trial court, and the plaintiffs appealed to the Connecticut Supreme Court.[95]

The Connecticut Supreme Court noted that the primary difference between *Buxton* and previous Connecticut birth control cases was that "here each plaintiff is asserting his own constitutional right, while in the *Nelson* and *Tileston* cases the doctors were attempting to assert the right of their patients to receive treatment." Buxton argued that he had a "constitutional right, distinct from that of his patients, to practice his profession free from unreasonable restraint," and the patients asserted their right to use birth control. The court believed that there was "no real difference in the nature of the right" claimed by Buxton and that of the patients. "The effect of regulation of a business or profession is to curtail the activities of both the dispenser and the user of goods or services. Both are deprived of some advantage they might otherwise have."[96]

The court again rejected the argument that a medical exception should be read into the statute. Such a construction would violate the separation of powers. "In our tripartite system of government, the judiciary accords to the legislature the right to determine in the first instance what is the nature and extent of the danger to the public health, safety, morals and welfare and what are the measures best calculated to meet the threat." Courts would overturn police power legislation only "when it clearly appears that the legislative measures taken do not serve the public health, safety, morals or welfare or that they deny or interfere with private rights unreasonably." According to the court, "it was out of respect for these fundamental principles" that no medical exception was found in *Nelson* and *Tileston*.[97]

The court noted that the legislature had repeatedly refused to amend the birth control statutes since *Tileston*.[98] The continued rejection of changes in the laws was significant, for "courts cannot, by the process of construction, abrogate a clear expression of legislative intent, especially when, as here, unambiguous language is fortified by the refusal of the legislature, in the light of judicial interpretation, to change it."[99]

Turning to the constitutionality of the statute, the court acknowledged that "the claims of infringement of constitutional rights are presented more dramatically than they have ever been before." Nevertheless, the claims were essentially the same as those in previous cases. The court reaffirmed its ruling in *Tileston* that, although contraceptives were "the best and safest preventative measure" for the plaintiffs, the legislature did not have to allow it when there was "another alternative, abstinence from sexual intercourse." According to the court, "We cannot say that the legislature, in weighing the considerations for and against an exception legalizing contraceptive measures in cases such as the ones before us, could not reasonably conclude that, despite the occasional hardship which might result, the greater good would be served by leaving the statutes as they are." In the court's view, the cases raised "an issue of public policy" reserved for the legislature: "Each of the separate magistracies of our government owes to the others a duty not to trespass upon the lawful domain of the others. The judiciary has a duty to test legislative action by constitutional principles, but it cannot, in that process, usurp the power of the legislature." For the court, overturning the birth control statutes would be such an improper judicial usurpation. Once again, the Connecticut Supreme Court deferred to a legislature that would prove to be unwilling to amend its statute. Following its precedents and finding no constitutional problems posed by the birth control ban, the court kept birth control clinics closed.[100]

In June 1961, a divided Supreme Court dismissed the appeal from the Connecticut ruling. Justice Felix Frankfurter, writing for a four-member plurality, found the case nonjusticiable because he believed there was no realistic threat of prosecution under the statutes. "The Connecticut law prohibiting the use of contraceptives has been on the State's books since 1879. During the more than three-quarters of a century since its enactment, a prosecution for its violation seems never to have been initiated, save in *State* v. *Nelson*."[101] The "unreality" of the case was further illuminated by the fact that certain contraceptives could be purchased in Connecticut drugstores. Frankfurter believed that Connecticut had practiced an "undeviating policy of nullification." He found that the lack of prosecutions under the statute "deprives these controversies of the immediacy which is an indispensable condition of constitutional adjudication. This Court cannot be umpire to debates concerning harmless, empty shadows." According to Frankfurter, "To find it necessary to pass on these statutes now, in order to protect appellants from the hazards of prosecution, would be to close our eyes to reality." [102]

Frankfurter appears to have been wrong regarding the lack of prosecutions other than *Nelson*. During oral argument, Connecticut Assistant Attorney General Raymond Cannon stated that he knew of "two cases in the police courts prosecuting proprietors of business establishments for having vending machines dispensing contraceptives." [103]

Justice Brennan provided the fifth vote to dismiss *Poe*. He recognized the issue at stake in the case, but not its implications. He was "not convinced, on this skimpy record, that these appellants as individuals are truly caught in an inescapable dilemma. The true controversy in this case is over the opening of birth-control clinics on a large scale; it is that which the State has prevented in the past, not the use of contraceptives by isolated and individual married couples." [104]

This impasse frustrated birth control advocates. As long as the law was on the books, it restricted the open prescription of contraceptives and therefore kept birth control clinics closed. As long as it was not actively enforced, its constitutionality could not be challenged, and birth control services would continue to be illegal.[105]

State *v.* Griswold

Planned Parenthood activists considered their next step. If Frankfurter was right that the state laws were "harmless, empty shadows," they could open clinics and operate freely. If Frankfurter was wrong, there would be prosecutions, and they would find themselves in court again. They decided to open a clinic and see what happened.[106]

The Planned Parenthood League of Connecticut opened a birth control clinic on November 1, 1961, at its Trumbull Street headquarters in New Haven. Dr. Buxton was its medical director and Estelle

Griswold served as executive director. Buxton told the *New York Times* that Frankfurter's opinion in *Poe* led him to believe that "all doctors in Connecticut may now prescribe child spacing techniques to married women when it is medically indicated." If Buxton was wrong and clinic personnel were prosecuted, Planned Parenthood officials were not concerned. Fowler Harper believed that "it would be a state and community service if a criminal action were brought. . . . I think citizens and doctors alike are entitled to know if they are violating the law." Meanwhile, the state's attorney in New Haven assumed that if there was a violation of the law, the local police would take action.[107]

The clinic served a heavy load of clients and prescribed a variety of contraceptives, including the new birth control pills.[108] In addition to its regular patients, on November 3, the clinic was visited by two detectives. The police acted after receiving a complaint by James G. Morris of West Haven, a Catholic who believed that "a Planned Parenthood Center is like a house of prostitution. It is against the natural law which says marital relations are for procreation and not entertainment."[109]

On November 10, police returned to arrest Griswold and Buxton. They were charged with violating the state birth control ban. The clinic was closed following the arrest. It had served seventy-five women in four sessions over the ten days it was open. At the time of the closing, the clinic was solidly booked for another month.[110]

Griswold and Buxton pled not guilty to the charges, and their attorney, Catherine Roraback, filed a demurrer, arguing that the prosecutions violated the state and federal constitutions.[111] Griswold and Buxton were tried on January 2, 1962. Three married women testified that they had attended the clinic, had received information and contraceptives, and had used the contraceptives.[112] The defendants were convicted of aiding and abetting the use of contraceptives. On appeal, the convictions were sustained by the Appellate Division of the Circuit Court. Roraback then filed an appeal to the Connecticut Supreme Court of Errors.[113]

The state supreme court disposed of the case briefly. The court found that the facts of the case indicated that there was "no doubt" that Griswold and Buxton "did aid, abet and counsel married women in the commission of an offense." The court was not sympathetic to their argument that Connecticut precedent on birth control should be reconsidered. According to the court, the state laws had "been under attack in this court on four different occasions in the past twenty-four years. . . . Every attack now made on the statute . . . has been made and rejected in one or more of these cases." The court followed its line of cases. "We adhere to the principle that courts may not interfere with the exercise by a state of the police power to conserve the public safety and welfare, including health and morals, if the law has a real and substantial relation to the accomplishment of those objects." Again, deference was appropriate. "The legislature is primarily the judge of the regulations required to that end, and its police statutes may be declared unconstitutional only when they are arbitrary or unreasonable attempts to exercise its authority in the public interest." The legislature had "not recognized that the interest of the general public calls for the repeal or modification of the statute as heretofore construed by us."[114]

Griswold and Buxton would, of course, go on to prevail in the Supreme Court, and *Griswold v. Connecticut* would become a landmark case establishing a constitutional right to privacy.[115] As far as the Connecticut court was concerned, however, the defendants' constitutional rights had not been violated, there was nothing unreasonable about the ban on contraceptives, and if birth control advocates wished to change the law, the proper forum was the legislature. One result, in the words of Dr. Buxton, was that in 1964 "women in Connecticut [were] still unnecessarily dying because of the statute."[116]

Conclusion

Several times between 1940 and 1964 the Connecticut Supreme Court considered the constitutionality of the state ban on contraceptives. Each time the court declined to scrutinize carefully the degree to which the state law reasonably served state purposes. The court refused to find state laws unreasonable or fundamental rights impaired when state legislation placed women's lives in jeopardy when they participated in marital sex. The central focus of the court's analysis was always on deference to the state legislature. And, due to decades of legislative gridlock on birth control reform, the court's deference left reproductive rights in Connecticut at a standstill.

The state court's answer to the dilemma Connecticut women found themselves in was that women's due process rights were not violated because of the existence of an alternative: abstinence from sexual intercourse. Many women avoided the harsh choices the court reserved for them by going out of state for a diaphragm, seeing a doctor willing to violate the law, or using the condoms and spermicides available over the counter. For those women unable to afford private medical care and for whom pregnancy was life-threatening, the success rates of over-the-counter contraceptives were insufficient. Consequently, though some forms of birth control were regularly sold in Connecticut drugstores, they did not work well enough for women who could not risk pregnancy. The result was that the Connecticut laws and the court's deferential posture took their toll on the lives of poor women in Connecticut in the form of unintended pregnancies and premature deaths.

Although the Connecticut law had harsh consequences, the courts and legislatures of other states were more permissive toward birth control. As a result, one might argue that the lesson to be learned from the history of state treatment of the right to use birth control is generally positive: overall, states have safeguarded reproductive rights on some level in the past. The contemporary treatment of abortion funding cases by some state courts reinforces this point.[117]

As the Supreme Court cuts back on the federal right to abortion, the state courts and state legislatures will be the only practical alternative. Nevertheless, the history of birth control in Connecticut illustrates the limitations of reliance on state courts for protection of fundamental rights. State courts, less insulated from majoritarian politics, are less willing or able to make unpopular decisions.[118] The Connecticut Supreme Court was unwilling to overturn the legislature when faced with a patently unjust and unreasonable law that was a source of great political controversy. That failure of will, according to Connecticut's leading gynecologist, cost women their lives. The women harmed by the statute were so invisible to the legal system that Justice Frankfurter thought of their concerns as "empty shadows."[119] It will again be these invisible women who will bear the burdens of restriction of the federal right to abortion. As did the women in Connecticut, they will bear them on their very real bodies, with their very real lives.

The question of the comparative sensitivity of state and federal courts to reproductive rights ultimately raises the issue of whether a unitary or decentralized constitutional system will provide greater protection for reproductive freedom. At the symposium "In Search of a Usable Past," Professor William Nelson asked participants what the "better" way would be for the Supreme Court to overturn *Roe v. Wade.* If the Court were so inclined, should it hold that the right to abortion is not protected under the U.S. Constitution and turn the matter back to the states? The result would be that abortion would remain legal in some states but would be illegal in others.[120] Decentralization would therefore mean that women fortunate to live in the right states and those wealthy enough to travel to a location where abortion is permitted will continue to have meaningful access to abortion. Others will not. The class-based nature of the right would be reinforced as states permitting abortion enacted regulations that made it more expensive.[121] In such circumstances, the history of birth control in Connecticut suggests that those harmed are also those least likely to be heard in the political process and in the courts. The implications for women with few financial resources whose lives will be altered by unintended pregnancies they are unable to terminate are chilling.

So one is unwillingly drawn to consider Nelson's second alternative: would it be "better" for the Court to hold that a fetus is a person entitled to constitutional protection and therefore that it is unconstitutional for states to permit abortions? The immediate effect of such a ruling would be devastating, but it would be devastating in every neighborhood of every state. As restrictions on reproductive rights personally touched the lives of more women and men, and more politically powerful women and men, the ultimate effect might be to galvanize broad-based political action. The unitary restriction on reproductive rights might be transformed, through a constitutional amendment, into unitary protection for all women in every neighborhood of every state.

Perhaps it is fear for women's lives, mixed with an unfounded hope that the decentralized political process will not mirror the callousness of the past, that makes me shy from such an alternative. Nevertheless, for reproductive rights to be more than an abstraction for low-income women, there is no substitute for strong, unitary constitutional protection. The difficult question at this point in time is how, and when, that may come to be.

Notes

I am very grateful to Brooks Ammerman, Martha Chamallas, and Linda Kerber for their helpful comments on previous drafts of this essay. I also benefited from discussions about the essay with participants in the symposium "In Search of a Usable Past," held at Albany Law School in October 1988. Thanks also go to Larry Burch, Kate Corcoran, Pat McCarley, Peter Parry, and Jim Spounias, who contributed to the research, and Rita Jansen, who typed the final drafts.

1. 109 S.Ct. 3040 (1989).
2. 410 U.S. 113 (1973). In *Webster* v. *Reproductive Health Services,* 109 S.Ct. 3040 (1989), the solicitor general of the United States argued that the Supreme Court should overturn *Roe.* 57 *U.S.L.W.* 3715–16 (1989); *New York Times,* late ed., April 27, 1989, pp. B14–16, cols. 1–6. Although the Court declined to overturn *Roe* in that case, three members of the Court have called for the decision to be overruled. See *Webster,* 109 S.Ct. at 3064 (Scalia, J., concurring); *Thornburgh* v. *American College of Obstetricians and Gynecologists,* 476 U.S. 747, 788 (1986) (White, J., dissenting) (joined by Justice Rehnquist). In addition, Justice O'Connor harshly criticized *Roe*'s reasoning in *City of Akron* v. *Akron Center for Reproductive Health, Inc.,* 462 U.S. 416, 452–59 (1983) (O'Connor, J., dissenting). The Court continued the trend of giving states greater leeway in restricting abortion rights in *Hodgson* v. *Minnesota,* 110 S.Ct. 2926 (1990) and *Ohio* v. *Akron Center for Reproductive Health,* 110 S.Ct. 2972 (1990).
3. See *Newsweek,* July 17, 1989, pp. 16–24; *Time,* July 17, 1989, p. 64; *New York Times,* July 4, 1989, p. 1, col. 5.
4. In *Harris* v. *McRae,* 448 U.S. 297, 326 (1980), the United States Supreme Court held that the Hyde Amendment, which prohibited federal Medicaid reimbursement for abortions unless the life of the woman was endangered by pregnancy or the pregnancy was the result of rape or incest, was constitutional. In *Maher* v. *Roe,* 432 U.S. 464, 474 (1977), the Court upheld a Connecticut statute providing state Medicaid reimbursement for childbirth but not for abortions that were not medically necessary. In contrast, some state courts have found similar funding restrictions under state law to violate state constitutions. *Doe* v. *Maher,* 40 Conn. Supp. 394, 450, 515 A.2d 134, 162 (1986); *Right to Choose* v. *Byrne,* 91 N.J. 287, 318, 450 A.2d 925, 941 (1982); *Committee to Defend Reproductive Rights* v. *Myers,* 29 Cal.3d 252, 285, 625 P.2d 779, 799, 172 Cal. Rptr. 866, 886 (1981); *Moe* v. *Secretary of Administration and Finance,* 382 Mass. 629, 654, 417 N.E.2d 387, 402 (1981); *Planned Parenthood* v. *Department of Human Services,* 63 Or. App. 41, 62, 663 P.2d

1247, 1261 (1983), *aff'd on other grounds,* 297 Or. 562, 687 P.2d 785 (1984). See also *Dodge* v. *Department of Social Services,* 657 P.2d 969 (Colo. App. 1982) (ruled against taxpayers' argument that state practice of funding all abortions was not authorized by state statutes); *Kindley* v. *Governor of Maryland,* 289 Md. 620, 426 A.2d 908 (1981) (same). But see *Fischer* v. *Department of Public Welfare,* 509 Pa. 293, 502 A.2d 114 (1985) (state funding formula based on Hyde Amendment criteria does not violate Pennsylvania Constitution); but see also *Stam* v. *State of North Carolina,* 302 N.C. 357, 275 S.E.2d 439 (1981) (county tax to fund elective abortions exceeded statutory authority). See generally Note, "The Evolution of the Right to Privacy after *Roe v. Wade,*" *American Journal of Law and Medicine* 13 (1987): 365, 436–66.

5. For example, the courts of some states were more likely to admit women to the practice of law in the late nineteenth century. The U.S. Supreme Court upheld the Illinois Supreme Court's denial of a license to practice law to Myra Bradwell in 1872. *Bradwell* v. *Illinois,* 83 U.S. (16 Wall.) 130 (1872). The Court denied Belva Lockwood admission to the bar of the U.S. Supreme Court itself in 1876 because "none but men are admitted to practice before it." Karen Berger Morello, *The Invisible Bar: The Woman Lawyer in America, 1638 to the Present* (Boston: Beacon Press, 1986), 33. In contrast, the Iowa Supreme Court admitted Belle Mansfield to the state bar in 1869, even though Iowa law restricted bar admission to "any white male person" meeting other qualifications. Ibid., 12. The Territory of Washington admitted Mary Leonard to the practice of law in the 1880s. Ibid., 28. Clara Foltz was admitted to practice before the supreme court of California in 1879. Barbara Babcock, "Clara Shortridge Foltz: 'First Woman,'" *Arizona Law Review* 30 (1988): 673, 715. See generally, Morello, *Invisible Bar,* 11–38; Babcock, "Clara Shortridge Foltz," 701–5.

6. *Buck* v. *Bell,* 274 U.S. 200 (1927). See Mary Dudziak, "Oliver Wendell Holmes as a Eugenic Reformer: Rhetoric in the Writing of Constitutional Law," *Iowa Law Review* 71 (1986): 833.

7. *Skinner* v. *Oklahoma,* 316 U.S. 535 (1942).

8. See Comment, "The History and Future of the Legal Battle over Birth Control," *Cornell Law Quarterly* 49 (1964): 275, 285–88 (written by Peter Smith).

9. See, e.g., *U.S.* v. *One Package,* 86 F.2d 737 (2d Cir. 1936).

10. See, e.g., *Commonwealth* v. *Gardner,* 300 Mass. 372, 15 N.E.2d 222 (1938); *appeal dismissed,* 305 U.S. 559 (1938).

11. See, e.g., *Tileston* v. *Ullman,* 129 Conn. 84, 26 A.2d 582 (1942); *appeal dismissed,* 318 U.S. 46 (1943).

12. 381 U.S. 497 (1965).

13. A recent example is statements made by Robert Bork in his confirmation hearings. See *Nomination of Robert H. Bork to Be Associate Justice of
the Supreme Court of the United States: Hearings Before the Senate Committee
on the Judiciary*, 100th Cong., 1st sess., 116, 241 (1987) (hereinafter cited
as *Bork Hearings*). See also Harriet Pollack, " 'An Uncommonly Silly
Law': The Connecticut Birth Control Cases in the U.S. Supreme Court"
(Ph.D. dissertation, Columbia University, 1968).

14. This was essentially the view expressed by the Supreme Court in *Poe* v.
Ullman, 367 U.S. 497 (1961).

15. *Bork Hearings*, 116.

16. Pollack, " 'Uncommonly Silly Law,' " 67.

17. C. Thomas Dienes, *Law Politics and Birth Control* (Urbana: University of
Illinois Press, 1972). See also Susan Hartmann, *The Home Front and Beyond: American Women in the 1940s* (Boston: Twayne, 1982), 171; Jonathan
Daniels, "Birth Control and Democracy," *Nation*, November 1, 1941,
p. 429.

18. Sylvia Law powerfully develops the argument that restrictions on re-
productive rights deny women their constitutional right to equality in
"Rethinking Sex and the Constitution," *University of Pennsylvania Law
Review* 132 (1984): 955.

19. See generally Linda Gordon, *Woman's Body, Woman's Right: A Social
History of Birth Control in America* (New York: Penguin Books, 1977).

20. Margaret Sanger, *The New Motherhood* (1922; rpt. Elmsford, N.Y.: Maxwell Reprint Co., 1977), 102, 109–10.

21. See Dienes, *Law Politics*, 78–88. See generally David Kennedy, *Birth
Control in America: The Career of Margaret Sanger* (New Haven: Yale University Press, 1970).

22. 17 Stat. 598 (1873).

23. See Abraham Stone and Harriet Pilpel, "The Social and Legal Status of
Contraception," *North Carolina Law Review* 22 (1944): 212, 220.

24. *U.S.* v. *One Package*, 86 F.2d 737 (2d Cir. 1936). "Illegal contraception"
would include the use of contraceptives in sex outside of marriage.

25. 222 N.Y. 192, 118 N.E. 637 (1918).

26. Ibid., 637.

27. Ibid., 638. The alternative would be to construe *disease* to mean sexually
transmitted diseases.

28. See Comment, "Legal Battle over Birth Control," 285. Massachusetts
was the one state other than Connecticut in which the courts construed
state law as forbidding the prescription of contraceptives by doctors
when the health of a patient required them. See *Commonwealth* v. *Gardner*, 300 Mass. 372, 15 N.E.2d 222 (1938).

29. Use of contraceptives came to be more widely accepted during a period

when, largely at the impetus of the medical profession, access to abortion was becoming difficult. Elaine Tyler May, *Homeward Bound: American Families in the Cold War Era* (New York: Basic Books, 1988), 153.

30. Stone and Pilpel, "Contraception," 215; May, *Homeward Bound,* 149.

31. Henry Pringle, "What Do the Women of America Think About Birth Control?" *Ladies' Home Journal,* March 1938, p. 14. See also Stone and Pilpel, "Contraception," 218; John D'Emilio and Estelle Freedman, *Intimate Matters: A History of Sexuality in America* (New York: Harper & Row, 1988), 248.

32. See Gordon, *Woman's Body, Woman's Right,* 186–245.

33. May, *Homeward Bound,* 149; D'Emilio and Freedman, *Intimate Matters,* 248.

34. May purposely uses the Cold War term *containment* to illustrate the connection between sexual values and postwar anticommunism. During the Cold War, many believed that "moral weakness was associated with sexual degeneracy, which allegedly led to communism. To avoid dire consequences, men as well as women had to contain their sexuality in marriage where masculine men would be in control with sexually submissive competent homemakers at their side." May, *Homeward Bound,* 99.

35. D'Emilio and Freedman, *Intimate Matters,* 265–74, 249. Although the birth rate climbed during the 1940s and 1950s, the size of individual families increased only from an average of 2.4 to 3.2 children. "What made the baby boom happen was that *everyone* was doing it—and at the same time." May, *Homeward Bound,* 135–61, quote on 152.

36. See below at text accompanying notes 40–42, 70–78.

37. Comment, "Legal Battle over Birth Control," 279.

38. The law was originally enacted as part of a broader obscenity statute. 1879 Conn. Pub. Acts ch. 78. In 1888, during a revision of Connecticut general statutes, the birth control law was removed from the general obscenity law and placed in a separate section. See Comment, "Legal Battle over Birth Control," 279. The statute, which would remain unchanged until it was invalidated in *Griswold,* read as follows: "Any person who uses any drug, medicinal article or instrument for the purpose of preventing conception shall be fined not less than fifty dollars or imprisoned not less than sixty days nor more than one year or be both fined and imprisoned." Conn. Gen. Stat. Rev. § 53–32 (1958).

39. Conn. Gen. Stat. Rev. § 54–196 (1958).

40. Pollack, " 'Uncommonly Silly Law,' " 80. Pollack's account of the *Nelson* case is based on an interview with J. Warren Upson, counsel for Dr. Roger B. Nelson. Ibid., 139. Their lawyer would be proven wrong. See below at text accompanying notes 42, 47. This was not the first

Connecticut Birth Control League clinic. One had been opened in Hartford in 1935, and there were others in Greenwich, New Haven, Stamford, Danbury, Westport, Norwalk, and Bridgeport. Ibid., 79–80.

41. Cornelius Trowbridge, "Catholicism Fights Birth Control," *New Republic,* January 22, 1945, p. 107. See also Dienes, *Law Politics,* 137.

42. Pollack, " 'Uncommonly Silly Law,' " 80–81. Dienes, *Law Politics,* 137; Trowbridge, "Catholicism," 107.

43. *State* v. *Nelson,* 126 Conn. 412, 415–16, 11 A.2d 856, 858 (1940). They also argued that the statute failed to fix a reasonably precise standard of guilt and failed to fix a maximum fine.

44. Id. At biannual legislative sessions from 1921 through 1931, bills were introduced that would have allowed contraceptives when prescribed by a physician. In 1933 and 1935, bills were introduced that would have allowed physicians to prescribe birth control only when pregnancy would be harmful to the health of a woman or her child. Id. at 416–18, 11 A.2d at 858–59.

45. Id. at 422–24, 11 A.2d at 860–61.

46. 227 Mass. 57, 62, 116 N.E. 265, 266 (1917).

47. *Nelson,* 126 Conn. at 425, 11 A.2d at 862 (quoting *Allison,* 227 Mass. at 62, 116 N.E. at 266). The court also rejected the defendants' arguments that the statute was unconstitutional because it did not set a maximum fine. The dissenters in *Nelson* did not file an opinion. Id. at 427, 11 A.2d at 863.

48. Id. at 418, 11 A.2d at 859.

49. Pollack, " 'Uncommonly Silly Law,' " 87. See *Poe* v. *Ullman,* 367 U.S. 497, 532–33 (Harlan, J., dissenting) (discussing the *Nelson* prosecution).

50. Trowbridge, "Catholicism," 107.

51. Pollack, " 'Uncommonly Silly Law,' " 89.

52. *Tileston* v. *Ullman,* 129 Conn. 84, 84, 86, 26 A.2d 582–84 (1942). Tileston worked with the Connecticut Birth Control League in bringing the suit. Pollack, " 'Uncommonly Silly Law,' " 89.

53. 129 Conn. at 84, 87, 26 A.2d at 583–85.

54. Id. at 92, 26 A.2d at 586 (citations omitted).

55. Id.

56. Id. at 96, 26 A.2d at 588.

57. Conn. Gen. Stat. §§ 6056 and 6057 (1930). The court believed that there was an important difference between medically necessary abortion and contraception. In the event that an ongoing pregnancy threatened a woman's life, "there was no alternative" other than abortion or harm to the woman's health. In contrast, before becoming pregnant, there was another alternative: abstinence from sex. 129 Conn. at 86, 93, 26 A.2d at 584–87.

58. 129 Conn. at 102, 26 A.2d at 590.

59. *Tileston* v. *Ullman*, 318 U.S. 44, 46 (1943).

60. See "The Accident of Birth," *Fortune*, February 1938, pp. 83, 108–14; Stone and Pilpel, "Contraception," 219.

61. Stone and Pilpel, "Contraception," 219.

62. "Accident of Birth," 85. According to the report, "The reliable manufacturers . . . are surrounded by fly-by-nights with no scruples. The industry's conventional outlets are drugstores, but these keep prices jacked up beyond reason." See James Reed, *From Private Vice to Public Virtue: The Birth Control Movement in American Society Since 1830* (New York: Basic Books, 1978), 239–46.

63. Stone and Pilpel, "Contraception," 219.

64. Catholic and non-Catholic doctors often differed in their willingness to prescribe birth control, and women in the state would discuss among themselves the differences between doctors on the subject of birth control. Telephone interview conducted by author with Louise Trubek, plaintiff in *Trubek* v. *Ullman*, 147 Conn. 633 (1960), *appeal dismissed*, 367 U.S. 907 (1961), August 30, 1988. See below, note 92 for a discussion of the *Trubek* case.

65. Telephone interview conducted by author with Catherine Roraback, counsel to Planned Parenthood in *Buxton* v. *Ullman*, 147 Conn. 48, 156 A.2d 508 (1959), *appeal dismissed sub. nom. Poe* v. *Ullman*, 367 U.S. 497 (1961), *reh'g denied*, 368 U.S. 869 (1961), and *Griswold* v. *Connecticut*, 381 U.S. 479 (1965), September 2, 1988; Daniels, "Birth Control and Democracy," 429.

66. *New York Times*, late ed. September 19, 1987, p. 10, cols. 2–5; Pollack, " 'Uncommonly Silly Law,' " 99.

67. See below at text accompanying notes 87–88.

68. See *Buxton* v. *Ullman*, 147 Conn. 48, 56–57 n. 2, 156 A.2d 508, 513 n. 2 (1959) (listing bills introduced and ultimately defeated in the 1943, 1945, 1947, 1949, 1951, 1953, 1955, 1957, and 1959 legislative sessions).

69. Comment, "Birth Control," 280–81, note 49.

70. Dienes, *Law Politics*, 106, 147. The church was also an important force in birth control politics in Massachusetts. Eugene Belisle, "Birth Control in Massachusetts," *New Republic*, December 8, 1941, p. 759.

71. "Defeat in Connecticut," *Outlook and Independent*, April 15, 1931, p. 518.

72. "The Law in Connecticut," *Time*, April 21, 1947, p. 58.

73. "68 Years," *New Republic*, May 19, 1947, p. 8; *New York Times*, late ed., May 5, 1947, p. 25, col. 2.

74. Gereon Zimmerman, "Contraception and Commotion in Connecticut," *Look*, January 30, 1962, p. 83.

75. "The Law in Connecticut," *Time*, April 21, 1947, p. 58. The removals

were protested by ministers of other faiths. Seventeen Protestant ministers, two rabbis, and a social worker signed a statement "commending the six doctors for refusing to retract 'a principle of conscience.' " Ibid. Similar hospital firings happened in other states. For example, four staff physicians at Mercy Hospital in Springfield, Massachusetts, were dismissed in 1947 for giving birth control advice to their patients. *New York Times*, late ed., June 18, 1947, p. 23, col. 2. In Poughkeepsie, New York, in 1952, seven doctors were told to sever their ties with Planned Parenthood or resign from the St. Francis Hospital staff. One doctor quickly resigned from the local chapter's medical advisory board because "he had 'four operation cases' in the hospital and did not want to 'distress them.' " *New York Times*, late ed., February 1, 1952, p. 1, cols. 6–7.

76. *New York Times*, late ed., November 1, 1948, p. 15, cols. 3–6; ibid., late ed., November 2, 1948, p. 3, col. 1. The Sixth Commandment is "Thou shalt not commit adultery." Exod. 20:14.

Similarly, in 1942 and 1948, Catholic priests were heavily involved in fighting birth control referenda in Massachusetts. Both measures, which would have allowed doctors to prescribe contraceptives for their patients when pregnancy would jeopardize their health, were defeated. Eugene Belisle, "The Cardinal Stoops to Conquer," *New Republic*, November 30, 1942, p. 710; *New York Times*, late ed., November 3, 1948, p. 2, col. 1. Archbishop Richard J. Cushing stated that those opposing the 1948 referendum had spent "well over $50,000" to defeat the measure. This disclosure prompted the Massachusetts Planned Parenthood League to question the church's tax-exempt status. *New York Times*, late ed., November 13, 1948, p. 16, cols. 6–7.

During the 1942 campaign, priests used the pulpit to encourage citizens to register to vote. The *Springfield Union* reported that parishioners at Sacred Heart Church were told that "Catholics had a moral obligation to vote against the referendum and *that any Catholic who knowingly voted in favor of it could not expect absolution.*" Quoted in Belisle, "The Cardinal Stoops to Conquer," 712. Monsignor Splaine told the St. Mary's Church congregation that it was a sin to vote in favor of the referendum. The newsletter of the Archdiocese of Boston ran weekly editorials against the measure from July 1942 until the election. But the referendum's proponents sometimes had difficulty finding a forum. After the owner of radio station WESX in Salem sold air time to referendum supporters, a Salem priest urged parishioners not to listen to the station or buy anything advertised on it. In another incident, eleven priests protested to the Catholic owner of an Italian newspaper after he sold space to the Mother's Health Committee, which supported the referendum.

77. See *New York Times*, late ed., May 19, 1963, p. 81, col. 5.

78. Comment, "Legal Battle over Birth Control," 281 (quoting report of the Legislative Committee of the Planned Parenthood League of Connecticut, from the files of the Planned Parenthood Federation of America, New Haven, Connecticut). Dienes, *Law Politics*, 144–47.

79. When *Nelson* was before the court, Justices Maltbie, Avery, Brown, Hinman, and Jennings were members of Protestant churches. Howard W. Alcorn, "Obituary Sketch of William M. Maltbie," 148 Conn. 740, 745 (1961); Allyn L. Brown, "Obituary Sketch of Christopher L. Avery," 143 Conn. 735, 736 (1956); Robert P. Anderson, "Obituary Sketch of Allyn L. Brown," 164 Conn. 713 (1973); John H. King, "Obituary Sketch of George E. Hinman," 148 Conn. 737, 740 (1961); Biographical sketch of Newell Jennings, *National Cyclopedia of American Biography* 52 (1970): 576. When *Tileston* was decided, Justice Ellis, also a member of a Protestant church, had replaced Justice Hinman. See Allyn W. Brown, "Obituary Sketch of Arthur F. Ellis," 151 Conn. 747, 749 (1956).

80. Ernest A. Inglis, "The Selection and Tenure of Judges," *Connecticut Bar Journal* 22 (1948): 106, 111.

81. See Editorial, "The Selection of Judges," *Connecticut Bar Journal* 21 (1947): 355. In 1986 Connecticut adopted a constitutional amendment changing the judicial selection process to one in which the governor nominates judges recommended by a Judicial Selection Commission. Conn. Const. amend. XXV.

82. Between 1900 and 1977, forty-six of the forty-eight people appointed to the state supreme court were superior court judges. Forty of them had the most seniority among superior court judges at the time. Peter Adomeit, "Selection by Seniority: How Much Longer Can a Custom Survive That Bars Blacks and Women from the Connecticut Supreme Court?" *Connecticut Bar Journal* 51 (1977): 295, 300.

    Connecticut Governor Ella Grasso departed from this tradition and that of appointing politicians when she nominated Justice Ellen Peters, formerly a Yale Law School professor, to the Connecticut Supreme Court in 1978. See *Connecticut State Register and Manual* (1979), 140.

83. Editorial, "Selection of Judges," 355–57. See also Inglis, "Selection and Tenure of Judges," 116 (suggesting that politics played an "important part" in judicial selection in Connecticut).

84. At the time *Nelson* was decided, three of the five justices on the Supreme Court of Errors had previously been elected to the General Assembly. Among them was Justice Christopher Avery, who dissented. See Alcorn, 148 Conn. at 741; Anderson, 164 Conn. at 713; Brown, 143 Conn. at 736. A fourth justice served for seven sessions as a clerk to the General Assembly. King, 148 Conn. at 737. The fifth member of the

court, Justice Newell Jennings, did not serve in the state legislature. See Raymond E. Baldwin, "Obituary Sketch of Newell Jennings," 152 Conn. 749 (1965). Justice Jennings dissented in *Nelson.*

At the time *Tileston* was decided, only Justice Jennings, who dissented, had not been elected to the General Assembly. See Brown, 151 Conn. at 748; Alcorn; Anderson; Brown; Baldwin.

During the years when *Buxton* v. *Ullman,* 147 Conn. 48 (1959), *Trubek* v. *Ullman,* 147 Conn. 633 (1960), and *State* v. *Griswold,* 151 Conn. 544 (1964), were decided, three of the five members of the court had previously served in the General Assembly either as law clerks or members of the legislature. See *Connecticut State Register and Manual* (1959), 107; *Connecticut State Register and Manual* (1964), 123.

85. *New York Times,* late ed., June 7, 1958, p. 10, col. 2.
86. C. Lee Buxton, "Birth Control Problems in Connecticut: Medical Necessity, Political Cowardice and Legal Procrastination," *Connecticut Medicine* 28 (August 1964): 581. I am indebted to Marion Stillson, see below, note 109, for leading me to Buxton's very helpful article.
87. Steven M. Spencer, "The Birth Control Revolution," *Saturday Evening Post,* January 15, 1966, p. 70.
88. Buxton, "Birth Control Problems," 581–82. It was considered too dangerous to do cardiac surgery during this woman's pregnancy.
89. Ibid., 583.
90. Interview with Catherine Roraback, September 2, 1988; Spencer, "Birth Control Revolution," 70. In part because Planned Parenthood supporters gathered together and planned litigation strategy and because of the involvement of the Planned Parenthood organization in the birth control litigation, some have dismissed the cases as unimportant "test cases" that did not involve real issues. See *Bork Hearings,* 116, 241. Prelitigation strategy sessions and involvement of interested organizations, however, have been an important aspect of other twentieth-century civil rights litigation efforts. See e.g., Mark Tushnet, *The NAACP's Legal Strategy Against Segregated Education, 1925–1950* (Chapel Hill: University of North Carolina Press, 1987). It was also not extraordinary at this time for a group to set its sights on invalidation of state laws in the U.S. Supreme Court. The school desegregation cases brought by the NAACP are perhaps the most well-known example of such a strategy. See ibid.; Richard Kluger, *Simple Justice: The History of Brown v. Board of Education and Black America's Struggle for Equality* (New York: Random House, 1977).
91. Anonymity was important. At the time *Tileston* was litigated, birth control advocates had difficulty finding people willing to participate in the case. Pollack, " 'An Uncommonly Silly Law,' " 89–90. Some feared re-

taliation. One *Buxton/Poe* plaintiff was afraid her husband would lose his job if her participation in the case became public. Ibid., 102 n. 45.

92. *Buxton v. Ullman,* 147 Conn. 48, 52–53, 156 A.2d at 511 (1959), *appeal dismissed* 367 U.S. 497 (1961), *reh'g denied,* 368 U.S. 869 (1961).

93. Pollack, "'Uncommonly Silly Law,'" 101. This plaintiff's case was later mooted when she moved from the state. As a substitute, David and Louise Trubek, who were Yale law students, filed suit. A married couple, they stated that they wished to postpone childbearing for economic and personal reasons and because pregnancy at that time would interfere with Louise Trubek's legal education. See *Trubek v. Ullman,* 147 Conn. 633, 636, 165 A.2d 158, 159 (1960) *appeal dismissed* 367 U.S. 907 (1961); Comment, "Legal Battle over Birth Control," 289; *New York Times,* late ed., May 27, 1959, p. 23, cols. 5–6. A demurrer to their complaint was sustained by the trial court and upheld by the Connecticut Supreme Court. *Trubek,* 147 Conn. at 635, 637, 165 A.2d at 159. The U.S. Supreme Court dismissed their appeal. *Trubek v. Ullman,* 367 U.S. 907 (1961). In contrast with other plaintiffs who wished to remain anonymous, the Trubeks "saw no reason not to" sue under their own names. Interview with Louise Trubek, August 30, 1988.

94. Pollack, "'Uncommonly Silly Law,'" 100–101. A separate suit was filed by three members of the clergy. They argued that the birth control ban interfered with their liberty, freedom of speech, and freedom of religion by making it illegal for them to counsel parishioners about birth control in premarital counseling. *New York Times,* late ed., May 5, 1959, p. 24, cols. 6–7. This case was delayed pending the outcome of the other litigation and ultimately was never tried. See Dienes, *Law Politics,* 153 n. 10.

95. *Buxton,* 147 Conn. at 50, 156 A.2d at 510.

96. Id. at 54, 156 A.2d at 512.

97. Id. at 55, 156 A.2d at 512.

98. Id. at 56, 156 A.2d at 513. In a footnote, the court listed the unsuccessful birth control reform bills introduced in the legislature from 1943 through 1959. Id. at 56–57 n. 2, 156 A.2d at 513 n.2.

99. Id. at 57, 156 A.2d at 513–14.

100. Id. at 58–59, 156 A.2d at 514.

101. *Poe v. Ullman,* 367 U.S. 497, 501 (1961). According to Frankfurter, the circumstances of *Nelson* proved "the abstract character of what is before us." He considered *Nelson* to be a "test case . . . brought to determine the constitutionality of the Act." After the state law was upheld by the state court, the prosecutions were dismissed. Id. at 501–2. As Justice Harlan noted in his dissent, however, "the respect in which *Nelson* was a test case is only that it was brought [by the state] for the purpose of

making entirely clear the State's power and willingness to enforce [the statute] against '*any* person, whether a physician or layman.' " 367 U.S. at 533 (Harlan, J., dissenting). See above at text accompanying note 49.

102. 367 U.S. at 502, 508.

103. *Poe* v. *Ullman,* 29 U.S.L.W. 3257, 3259 (March 7, 1961) (arguments before the Supreme Court). See *Poe,* 367 U.S. at 512–13 (Douglas, J., dissenting).

104. Id. at 509 (Brennan, J., concurring in the judgment). Justices Black, Douglas, Harlan, and Stewart dissented.

105. See *New York Times,* late ed., November 3, 1961, p. 37, col. 4.

106. Interview with Catherine Roraback, September 2, 1988. According to Roraback, the Connecticut attorney who handled the *Buxton/Poe* and *Griswold* litigation in the state courts, the purpose behind opening the clinic "was to provide services in Connecticut," not to generate a lawsuit to give Yale law professors a chance to argue the case, as was suggested in the Bork hearings. See *Bork Hearings,* 116 (quoting Robert Bork as suggesting that the litigation was "framed by Yale professors" simply "because they like this type of litigation").

107. *New York Times,* late ed., November 3, 1961, p. 37, col. 4.

108. See Marion Stillson, "The Confluence of Choice and Chance in the Construction of a Successful Legal Strategy: A Case-Study of *Griswold v. Connecticut* " (unpublished paper, Georgetown University Law Center, 1986), 22. I am grateful to Wendy Williams for providing me with a copy of Stillson's helpful paper.

109. Zimmerman, "Contraception," 80–81; Pollack, " 'Uncommonly Silly Law,' " 115. New Haven prosecutors later indicated that they would have acted with or without Morris's complaint. Ibid., 116.

110. *New York Times,* late ed., November 11, 1961, p. 25, col. 1. The clinic was open three times a week.

111. *New York Times,* late ed., November 25, 1961, p. 25, col. 8.

112. *State* v. *Griswold,* 151 Conn. 544, 546, 200 A.2d 479, 480 (1964), *rev'd* 381 U.S. 479 (1965). In addition, a detective testified that when he visited the clinic, Griswold explained its functions to him and gave him literature and contraceptives. *New York Times,* nat. ed., January 3, 1963, p. 16.

113. *Griswold,* 151 Conn. at 545, 200 A.2d at 480; *New York Times,* western ed., January 18, 1963, p. 2, col. 1. Planned Parenthood attorneys did not expect the state supreme court to overturn the statute on privacy grounds. They hoped that the court would overturn *Tileston* and construe the statute as containing an implied exception when pregnancy jeopardized life. Interview with Catherine Roraback, September 2, 1988.

114. *Griswold,* 151 Conn. at 546–47, 200 A.2d at 480.

115. See *Griswold* v. *Connecticut,* 381 U.S. 479 (1965).

116. Buxton, "Birth Control Problems," 583.

117. See above, note 4.

118. Burt Neuborne, "The Myth of Parity," *Harvard Law Review* 90 (1977): 1105.

119. *Poe* v. *Ullman,* 367 U.S. at 508.

120. See *Newsweek,* July 17, 1989, p. 24; *New York Times,* July 4, 1989, p. 1, col. 5.

121. For example, in a case currently before the Supreme Court, the state of Illinois enacted regulations requiring doctors to perform first-trimester abortions only in facilities that meet complex and expensive licensing requirements. The Court of Appeals found that the regulations unconstitutionally burdened the right to choose an abortion. *Ragsdale* v. *Turnock,* 841 F.2d 1358, 1360–63, 1370–75 (7th Cir. 1988), *deferred,* 110 S.Ct. 532 (1989). The case was settled pending appeal to the Supreme Court. *New York Times,* late ed., November 23, 1989, p. 1, col. 1.

Supreme Court Jury Discrimination Cases and State Court Compliance, Resistance, and Innovation

Charles J. Ogletree

Although many celebrated the Constitution's two hundredth birthday, Justice Thurgood Marshall, the only black to serve on the Supreme Court, took a more sober approach to the event. Commenting on the celebration, Justice Marshall stated: "This is unfortunate—not the patriotism itself, but the tendency for the celebration to oversimplify, and overlook the many other events that have been instrumental to our achievements as a nation. The focus of this celebration invites a complacent belief that the vision of those who debated and compromised in Philadelphia yielded the 'more perfect union' it is said we now enjoy." Justice Marshall harshly criticized the founding fathers' view of our republic:

> I do not believe that the meaning of the Constitution was forever "fixed" at the Philadelphia convention. Nor do I find the wisdom, foresight, and sense of justice exhibited by the framers particularly profound. To the contrary, the government they devised was defective from the start, requiring several amendments, a civil war, and momentous social transformation to attain the system of constitutional government, and its respect for the individual freedoms and human rights, that we hold as fundamental today.[1]

The founding fathers' adoption of the United States Constitution has been viewed as a major example of democracy at work. Yet although the Constitution begins with the words, "We the People," the framers deferred to the states the most fundamental right, the decision about who had the right to vote, so that women, most blacks, and poor whites were generally excluded. In several clauses of the Constitution they recognized and protected slavery.[2] Rather than celebrate the Constitution, Marshall called for a serious examination of the document.[3]

Justice Marshall, nonetheless, acknowledged that the post–Civil War constitutional amendments provided hope for justice and equality.[4] The Fourteenth Amendment protected the life, liberty, and property of all Americans against deprivations without due process and guaranteed all Americans equal protection of the laws.[5] Justice Marshall pointed to the dramatic progress made since the end of slavery and suggested that it will continue.[6]

Justice Marshall's criticism of the founding fathers is warranted, although his forecast of continuing progress in the elimination of racial discrimination may be overly optimistic. The Supreme Court's incremental progress in grappling with some forms of racial discrimination in the selection of jurors in criminal cases gives some force to criticisms made by Frederick Douglass more than a century ago. The Supreme Court contributes to the problem of discrimination in jury selection by leaving considerable discretion to the states to implement broad constitutional commands and often providing state courts with little guidance and infrequent review of state court decisions that seem to circumvent Supreme Court precedent.

This essay focuses on state court responses to Supreme Court jury discrimination cases, with special reference to three cases addressing discrimination against blacks in the jury selection process. The three cases span more than a century, beginning with the first instance in which the Court applied the Fourteenth Amendment in a race relations context and ending with the Court's attempt to develop a test to prevent discriminatory use of peremptory challenges. State court responses to these decisions will be analyzed. I will trace the dialectic between the Supreme Court and state courts in responding to jury discrimination in criminal cases. The Supreme Court's failure to take a stronger antidiscrimination stance or to devise a more efficacious remedy to the pervasive practice of excluding blacks from jury service will be considered. Although the Supreme Court will be criticized for its failure to proscribe discrimination adequately, state courts are also criticized for employing the discretion accorded to them in ways that have tolerated the exclusion of blacks from jury service through purposely discriminatory methods.

In some instances, state courts appear to follow the letter and spirit of Supreme Court decisions. In others, they seem bent on resisting Supreme Court decisions in jury discrimination cases by establishing criteria for jury selection that have a disparate impact on blacks, such as poll taxes and character and fitness tests. In still other cases, the discrimination is obvious and pervasive. Jury commissioners were permitted to maintain black and white jurors on separate lists and choose no blacks to serve. In some counties with a sizable black population of qualified jurors, at least until recently, no black was selected to serve on a jury. In still other cases, state courts have looked to state constitutions for remedies when the Supreme Court has been silent or equivocal. The result of these practices at the state court level is that qualified blacks are still grossly unrepresented on juries, and jury discrimination challenges are rarely successful. This essay posits that the Supreme Court must set out clearer guidelines to avoid the continuation of this pattern of discrimination, or other race-conscious measures must be devised to remedy the situation.

The Equal Protection Clause and Jury Discrimination

The three federal cases the response to which is studied in this essay are *Strauder* v. *West Virginia*,[7] *Swain* v. *Alabama*,[8] and *Batson* v. *Kentucky*.[9] In *Strauder*, the Supreme Court invalidated on equal protection grounds a state statute that explicitly excluded blacks from jury service. Eighty-five years later in *Swain*, the Court placed a "nearly insurmountable" burden on defendants seeking to prove an equal protection violation in the use of peremptory challenges.[10] In 1986, in *Batson* the Supreme Court overruled *Swain*, holding that prosecutorial use of peremptory challenges to exclude jurors on the basis of their race violates the equal protection clause.[11]

Strauder, *Swain*, and *Batson* present interesting similarities. All arose in southern states and in each case the defendant was a black male.[12] Each defendant raised the issue of discriminatory exclusion of blacks from jury service. In each case, the Supreme Court analyzed the evidence supporting claims of discrimination in jury selection and provided some principles to guide state courts in handling future cases.

An issue of principal concern in each case is the degree to which state courts followed the guidelines delineated by Supreme Court edict or pursued what appear to be contrary or independent bases of analysis.

Strauder *v.* West Virginia: *Discriminatory Exclusion from the Jury Venire*

Strauder v. *West Virginia* was the first case in which the United States Supreme Court applied the equal protection clause of the Fourteenth Amendment to benefit a racial minority. In *Strauder,* the defendant appealed his murder conviction by an all-white (and male) jury, claiming that the statutory exclusion of blacks from serving on juries violated the equal protection clause.[13] The Supreme Court agreed, observing that

> the very fact that colored people are singled out and expressly denied by statute all right to participate in the administration of the law, as jurors, because of their color, though they are citizens, and may be in other respects fully qualified, is practically a brand upon them, affixed by the law, an assertion of their inferiority, and a stimulant to that race prejudice which is an impediment to securing to individuals of the race that equal justice which the law aims to secure to all others.[14]

The Court's strong language in *Strauder* did not eliminate racial discrimination in the jury selection process in state courts.[15] Equally important, the Supreme Court's focus on the pervasive practice of excluding blacks from jury service was only a modest assertion of the antidiscrimination principle. Although exclusion was strongly condemned, little was said or done to ensure the affirmative inclusion of blacks on juries after *Strauder*. Although treating blacks equally was a laudable first step, the Supreme Court did not assert that black defendants have any right to an integrated jury.[16] For many years after *Strauder,* some state courts approved jury selection procedures that, although not explicitly prohibiting racial minorities from serving on juries, nonetheless restricted the eligibility of blacks to serve on juries.[17] Delaware, for example, chose jurors from "sober and judicious persons" on the voting rolls.[18] Though such qualifications appear eminently reasonable and objective, these procedures were routinely used to exclude blacks from jury service. Even in states that did not prohibit minorities from voting, their widespread disfranchisement excluded them from serving on juries because state selection procedures relied on voter lists.[19] States also employed highly discretionary procedures in which jury commissioners would select "qualified" candidates to be eligible for jury service.[20] Qualifications included "intelligence, sobriety and integrity,"[21] or "good moral character."[22] The result of these and other procedures was that thirty years after *Strauder*, blacks were still uniformly excluded from jury service in many states.[23] Fifty years after *Strauder*, the presence of blacks on juries was rare,[24] and over a century after *Strauder*, minorities continue to be underrepresented on juries throughout the nation.[25]

Strauder left the ultimate responsibility for implementing its antidiscrimination command in the hands of state courts. Under an 1875 revision[26] of the Civil Rights Act of 1866 as part of a compilation of statutes, Congress had allowed removal of cases to federal court only as a pretrial jurisdictional remedy.[27] In *Virginia* v. *Rives,* the Court held that the removal could be based on the denial of rights by state statutes or state constitutional revisions but not on the denial of rights at the state trial court level. Federal court evaluation of jury discrimination claims was therefore limited to Supreme Court appellate jurisdiction—review that tended to be very deferential. After *Strauder*, state courts were responsible for the crucial factual determinations of whether jury discrimination had been demonstrated, and little opportunity existed for federal court review.[28]

State court interpretation of *Strauder's* nondiscrimination principle was therefore critical to its success. Unfortunately, most state courts were reluctant to find state jury selection systems unconstitutional.[29] When confronted with evidence that very few minorities served on juries, state courts were usually willing to assume that the vast majority of black persons were not qualified to serve.[30] State courts refused to find constitutional violations despite fairly clear evidence demonstrating the exclusion of minorities. When the Supreme Court reviewed state court decisions, it showed extraordinary deference to dubious factual findings of the state courts. For example, in *Thomas* v. *Texas,* a unanimous Supreme Court observed:

> Whether such discrimination was practiced in this case was a question of fact, and the determination of that question adversely to plaintiff in error by the trial court and by the Court of Criminal Appeals was decisive, so far as this court is concerned, unless it could be held that these decisions constitute such abuse as amounted to an infraction of the Federal Constitution, which cannot be presumed, and which there is

no reason to hold on the record before us. On the contrary, the careful opinion of the Court of Criminal Appeals, setting forth the evidence, justifies the conclusion of that court that the negro race was not intentionally or otherwise discriminated against in the selection of the grand and petit juries.[31]

In 1903, for example, the Texas Court of Criminal Appeals refused to find unconstitutional exclusion despite evidence that of approximately ten thousand voters in the county, six hundred were black, but no blacks were drawn for the grand jury and, to the knowledge of several witnesses, none had ever been drawn to serve on a grand jury.[32] After *Strauder*, the Supreme Court rarely granted certiorari in state court cases raising claims of discrimination in jury selection. When claims were raised, successful challenges seemed to flow from the Supreme Court's refusal to be deferential; when the Supreme Court took an independent review of the record, claims of discrimination seemed to have a greater chance of success.

In 1935, the Supreme Court decided *Norris* v. *Alabama*.[33] In *Norris*, the defendant challenged his indictment on the ground that blacks were systematically excluded from grand and petit jury service. At an evidentiary hearing, Norris presented substantial evidence demonstrating the systematic exclusion of blacks from the jury rolls in Alabama.[34] Although the Alabama jury commissioner acknowledged that jury rolls did not contain blacks, he attempted to justify this result by stating that "I do not know of any negro in Morgan County over 21 and under 65 who is generally reputed to be honest and intelligent and who is esteemed in the community for his integrity, good character and sound judgment, who is not an habitual drunkard, who isn't afflicted with a permanent disease or physical weakness which would render him unfit to discharge the duties of a juror, and who can read English, and who has never been convicted of a crime involving moral turpitude."[35] The Alabama judge accepted the commissioner's argument, concluding that more white citizens possessed the requisite qualifications for jury service than did blacks. Therefore, the Alabama court held, the exclusion of blacks from jury service was justified. The Supreme Court disagreed:

> We think that the evidence that for a generation or longer no negro had been called for service on any jury in Jackson County, that there were negroes qualified for jury service, that according to the practice of the jury commission their names would normally appear on the pre-

liminary list of male citizens of the requisite age but that no names of
negroes were placed on the jury roll, and the testimony with respect
to the lack of appropriate consideration of the qualifications of negroes,
established the discrimination which the Constitution forbids.[36]

The Supreme Court examined the record behind the assertions of
Alabama officials, the Alabama trial court, and the Alabama Supreme
Court and reversed the Alabama Supreme Court.[37] After *Strauder,
Norris* was an important example of the Supreme Court's nondefer-
ential assessment of state court conclusions that discrimination in
jury selection had not occurred.[38] After *Norris,* however, the Supreme
Court did on occasion revert to being deferential to state courts. In
Akins v. *Texas,* for example, the defendant presented substantial evi-
dence of discrimination in the jury selection process in Texas, but the
Supreme Court chose to defer to the state court's finding.[39]

Swain *v.* Alabama

Efforts to prohibit all racial discrimination in jury selection suffered a
serious blow in the decision in *Swain* v. *Alabama.*[40] In *Swain,* the defendant was convicted of rape by an all-white jury in the circuit court
of Talladega County, Alabama, and was subsequently sentenced to
death. Cognizant of the apparent racial discrimination against blacks
eligible for jury service in Alabama, Swain sought on appeal to invoke
the constitutional principles outlined in *Strauder.* Swain demonstrated
that, although 26 percent of the eligible jurors in the jurisdiction were
black, only 10 to 15 percent of those on the county's jury panels were
black. He also showed that not a single black had served on a petit
jury in a criminal case "since about 1950."[41]

Despite this evidence of widespread exclusion, the Supreme
Court held that Swain had not demonstrated purposeful discrimination. The Court stated: "Undoubtedly, the selection of prospective
jurors was somewhat haphazard and little effort was made to ensure
that all groups in the community were fully represented. But an imperfect system is not equivalent to purposeful discrimination based
on race. We do not think that the burden of proof was carried by
petitioner in this case."[42]

Swain also established that the prosecutor in his particular case
excluded blacks from the jury by using peremptory challenges on all
six blacks on the venire. The plurality held, however, that, in any

given case, a presumption exists that the prosecutor has used peremptory challenges in a fair and impartial manner. To overcome this presumption, the defendant must show that the prosecutor consistently removed qualified blacks who would have survived challenges for cause. The Supreme Court concluded that Swain did not establish intentional discrimination on the part of the prosecutors in excluding all blacks from jury service but did not specify the appropriate burden of proof that must be met by a defendant who makes such a claim. The Court simply stated that it was "readily apparent" that Swain had failed to meet the burden in his case.[43]

State Court Responses to Swain

The requirement in *Swain* that a defendant demonstrate systematic exclusion proved insurmountable in the vast majority of cases.[44] The Supreme Court's unwillingness to prohibit the discriminatory use of peremptory challenges in *Swain* gave the states an opportunity to go beyond *Swain* and find further protections in state constitutional provisions and other federal constitutional provisions.[45] The California Supreme Court led the way in *People* v. *Wheeler*.[46] Relying on the jurisprudence of both the Sixth Amendment to the federal Constitution and Article 1, section 16, of the California Constitution,[47] the California Supreme Court held that "the use of peremptory challenges to remove prospective jurors on the sole ground of group bias violates the right to trial by jury drawn from a representative cross-section of the community article I, section 16 of the California Constitution."[48]

The court's analysis in *Wheeler* turned on a distinction between group and specific bias. The court identified group bias as that which a prospective juror is thought to have simply because of being a member of a particular group. Specific bias, by contrast, relates to the particular case on trial or the parties and witnesses involved.[49] The California court ruled that peremptory challenges may be exercised on the basis of a specific bias but not on the basis of group bias.

As in *Swain,* the California Supreme Court acknowledged that in any particular case there must be a presumption that a party is exercising peremptory challenges in a constitutionally permissible manner.[50] Unlike the United States Supreme Court, however, the *Wheeler* court set reasonable requirements for demonstrating a prima facie case of discrimination. The court said that parties who believe their opponent is using peremptory challenges based on a group bias must raise the point in a timely manner, make a complete record of the circumstances, and then show that the persons excluded are members of a cognizable group and show a *strong likelihood* that such persons are being challenged because of their group association rather than because of any specific bias.[51]

Whereas the *Swain* Court required a showing that the prosecutor consistently used peremptory challenges to remove qualified black jurors, under *Wheeler* a party could establish a strong likelihood of the use of peremptories based on group bias by providing evidence demonstrating that the party struck "most or all the members of the identifiable group"; "the jurors in question share only this one characteristic—their membership in the group"; the party failed to question the challenged jurors in more than a desultory manner; and the defendant is a member of the excluded group, especially if the victim is a member of the group to which a majority of the jurors belong.[52] Thus a defendant could prevail simply by showing improper conduct in the case at hand.[53]

Once a trial court finds a prima facie case of discrimination, the burden shifts to the party using the peremptory challenges to show that the challenges in question were not predicated on group bias alone. In other words, the party must convince the court that the peremptories were based on grounds "reasonably relevant to the particular case on trial or its parties or witnesses."[54]

Six states adopted the *Wheeler* approach with little modification: Alabama,[55] Delaware,[56] Florida,[57] Massachusetts,[58] New Jersey,[59] and New Mexico.[60] Five states (Arizona, Illinois, Kansas, Rhode Island, and Wisconsin) explicitly rejected the *Wheeler* approach.[61]

Despite the responses of some state courts to the inadequacies of *Swain*, discriminatory use of peremptory challenges continued in many jurisdictions.[62] In many jurisdictions, prosecutors used over 80 percent of their peremptory challenges to exclude minority venirepersons.[63] The use of these challenges disproportionately excluded minorities.[64] Some prosecutors openly acknowledged their policy of eliminating any member of a minority group from juries.[65] The unwillingness of many state and lower federal courts to curb the abuse of peremptory challenges and the obvious disarray in state and federal courts following the *Swain* opinion set the stage for action from the Supreme Court.

Batson *v.* Kentucky

In 1986, the Supreme Court issued its landmark opinion in *Batson* v. *Kentucky*.[66] In a 7 to 2 opinion written by Justice Lewis F. Powell, Jr., the Supreme Court reexamined *Swain*[67] and held that prosecutorial use of peremptory challenges to exclude potential jurors on the basis of race violated the equal protection clause.[68] The court stated that "although a prosecutor ordinarily is entitled to exercise permitted peremptory challenges 'for any reason at all, as long as that reason is related to his view concerning the outcome of the case to be tried' . . . the Equal Protection clause forbids the prosecutor to challenge potential jurors solely on account of their race or on the assumption that black jurors as a group will be unable impartially to consider the State's case against a black defendant."[69]

After *Batson*, to establish a prima facie case of discriminatory use of peremptory challenges, a defendant must show that he or she is a member of a cognizable racial group, that the prosecutor has exercised peremptory challenges to remove members of the defendant's race from serving as jurors in the defendant's case, and that these facts and any other relevant circumstances raise an inference that the prosecutor removed venirepersons on account of their race. Once the defendant makes this prima facie showing, the burden shifts to the prosecution to provide a neutral explanation for the challenges.[70]

Batson was viewed as a major accomplishment in the effort to eliminate jury discrimination against minorities. In the majority opinion, Justice Powell noted that the required evidentiary standard under *Swain* imposed a "crippling burden of proof" that was "inconsistent with standards that have been developed since *Swain* for assessing a prima facie case under the Equal Protection clause."[71]

Although in his concurring opinion, Justice Marshall acknowledged that *Batson* "takes a historic step towards eliminating the shameful practice of racial discrimination in the selection of juries,"[72] he was not as optimistic about the likelihood of it eliminating the vestiges of discrimination in jury cases.[73] He was skeptical of the states' willingness to carry out *Batson*'s mandate.[74] He noted that the states had developed similar tests designed to limit the ability of prosecutors to discriminate in the use of peremptory challenges but that in many instances the state courts did not find constitutional violations.[75]

Justice Marshall was concerned that prosecutors would find ingenious ways to circumvent *Batson*'s mandate. He concluded that if the state courts permitted prosecutors to strike blacks because they were "uncommunicative, or never cracked a smile, or failed to 'possess the sensitivities necessary to realistically look at the issues and decide the facts in this case' as justifications for eliminating blacks as jurors when blacks were defendants in cases, then the protection apparently established by the court in *Batson* was only illusory." Justice Marshall was not merely concerned that prosecutors might lie in stating their basis for striking blacks but also that their unconscious racism might lead them to conclude that prospective black jurors were incapable of fairly reaching a verdict in a black defendant's case. Furthermore, a judge's own conscious or unconscious racism might lead the judge to conclude that the prosecutor's basis for the removal of black jurors was justified.[76]

The *Batson* Court left the important issue of determining whether a defendant had established a prima facie case of discrimination and whether the prosecution had rebutted that prima facie showing to the trial courts.[77] The Court provided lower courts with little guidance regarding those determinations and thereby created opportunities for state and lower federal courts to interpret the commands of *Batson* differently and, in some cases, to undermine the protection it offered.

Lower Court Compliance with Batson

State and lower federal courts have, in fact, shown widely different views regarding the existence of a prima facie case under *Batson*. The first two elements of the prima facie case—that the defendant is a member of a cognizable racial group and that the prosecutor has exercised a peremptory challenge or challenges to remove members of the defendant's race from the venire[78]—are straightforward and provide little room for differing interpretations.[79]

Different interpretations stem from the third required element, "that these facts and any other relevant circumstances raise an inference that the prosecutor used that practice to exclude the veniremen from the petit jury on account of their race."[80]

Courts in some states have indicated that certain factors create an inference of discrimination.[81] Most courts will find an inference of discrimination if a prosecutor has eliminated all members of the defendant's race from the jury.[82] Some courts will find an inference of discrimination when a disproportionate number of strikes are used against members of a defendant's minority group.[83] One court has held that a substantial underrepresentation of the defendant's race on the jury raises an inference of discrimination.[84] Other courts, however, have insisted that numbers alone do not raise an inference of discrimination.[85] Some have also found that the presence of jurors of the defendant's race rebuts any inference of discrimination.[86]

Courts will sometimes look beyond the numbers to find inferences of discrimination. Courts have inferred discrimination from the past conduct of the prosecutor, the type and manner of questions during voir dire, and the fact that the only thing the challenged jurors have in common is their race.[87]

State courts have also differed about the context in which they will consider the reasons a prosecutor offers to support the use of peremptory challenges in determining whether the defendant has established a prima facie case or whether the prosecutors' reasons will be considered under a heavier burden, after a prima facie case has been established.[88]

By considering the prosecutor's reasons in determining whether a prima facie case of discrimination exists, some courts have changed the nature of *Batson*'s protection and made it less stringent. In *Batson*, the Court created a system of presumptions. The Supreme Court told lower courts to begin with a presumption that prosecutors exercise their peremptories in a fair and racially neutral manner[89] and then, if a defendant established a prima facie case, to shift the presumption and place the burden on the prosecution to show that challenges were exercised in a race-neutral manner.[90] But the lower courts show little evidence of taking this final crucial step. If the requirement of a prosecutorial explanation becomes a requirement for a mere pretext and not for a reason sufficiently stringent to withstand scrutiny, then such an inquiry substantially undermines the protection envisioned in *Batson*.[91]

The Court also provided little guidance to trial courts regarding what prosecutorial explanations they should accept as rebutting a prima face showing. Although the Court said that prosecutors could not rebut a prima facie showing merely by saying that they assumed the challenged jurors would be partial to the defendant because they shared the defendant's race, or by simply affirming their good faith in making the challenges, the Court did not provide sufficient guidance to state courts. It simply directed trial courts to ensure that prosecutors articulate a neutral explanation related to the case being tried.[92]

Batson's effect on the elimination of discriminatory use of peremptory challenges therefore depends in large part on trial courts' interpretation and application of *Batson's* standards. Placing so much reliance on trial court determinations is particularly problematic because those decisions are largely unreviewable and in light of the long history of deference to state court factual findings that are clearly dubious. Because the evaluation of prosecutorial explanations in a *Batson* hearing is a determination of fact, trial court determinations are accorded highly deferential treatment by appellate courts.[93] They will be reversed only if they are found to be "clearly erroneous."[94]

Justice Marshall's concern that prosecutors might fabricate facially neutral reasons for striking minority jurors that trial courts would have difficulty evaluating[95] has become an issue in some cases. This problem is twofold. First, some state trial courts frequently accept explanations that appear to be no more than after-the-fact rationalizations for challenges that appear to be subconsciously made on racial grounds. Additionally, the appellate courts have been reluctant to review arguably plausible challenges by prosecutors when such challenges have a disparate effect on black jurors. In Alabama, for example, although the state supreme court has insisted that "no merely whimsical or fanciful reason will suffice as an adequate explanation"[96] and has directed trial judges to "consider whether the facially neutral explanations [offered] are contrived to avoid admitting acts of group discrimination,"[97] state trial courts have not always scrutinized prosecutorial explanations closely. In *Wallace* v. *State*,[98] for example, the prosecutor explained that he challenged one young black woman because she was a homemaker and lacked knowledge of what life was like out on the street. He challenged another because she was a student without the "necessary experience." An older black woman was struck because she was a "grandmotherly type" who might be overly sympathetic. A middle-aged black woman was struck because she appeared to be the same age as the defendants' parents. The prosecutor also challenged a young black man because he had a beard and a middle-aged black man because he was unemployed and therefore might be irresponsible.[99] The trial court found the prosecutor's explanations sufficient to rebut the prima facie case of discrimination, and the Alabama Court of Criminal Appeals affirmed. In other cases, courts have accepted prosecutors' explanations that a juror was challenged because of his or her demeanor.[100] Similarly dubious explanations have been accepted in many states.[101] State trial courts frequently accept prosecutorial explanations that, although somewhat plausible, have a disparate effect on minorities and therefore may become convenient excuses for rationalizing challenges against minorities. For example, in *State* v. *Alexander*,[102] a prosecutor explained that he challenged a black juror because the juror was unemployed, did not understand one of the questions asked during voir dire, and lived in a high-crime neighborhood.[103] Unemployment, lower education, and crime are found more frequently in minority communities, yet the court seemed unconcerned that minorities might be excluded disproportionately because of them. In *New Jersey* v. *Pemberthy*,[104] a prosecutor explained that he challenged Spanish-speaking jurors because a Spanish translation would be at issue in the trial.[105] Excluding foreign-speaking jurors will obviously have a disparate effect on minorities. Many state trial courts have accepted explanations that are based on these or other characteristics that correlate with race.[106] Particularly troubling is the acknowledgment by at least one court that mere subjective neutrality will suffice. By rejecting a requirement that a prosecutor proffers an objectively neutral reason for a challenge, this court has in effect given the state a license to indulge the very racial stereotypes *Batson* sought to eliminate.[107]

Remedial Measures to Eliminate Jury Discrimination

Batson did not provide an adequate solution to the problem of discriminatory use of peremptory challenges. States are willing to interpret *Batson*'s requirements loosely and allow discrimination to continue. This is unfortunate, but it is not surprising given the history of state court efforts to subvert Supreme Court decisions designed to eliminate racial discrimination in jury selection.

Some state courts have, however, provided standards for lower courts to use in assessing prosecutorial reasons for challenges. For example, in the wake of *Wheeler*, California courts have developed more rigid requirements for prosecutorial explanations.[108] Similarly, in *State* v. *Goode*,[109] the New Mexico Supreme Court instructed its lower courts that prosecutorial reasons should be found to be mere pretext for discrimination if they are reasons that applied equally to jurors that were not challenged; the prosecutor failed to question the challenged juror about the concerns leading to the challenge;[110] or the challenges were based on assumptions of group bias.[111]

Additionally, in *State* v. *Slappy*,[112] the Florida Supreme Court held that mere pretext for discrimination should also be found when certain jurors are singled out in voir dire and asked special questions designed to evoke a particular response, which could then be used to explain a challenge, or when the reasons given for a challenge are unrelated to the factors of the case at trial.[113]

Conclusion

Although the Supreme Court has attempted to elucidate important antidiscrimination principles in its jury discrimination cases, the Court's lack of a forceful and clear set of principles has led to inconsistent and conflicting interpretations of those rules in the state courts. From *Strauder* v. *West Virginia,* to *Swain* v. *Alabama,* to *Batson* v. *Kentucky,* the Supreme Court has articulated the guidelines for handling jury discrimination cases and left considerable discretion to state courts in implying and enforcing those guidelines. As a result of the Supreme Court's lack of clear and authoritative direction, the state courts have often ignored the Supreme Court's guidelines, or have come up with creative methods for avoiding the guidelines, or, on some occasions, have decided to go beyond Supreme Court guidelines and find independent state constitutional grounds to prevent jury discrimination.

By providing state courts with considerable discretion, the Supreme Court has witnessed and acknowledged that the state courts have been operating without any clear sense of the Supreme Court's mandate. After *Strauder* v. *West Virginia,*[114] state courts were prohibited from intentionally discriminating against blacks in jury selection, but they were given considerable discretion in establishing qualifications for jury service. Those qualifications ultimately were used to disqualify a substantial number of blacks from serving on juries, without any valid legal justification. State court judges would hear testimony from jury commissioners about the absence of any sober, judicious, and conscientious black jurors on the jury rolls and accept those statements as a legitimate basis to deny a black defendant's claim that black jurors were being systematically excluded from jury service. Moreover, when the Supreme Court issued guidelines for litigants to follow, in *Swain* v. *Alabama*,[115] jury commissioners were again given the authority to determine whether the absence of significant numbers of blacks in the jury pool was evidence of intentional discrimination. The Court imposed an impossible burden on litigants after *Swain*, and accordingly discrimination against blacks in jury selection was permitted to flourish.

Finally, in *Batson* v. *Kentucky*,[116] the Supreme Court realized that the burden it had imposed in the *Swain* case could not reasonably be met by litigants and established a test for courts to apply to prevent future discrimination in jury service. Despite the Court's laudable efforts in *Batson*, however, prosecutors were able to support implausible and indefensible rationales for striking black jurors through these peremptory challenges, and state courts have consistently upheld the reasons for prosecutory challenges.

One possible means of remedying this situation is for the Supreme Court to take a different posture in dealing with jury discrimination than it has taken in the past. For example, the Court's effort to present an antidiscrimination principle to protect the interest of blacks may not go far enough. Just because blacks are now eligible to serve on juries does not ensure that there will be a cross-sectional representation of minorities on juries. Accordingly, a possible remedy for the exclusion of blacks from juries might be affirmatively to require that black jurors serve in certain cases. A variety of affirmative proposals to ensure black presence on juries have been offered,[117] but in light of the serious constitutional problems, it is unlikely that any will be adopted.[118]

If a specific proposal requiring a certain percentage of minorities to serve on juries is unworkable in light of the clear possible constitutional challenges, the alternative remedy would be for the Supreme Court to grant certiorari in a jury discrimination case and to lay out with some clarity and detail the steps that judges must take to ensure that prosecutors do not use peremptory challenges to discriminate against blacks. Unless and until the Supreme Court gives a clear indication of the constitutional limits on the use of discriminatory procedures and tactics for striking black jurors, we will continue to see a process lamented by Frederick Douglass when he noted that the continued discriminatory practice in jury selection would require a black man, when he happens to be on trial in America, to prove his innocence, rather than requiring the state to prove his guilt. For such a practice to be tolerated offends the Constitution and our sense of justice and fair play.

Notes

1. Thurgood Marshall, "Reflections on the Bicentennial of the United States Constitution," *Harvard Law Review* 101 (1987): 1, 2 (text of speech delivered at Annual Seminar of San Francisco Patent and Trademark Law Association, Hawaii, May 6, 1989).
2. See William M. Wiecek, "The Witch at the Christening: Slavery and the Constitution's Origins," in *The Framing and Ratification of the Constitution*, ed. Leonard W. Levy and Dennis J. Mahoney (New York: Macmillan, 1987), 167–84; and Paul Finkelman, "Slavery and the Constitutional Convention: Making a Covenant with Death," in Richard Beeman et al., *Beyond Confederation: Origins of the Constitution and American National Identity* (Chapel Hill: University of North Carolina Press, 1987), 188–225.
3. Marshall, "Reflections of the Bicentennial," 1–2.
4. Ibid., 4.
5. The Fourteenth Amendment provides, in pertinent part: "Nor shall any State deprive any person of life, liberty, or property without due process of law; nor deny to any person within its jurisdiction the equal protection of the laws." U.S. Const. amend. XIV, § 1.
6. Marshall, "Reflections of the Bicentennial," 5.
7. 100 U.S. 303 (1880).
8. 380 U.S. 202 (1965).
9. 476 U.S. 79 (1986).
10. See Note, "Developments in the Law: Race and the Criminal Process," *Harvard Law Review* 101 (1988): 1573.
11. *Batson*, 476 U.S. at 93–97.
12. In 1874, Taylor Strauder was indicted for murder in the Circuit Court of Ohio County, West Virginia. See *Strauder*, 100 U.S. 304. Robert Swain was indicted for rape in the Circuit Court of Talladega County, Alabama. See *Swain*, 380 U.S. 203. James Batson was indicted on charges of second-degree burglary and receipt of stolen goods in the Circuit Court of Jefferson County, Kentucky. See *Batson*, 476 U.S. 79.
13. The statute declared: "All white male persons who are twenty-one years of age and who are citizens of this state shall be liable to serve as jurors." W. Va. Acts of 1872–73, p. 102, see *Strauder*, 100 U.S. at 305.

14. Id. at 308. Although the Court stressed the stigma aspect of racial exclusion, the exclusion of minorities from jury service also undermines the minority defendant's right to a fair trial. *Thiel* v. *Southern Pac. Co.*, 328 U.S 217, 227 (1946) (Frankfurter, J., dissenting) ("The broad representative character of the jury should be maintained, partly as assurance of a diffused impartiality"). Empirical evidence indicates that white jurors are more likely to convict black defendants than white defendants. See Harry Kalven and Hans Zeisel, *The American Jury* (Boston: Little, Brown, 1966), 210–11; Note, "Developments in the Law," 1559–60; see also Gunnar Myrdal, *An American Dilemma*, 2d ed. (New York: Harper & Row, 1962) (need parenthetical).

15. Benno C. Schmidt, "Juries, Jurisdiction and Race Discrimination: The Lost Promise of Strauder v. West Virginia," *Texas Law Review* 61 (1983): 1401, 1429 ("Rarely, if ever, in the Supreme Court's history has there been a decision that so forces our attention to the gulf between explication and implementation of constitutional rights"). See also Gilbert T. Stephenson, *Race Distinctions in American Law* (New York: AMS Press, 1910), 247, 272.

16. See, e.g., Randall L. Kennedy, "Race and the Fourteenth Amendment: The Power of Interpretational Choice," in *A Less Than Perfect Union*, ed. Jules Lobel (New York: Monthly Review Press, 1988), 276–77.

17. See, e.g., *Eubanks* v. *Louisiana*, 356 U.S. 584 (1958); *Hernandez* v. *Texas*, 347 U.S. 475 (1954) (noting that no Mexican-American juror had served in twenty-five years); *Patton* v. *Mississippi*, 332 U.S. 463 (1947); *Hale* v. *Texas*, 316 U.S. 400 (1942); *Williams* v. *Mississippi*, 170 U.S 213 (1898); see also Note, "Developments in the Law," 1567–73. See, however, Donald Nieman, "Black Political Power and Criminal Justice: Washington County, Texas, 1868–1884," *Journal of Southern History* 55 (1989): 391 (discussing black jurors in a Texas county both during and after Reconstruction).

18. Del. Rev. Stat. ch. 109 §§ 1, 2 (1853). The act was republished in 1874. See *Neal* v. *Delaware*, 103 U.S. 370, 377, 380 (1881).

19. This problem became acute after 1890. See Schmidt, "Juries, Jurisdiction and Race Discrimination," 1401, 1406, 1463–1464, 1468 (explaining how the widespread disfranchisement of blacks in Mississippi during the 1890s resulted in black exclusion from jury service). See also Stephenson, *Race Distinctions*, 271 ("The great majority of the Negroes have been unable to satisfy the suffrage tests and have been disenfranchised. They are, consequently, not electors and not eligible to serve as jurors"). Even today most states rely on voter lists and tax roles to generate jury rolls, which underrepresent minorities. See National Jury Project, *Jury Work: Systematic Techniques*, ed. Elissa Krauss and

Beth Benora, 2d ed. (New York: Clark Boardman, 1987), §5.02, at 5–4 (noting that reliance on voter lists continues to exclude racial minorities disproportionately).

20. Roger Kuhn, "Jury Discrimination: The Next Phase," *Southern California Law Review* 41 (1967–68): 235, 266–68.

21. *Cooper* v. *State*, 64 Md. 40, 20 A. 986 (1885) (upholding jury selection system with these requirements under an 1867 act because it did not explicitly prevent the selection of colored men as jurors).

22. See, e.g., *Franklin* v. *State of South Carolina*, 218 U.S. 161 (1910) (holding that the jury selection system was not unconstitutional); Kuhn, "Jury Discrimination," 282 (" 'The good morals requirement is so vague and subjective that it has constituted an open invitation to abuse at the hands of voting officials.' The invitation is just as clear where jury selection is concerned." Quoting *South Carolina* v. *Katzenbach*, 383 U.S. 301, 312–313 [1966]).

23. Stephenson, *Race Distinctions*, 253–72; Schmidt, "Juries, Jurisdiction and Race Discrimination," 1407.

24. Schmidt, "Juries, Jurisdiction and Race Discrimination," 1419.

25. Note, "Developments in the Law," 1558.

26. U.S. Rev. Stat. 641 (1875).

27. Schmidt, "Juries, Jurisdiction and Race Discrimination," 1432.

28. *Virginia* v. *Rives*, 100 U.S. 313, 319 (1880); Schmidt, "Juries, Jurisdiction and Race Discrimination," 1434, 1462, 1436. ("It is when the denial [of equal protection] rests instead on hidden, stubborn administrative discrimination, when assessment and correction depends on unbiased, careful fact-finding, and when an inadequate record effectively immunizes the denial from the appellate correction, that federal trial court jurisdiction is most needed").

29. Schmidt, "Juries, Jurisdiction and Race Discrimination," 1482. ("*Strauder*'s non-discrimination principle was vitiated by state courts' concerted refusal to undertake fair inquiry into the methods of jury selection, by the state jury commissions' capacity to hide systematic racial exclusion behind general assertations, and by the ineptitude and passivity of the mostly white counsel for black defendants").

30. See, e.g., *Thomas* v. *State*, 49 Tex. Crim. 633, 95 S.W. 1069 (Tex. Crim. App. 1906) *aff'd*, *Thomas v. Texas*, 212 U.S. 278 (1909); *Smith* v. *State*, 45 Tex. Crim. 552, 78 S.W. 1069 (Tex. Crim. App. 1904); cf. *State* v. *Gill*, 186 La. 339, 172 So. 412 (presuming that the jury list was selected by commissioners in a fair effort to select the most qualified persons even though all but a few persons listed were white), *cert. denied*, 301 U.S. 685 (1937).

31. 212 U.S. 278, 282–83 (1909).

32. *Thompson* v. *State*, 45 Tex. Crim. 397, 77 S.W. 449 (Tex. Crim. App. 1903). In 1945, the Georgia Supreme Court refused to find an equal protection violation despite a more extreme disparity. Evidence indicated that 42 percent of the county population was black, yet only 1.8 percent of those on the jury rolls were black. The Georgia court refused to find discrimination absent evidence indicating the number of black residents qualified for jury duty and evidence indicating the number of "upright" and "intelligent" white men not on the jury roll. *Watkins* v. *State*, 199 Ga. 81, 33 S.E.2d 325 (1945). Thus though the statistical evidence of juror selection raised serious questions of discrimination on racial grounds, the state court found the records legally insufficient to rule on the merits in some cases.

33. 294 U.S. 587 (1935). Clarence Norris, the defendant, was one of the codefendants in the well-publicized Scottsboro Boys rape trial.

34. Id. at 588, 590–99. Norris presented evidence documenting that, of the 8,801 males over age twenty-one in Jackson County, 666 were black. Id. at 590. Norris established that "no black person served on a grand or petit jury in [Jackson] County within the memory of witnesses who had lived there all their lives." Id. at 591. Norris also documented the exclusion of blacks from jury service in Morgan County, the location of his trial in the case. This evidence was uncontroverted and provided the basis for the court's reversal of Norris's conviction. Id. at 596–97.

35. Id. at 598–99.

36. 294 U.S. at 596 reversing *Norris* v. *State*, 229 Ala. 226, 156 So. 556 (1933).

37. *Norris* v. *State*, 229 Ala. at 226.

38. See, e.g., Schmidt, "Juries, Jurisdiction and Race Discrimination," 1479.

39. *Akins* v. *Texas*, 325 U.S. 398, 402 (1945). ("We accord . . . great respect to the conclusions of the state judiciary"). Still, the Court did not ignore clear evidence of discrimination. In *Avery* v. *Georgia*, 345 U.S. 559 (1953), for example, the jury commissioners drew the jury lists from county tax returns. The names of potential white jurors were printed on white ballots, and the names of potential black jurors were printed on yellow ballots. Id. at 560. The accused demonstrated that no black juror was selected to serve on the panel of sixty that was drawn to decide his fate and that the use of different colored ballots presented an opportunity to discriminate. The court ruled that the accused had presented a prima facie case of racial discrimination in the selection of his jury and accordingly reversed his conviction. Id. at 562.

40. 380 U.S. 202 (1965).

41. Id. at 205.

42. Id. at 209 (citations omitted).

43. Id. at 222, 224.

44. *Batson,* 476 U.S. at 92 and n. 17; *Wheeler,* 22 Cal. 3d at 286 (quoting Annotation, *Use of Peremptory Challenges to Exclude from Jury Persons Belonging to a Class or a Race,* 79 A.L.R. 3d 14, 56–73 (1975); See also *United States* v. *Childress,* 715 F.2d 1313, 1316 (8th Cir. 1983) ("Although case law repeatedly describes the defendant's burden of proof [under *Swain*] as 'not insurmountable' . . . a defendant has successfully established systematic exclusion in only two cases since *Swain* was decided in 1965," citing *State* v. *Brown,* 371 So. 2d 751 [La. 1979], and *State* v. *Washington,* 375 So. 2d 1162 [La. 1979], *cert. denied,* 464 U.S. 1063 [1984]. See also Frederick L. Brown, Frank T. McGuire, and Mary S. Winters, "The Peremptory Challenge as a Manipulative Device in Criminal Trials: Traditional Use or Abuse?" *New England Law Review* 14 (1978): 192, 197. The court's opinion in *Swain* was the subject of near universal criticism. See, e.g., Note, "Developments in the Law," 1573; Toni M. Massaro, "Peremptories or Peers?—Rethinking Sixth Amendment Doctrine, Images and Procedures," *North Carolina Law Review* 64 (1986): 501, 525, 502 and n. 7; Sheri Lynn Johnson, "Black Innocence and the White Jury," *Michigan Law Review* 83 (1985): 1611, 1666.

45. Although this essay focuses on state court efforts to expand the protection of minorities in instances when the Supreme Court has provided limited protection, some lower federal courts also made efforts to protect the rights of defendants against the discriminatory exercise of peremptory challenges by prosecutors. See *Booker* v. *Jabe,* 775 F.2d 762, 770 (6th Cir. 1965) ("The sixth amendment guarantees that a criminal charge will not be tried before a jury that fails to represent a cross-section of the community as a consequence of a method of jury selection that systematically excludes a cognizable group from jury service"); *McCray* v. *Abrams,* 750 F.2d. 1113 (2d Cir. 1984) (departing from *Swain's* restriction on challenges and relying on the Sixth Amendment to increase the scrutiny of prosecutorial peremptory challenges). But see *United States* v. *Leslie,* 783 F.2d 541 (5th Cir. 1981) (rejecting a Sixth Amendment challenge).

46. 22 Cal. 3d 258, 148 Cal. Rptr. 890, 583 P.2d 748 (1978).

47. Id. at 755–58. Article I, section 16, reads in relevant part that "trial by jury is an inviolate right and shall be secured to all."

48. Id. at 761–62.

49. 583 P.2d at 761.

50. Id. at 762. See *Swain* v. *Alabama,* 380 U.S. 202, 222 (1965).

51. *Wheeler,* at 764.

52. Id. These are not the requirements of the prima facie case, but rather indications of evidence that is relevant to the determination of whether there is a strong likelihood that persons were challenged based on

group bias. In particular, a defendant need not be a member of the excluded group and the victim need not be a member of the group to which the majority belongs.

53. *Wheeler*, 22 Cal. 3d at 285–86.

54. Id. at 764–65.

55. *Jackson* v. *Alabama*, 516 So. 2d 768, 772 (Ala. 1986).

56. *Riley* v. *State*, 496 A. 2d 997 (Del. 1985) *cert. denied*, 478 U.S. 1022 (1986).

57. *State* v. *Neil*, 457 So. 2d 481 (Fla. 1984).

58. *Commonwealth* v. *Soares*, 377 Mass. 461, 387 N.E.2d 99, *cert. denied* 444 U.S. 881 (1979).

59. *State* v. *Gilmore*, 199 N.J. Super. 389, 489 A. 2d 1175 (1985), *aff'd* 103 N.J. 508, 511 A.2d 1150 (1986).

60. *State* v. *Crespin*, 94 N.M. 486, 612 P.2d 716 (Ct. App. 1980).

61. *State* v. *Wiley*, 144 Ariz. 525, 698 P.2d 1244 (1985); *People* v. *Williams*, 97 Ill. 2d 252, 454 N.E. 2d 441, 443 N.E. 2d 915 (1982) *cert. denied* 461 U.S. 961 (1983); *State* v. *Raymond*, 446 A. 2d 743 (R.I. 1982); *State* v. *Stewart*, 225 Kan. 410, 591 P. 2d 166 (1979). See also *State* v. *Grady*, 93 Wis. 2d 1, 286 N.W. 2d 607 (Ct. App. 1979) (rejecting *Wheeler* doctrine at the appellate court level).

62. *Batson*, 476 U.S. at 103–4 (Marshall, J., concurring) (detailing cases in which prosecutors have used peremptory challenges to exclude minorities); Paula DiPerna, *Juries on Trial* (New York: Dembner Press, 1984), 175 (reporting that St. Louis prosecutors used peremptory challenges to eliminate 74 percent of blacks in the jury pool); George Hayden, Joseph Sonna, and Larry Siegel, "Prosecutorial Discretion in Peremptory Challenges: An Empirical Investigation of Information Use in the Massachusetts Jury Selection Process," *New England Law Review* 13 (1978): 768, 790–91; Frantz, "Many Blacks Kept Off Juries Here," *Chicago Tribune*, August 5, 1984, p. 1, col. 3 (reporting that prosecutors in Cook County, Illinois, eliminated black jurors at more than twice the rate that they excluded white jurors during one month).

63. *United States* v. *Carter*, 528 F.2d 844, 848 (8th Cir. 1975) (reporting that in fifteen cases in 1974 in the Western District of Missouri involving black defendants, prosecutors peremptorily challenged 81 percent of black jurors), *cert. denied*, 425 U.S. 961 (1976); *United States* v. *Robinson*, 421 F. Supp. 467, 469 (D. Conn. 1976) (reporting that Connecticut prosecutors struck 59.2 percent of blacks in cases involving white defendants and 84.8 percent in cases involving black or Hispanic defendants); *McKinney* v. *Walker*, 394 F. Supp. 1015, 1017–18 (S.C. 1974) (reporting that in thirteen criminal trials in 1970–71 in Spartanburg County, South Carolina, involving black defendants, prosecutors peremptorily challenged 82 percent of black jurors), *aff'd* 529 F.2d 516 (4th Cir. 1975).

64. See, e.g., *Batson*, 476 U.S. at 104 (Marshall, J., concurring) ("In 100 felony trials in Dallas County in 1983–84, prosecutors peremptorily struck 405 out of 467 eligible black jurors; the chance of a qualified black sitting on a jury was 1 in 10, compared with 1 in 2 for a white"); *United States* v. *McDaniels*, 379 F. Supp. 1243 (E.D. La. 1974) (indicating that in fifty-three criminal cases between 1972 and 1974 in that district involving black defendants, federal prosecutors used 68.9 percent of their peremptory challenges against black jurors, who made up less than 25 percent of the venire).

65. See *Batson*, 476 U.S. at 104 (Marshall, J., concurring) (quoting an instruction book used by prosecutors in Dallas County, Texas, which explicitly advises prosecutors to conduct jury selections so as to eliminate "any member of a minority group").

66. 476 U.S. 79 (1986).

67. 380 U.S. 202 (1965).

68. *Batson*, 476 U.S. at 93–97. The Supreme Court reserved judgment on the exercise of peremptory challenges by defense counsel, but the question of whether the government may require defense counsel to explain their use of peremptory challenges has been the subject of some discussion. See, e.g., Katherine Goldwasser, "Limiting a Criminal Defendant's Use of Peremptory Challenges," *Harvard Law Review* 102 (1989): 808; Note, "Discrimination by the Defense: Peremptory Challenges After *Batson v. Kentucky*," *Columbia Law Review* 88 (1988): 355. Moreover, some state court decisions prohibit the discriminatory use of peremptory challenges by both defense counsel and prosecutors. See, e.g., *People* v. *Kern*, 75 N.Y. 2d 638, 554 N.E. 2d 1235 (1990) (holding that judicial enforcement of defendant's racially discriminatory use of peremptories is state action and that jury service is a civil right which the prosecution may properly defend on an individual juror's behalf); *People* v. *Wheeler*, 22 Cal. 3d 258, 276–77, 583 P.2d 748, 761–62 (1978); *State* v. *Neil*, 457 So. 2d 481, 486 (Fla. 1984); *Commonwealth* v. *Soares*, 377 Mass. 461, 486, 387 N.E.2d 499, 513 (1979). *Batson* itself suggests two interests—the individual's interest in participating in jury service and the state's interest in public confidence in the fairness of the judicial system, see *Batson*, 476 U.S. at 87—that argue against a defendant's discriminatory use of peremptory challenges as well. The Supreme Court recently held that the Sixth Amendment right to trial by an impartial jury provides no additional protection against the discriminatory use of peremptory challenges. *Holland* v. *Illinois*, 110 S.Ct. 803 (1990).

69. *Batson*, 476 U.S. at 97.

70. Id. at 96–97.

71. Id. at 92–93.

72. Id. at 102 (Marshall, J., concurring). Justice Powell's majority opinion disagreed with Justice Marshall. Justice Powell was convinced that the Court's holding would eliminate the discriminatory use of peremptory challenges. Id. at 99 n. 22.

73. Id. at 102–3 (Marshall, J., concurring). "The decision today will not end the racial discrimination that peremptories inject into the jury-selection process. That goal can be accomplished only by eliminating peremptory challenges entirely."

74. Id. at 102–8. Justice Marshall's less than enthusiastic endorsement of the *Batson* opinion obviously flows from realism born of experience, coupled with frustration at the slow pace of change.

75. *Batson*, 476 U.S. at 105–6 (Marshall, J., concurring); see also *People* v. *Hall*, 35 Cal. 3d 161, 197 Cal. Rptr. 71, 672 P. 2d 854 (1983); *People* v. *Rousseau*, 129 Cal. App. 3d 526, 536–37, 179 Cal. Rptr. 892, 897–98 (1982); *Commonwealth* v. *Robinson*, 382 Mass. 189, 195, 415 N.E.2d 805, 809–10 (1981); *King* v. *County of Nassau*, 581 F. Supp. 493, 501–2 (E.D.N.Y. 1984).

76. *Batson*, 476 U.S. at 106. Justice Powell's majority opinion disagreed, believing that both prosecutors and judges would apply *Batson* standards fairly and conscientiously. Id. at 99 n.22.

77. Id. at 97–98.

78. Id. at 97.

79. One area of disagreement, however, is whether the defendant may object to the removal of members of a distinct racial group from the venire if the defendant is not a member of that racial group. Lower courts have provided a variety of answers to the question. Compare *Clark* v. *City of Bridgeport*, 645 F. Supp. 890 (D. Conn. 1986) (white plaintiff in civil suit has standing); *U.S.* v. *Townley*, 843 F.2d 1070 (8th Cir. 1988) (two white defendants have standing to join in black codefendant's challenge); *Seubert* v. *State*, 749 S.W. 2d 585, 588 (Tex. Ct. App. 1988) (citing *Peters* v. *Kiff*, 407 U.S. 493 [1972], holds that due process clause offers equivalent protection against discriminatory use of peremptories and gives standing to white defendant); *State* v. *Gardner*, 156 Ariz. 512, 515, 753 P.2d 1168, 1170 (1987) (holding that a white defendant has standing to challenge the exclusion of black venirepersons but implying that there is not as strong an evidentiary inference of purposeful discrimination when the defendant is white); *Pope* v. *State*, 255 Ga. 195, 345 S.E. 2d 831 (1986) (holding that a white defendant cannot establish a prima facie case if not a member of a cognizable racial group); *People* v. *Zayas*, 159 Ill. App. 3d 554, 110 Ill. Dec. 94, 510 N.E.2d 1125 (1987) (holding that a Hispanic defendant lacked standing to challenge partial exclusion of blacks from the jury); *State* v. *Bolands*, 743 S.W.2d 442 (Mo. App. 1987)

(holding that the *Batson* rule does not apply to a Hispanic defendant's challenge to the state's use of peremptories to strike black venire-persons); *State* v. *Christensen*, 720 S.W.2d 738 (Mo. App. 1986) (holding that a white defendant cannot establish a prima facie case of discrimination if not a member of a cognizable racial group); *State* v. *Agudelo*, 89 N.C. App. 640, 647, 366 S.E.2d 921, 925 (1988) (holding that Hispanic defendants were not entitled to challenge the exclusion of blacks under *Batson*); *U.S.* v. *Vaccaro*, 816 F. 2d 443, 457 (9th Cir.), *cert. den.*, 484 U.S. 914 (1987) (white defendant lacks standing); *U.S.* v. *Sgro*, 816 F.2d 30, 33 (1st Cir. 1987); *Wilson* v. *Cross*, 845 F.2d 163 (8th Cir. 1988); *U.S.* v. *Chavez-Vernaza*, 844 F.2d 1368, 1375–76 (9th Cir. 1987) (refusal to allow Peruvian to challenge exclusion of black jurors). Justice Kennedy's concurrence in *Holland* v. *Illinois*, 110 S.Ct. 803, appeared to presage an answer to this question, as Kennedy noted in dictum that he saw "no obvious reason to conclude that a defendant's race should deprive him of standing in his own trial to vindicate his own jurors' right to sit." 110 S.Ct. at 812. Because Justices Marshall, Brennan, Blackmun, and Stevens endorsed this position, see id. at 814 (Marshall, J., dissenting) and 821 (Stevens, J., dissenting), a majority of five justices share this belief that a defendant's race was irrelevant to his standing to assert a *Batson* claim. The recent resignation of Justice Brennan, however, has dissolved that majority and the future of the dicta in *Holland* has therefore become uncertain. The issue is squarely presented to the Court in a case scheduled for argument in the October 1990 term. *Powers* v. *Illinois*, *cert. granted*, 110 S.Ct. 1109 (1990).

80. *Batson*, 476 U.S. at 97.

81. See, e.g., *Ex parte Branch*, 526 So.2d 609, 622–23 (Ala. 1987); *State* v. *Goode*, 107 N.M. 298, 756 S.E.2d 578, 581 (1988).

82. See, e.g., *Ex parte Branch*, 526 So. 2d at 623; *Gamble* v. *State*, 257 Ga. 325, 327, 357 S.E.2d 792, 794 (1987); *People* v. *Parker*, 166 Ill. App. 3d 123, 116 Ill. Dec. 635, 519 N.E.2d 703, 705 (1988); *State* v. *Hood*, 242 Kan. 115, 119–20, 744 P.2d 816, 820 (1987); *Stanley* v. *State*, 313 Md. 50, 72, 542 A.2d 1267, 1284 (1988) *State* v. *Goode*, 107 N.M. 298, 301, 756 P.2d 578, 581 (1988).

83. See, e.g., *Ex parte Branch*, 526 So. 2d at 622 (holding that a pattern of strikes raises an inference of discrimination); *Swain* v. *State*, 504 So. 2d 345, 350 (Ala. App. 1987) (holding that striking a disproportionate number of members of defendant's minority group may raise an inference of discrimination); *Stanley* v. *State*, 313 Md. 50, 72, 542, A.2d 1267, 1284 (1988) (finding an inference of discrimination when 80 percent of strikes were used against blacks who constituted only 25 percent of the venire).

84. *State* v. *Goode*, 107 N.M. 298, 301, 756 P.2d 578, 581 (1988).

85. The federal courts have shied away from requiring specific numbers or percentages of strikes as a trigger. See National Jury Project, *Jurywork* at § 4.03 [4] [a], 4–25; *United States* v. *Clemens*, 843 F.2d 741, 746 (3d Cir. 1988). *Smith* v. *State*, 294 Ark. 357, 360, 742 S.W. 2d 936, 937 (1988) ("There were no questions or statements made during the voir dire examination that support an inference of discriminatory purpose. . . . The striking of two jurors, standing alone is not sufficient to establish a *Batson* 'pattern' "); *Blackshear* v. *State*, 504 So. 2d 1330, 1331 (Fla. App. 1987) ("The mere exclusion of a number of blacks by itself is insufficient to entitle a party to an inquiry into the other party's use of peremptories"); *Thorne* v. *State*, 509 N.E.2d 877, 881 (Ind. App. 1987) ("The removal of two black jurors by the use of peremptories does not, by itself, raise an inference of racial discrimination").

86. See *United States* v. *Montgomery*, 819 F.2d 847 (8th Cir. 1987) (citing the government's acceptance of a jury with two blacks when it had peremptory challenges remaining as the basis for denying a prima facie case); *Williams* v. *State*, 257 Ga. 788, 364 S.E.2d 569 (1988) (finding no prima facie case when there were seven black jurors); *State* v. *Thompson*, 516 So.2d 349, 354 (La. 1988) (four of twelve jurors were black and prosecutor accepted three additional black jurors excluded by defendants). But see *United States* v. *Battle*, 836 F.2d 1084 (8th Cir. 1987) (striking even one black juror may suffice for a prima facie case even if the other blacks are impaneled or dismissed for valid reasons).

87. See *Ex parte Branch*, 526 So. 2d 609, 623, 622 (Ala. 1987).

88. Compare *State* v. *Antwine*, 743 S.W.2d 51 (Mo. 1987) (considering prosecutorial reasons) and *Gray* v. *Commonwealth*, 233 Va. 313, 356 S.E.2d 157 (1987) with *People* v. *Granillo*, 197 Cal. App. 3d 110, 242 Cal. Rptr. 639 (1987) (refusing to consider reasons in determining prima facie case) and *State* v. *Goode*, 107 N.M. 298, 756 P.2d 578 (1988).

89. *Batson*, 476 U.S. at 91, 96–97; *Swain* v. *State*, 504 So.2d 347, 351 (Ala. App. 1987).

90. *Batson*, 476 U.S. at 97.

91. Such a procedure stands in marked contrast to the method of proving illegal discrimination under Title VII law, although the *Batson* Court referred to its Title VII decisions in illustrating procedures for attacking a peremptory challenge. In Title VII cases, plaintiff's proof of a prima facie case is followed by distinct stages in which defendant must proffer a neutral explanation and in a third distinct stage the plaintiff must prove that this explanation is pretextual. In jury discrimination cases, however, these final stages are often lacking. See National Jury Project, *Jurywork*, § 4.04 [4] at 4–45. Some federal courts have even held

that prosecutors may offer their reasons in an ex parte hearing, thereby depriving defendants of an opportunity to contest them. See *United States* v. *Tucker*, 836 F.2d 334, 338–40 (7th Cir. 1988); *United States* v. *Davis*, 809 F.2d 1194 (6th Cir. 1987). But see *United States* v. *Garrison*, 849 F.2d 103 (4th Cir. 1988), *cert. den.*, 109 S.Ct. 566 (requiring adversarial hearing on prosecutor's explanation absent compelling reasons for secrecy).

92. 476 U.S. at 97–98.

93. See, e.g., *Batson*, 476 U.S. at 98 n. 21; *State* v. *Rogers*, 753 S.W.2d 607 (Mo. App. E.D. 3 Div. 1988); *People* v. *King*, 195 Cal. App. 3d 923, 436 (1987) (Poche, J., dissenting) (criticizing the court's fanatic devotion to the doctrine of deference to the trial court).

94. See, e.g., *United States* v. *Garrison*, 849 F.2d 103 (4th Cir. 1988), *cert. den.*, 109 S. Ct. 566; *State* v. *Rowe*, 228 Neb. 663, 423 N.W.2d 782, 786 (1988); *Rogers* v. *State*, 725 S.W.2d 477, 480 (Tex. App. 1 Dist. 1987).

95. See *Batson*, 476 U.S. at 106 (Marshall, J., dissenting).

96. See *Jackson* v. *Alabama*, 516 So. 2d 768 (Ala. 1986).

97. See *In re Branch* v. *State of Alabama*, 526 So. 2d 609 (Ala. 1987).

98. 530 So. 2d 849 (Ala. Crim. App. 1987), *cert. den.*, 530 So. 2d 856 (Ala. 1988).

99. Id. at 851–52.

100. See *United States* v. *Forbes*, 816 F.2d 1006, 1010 (5th Cir. 1987) (finding a challenge to have been racially neutral when the prosecutor "sensed by [the juror's] posture and demeanor that she was hostile to being in court"); *People* v. *Talley*, 152 Ill. App. 3d 261, 121 Ill. Dec. 800, 504 N.E.2d 1318, 1327–28 (1987) (finding a challenge to have been exercised for racially neutral reasons when the prosecutor explained that he was "not happy with [the juror's] demeanor"). *Chambers* v. *Texas*, 711 S.W. 2d 240 (Tex. Ct. App. 1986) ("body English" can provide the basis for a challenge); *Commonwealth* v. *Lathimore*, 396 Mass. 446, 486 N.E. 2d. 723 (1985) (accepting a peremptory challenge because the prosecutor did not like the juror's looks). But see *People* v. *Washington*, 234 Cal. Rptr. 204 (Cal. Ct. App. 1987) (mere "subjective conclusory nuances" regarding juror's soft-spokenness and unmarried status not enough).

101. For example, in *State* v. *Rogers*, 753 S.W.2d 607 (Mo. App. 1988), the Missouri Appellate Court accepted the prosecutor's explanation that he struck two black men because they had incarcerated relatives, even though two unchallenged white jurors had relatives who had been incarcerated. See id. at 610. The court accepted the prosecutor's explanation that the white jurors were different because their relatives were no longer in jail. The court also allowed a challenge to a black juror because his younger brother had been convicted of a crime and

therefore might harbor ill feelings toward the police. The court accepted this explanation despite acknowledging that the white jurors
with formerly incarcerated relatives might have similar feelings. The
court simply said that "differences in age, sex and occupation are also
factors for consideration" but did not explain why those factors would
justify the challenge of the black juror. See id.; see also *U.S.* v. *Love*, 815
F.2d 52, 54 (8th Cir. 1987) (upholding a challenge to the lone black juror
"because he had heard of a business owned by a person [who] the government expected would be called as an alibi witness" in a related case
"who might be sympathetic to appellant as well"). See also *Rogers* v.
State, 725 S.W.2d 477, 481 (Tex. Ct. App. 1987) (accepting a prosecutor's
explanation that she struck a black venireperson because she "felt that
he distrusted her and that something seemed unfavorable").

102. 755 S.W. 2d 397 (Mo. App. 1988).
103. Id. at 398.
104. 224 N.J. Super. 280, 540 A.2d 227 (1988).
105. Id. at 232–34; see also *People* v. *Hernandez*, 528 N.Y.S. 625 (N.Y. App.
Div. 1988) (accepting the challenges of two Hispanic venirepersons
because they spoke Spanish and indicated during voir dire that they
might have difficulty accepting as final and authoritative the court interpreter's translations of testimony). It seems bizarre that courts would
allow the challenge of Spanish-speaking jurors whenever there will
be Spanish testimony but would not think it appropriate to remove
English-speaking jurors when there will be English testimony.
106. See, e.g., *People* v. *Taylor*, 171 Ill. App. 3d 261, 121 Ill. Dec. 168, 524
N.E.2d 1216, 1220 (1988) (accepting a prosecutor's explanation that
a juror had been challenged in part because the juror was young—
twenty-seven—and had been employed for only a short period of
time); *People* v. *Cartagena*, 128 A.D.2d 797, 513 N.Y.S.2d 497 (N.Y. App.
Div. 1987) (accepting a prosecutor's explanation that he had challenged
four black jurors on the basis of their educational backgrounds, their
employment histories, the employment of their spouses and children,
and their criminal records, if any); *State* v. *Martinez*, 294 S.C. 72, 362
S.E.2d 641 (1987) (holding that a prosecutor's challenge of one black
juror was sufficiently explained by his chronic unemployment and
that two other black jurors were acceptably challenged because they
were of the same sex and age group as the defendant and had "possible criminal records"); *Chambers* v. *State*, 724 S.W. 2d 440 (Tex. App.
1987) (accepting the explanation that prosecutor struck a black woman
because she was unmarried and had two children); *Taitano* v. *Commonwealth*, 4 Va. App. 342, 358 S.E.2d 590, 592–93 (1987) (holding that the
challenge of a black man because he lived near the defendant or near

the scene of the crime or in an area of high crime was acceptable under *Batson*).

107. *State* v. *Algarin*, 47 *Criminal Law Report* (BNA), 1369 (Ill. App. Ct., 1st Dist., 3d Cir.).

108. *People* v. *Turner*, 42 Cal.3d 711, 720 n. 6, 230 Cal. Rptr. 656 (1986) (noting that although appellate courts must ordinarily defer to trial courts' evaluations of prosecutorial reasons, such deference is not inevitable, for whether a particular explanation is sufficient remains a question of law); *People* v. *Washington*, 234 Cal. Rptr. 204 (Cal. Ct. App. 1982) (rejecting "subjective conclusory nuances" such as soft-spokenness as bases for justifying challenges). See generally National Jury Project, *Jurywork* at §4.04 [2], 4–32 to 4–39.

109. 107 N.M. 298, 756 P.2d 578 (1988).

110. See 107 N.M. at 302; see also *State* v. *Slappy*, 13 F.L.W. 184, 522 So. 2d 18 (1988); *Gamble* v. *State*, 257 Ga. 325, 357 S.E.2d 792 (1987).

111. See *Goode*, 107 N.M. at 303, 756 P.2d at 583; see also *Ex parte Branch*, 526 So.2d at 624; *Slappy*, 522 So.2d at 22.

112. 13 F.L.W. 184, 522 So.2d 18 (1988).

113. 522 So.2d at 22; see also *Ex parte Branch*, 526 So. 2d at 624.

114. 100 U.S. 303 (1880).

115. 380 U.S. 202 (1965).

116. 476 U.S. 79 (1986).

117. See E. G. Johnson, "Black Innocence and White Juries," *University of Michigan Law Review* (1969); Derrick A. Bell, *Race, Racism and American Law*, 2d ed. (Boston: Little, Brown, 1980).

118. The Court has repeatedly rejected arguments that there is any con-stitutional right to a petit jury, as opposed to a venire, of a particular composition. See, e.g., *Holland* v. *Illinois*, 110 S.Ct. 803 (1990).

Part Five

Assessments

State Protection of Personal Liberty

Remembering the Future

William M. Wiecek

Kermit Hall offers a pessimistic view of the possibilities that state constitutions provide for the protection of individual rights and liberties.[1] I maintain, in contrast, that the states' constitutional experience actually suggests numerous possibilities, both benign and destructive, for the protection of liberty. In the states' constitutional order, we have found a far richer basis for the development of rights than the gloomy prognosis provided by Professor Hall.

To demonstrate this point, a survey of all or even several states would prove uselessly superficial. Instead, let me recapitulate all too briefly the experience of one state in developing guarantees for liberty and rights: New York. As one of the original mainland colonies, New York provides a historical span of nearly four centuries, dating back to the period of Dutch settlement in the seventeenth century. I will concentrate on the earlier period of New York history, in part because that is the era most familiar to me and in part because Vincent Bonventre's work on the New York Court of Appeals surveys the modern period.[2] I will enumerate a dozen instances or subjects before the twentieth century that have expanded or contracted the scope of liberties enjoyed by people in the colony, province, and state of New York. The impact of these incidents was not confined to free citizens; slaves, disfranchised residents, nonresidents, and foreigners were often the principal beneficiaries or victims of New York's legal tradition.

My survey offers two conclusions about the potential for state protection of individual liberty. First, state constitutional development, as exemplified by New York, has had a profound and extensive impact on personal liberties. Second, from a libertarian perspective, that impact cuts both ways. Some of the incidents I will note have expanded personal liberties, but not all of them have. Neither New York nor any other state is a haven of libertarian perfection, and the shortfalls I review remind us that even a progressive state has skeletons in its historical closets.

We often assume that only public law—constitutional law, administrative law, criminal law and its procedure—is relevant to the protection of liberty. Chief Justice Ellen Peters of the Connecticut Supreme Court has made the point I am about to survey, but my repetition here will serve to emphasize its importance. Private law—those domains of law that are concerned with contracts, property, torts, family relationships, corporations, and so on—is of at least as much interest to those concerned with the boundaries of liberty as public law. Chief Justice Peters has convincingly demonstrated that the quarries of private law, in Connecticut as elsewhere, furnish materials as ample and important to our rights as do the sources of public law.[3] With that said, I proceed to a review of highlights in New York's history of protecting the scope of human liberty.

The New York Charter of Libertyes of 1683 adopted several significant elements of the English libertarian tradition, including chapter 39 of Magna Charta, as well as the grand and petit juries. It also contained important innovations such as a representative assembly whose consent was necessary for the imposition of taxes, a primitive homestead exemption, a forerunner of the Third Amendment, a guarantee of dower, and a provision for religious toleration.[4] The title "Charter" was a misnomer, and the document itself proved abortive. It was a statute adopted by the people of New York meeting through their representatives in a specially convened "legislative" session representing all the then-settled places in the colony of New York (plus some areas that have since become parts of other states: Martha's Vineyard, Nantucket, and eastern Maine). Though he approved the document when he was Duke of York (and therefore proprietor of the colony that was his namesake), King James II on his accession to the throne in 1685 disallowed the charter in favor of a brief interlude of authoritarian administrations under Thomas Don-gan, Edmund Andros, and Francis Nicholson. This experiment in arbitrary government was cut short by the transatlantic reverberation of the Glorious Revolution in New York, Leisler's Rebellion (1689–91).

When the political turmoil of the Glorious Revolution subsided, Yorkers turned to the reform of their civil administration. One of the most important accomplishments of this reform effort was the land-mark Judiciary Act of 1691,[5] which gave justices of the peace a petty civil jurisdiction. To the twentieth-century mind, this may not seem very significant, but in its time it made legal process available to all people, cheaply and near their residence. This was an achievement of no small moment when we recall that remote and expensive justice continued to be a grievance in other colonies through the American Revolution (consider, for example, the Regulation in South Carolina [1767–69] and Shays' Rebellion in Massachusetts [1786–87]). Suzanna Sherry notes that ordinary people demand courts of justice, not courts of law. That is just what the residents of New York got in the 1691 Judiciary Act.

New York led the way in development of judicial review, that prerequisite in the American legal system for limited government and the rule of law. Alexander Hamilton played a preeminent role in this development—as befits the author of *Federalist* No. 78, the great de-fense of judicial review. While engaged in private practice in New York City,[6] Hamilton argued the case of *Rutgers* v. *Waddington* (1784). He insisted that a court could refuse to give effect to a statute on the grounds that the act conflicted with the state constitution, as well as with the treaty of peace concluded the previous year with Great Britain.[7] Along with the 1787 North Carolina case of *Bayard* v. *Single-ton*,[8] Hamilton's argument in *Rutgers* led the way in establishing the principle of judicial review.

Hamilton also contributed to the nascent tradition of freedom for political debate through his appearance as counsel for the de-fense in the criminal prosecution of Federalist editor Harry Croswell for seditious libel in 1803. (Croswell had nettled President Thomas Jefferson and local Republicans with his barbed editorials and politi-cal doggerel.) Hamilton there argued that truth constituted a defense: "It is inherent in the nature of things," he insisted, "that the asser-tion of truth cannot be a crime."[9] This idea echoed the arguments of more than a half-century earlier by Andrew Hamilton (no relation) in John Peter Zenger's celebrated case.[10] Alexander Hamilton's 1804 argument had a long-lived impact on free press doctrine. The state adopted Hamilton's position in a statute of 1805[11] and then wrote it into the constitutions of 1821 and 1846,[12] where it served as a model for guarantees of freedom of the press incorporated into other state constitutions.

Freedom of political discourse was secured in New York at an early date, but religious liberty was harder to establish. New York's greatest nineteenth-century jurist, James Kent, upheld a prosecution for blasphemy in *People v. Ruggles* (1811), providing an elaborate defense of the conservative position that a religious majority ought to be able to prosecute religious dissidents for rejecting the beliefs of the dominant sects. "Nothing could be more offensive to the virtuous part of the community, or more injurious to the tender morals of the young, than to declare such profanity lawful," Kent wrote. As for the guarantee of religious freedom in Article 38 of the 1777 New York Constitution, he went on, "to construe it as breaking down the common law barriers against licentious, wanton, and impious attacks upon christianity itself, would be an enormous perversion of its meaning."[13] This case and the experience of Abner Kneeland, an early nineteenth-century freethinker in Massachusetts, demonstrated that state courts would still tolerate the use of the state's coercive power to suppress challenges to religious orthodoxy. The obvious uselessness of persecution for religious utterance and its inconsistency with the ideas of the revolutionary-era declarations of rights in the state constitutions were insufficient to deter the New York legislature from criminalizing "sacrilegious" expression until the United States Supreme Court sharply curtailed the discretion of the censor in the Empire State in *Joseph Burstyn, Inc. v. Wilson* (1952).[14]

New York has had a curiously uneven record in the domain of race relations. In the colonial period, the statutory basis of its law of slavery was relatively moderate, though slavery itself was extensive in the colony, but the application of law to slaves and free blacks may have been the harshest of the mainland colonies. Yet New York fairly quickly abolished slavery. Although it discriminated against free blacks in the antebellum period, it also provided generous safeguards to protect alleged fugitive slaves. And when its legal system was threatened from without by the slavocracy, it reacted vigorously to prevent the intrusion of slavery into the Empire State. Though some of New York's political leaders and many of its citizens led the movement for the abolition of slavery and the protection of black freedom, its antebellum history of race relations reveals many retrograde moments.

When the English supplanted Dutch rule in New Amsterdam in the late seventeenth century, they introduced a form of slavery far more harsh than the relatively mild sort practiced by the Dutch.[15] One consequence of the introduction of the more brutal Anglo-American slavery was violent overreaction to the supposed New York City slave insurrections of 1712 and 1741.[16] The 1741 incident resulted in hideous tortures and executions of innocent slaves to propitiate a spasm of white paranoia.

Independence presented Yorkers with an opportunity to reconsider slavery's existence in their state in the light of revolutionary ideals. They responded with less enthusiasm than the neighboring states of Vermont and Pennsylvania, as well as the Confederation Congress, but they did at least begin the process of gradual abolition within fifteen years after independence. Yorkers considered the present state of Vermont to be part of their province through the Revolution, a claim they did not finally abandon until the area's admission to the Union as a state in 1791. In 1777, the Vermonters, declaring themselves a republic independent of New York, rival claimant New Hampshire, and the other mainland colonies, adopted a constitution with a Declaration of Rights that was modeled on Virginia's, that fecund mother of most of the other original state bills of rights. They borrowed Article 1 of the Virginia Declaration verbatim, but added to it the logical conclusion that slavery was abolished absolutely because "all men are born equally free and independent."[17] The Green Mountain Republic thereby became the first American state to eliminate slavery totally, immediately, and explicitly. Vermonters thus established a tradition of personal liberty well in advance of that of any other state and cultivated that tradition of freedom consistently to the Civil War. The Confederation Congress adopted the Northwest Ordinance in 1787, banning slavery from the Northwest Territory, the second example of immediate abolition in our early experience. And Pennsylvania began the process of gradual abolition in 1780 by enactment of its farsighted and liberal "Act for the Gradual Abolition of Slavery."[18] So it was not as if New York lacked nearby examples of abolition.

But New York did at least begin to make amends for its bloody colonial history of race relations, even if it was slower than adjacent states.[19] In 1776, Alexander Hamilton and others founded an institution whose name accurately announced its mission: the New-York Society, for Promoting the Manumission of Slaves and Protecting Such of Them as Have Been or May be Liberated. Together with its sibling, the Pennsylvania Abolition Society, the New-York Manumission Society performed yeoman service in promoting gradual emancipation, protecting the freedom of liberated Yorkers, thwarting kidnapping, and providing jobs and welfare services for free blacks. The society played an important role in securing adoption of New York's 1799 gradual emancipation act, a post-nati statute that freed children born to slave mothers but held them in servitude until age twenty-eight for males and twenty-five for females.[20] Within two decades, New York had liberated its remaining slaves, first extending to them some basic civil rights such as the right to contract marriage, the power of owning property, the ability to testify against whites, and the right to jury trial in all felony prosecutions. In 1817 the state converted all remaining slaves to servants with limited-term servitude; all would be completely free by 1827.[21]

New York's 1821 Constitution permitted some blacks to vote but left imposed on them a property qualification not similarly applicable to whites.[22] This raises again the question posed by Suzanna Sherry: do we regard the glass as half empty because blacks were discriminated against in access to the ballot, or half full because some of them were allowed to vote, in contrast to most northern and all southern states, which excluded them from the ballot entirely?

New York also enacted a progressive series of measures protecting blacks who were caught in the snare of the federal Fugitive Slave Act of 1793. In succession, it prohibited the kidnapping of free blacks, assured blacks the right of trial (and later jury trial) in state courts when captured as alleged fugitive slaves, provided state counsel in such trials, made available to blacks the writs of homine replegiando and habeas corpus, and refused to permit state officials or facilities to be used to restrain blacks captured as fugitives.[23] The 1851 rescue of the captured fugitive Jerry McHenry in Syracuse was the capstone of New York's resistance to enforcement of the harsh 1850 federal Fugitive Slave Act.

The Empire State proved to be fertile ground for the abolition movement.[24] The "Burned-Over District" along the Erie Canal was a hotbed of abolition sentiment, producing or welcoming many of the nation's preeminent abolitionists of the 1840s, including among others Frederick Douglass, who published the *North Star* in Rochester; Alvan Stewart, the earliest proponent of the Fifth Amendment's due process clause as an antislavery weapon; Gerrit Smith, the generous if mad benefactor of the movement and, for a brief moment, an abolitionist congressman; and Myron Holley, upstate lawyer.

Paul Finkelman has recently traced New York Governor William Seward's efforts in the extradition tugs-of-war with Virginia and Georgia.[25] The escalating hostility revealed fatal sectional antagonisms that rose like evil vapors out of the miasma of fugitive slave captures. Historians have emphasized Seward's role in the sectional controversy as United States senator, presidential candidate, and secretary of state. Finkelman has made an invaluable contribution by restoring Seward's role as a state figure, an official representative of New York's antislavery impulses. Seward made the oral arguments before the United States Supreme Court in *Jones v. Van Zandt* (1847), though Salmon Chase's printed argument in that case has diverted much of the credit and all the attention to him rather than to Seward.[26]

New York's last major contribution to the controversy over slavery came in the litigation of *People v. Lemmon* (1860).[27] Repudiating the views of Chief Justice of the United States Roger B. Taney in the *Dred Scott* case of 1857,[28] a majority of the judges of the New York Court of Appeals held that slaves brought voluntarily into the state became free because there was no state law that enslaved them and they consequently reassumed their natural condition, freedom. *Lemmon* was immediately overtaken by secession and the Civil War, but had both been delayed a few years, the case might have become the vehicle by which the antislavery policies of the free states of the North confronted the proslavery constitutionalism of the Taney Court, with results that can only remain speculative.

As one of the largest and richest states of the early Union, New York played a prominent role in pioneering experiments with economic regulation. This topic did not have the immediate and obvious impact on personal liberty that the law of race relations had, but it was nonetheless important for establishing the boundaries between state control and individual freedom. Willard Hurst's classic essay "The Release of Energy" has sensitized us to the importance of economic affairs in the nineteenth century's conception of human freedom.[29] Thus a review of the state's economic regulatory activities will disclose an impact on human liberty not at first obvious.

New York's development of labor law before the Civil War provides a socially reactionary contrast with what was otherwise a generally progressive course of constitutional development. In the New York City *Cordwainers Case* of 1810, De Witt Clinton, presiding over the Mayor's Court of New York City, upheld a conviction for common law conspiracy of shoemakers to organize for the purpose of demanding higher wages for piecework.[30] Justice John Savage of the New York Supreme Court reiterated the point in the 1835 case of *People* v. *Fisher*, reinforcing his legal conclusion with assumptions based on classical market economics. Savage condemned the workers' "extravagant demands for wages," insisting that only the market, and not the legislature or private associations like unions, could efficiently accomplish what today would be called equilibrium pricing. As he put it, "it is important to the best interests of society that the price of labor be left to regulate itself, or rather, be limited by the demand for it."[31]

These leading precedents encouraged a climate of hostility to labor organization that was shortly challenged in Massachusetts by Chief Justice Lemuel Shaw's opinion in *Commonwealth* v. *Hunt* (1842), rejecting the idea that labor organization for higher wages was per se an actionable common law conspiracy.[32] But New York jurists remained unaffected by Shaw's enlightened approach. Until World War I, judges of the Empire State led a reactionary movement of hostility to union organization and to legislative attempts to meliorate the harsh lot of workers victimized by industrialization.

In the history of the New York bench, James Kent was a giant, wielding an influence not equaled until the appointment of Benjamin N. Cardozo to the New York Court of Appeals in 1913. Kent was a major voice in the antebellum debate over which of differing models of economic development the law should encourage. His most conspicuous opportunity to air his views favoring monopolies took place in *Livingston* v. *Van Ingen* (1812),[33] the state court predecessor to the celebrated United States Supreme Court decision in *Gibbons* v. *Ogden* (1824).[34] The *Livingston* decision was rendered by that judicial hybrid and predecessor of the Court of Appeals, the New York Court for the Trial of Impeachments and the Correction of Errors. Judges on that body delivered their opinions seriatim, presenting the opportunity for a face-to-face confrontation between Kent, exponent of the backward-looking monopoly theory, and Chancellor John Lansing, who promoted the competition model.

Kent argued that the law should honor monopolistic grants by the legislature as the surest way to encourage venture capitalists to seek innovative investment opportunities. "The power [to grant monopolies] is important in itself, and may be most beneficially exercised for the encouragement of the arts," Kent contended; "and if well and judiciously exerted, it may ameliorate the condition of society, by enriching and adorning the county with useful and elegant improvements." Lansing rejected state support of monopolies, arguing that instead the law should stand back to permit the market to regulate the scramble for economic opportunity. Kent's view gradually gave way to Lansing's, but judicial conservatives, including Joseph Story, waged a stubborn campaign on its behalf from the bench.

Governor De Witt Clinton's promotion of the Erie Canal, opened in 1825, had an immeasurable effect on the development of New York City, the state, and the nation as a whole.[35] "Clinton's Ditch" made New York City the unrivaled financial and shipping headquarters of the nation for over a century. The canal linked the interests of the states carved out of the Northwest Territory inseparably with the East rather than the South. It provided one of the most important infrastructural components that were essential to industrialization in midcentury. It promoted settlement of the Middle West. And not least, it became a highway of ideas as well as of commerce, an intellectual path that bore the doctrines of millennial religion, abolition, and a hundred reform isms from New England and New York throughout the upper Ohio and Mississippi valleys. The canal was important in other ways. It and its daughter waterways were an impetus for the development of administrative agencies through the creation of canal commissions in the 1840s.[36] Though all were short-lived, these earliest regulatory commissions marked the beginning of that modern leviathan, the administrative state.

We must beware the tendency to assume that constitutional development, especially in economic matters, was the monopoly of the legal elite. As the abolitionists and temperance reformers of New York State demonstrated, ordinary people had an influence on the content of their public law. A dramatic example was the so-called Rent Wars of the late 1830s in the Helderberg Mountains south of Albany.[37] The farmers of the region resented the quitrents that they were obliged to pay to the descendants of the Dutch patroons who had engrossed so much land in the Hudson and Mohawk valleys. The farmers demanded fee simple ownership of their holdings. Their inability to secure changes in the patterns of ownership of agricultural land led them to take matters into their own hands and revive the eighteenth-century tradition of "the people out of doors," as it was then called, whereby controlled mobs took purposive action to secure political goals with a minimum of violence.[38]

The farmers' grievances expressed in the Rent Wars were redressed in the nineteenth century's most innovative and influential constitutive document, the New York Constitution of 1846.[39] Itemizing some changes wrought by this instrument will demonstrate how significant constitutional change at the state level was for the protection of individual liberty before the Civil War. Among other things, the 1846 Constitution abolished legislative divorce; prohibited lotteries; did away with feudal tenures (the focus of the Rent Wars grievances), replacing them with fee simple tenure of allodial land and prohibiting long-term agricultural leases; mandated the creation of a commission to codify the state's procedural law (the origin of the Field codes that replaced common law pleading); confirmed universal white manhood suffrage, with liberal residence requirements but with a property qualification for blacks; experimented with what is now called alternative dispute resolution through the creation of "tribunals of reconciliation"; severely restricted state indebtedness; authorized general incorporation acts; and prohibited special legislative charters for all but banking corporations.

By far the most significant intersection of law and economic regulation was the growth of the legal doctrine of substantive due process and its conflict with the state police power. The struggle of these two antithetical doctrines provided the principal dynamic for American constitutional law after slavery had been abolished. A New York judge, Chancellor Reuben Walworth, first articulated one of the most important components of state police power doctrine, the concept of eminent domain, in the 1831 case of *Beekman* v. *Saratoga and Schenectady Railroad*.[40] He held that government might take any property for public use and upon payment of just compensation. The people through their government "have a right to resume the possession of the property in the manner directed by the Constitution and the laws of the State, whenever the public interest requires it." Walworth thereby reaffirmed the power of government to regulate for the common good, subject only to the explicit restraints embedded in the Constitution. This was an important precursor to the doctrine of the police power that was expressed two decades later by Chief Justice Shaw in the Massachusetts case of *Commonwealth* v. *Alger* (1851). Shaw there identified "the police power [as] the power vested in the legislature by the constitution, to make . . . all manner of wholesome and reasonable laws . . . not repugnant to the constitution, as they shall judge to be for the good and welfare of the commonwealth."[41]

No state played as important a role in the evolution of higher law ideas into substantive due process as did New York. Her jurists were unusually hospitable to doctrines embedded in American constitutional law by the 1798 United States Supreme Court decision of *Calder* v. *Bull*. In that case, Justice Samuel Chase maintained that "certain vital principles in our free republican governments" and "the general principles of law and reason" provided a basis for holding state laws unconstitutional, even without textual warrant in the state or federal constitutions.[42] It should be no surprise that a conservative jurist like Chancellor Kent should be an enthusiast for higher law doctrines then mutating into substantive due process. In *Gardner* v. *Newburgh* (1816), he held that riparian rights were "part of the freehold, of which no man can be disseised 'but by lawful judgment of his peers, or by due process of law.' This is an ancient and fundamental maxim of the common law to be found in Magna Charta."[43]

Enthusiasm for substantive due process is often inversely proportional to democratic sympathies. A judge like Kent who extols limitations on legislative power can be expected to display little sympathy for democracy. And so it was that Kent, as a delegate to New York's 1821 constitutional convention, participated prominently, on the backward-looking and losing side, in the struggle over democratization of the suffrage in New York State. The convention considered scrapping or reducing the property qualification for suffrage that had been part of the original 1777 Constitution on the grounds that what was conformable with republican ideology in the revolutionary era had become incompatible with the nineteenth century's spirit of democracy celebrated by Andrew Jackson and Alexis de Tocqueville. Disdaining to court popularity, Kent denounced universal suffrage as "that extreme democratic principle" that would "jeopardize the rights of property and the principles of liberty." He darkly warned of the dangers of a communistic redistribution of property: a legislature elected by universal suffrage would "divide the whole capital [of society] upon the principles of an agrarian law."[44]

We have already seen how metaconstitutional ideas about higher law affected early labor law in New York in the *Cordwainers* and *Fisher* cases. Two other subjects also had an irresistible appeal to conservative jurists seeking to replace legislative policy making with their own economic views: the Married Women's Property Acts and the movement to outlaw alcoholic beverages. In both areas, New York courts led the way in applying higher-law doctrines.

In *White* v. *White* (1849), the New York Supreme Court indignantly struck down a statute that divested husbands of rights in the property of their wives, stating that "the security of the citizen against such arbitrary legislation rests upon the broader and more solid ground of natural rights" and does not require explicit support in the state constitution.[45] But contemporary jurists recognized that such ethereal notions would not long withstand the onslaught of Jacksonian Democratic ideas about legislative superiority. In the 1856 case of *Wynehamer* v. *The People*, involving a prohibition statute, the New York Court of Appeals secured higher law in the more solid ground of provisions in the state constitution, becoming thereby the first American court to articulate the doctrine of substantive due process. The court construed the law-of-the-land and due process clauses of the state constitution to mean "that where rights are acquired by the citizen under the existing law, there is no power in any branch of the government to take them away."[46]

After the Civil War, New York judges continued to expound the idea that the due process clause was a check on the substance of state legislation. In the 1885 case of *In re Jacobs*, the Court of Appeals struck down a statute that prohibited the manufacture of cigars in residential tenements, declaring that "under the mere guise of police regulations, personal rights and private property cannot be arbitrarily invaded, and the determination of the legislature is not final or conclusive."[47] Four years later, Judge Rufus Peckham of the New York Court of Appeals attempted to dethrone the United States Supreme Court's reasoning in *Munn* v. *Illinois* (1877),[48] denouncing legislative rate regulation as "vicious in its nature [and] communistic in its tendency" (*People* v. *Budd* [1889], Peckham, J., dissenting).[49]

Peckham had the opportunity to ensconce his views as constitutional dogma when he was elevated to the United States Supreme Court by President Grover Cleveland (himself a New Yorker). In doing so, Peckham projected New York's development of substantive due process in its most virulently reactionary form onto the nation's public law. In *Allgeyer v. Louisiana* (1897),[50] Peckham created the doctrine of liberty of contract, a child of substantive due process that outgrew its parent and became responsible for gutting innumerable pieces of regulatory legislation through the New Deal. But the apotheosis of substantive due process came in another Peckham opinion, speaking for the majority in *Lochner v. New York* (1905),[51] where he condemned New York maximum hours legislation as "mere meddlesome interferences with the rights of the individual."

Finally, the New York Court of Appeals once again attained some *ne plus ultra* of substantive due process judicial lawmaking in *Ives v. South Buffalo Railway* (1911) by striking down New York's Worker's Compensation statute on substantive due process grounds.[52] This went too far for even so conservative a political leader as President William Howard Taft, who conceded that the decision typified "a hidebound and retrograde conservatism on the part of courts in decisions which turn on the individual economic or sociological views of the judges."[53]

These higher law/substantive due process decisions of New York courts and judges pose an uncomfortable challenge to the libertarian values of the present. Nearly all people, even judicial conservatives like Chief Justice of the United States William H. Rehnquist, condemn *Lochner* and its ilk as judicial arrogation of policy-making power properly belonging to the legislature.[54] Yet at the same time, nearly all Americans espouse some role for courts in refusing to give effect to legislative policy that deprives individuals of substantive rights guaranteed by the Constitution explicitly (e.g., speech) or implicitly (e.g., privacy). How do we identify and reject what was wrong with this line of New York jurisprudence and retain the juristic achievements of the New York courts that derived from permanent values in the American constitutional tradition?

What lessons may we legitimately draw from this survey of the impact of New York law on individual liberty before the twentieth century? First, a historian's caveat: the theme of this book is the search for a usable past. Such talk makes most historians uneasy. We are uncomfortable with the idea of *using* the past. It sounds manipulative. Lawyers, by contrast, gladly use the past; why not? What are briefs, arguments before legislative committees, and judicial opinions but reflections on the past and efforts to draw lessons from that past to guide future conduct? But the historian does not see it that way. The past may be explored, understood, interpreted. It teaches us and is our master, not the other way around. The past just does not lend itself to being used by historians. When we try to do so, it turns into a rope of sand in our hands. Jefferson Powell reminds us that the past is a mirror that demonstrates to us the contingency of the present.[55] Its principal lesson is that things did not have to turn out the way they did in our time. And that, I think, is all that the past can be used for.

But though history cannot be used, it has much to teach us. One of the principal lessons we find there is that the states have played an important role in protecting or limiting the content of individual liberties. Far from being the only player in the game, the federal government before the twentieth century was not even the most important one. Its role has greatly expanded since World War I, but even today it has not entirely eclipsed the states. Nor will it. The states retain great potential as sources for the growth or diminution of our liberties in the twenty-first century. But as with every other aspect of human affairs, nothing is inevitable. Whether the states in fact realize that potential depends on us, the American people, and our evolving understanding of the federal system in which our law functions. We can discard the role of the states if we wish, but I believe, with Louis Brandeis, that that decision would be a tragedy. Whether a century from now Professor Hall's view or mine will have prevailed will depend not on how we use the past but on the lessons we draw from it. To paraphrase slightly Benjamin Franklin's bon mot quoted so often in the past constitutional bicentennial year, we have republics, if we can keep them.

Notes

The title of this essay is taken from Sir Lewis Namier, "Symmetry and Repetition," in Namier, *Conflicts: Studies in Contemporary History* (London: Macmillan, 1942), 70.

1. Kermit L. Hall, "Mostly Anchor and Little Sail: The Evolution of American State Constitutions," in this volume.

2. Vincent Bonventre, "State Constitutionalism in New York: A Non-Reactive Tradition," *Emerging Issues in State Constitutional Law* 2 (1989): 31.

3. Hon. Ellen A. Peters, "Common Law Antecedents of Constitutional Law in Connecticut," in this volume.

4. The charter is reprinted in *Sources and Documents of United States Constitutions* (Dobbs Ferry, N.Y.: Oceana Publications, 1973–78), 7:164–67; see David S. Lovejoy, "Equality and Empire: The New York Charter of Libertyes, 1683," *William and Mary Quarterly* 3d ser., 21 (1964): 493–515.

5. An Act for Establishing Courts of Judicature (1691), in *Colonial Laws of New York from 1664 to the Revolution* (Albany: J. B. Lyons State Printer, 1894), 1:226; see Note, "Law in Colonial New York: The Legal System of 1691," *Harvard Law Review* 80 (1967): 1757.

6. See generally Paul Finkelman, "Alexander Hamilton, Esq.: Founding Father as Lawyer," *American Bar Foundation Research Journal* (1984): 229–52.

7. *Rutgers* v. *Waddington*, N.Y. Mayor's Court, 1784, in *The Law Practice of Alexander Hamilton: Documents and Commentary*, ed. Julius Goebel, Jr. (New York: Columbia University Press, 1964), 1:304–6, 338ff. On judicial review, see also H. Jefferson Powell, "The Uses of State Constitutional History: A Case Note," in this volume.

8. 1 N.C. (Mart.) 42 (1787).

9. *People* v. *Croswell*, N.Y. Sup. Ct. 1803–4; Hamilton quoted in *Law Practice of Hamilton*, ed. Goebel, 1:818. Croswell's prosecution was eventually abandoned.

10. *A Brief Narrative of the Case and Trial of John Peter Zenger*, ed. Stanley N. Katz (Cambridge, Mass.: Belknap Press of Harvard University Press, 1972), 65–79.

11. Laws of N.Y. 1805, ch. 90.

12. N.Y. Const. 1821, art. VII, §8; N.Y. Const. 1846, art. I, §8, in *Sources and Documents*, ed. Swindler, 7:187, 193.

13. *People* v. *Ruggles*, 8 Johns. 290 (N.Y. Sup. Ct. 1811).

14. 343 U.S. 495 (1951).

15. David Kobrin, *The Black Minority in Early New York* (Albany: University of the State of New York, State Education Department Office of State History, 1971), 11–13.

16. Kenneth Scott, "The Slave Insurrection in New York in 1712," *New-York Historical Society Quarterly* 45 (1961): 43–74; Daniel Horsmanden, *The New-York Conspiracy*, ed. Thomas J. Davis (1744; rpt. 1810; rpt. Boston: Beacon Press, 1971).

17. Vt. Const. 1777, ch. 1, I, in *Sources and Documents*, ed. Swindler, 9:489.

18. Reprinted in *The First Laws of the Commonwealth of Pennsylvania*, ed. John D. Cushing (Wilmington, Del.: Glazier Publishing, 1984), 282–87.

19. On the history of slavery and its abolition in New York, see Edgar J. McManus, *A History of Negro Slavery in New York* (Syracuse: Syracuse University Press, 1966); A. Leon Higginbotham, *In the Matter of Color: Race and the American Legal Process, The Colonial Period* (New York: Oxford University Press, 1978), 100–150; and Arthur Zilversmit, *The First Emancipation: The Abolition of Slavery in the North* (Chicago: University of Chicago Press, 1967).

20. N.Y. Laws 1799, ch. 62.

21. N.Y. Laws 1817, ch. 137.

22. N.Y. Const. 1821, art. II, §1, in *Sources and Documents*, ed. Swindler, 7:183. Before 1821, both blacks and whites labored under the same suffrage requirement. Its abolition for whites in 1821 by adoption of white manhood suffrage left blacks under the old disability.

23. N.Y. Laws 1840, ch. 224.

24. For upstate abolitionist activity, see Gerald Sorin, *The New York Abolitionists: A Case Study of Political Radicalism* (Westport, Conn.: Greenwood, 1971). Bertram Wyatt-Brown, *Lewis Tappan and the Evangelical War against Slavery* (Cleveland: Press of Case Western Reserve University, 1969), covers the New York City node of the abolitionist movement.

25. See his "States Rights North and South in Antebellum America," in *An Uncertain Tradition: Constitutionalism and the History of the South*, ed. Kermit Hall and James W. Ely, Jr. (Athens: University of Georgia Press, 1989), 141–44; and "The Protection of Black Rights in Seward's New York," *Civil War History* 34 (1988): 211–34.

26. 5 How. (46 U.S.) 215 (1847); Salmon P. Chase, *Reclamation of Fugitives from Services . . .* (Cincinnati: B. P. Donough, 1847).

27. 20 N.Y. 562 (1860).

28. 60 U.S. (19 How.) 393 (1856).

29. James Willard Hurst, *Law and the Conditions of Freedom in the Nineteenth-Century United States* (Madison: University of Wisconsin Press, 1956), chap. 1.

30. *Trial of the Journeymen Cordwainers of the City of New York for a Conspiracy to Raise Their Wages* (1810), reprinted in John R. Commons et al., *A Documentary History of American Industrial Society* (Cleveland: A. H. Clark Co., 1910–11), 3:251–385.

31. 14 Wend. 6 (N.Y. 1835).

32. 45 Mass. (4 Met.) 45.

33. 9 Johns. 507 (seriatim opinions of Lansing, Ch. and Kent, C.J.).

34. 22 U.S. (9 Wheat.) 1 (1824).

35. Curiously, this immensely important subject has never received the treatment it deserves, uniting a review of its various economic, geo-

political, social, intellectual, religious, and technological impacts. The
Erie Canal cries for treatment in the grand manner.

36. The foremost treatment is Harry N. Scheiber, *Ohio Canal Era: A Case
Study of Government and the Economy, 1820–1861* (Athens: Ohio University Press, 1968).

37. Henry Christian, *Tin Horns and Calico: A Decisive Episode in the Emergence
of Democracy* (New York: Holt Publishing, 1945).

38. Pauline Maier, "Popular Uprisings and Political Authority in Eighteenth-
Century America," *William and Mary Quarterly* 3d ser., 27 (1970):
3–35.

39. N.Y. Const. 1846, in *Sources and Documents*, ed. Swindler, 7:192–208.

40. 3 Paige Ch. 42 (N.Y. Ch., 1831).

41. 61 Mass. (7 Cush.) 53 (1851).

42. 3 U.S. (3 Dall.) 386 (1798).

43. 2 Johns. Ch. 162 (N.Y. Ch., 1816).

44. *Democracy, Liberty, and Property: The State Constitutional Conventions of
the 1820s*, ed. Merrill D. Peterson (Indianapolis: Bobbs-Merrill, 1966),
194, 196.

45. 5 Barb. Ch. 474 (N.Y. Ch., 1849).

46. 13 N.Y. 378 (1856).

47. 98 N.Y. 98 (1885).

48. 94 U.S. 113 (1877).

49. 117 N.Y. 1 (1889).

50. 165 U.S. 578 (1897).

51. 198 U.S. 45 (1905).

52. 201 N.Y. 271 (1911).

53. Taft veto of Arizona Enabling Act (1911) in *The Messages and Papers of the
Presidents*, comp. James D. Richardson (New York: Bureau of National
Literature and Art, 1897–1907), 11:7637–44.

54. William H. Rehnquist, "The Notion of a Living Constitution," *Texas
Law Review* 54 (1976): 693.

55. Powell, "Uses of State Constitutional History."

Mostly Anchor and Little Sail

The Evolution of American State Constitutions

Kermit L. Hall

 In 1857 the English historian Thomas Babington Macaulay described the American Constitution as "all sail and no anchor."[1] Macaulay believed that centrifugal social demands, most notably slavery, would ultimately rip the fabric of America's ruling document. In the short run, he was prescient; little more than four years later the nation exploded in its greatest constitutional crisis, the Civil War. Over the longer term, however, the forces of sail and anchor balanced one another far more effectively than Macaulay imagined. No other nation today has had a longer history of government under a written constitution, a development that scholars attribute either to the framers' foresight, the structure of the Constitution itself, or both.[2] The difficult amending process in Article V, for example, has shielded the Constitution from abrupt change, and the Supreme Court, sitting as a kind of continuing constitutional convention, has invoked judicial review to forge broad changes in public life through appeal to the rule of law.[3] Sir William Gladstone, another nineteenth-century Englishman, concluded that the resulting combination of stability and adaptability formed the "genius" of the Constitution. He described the document as "the most remarkable work . . . to have been produced by the human intellect, at a single stroke."[4]

Much present-day scholarship echoes this Gladstonian analysis by interpreting the nation's constitutional history and public law as the unfolding majesty of the federal document.[5] State constitutions, however, have received short shrift, even though they were by more than a decade the "first" American constitutions, even though they provided the crucial working models for the framers in Philadelphia, and even though they have historically provided much of the grist for the nation's rich constitutional politics. The Massachusetts Constitution of 1780, for example, is the world's oldest working written frame of government.[6] Despite this inheritance, state constitutions have claimed neither the same level of scholarly attention nor of public prestige as has the federal document. Law schools, where such matters should be taken seriously, devote far more attention to federal constitutional law than to the public law of the states.[7] Scholars from other disciplines have proven only slightly more attentive.[8]

The scholarly problem of state constitutions involves more than neglect. Rather, an appreciation of them promises to shed new light on the extent to which the genius—the ability to be both anchor and sail—of the federal Constitution has been shared by its state counterparts and what, if anything, the federal document has contributed to their development. Both the federal Constitution and state constitutions (and the constitutional systems they have established) have resonated to social and economic demands.[9] Although scholars wrestle with the problem of how social demands shape public law, there seems little doubt that American constitutional history has been more like a river than a rock.[10] But to say that state constitutions tended to mirror social demands, like the assertion that they have been neglected, is only the beginning of wisdom.

This essay explores some of the implications of the federal and state documents for each other and for the political process they have shaped. First, it examines some state-level developments related to specific provisions in the federal document. Second, it probes the ways in which state-level constitutional provisions served to "fill in" the blank pages left intentionally incomplete by the framers in Philadelphia.[11] Third, it charts the consequences for the federal system of the states filling in these blank pages by examining the history of state constitutional traditions. The essay concludes that in some ways the genius of the Constitution backfired insofar as state constitutions were concerned. Populist and majoritarian impulses in the states produced documents of ever greater length that were more like codes than fundamental laws. They constrained the operations of state governments and prompted social and economic minorities to secure federal constitutional authority to regulate the consequences of industrialization and to fulfill the rising expectations for social equality. Stronger central government was the ironic consequence of the propensity of state constitutions to become more anchor than sail.

The Relationship of the Federal and State Constitutions

State-Level Constitutional Developments Related to Specific Federal Constitutional Provisions

On first impression, the federal Constitution would seem to have had a huge impact on the state documents, so much so that the former would seem to swallow up the latter. The federal Constitution is, as Article VI proclaims, supreme; the states cannot with impunity violate its explicit mandates.[12] The Constitution is subordinate only to the people of the United States, but the state constitutions are subordinate to the national Constitution in substantial ways, as well as to the people of the states. Even accepting that the federal document is one of enumerated powers (considerably expanded by the necessary and proper clause in Article I), the fact remains that the framers of state constitutions have crafted their constitutional identities within this national framework.[13]

The original text and amendments to the Constitution constitute a mix of restrictions and guarantees that have defined the boundaries of state constitutions. Today, for example, the federal document prohibits states from abridging individual rights, granting titles of nobility, coining money, conducting foreign policy, engaging in war, laying duties on tonnage, maintaining troops and a navy, making compacts with other states, and collecting poll taxes in federal elections.[14] These prohibitions are real limitations on the discretion of state constitution makers. Perhaps the most vivid evidence of the shaping influence of the text of the federal document appeared during Reconstruction in the states of the former Confederacy. To gain readmittance to the Union, these states had to abjure the "right" of secession and embrace the broad commands of the Fourteenth Amendment. As the North Carolina Constitution of 1868 proclaimed: "Every citizen of this

State owes paramount allegiance to the Constitution and Government of the United States."[15] In more recent times, passage of the Sixteenth Amendment, authorizing a federal income tax, has produced a series of "federalized" amendments to state constitutions authorizing the definition or computation of income for state tax purposes by reference to federal law.[16]

The text of the federal Constitution also provides certain guarantees to the states that, just as much as the prohibitions, tailor their fundamental laws. Article IV, for example, guarantees every state a republican form of government and the privilege of calling upon the federal government to protect it from internal domestic upheaval.[17] The federal government pledges to protect the states from foreign invasion and to ensure equality for a citizen of one state in another state. The federal Constitution, in section 2 of the Fourteenth Amendment, guarantees that apportionment in the national Congress shall be based on population in the states.[18]

The federal Constitution also has a symbolic and analogic relationship to state constitutions. The federal Constitution was, in many of its provisions, the creation of the framers' initial experience with state constitution making. As Willi Paul Adams has shown, in matters such as separation of powers, popular sovereignty, and an independent judiciary, the framers in Philadelphia borrowed heavily from that experience.[19] Thereafter, as a growing and restless American population spread across the continent, the states of the ever-moving West mimicked their eastern counterparts. But they also copied, in form and spirit, the broad principles of constitutionalism embodied in the federal document. A sort of cult of the Constitution appeared almost immediately, and the framers of subsequent state constitutions believed that their documents reflected the same spirit of republican government that had informed events in Philadelphia.[20]

The federal courts and Congress have translated federal constitutional provisions into meaningful, if often hotly disputed, guidelines for state constitution makers. The Thirteenth, Fourteenth, and Fifteenth amendments, for example, clothed federal judges and Congress with substantial authority, if they wished to invoke it, to alter state constitutional practices dealing with race relations and the distribution of political power. In the last part of the nineteenth century, southern constitution makers fashioned fundamental frames of government that aimed to preserve white supremacy. Racial segregation

became a matter of fundamental law, and the Supreme Court countenanced it as such. As early as 1870, the Tennessee Constitution
provided that no school aided by the state "shall allow white and
negro children to be received as scholars together." [21] Segregation and
disfranchisement went hand-in-hand. The Mississippi Constitution of
1890 set up a poll tax of two dollars and imposed reading requirements on all electors. The federal courts tested many of these provisions, finding a few wanting but sustaining most. Thus in *Williams* v.
Mississippi (1898) the Supreme Court approved both the literacy and
poll-tax provisions of the Mississippi Constitution,[22] but it ruled as unconstitutional so-called grandfather clauses in several southern state
constitutions that excused the sons and grandsons of Civil War white
voters from having to meet educational and property qualifications.[23]
In the mid-twentieth century, the Court reversed its direction and
wiped out, through its decision in *Brown* v. *Board of Education of Topeka,
Kansas* and subsequent cases, entire sections of southern state constitutional law.[24]

Congress, too, has frequently shaped state constitutional development. After the creation of the Union by the original thirteen states,
the process of admitting new states became a function wholly controlled by the national government, and Congress specifically. Article
IV, section 4, of the U.S. Constitution required the federal government
to guarantee that each new state had a "Republican form of Government." [25] Because the vastness of the continent created anxiety over the
coherence and stability of a nation of individual republics, Congress
took care to ensure that the people of the new states would understand themselves to be citizens of the larger nation, sharing not only a
commitment to republican rights and liberties but also an allegiance to
the larger polity based on those principles. One consequence was an
extraordinary degree of mimesis by state constitution makers. After
all, their chief objective was to gain admission to the Union, and they
paved the road to statehood by adopting the constitutional provisions
of existing states.[26]

Moreover, when combined with the guarantee clause, the constitutional authority of Congress to set terms of admission of new states
shaped substantive state policies. Public education was a notable example. The federal government supported under the guarantee clause
the working assumption that public education was an "essential feature of a republican government based upon the will of the people." [27]

In the nineteenth century, building on the experience of the North-west Ordinance of 1787, Congress enforced this goal through grants of public lands to the states, stipulating that the states would de-vote part of the public domain to foster public education. Nineteenth-century state constitution makers responded by devising ever more elaborate provisions guaranteeing public education and mandating bureaucratic structures in detailed constitutional provisions. Thus the federal document, through congressional initiative, pressed upon the states specific requirements to provide educational institutions.

The Implications of the Incomplete Federal Constitution for
State Constitutions

The inherent supremacy of the federal Constitution belies the con-siderable discretion enjoyed by the states, both in chartering their constitutional course and, as the experience with the Civil War and Reconstruction amendments suggests, in diluting the force of federal pronouncements. Moreover, though the federal Constitution men-tions the states some fifty times, it does not specify anything about the operation of state government, save that it should be republican in character. The federal Constitution, as Donald Lutz reminds us, was *"by design* an incomplete document." [28] By this phrase, Lutz meant that the Constitution did not describe fully the operation of government and politics throughout the nation. The framers purposefully left that task to state constitution makers, a responsibility that meant that the states forged the main lines of the American political process and provided for day-to-day governance of a host of social and economic matters.

Much of the constitutional history of the states (not to mention of the nation through the states) can be understood as a working out of the implications of the incomplete nature of the federal document. Succeeding generations of Americans have adapted their organic laws to changing social and economic circumstances. The proximity of the states to these pressures meant that constitutional experimentation became much more brisk there than at the federal level. These inno-vations included, among others, popular election of judges, women's suffrage, equal rights for women, black disfranchisement and black suffrage, the income tax, and prohibition. In this vein, proposed amendments to today's federal Constitution calling for a balanced federal budget and the line-item veto merely confirm an existing pattern of borrowing by the nation from the states.[29]

The states have been the world's oldest and most active laboratories of constitutional experimentation. Despite social, geographical, and economic differences, they have had remarkably similar experiences. All state constitutions have organized the polity, the relations between the state and its people, and the responsibilities of its officers. They also have been documents of constitutional law that embrace concepts such as sovereignty, individual rights, separation of powers, and judicial review. Each has provided for a legislature (and all of them today except Nebraska's are bicameral), an elected chief executive, and a judiciary. In these respects, they have generally mirrored the federal Constitution, and their provisions underscore that even the incomplete nature of that document did not make state constitutional development a free-for-all. Moreover, like the federal Constitution, state constitutions have rested government authority on popular consent.[30]

State constitutions derive from several historical epochs. Although most can be dated from the nineteenth century, the heyday of state constitutional development, eighteen were either created or totally rewritten in the twentieth century. Three documents—the constitutions of Massachusetts (1780), New Hampshire (1784), and Vermont (1793)—are products of the eighteenth century. Fifteen state constitutions were formulated during the last quarter of the nineteenth century, eleven date from the period 1860 to 1874, and three from the first half of the nineteenth century.[31]

Most state constitutions have also been remarkably pliable, a quality essential to their function of filling the vacant spaces of the federal document. Revision of the federal Constitution has proceeded gradually and incrementally. There has never been a second federal constitutional convention. The state experience has been the opposite; states have easily shed one organic law for an entirely new one. There have been 239 separate constitutional conventions, and since the beginning of the republic there has never been a three-year period in which at least one state constitutional convention or, more recently, a constitutional revision commission has not met. Since 1776 the fifty states have operated under no fewer than 146 constitutions and thirty-one of the fifty states have had 2 or more constitutions. Eighteen states have had 4 or more constitutions, with Louisiana topping the list with 11. On average, each state constitution has been amended four times more frequently than the federal document. Through 1985 more than eight thousand amendments to state constitutions were voted on and more than five thousand of these were adopted.[32]

All this activity suggests a key feature of state constitutions: they have increasingly become codes rather than fundamental frames of government. The federal Constitution today contains approximately 7,300 words; only the Vermont constitution among the states is shorter at an estimated 6,600 words. In 1776 the average length of state constitutions was 7,150 words; by 1985 it had ballooned to approximately 26,150 words. The present Alabama Constitution, at approximately 250,000 words, is now the nation's longest, a distinction that the quarter-million-word Louisiana Constitution claimed until it was drastically shortened in 1974.[33]

State constitutions, unlike the federal document, have evolved into lengthy documents of modest age that have been repeatedly amended and frequently recreated entirely. As stable representations of fundamental principles and timeless structures they pale before the federal Constitution.

The federal character of the national document encouraged this development by granting the states significant discretion in shaping their own constitutions.[34] As documents essential to the functioning of the incomplete federal Constitution and as subordinate entities to it, state constitutions evolved at least five distinctive regional traditions or patterns of development. Each of these reveals the way in which state constitution makers at particular places and times adapted fundamental law to constituent social and economic pressures, prevailing ideological assumptions about the nature of government, and the dictates as well as the opportunities created by the incomplete federal Constitution.

The Traditions of State Constitutional Adaptation Within the Federal Constitutional System

The Genesis of the State Constitutionalism: The Whig-Republican Tradition

The first of these constitutional traditions emerged from the same matrix of colonial precedent, English political dissent, and revolution that fostered the federal Constitution.[35] The Whig-republican tradition appeared between 1776 and 1800, and it mixed notions of re-publicanism, popular sovereignty, distrust of executive authority, and communitarianism through social contract theory.[36] It set standards for representation that abetted political inequality as we understand it today because it excluded women and blacks from political partici-pation, often required a modest freehold to vote and hold office, and every state but New York and Virginia required a religious test for officeholding. The federal Constitution, of course, addressed none of these matters specifically, other than the exclusion of religious tests. The legislative branch had great authority to determine community goals and to enforce compliance. The state took precedence over the individual, but these documents also made the protection of rights one of the primary purposes of government. Hence by about 1800, formal bills of rights, which limited state interference with individuals (and which had not been part of many of the first state constitutions), became common.[37]

The Whig-republican tradition incorporated such concepts as small electoral districts, short tenure in office, many elective offices, sharp separation of powers (including an independent judiciary), and constituent instruction of representatives. These brief documents, like the federal Constitution that was so extensively based on them, broadly stated the first principles of government and left to subse-quent generations the task of adapting them to the exigencies of social and economic change.[38] Over time, of course, the federal judiciary (and Congress) performed this task at the national level, while in the states more formal modes of direct constitutional change—constitu-tional conventions, amendments, and direct popular control through the initiative and referendum—eventually took hold.

The Federalist delegates to the Philadelphia Convention in 1787 challenged many features of this Whig-republican tradition. The domi-nant group, led by James Madison of Virginia, crafted provisions in the federal document designed to stem radical majoritarianism in the states and to enhance the authority of the new national Union. These Federalists, like spokesmen for the Whig-republican tradition in the states, embraced the idea that all powers of government derived from the people, but they purposefully curbed the direct impact of popu-lar sovereignty on the national government. They did so by asserting the supremacy of the federal Constitution and then balancing indi-vidual and group interests by means of larger electoral districts, longer tenures of office, an independent judiciary (which held office during good behavior), limited numbers of elective offices, and a system of separated institutional sharing of powers.[39]

A second group of Federalists, led by Alexander Hamilton, believed in an even more comprehensive expansion of national powers. Their goal was to enhance the wealth of the nation by protecting property holders and promoting the nation's commercial interests through government action. They were even more critical than the Madisonians of what they perceived to be the great authority exercised by state legislatures. They succeeded in the federal Constitution in strengthening the executive at the expense of the legislative branch, a development that also became common in the states by about 1800. These Federalists embraced what Daniel Elazar has called the "managerial tradition."[40] Principles of commerce were central to this conception of constitutionalism because the purpose of the polity was to support the commercial classes. Hamilton accepted that popular will should be the basis of sovereign authority, but he also believed that the wishes of the people should be virtually rather than actually represented. Thus a strong chief executive, whether president or governor, was supposed to administer public affairs rationally, free from political and popular influence. The growing wealth of the American commercial empire would redound eventually to the benefit of all citizens. Of course, the Anti-Federalists who opposed the Constitution rejected just this view of representation and of executive authority, but the managerial tradition posed an important challenge to the much more democratic and localistic Whig-republican tradition.[41]

The Whig-republican tradition took firmest root in New England, where it remains important today.[42] But modifications, as the federalist and managerial patterns suggest, quickly appeared. State political leaders adapted their fundamental laws to correspond to particular social and economic interests. These early constitutions, of course, were conceptual documents that, like the federal Constitution, broadly stated their objectives. They were as much shaped, however, by interest as by abstract ideas. State constitutions in almost every instance, save for New England, where the Whig-republican tradition persisted, became increasingly specific and lengthy, reflecting in their mounting detail not only changing conceptions of the role of government but the consequences of moving from an eighteenth-century agrarian society to the postindustrial present.

Nineteenth-Century Patterns of State Constitutional Development

This process of adaptation, given the social, economic, political, and cultural diversity of the regions of the new nation, spawned four major constitutional patterns, each of which was a variation upon and a blending of the Whig-republican, federalist, or managerial models.[43]

The Whig-republican tradition underwent the least modification in New England, a region that has historically had the briefest constitutions and the ones least responsive to fads in government. These documents embraced a distinctively American principle, that of the commonwealth. Despite their brevity, they did more than sketch a basic framework of government and provide for individual rights. They also encouraged legislative activism with a view to harnessing a state's resources to release the creative potential of its people.[44] The "commonwealth idea," Leonard W. Levy has written, "was essentially a quasi-mercantilist conception of the state within a democratic framework." In Europe, where the state was not responsible to the people and was the product of remote historical forces, mercantilism served the ruling classes who controlled the state.[45] In America, under the commonwealth theory of constitutional government, the state was no night watchman; instead, it was an intensely real and immediate force in the day-to-day lives of the citizens it served. The state was the "common wealth" of all the people, and government was responsible for giving effect to it.

Massachusetts became the model of this commonwealth tradition. There, for example, the state legislature drew upon the extensive police powers granted it in the Constitution to regulate weights and measures, provide standard measures for commodities, establish rules for packaging, and provide for inspection to ensure that laws were followed. Typical was the remarkably detailed regulation of the nailmaking industry in Massachusetts. In a series of statutes, the General Court (the legislature of the state) set exacting standards for the number, size, and weight of iron nails to be packed in casks.[46]

This commonwealth principle strongly influenced the antebellum free northern states, but in at least eight of them a variant pattern, that of commercial republicanism, appeared. This model, which took its most notable form in Ohio and Wisconsin, stressed the role of government in promoting private commercial activity while leaving other areas of human activity free of state interference. At the same time, the slave states of the South, which were much more sympathetic to the federalist model, fashioned a southern contractual pattern. The ruling documents of these states, though predicated as much as those in the North on popular sovereignty, stressed the limiting influence of the social contract on the authority of the states to interfere with basic institutions, most notably slavery.[47] Both of these patterns underscored the adaptive process by which the interests and ideals of migrants from the settled states were redefined on a transcontinental scale.

The commercial republican tradition spread into the trans-Appalachian West and beyond as migrants from New England and the Middle States adapted their learned constitutional traditions to new surroundings. Throughout the nineteenth century these documents embodied compromises resulting from conflict among rival ethnic and economic interests and the overlapping tension generated between the growing commercial cities and the still influential agricultural regions within each state. The constitutions of the commercial republican tradition grew in length, in part because compromising these tensions required more rather than fewer words and in part because their framers pursued through them a mercantilist policy designed to promote commercial economic development. The pursuit of commercial wealth, as in the Illinois Constitution of 1848, shaped provisions such as the organization of local government, public education, and public welfare.[48] Like the constitutions of the commonwealth tradition, the new commercial-republican documents relied on promotion and regulation to enhance the economy, but they differed from the former in that they also sought compromise among contending economic groups (farmers and merchants) and rival ethnic groups.

The organic laws of the South also had mercantilist objectives, and they too grew in length in comparison to the simple documents of the Whig-republican tradition. Their framers had the additional burden of perpetuating a social and economic system first rooted in slavery and later in segregation. Constitution makers in these states, especially after Reconstruction, increasingly sought to maintain the social order by adding provisions involving race and economic matters that in most other regions of the country were left to legislative discretion. This southern contractual tradition was typified by a diffusion of authority among many offices to accommodate the swings between "oligarchy and factionalism characteristic of Southern state politics."[49]

Because of the fluctuating balance of factions in many southern states, the framers of their constitutions included materials typically the subject of ordinary legislation outside the section.[50]

The rise of mass political parties in the mid-1830s contributed to the diffusion of constitutional traditions, the increasing detail that filled most fundamental frames of government outside of New England, and the negative tone of these documents. As Morton Keller has observed, state constitutions of this era became "deeply mired in party politics and changing social and economic interests."[51] Whigs and Jacksonian Democrats in state constitutional conventions of this period, in comparison with the often benign factionalism and deferential politics of earlier gatherings, struggled to legitimate their partisan goals through recourse to constitutional authority. They politicized constitution making along partisan lines and developed the practice of constitutional legislation—that is, writing specific provisions that could not be won through the usual legislative processes into constitutions. The less troublesome, but nonetheless contentious, issues involved free public education, state support for the indigent, and an end to religious tests for political participation. In the South constitution makers formally recognized the institution of slavery, and in almost every state, as in the North at the same time, they extended the franchise to adult white males and disfranchised free blacks.[52] The notion of state constitutions as fundamental frames of government waned, and constitutional legislation appeared with greater frequency.[53]

The states' roles in economic development provoked the most serious partisan wrangling. The formal division of sovereignty in American federalism notwithstanding, the states exercised the most influence over public policy before the Civil War. State lawmakers formulated mercantilist policies under the police power, the concurrent power over interstate commerce, and the power of eminent domain. They broadly construed their constitutional authority to promote banking, internal improvements, and transportation. State appellate courts lent their support as well by embracing an instrumental conception of the common law that rewarded risk taking and freed the creative energies of individuals in the marketplace.[54]

The political aftershocks of the Panic of 1837, however, sparked many state constitution makers to curb mercantilist policies and spendthrift legislatures. The delegates to the Ohio constitutional convention of 1850–51, for example, had soured on the legislature's enthusiasm for public promotion of canals and railroads. They placed language in the new constitution that restricted the power of the state legislature to authorize theretofore popular "loans of credit" to local governments, clamped new limits on corporations, and generally proscribed state support of private enterprise of all kinds.[55]

This reaction to the Panic of 1837 had two important long-term consequences. First, state constitutions departed from the republican model by limiting the power of legislative bodies. More and more these documents became a litany of restrictions. These prohibitions, which aimed to reduce the influence of special interests on state government, dramatically increased the length of constitutions. The Ohio Constitution of 1851, for example, was almost twice as long as its predecessor. Constitutional revision increasingly became the conduct of legislation—or of politics—through other means, and the documents themselves resembled statutory codes rather than organic laws.[56]

Second, judicial and executive authority grew apace as state government evolved even more into a shared exercise of power among the three branches. The judiciary became popularly elected for limited terms of office, a reform that simultaneously made judges more accountable to public needs while granting them a popular base from which to scrutinize legislative enactments. Long-suffering chief executives received additional authority to veto legislation, to exercise the pardoning power, and to make appointments.[57]

Except in New England, where the commonwealth variant of the Whig-republican tradition persisted, state constitutions reflected a deep suspicion of government, itself a reaction to the growing influence of parties in American life. The quest for more democratic government during these years was nothing less than a search for greater popular accountability in government. The Mississippi Constitution of 1832, in a pattern that became unexceptional later in the nineteenth century, merged populism with a pervasive distrust of government. In essence, state constitutions became antigovernment, stripping from political officials the legal authority they needed to govern. The assumptions underlying state constitutions were not just laissez-faire; they were positively hostile, save in a few limited areas, to the exercise of government power either to regulate or promote. Increased openness in state government was accompanied, ironically, by growing antigovernmentalism. Mississippi, at the edge of the expanding southern frontier, provided for universal white manhood suffrage, the election of all state officers, the replacement of county courts by elected boards of police as county governing boards, and the election of all judges.[58] This new populism was not meant to empower but rather to limit government.

Persistent antigovernmentalism also surfaced in the increasingly difficult provisions made for constitutional amendment and in the acceptance of the idea that the work of constitutional conventions had to be submitted to the public for ratification. Having subdued legislative authority, mid-nineteenth-century constitution makers were loath to have their work easily undone. Constitutional conventions became all the more important and further politicized constitutional development.[59] Under such circumstances, constitutional conventions became arenas for the working out of particular, ongoing conflicts rather than restating fundamental principles.[60] Issues that proved intractable in the regular legislative process could be resolved only through constitutional conventions, and more often than not the solution was to limit the power of the state.

This populist approach to state constitutions rejected the older Whig-republican notion of communitarianism and substituted in its place an essentially negative, antigovernment conception that sought through public law to balance diverse social and geographical interests within the states. Like the national document, state constitutions exemplified the deep distrust with which state residents viewed their governments and the persons who represented them. But unlike the national document, these populistic state constitutions were far more susceptible to majority control.[61]

State constitutions began to lose the creative energy—the sail-like quality—of earlier decades at about the same time the expansive qualities of federal fundamental law became apparent. The pre–Civil War generation had enormous confidence in its ability to shape events through state constitutions, but these increasingly wordy frames of government offered, as their framers intended, limited interpretive possibilities. For example, the incidence of state appellate courts overturning legislative enactments rose dramatically in the 1850s because the judiciary had to apply the many restrictive provisions in state constitutions and because state appellate judges were typically elected and, therefore, poorly situated to expand significantly the active role of government.[62] At the same time, their more independent federal counterparts, led by Chief Justice John Marshall, creatively applied the open provisions of the federal document in adapting constitutional law to the exigencies of social and economic change.[63]

James Bryce in 1880 reported how far this process had gone. "We find a great deal of matter [in state constitutions]," he concluded, "which is in no distinctive sense constitutional law, but of general law. . . . We find minute provisions regarding the management and liabilities of banking companies, or railways, or of corporations generally." Bryce went on to observe that "the framers of these more recent constitutions have in fact neither wished nor cared to draw a line of distinction between what is proper for a constitution and what ought to be left to be dealt with by the State legislature."[64]

Bryce also concluded that as a result of these changes the states had begun to lose authority to the federal government. He argued that in the original "partionment of government functions between the nation and the States, [the] State got the most but the nation the highest, so the balance between the two [was] preserved."[65] But following the Civil War, Bryce detected a transformation in which not only did state constitutions gradually lose the power to mold conclusively the course of public policy in areas they once exclusively dominated, but their prestige in relation to the federal Constitution also plummeted.

The decline of state constitutions after the Civil War was also much a product of federal constitutional developments, with the growing rigidity of many state constitutions facilitating this development. Bryce was certainly right: the antigovernment, populist, and lengthy character of these documents made them codes rather than organic laws. But what he did not fully appreciate was that this change abetted a greater concentration of authority in the national government. For example, the justices of the Supreme Court employed the equal protection and due process clauses of the Fourteenth Amendment to inquire broadly into the states' attempts to regulate social and economic policies through their police powers. From the 1880s through the 1930s the justices invoked the doctrine of substantive due process to bolster property rights and to limit state economic regulation. Thereafter, when the composition and substantive agenda of the Court switched to matters of civil liberties and civil rights, the justices relied on the same amendment to supervise race relations and criminal justice, areas previously the domain of state government.[66]

State constitutional development in the post–Civil War nineteenth century, as in earlier periods, responded to social demands. In the southern states, for example, the contract model had to be modified to permit the seceded states to reenter the Union, to define the legal condition of millions of former slaves, and to take account of the enormous burden of public indebtedness incurred during the war.[67] Throughout the nation, moreover, state governments had to adapt to an emerging industrial market economy, urbanization, and the excesses of political corruption that accompanied both.

With the practice of partisan interference in state constitution making firmly established in the pre–Civil War era, competing social and economic interests in the 1870s and later aggressively competed to control state fundamental law, usually at the expense of legislative discretion. Many social reformers, workers, and farmers complained that state legislatures were vulnerable to big business, especially railroads. Merchants in growing urban areas were equally concerned that they were suffering at the hands of out-of-state railroad operators, who were seemingly free to set freight rates. The framers of the Illinois Constitution of 1870, for example, revamped the judiciary, strengthened the chief executive, and clamped twenty-three explicit prohibitions on the legislature.[68] A special article dealt in seven long sections with the regulation of grain elevators and warehouses. In still another section the constitution commanded the legislature to "correct abuses and prevent unjust discrimination . . . in the rates of freight and passenger tariffs on the different railroads in this State."[69]

The constitutions of the new western states were much the same, although their distance from the settled East and their small and relatively homogeneous populations encouraged the development of a fourth distinct constitutional tradition—the frame of government. The constitutions of these states embraced the republican and democratic impulses of the late nineteenth century, but they were much more businesslike than their eastern and southern counterparts, stressing as they did the structure of state government and the distribution of powers within it.[70] Special constitutional legislation and clear restraints on government also pervaded even these documents. The Washington Constitution of 1889 outlawed free railroad passes and admonished the legislature to "pass laws establishing reasonable maximum rates of charges for the transportation of passengers and freight and to correct abuses."[71] The Colorado Constitution of 1876 and the Idaho document of 1889, for example, provided specific protections for miners and prohibited the employment of children in underground mining.[72] Still other western constitutions established merit selection plans for civil servants, ordered the preservation of natural resources, and granted women the right to vote.[73]

States that had earlier pursued a promotional role in economic development now engaged in regulatory activity based on their police powers. The framers of state constitutions cast a wary eye on railroads and other business corporations and expected independent regulatory commissions to blunt the influence of big business. The delegates to the California constitutional convention of 1879, for example, sought to frustrate railroad magnate Collis P. Huntington's control over the state assembly by establishing an independent railroad commission to regulate passenger and freight rates within the state.[74] Administrative bureaucracy and antigovernmentalism were reciprocal and reinforcing concepts in late nineteenth-century America, although by the mid-twentieth century advocates of limited government made government bureaucracy itself an object of criticism.[75]

This antigovernment bias surfaced in other ways. For example, long-standing agitation over state courts culminated in elaborate judiciary articles that specified in great detail the jurisdiction and organization of these courts. Governors gained additional authority, most notably through longer terms of office and the line-item veto. They also lost some administrative control to the new regulatory agencies and some political power to civil service reforms.[76]

Antigovernmentalism also went hand in hand with localism. Rapid urbanization after the Civil War created new centers of local power. Between 1865 and 1875 local governments went on a borrowing binge to fund services for their rapidly growing populations and to provide an adequate infrastructure for economic development. The depression of 1873–77 ruined local and state credit ratings and fueled measures, even more far-reaching than those following the Panic of 1837, that clamped strict controls on public borrowing.

The framers of state constitutions added teeth to earlier limits on local borrowing and state liability in case of defalcation. At the same time, they granted home rule to towns and cities, a process begun in the Missouri Constitution of 1876. Home rule allowed communities to organize into corporations free to conduct their affairs as long as they abided by the applicable constitutional provisions. Although they were not sovereign entities, local governments further accentuated the trend in state government to balance and share powers.[77]

These state constitutions also had important social functions, especially in the South with its strong contractarian tradition of limited government. There constitution makers, who were skeptical of invoking state constitutional authority to empower government in fiscal and economic matters, were anxious to write racial policies into public law. A distinctively southern pattern emerged.[78] Immediately following the Civil War the former Confederate states experienced a decade of federally imposed constitution making. The radical state constitutions of the South disrupted the old centers of social and political power and created in their place new ones based on black votes. In the 1870s and afterward the section's Bourbon leaders "redeemed" these states by writing their obsession with white supremacy into state constitutions. These documents and the legislation they authorized prohibited intermarriage between the races, provided for segregation of schools, and imposed race-based suffrage requirements. After a period during the 1870s and 1880s in which some southern states experimented with less restrictive documents in economic and fiscal matters, the region as a whole in the 1890s clambered aboard the antigovernment bandwagon.[79]

By century's end state constitutions were substantial if cumbersome facts of public life. They had a very different place in the polity than their federal counterpart. Over the previous century they had evolved into diffuse, overly long, negative documents that generally prevented the positive exercise of public authority, especially in fiscal and economic matters. As Woodrow Wilson observed in 1887, "It is getting harder to *run* a constitution than to frame one."[80]

Progressive Constitutionalism in the First Half of the Twentieth Century

The most recent state constitutional tradition emerged at the beginning of the twentieth century. The Progressive model echoed many of the principles of Hamilton's managerial scheme, but it also incorporated features drawn from the frame of government tradition. Progressive constitutionalism, strongest in the Middle West and West, was the first truly national approach to state constitutions because it permeated every section and had a vigorous national spokesman in Senator Robert A. LaFollette of Wisconsin.[81] The Progressive tradition rejected corruption and partisanship in politics and urged greater efficiency through rational methods of bureaucratic administration and strong executive leadership.

Progressives proposed to destroy the antigovernment bias in state constitutions by making government at once more bureaucratic and democratic but less partisan. The result was an awkward mix of bureaucracy, democracy, and a commitment to rational administration of government on a scientific rather than partisan basis. Progressives, for example, urged adoption of the initiative, referendum, and recall, measures that opened state constitutions to direct popular revision and state officials to close public scrutiny. But they also sponsored constitutional provisions that required voters to register, required secret balloting, formed at-large electoral districts, and made some elective offices nonpartisan. For example, the emphasis on rational state government based on professional expertise surfaced in the nonpartisan election of judges and later in the less democratic Missouri plan of judicial recruitment. All these measures depressed the level of voters' participation.[82] The new documents also reorganized government services into a limited number of departments, created independent boards and commissioners, gave authority to the governor to appoint a single department head, and mandated executive budgets.[83]

The Progressive constitutional tradition had important theoretical implications for the character of state government, but as a practical matter its effect was limited. State constitutions continued to swell, and most documents remained essentially negative in character. Change most often came on a piecemeal basis. The voters ratified 60 percent of the more than twenty-five hundred amendments proposed during the first thirty-five years of the century. A significant portion of the public apparently remained attached to documents it knew, whatever their defects, and regularly rejected significant constitutional innovations that threatened established bases of power. Restricted state government had—and continues to have—a significant public following. Between 1900 and 1950 voters adopted twelve new constitutions (one each in four new states, two in Louisiana, and one each in six existing states), but they also rejected the same number.[84]

Post-Progressive Developments: The Resurgence of the Managerial Tradition

Since about 1950 Hamilton's managerial tradition, refracted in many cases through Progressive ideals, has received renewed attention. Between then and 1981 twenty states undertook to revise their fundamental documents, with the bulk of this activity coming in the 1960s and 1970s. The pressure for change came from several sources. Proponents of constitutional revision stressed the need not only for more efficient government but for the documents drawn in the nineteenth century to fit the social and economic realities of the mid-twentieth century. They pointed especially, but not exclusively, to federal Supreme Court decisions striking down traditional state practices of racial segregation and legislative malapportionment. The malleable quality of federal constitutional law, with its power to protect minority rights from local majorities, as was true in *Brown* v. *Board of Education* (1954), made state constitutional reform a national problem.[85]

There were other sources of change. Inefficiency along with inequality became the new code words for national reform of these state documents. The federally created Kestenbaum Commission on Intergovernmental Relations in 1955 offered a scathing indictment of state government that blamed outmoded constitutions for its inadequacies.[86] "Many State constitutions," the commissioners reported to President Dwight D. Eisenhower, "restrict the scope, effectiveness and adaptability of State and local action. . . . The Commission believes that most states would benefit from a fundamental review and revision of their constitutions to make sure that they provide for vigorous and responsible government, not forbid it."[87] The commission's report stressed that state constitutions were too long, too detailed, and almost wholly negative. Under such circumstances, the commission argued, the federal government had encroached on areas of government responsibility that were traditionally the province of the states.

The report rang true. The struggle over apportionment of state legislatures vividly dramatized the unresponsive and unrepresentative character of state government. Most state legislatures had not accommodated themselves to the twentieth-century population shift from rural to urban. As a result, rural and agricultural interests were dramatically overrepresented. The United States Supreme Court's decision in *Baker* v. *Carr* (1962) opened fresh opportunities for constitutional revision by reapportioning legislatures in ways that gave greater voice to urban and suburban voters.[88] The new crop of state legislators pressed for constitutional modernization based on the Progressive-managerial model.

Efforts to streamline state government through constitutional revision have met with mixed success. Twenty states engaged in significant reform during these years, and the products of their labors reflected the broad outlines of the model state constitution first proposed by the National Municipal League in the 1920s and updated many times since. Many of these state documents also underscore the growing realization that for state constitutions to succeed, they must embody some of the sail-like qualities of the federal document. Many new state constitutions, such as those in Illinois and Michigan, contain provisions that mandate that the public will be able on a regular basis (usually ten years) to vote on whether to call a constitutional convention or revision commission. The recent history of the constitutional initiative in California and elsewhere makes a similar point.

Antigovernmentalism and negative constitutional legislation remain persistent themes in American public life. The citizenry continues to balk at substantial revisions of these documents; voters have rejected about half of all constitutions put forward since 1950. A combination of special interests worried about losing favored positions under existing documents and public suspicion of the ability of government to tax and spend frustrated many reform efforts.[89] In present-day Mississippi, for example, some black political leaders, who have found their power enhanced as a result of the federal constitutional revolution in race relations since 1954, shun proposals by white business reformers who want to revamp the state's 1890 constitution, one of the most racist state constitutions in the nation.[90] In this context, successful black political leaders, whose strength lies in the rural areas and small towns of Mississippi, clearly worry about the political consequences of constitutional "reforms" that would centralize decision making in the state capital. The irony is that a more active state government might well lift the economic fortunes of all of the people of Mississippi, a state long condemned to second-class economic status in part because of the weak state government.

The contemporary claims by both conservatives and liberals to the authority of state constitutions underscores that these documents continue to shape and are shaped by the political process. State constitutional law remains alive and well, even if the documents upon which it rests command less respect than they did two centuries ago. Conservative critics, who believe the federal government has exceeded its authority, urge amendments to the federal Constitution that would emulate provisions in state constitutions restricting the taxing power, mandating a balanced budget, and equipping the chief executive with a line-item veto. Liberals have also laid claim to state constitutions. Proponents of enhanced civil liberties and civil rights, faced with a Supreme Court unwilling to proceed at the pace of the Warren Court, insist that the bills of rights that grace these state documents can be interpreted to raise the ceiling of rights well above the floor established by the federal Constitution.[91] Today, as was true centuries ago, political vision and constitutional legitimacy remain reciprocal and reinforcing.

Conclusion: The Irony of State Constitutions and the Incomplete Federal Constitution

State constitutions since the mid-nineteenth century have reflected the persistent localism and antigovernmentalism that underlie much of American political culture. Because of these pressures and because the framers of the federal Constitution left to the states the task of describing the substantive functions of government, these state documents have evolved in a quite different way from the federal Constitution. Instead of growing as flexible organic laws readily susceptible to judicial modification, they have, with the notable exception of those of the New England states, become codelike documents filled with prohibitions against government action.

This historical development is ironic. In some ways, the genius of the federal Constitution so ably captured by Macaulay and Gladstone backfired insofar as state constitutions were concerned. The blank pages of the incomplete federal document evolved in the hands of local majorities into often populistic codes that constrained the operations of state government. This development generated pressures on the federal government to fill the vacuum created by the inability of state governments to respond fully to the transformation of American society and economy that accompanied the Industrial Revolution. The result was a central government more powerful than most of the framers, save for Hamilton and his allies, would have wanted. The growing centralization of national decision making in our own day appears to be part of a larger historical trend that was one of the consequences of the framing of the Constitution more than two centuries ago.

The success of the federal Constitution and the relative unimportance of state constitutions have not been accidental. They have earned their reputations. Unless we are prepared to overhaul our federal system in fundamental ways (which seems unlikely), we are probably headed for a future in which the political process will be increasingly molded by the adaptive qualities of the federal Constitution rather than the codelike populism and antigovernmentalism of most state constitutions. The states have been, from time to time, creative laboratories of constitutional change that have foretold future developments in federal public law, but more often than not they have been mostly anchor and little sail.

Notes

1. Thomas Babington Macaulay to H. S. Randall, May 23, 1857, as quoted in *Familiar Quotations,* ed. John Bartlett, 13th ed. (Boston: Little, Brown, 1955), 494.
2. Alfred H. Kelly, Winfred A. Harbison, and Herman J. Belz, *The American Constitution: Its Origins and Development,* 6th ed. (New York: Norton, 1983), 86–106. For a discussion of the relevant literature, see ibid., 779–82.
3. Kermit L. Hall, *The Supreme Court and Judicial Review in American History* (Washington, D.C.: American Historical Association, 1985).
4. *Familiar Quotations,* ed. Bartlett, 534.
5. Harry N. Scheiber, "American Constitutional History and the New Legal History: Complementary Themes in Two Modes," *Journal of American History* 68 (September 1981): 337–50.
6. Paul C. Reardon, "The Massachusetts Constitution Marks a Milestone," *Publius: The Journal of Federalism* 12 (Winter 1982): 45–55.
7. Robert F. Williams, "Introduction: State Constitutional Law in Ohio and the Nation," *University of Toledo Law Review* 16 (Winter 1985): 391–404.
8. For a listing of the relevant historical literature, see *A Comprehensive Bibliography of American Constitutional and Legal History,* ed. Kermit L. Hall (Millwood, N.Y.: Kraus International Publications, 1984), 1:506–22. For the literature in other disciplines, see Albert L. Sturm, *Thirty Years of State Constitution Making: 1938–1968* (New York: National Municipal League, 1970); and Williams, "Introduction," 391–404.
9. Kermit L. Hall, *The Magic Mirror: Law in American History* (New York: Oxford University Press, 1989), 480–85.
10. "Discussion of 'The Politics of State Constitutional Revision, 1820–1930,'" in *The Constitutional Convention as an Amending Device,* ed. Ker-

mit L. Hall, Harold M. Hyman, and Leon V. Sigal (Washington, D.C.: American Historical Association and American Political Science Association, 1981), 87–112.

11. The concept of the "incomplete" federal Constitution is discussed further below. See Donald S. Lutz, "The Purposes of American State Constitutions," *Publius: The Journal of Federalism* 13 (Winter 1982): 38.

12. U.S. Const., art. VI.

13. Daniel Elazar, "State Constitutional Design in the United States and Other Federal Systems," *Publius: The Journal of Federalism* 12 (Winter 1982): 1–10; "Discussion of 'The Politics of State Constitutional Reform,' " 92–97.

14. For a complete listing of the various restraints and guarantees, see Daniel J. Elazar, *American Federalism: A View from the States,* 3d ed. (New York: Harper & Row, 1972), 38–39.

15. N.C. Const., 1878, art. I, § 4, in *Sources and Documents of United States Constitutions,* ed. William Swindler (Dobbs Ferry, N.Y.: Oceana Publications, 1973–78), 7:415.

16. Albert L. Sturm, "The Development of American State Constitutions," *Publius: The Journal of Federalism* 12 (Winter 1982): 93.

17. U.S. Const., art. IV.

18. Ibid., art. XIV, § 2.

19. Willi Paul Adams, *The First American Constitutions: Republican Ideology and the Making of the State Constitutions in the Revolutionary Era* (Chapel Hill: University of North Carolina Press, 1980).

20. Michael Kammen, *A Machine That Would Go of Itself: The Constitution in American Culture* (New York: Knopf, 1986), 22–23.

21. Tenn. Const., 1870, art. XI, § 12, in *Sources and Documents,* ed. Swindler, 9:186.

22. 170 U.S. 213 (1898).

23. *Guinn* v. *U.S.,* 238 U.S. 347 (1915).

24. 349 U.S. 294 (1954). For a discussion of how the *Brown* decision undermined existing racial guidelines in southern state constitutions, see Richard Kluger, *Simple Justice: The History of Brown* v. *Board of Education and Black America's Struggle for Equality* (New York: Knopf, 1976).

25. U.S. Const. art. IV, § 4. On the historical development of the guarantee clause, see William M. Wiecek, *The Guarantee Clause of the U.S. Constitution* (Ithaca: Cornell University Press, 1972).

26. James Willard Hurst, *The Growth of American Law: The Law Makers* (Boston: Little, Brown, 1950), 336.

27. David Tyack, Thomas James, and Aaron Benavot, *Law and the Shaping of Public Education, 1785–1954* (Madison: University of Wisconsin Press, 1987), 20.

28. Lutz, "The Purposes of American State Constitutions," 38.

29. Morton Keller, "The Politics of State Constitutional Reform," in *The Constitutional Convention as an Amending Device*, ed. Hall, Hyman, and Sigal, 93, 96. On the balanced budget and line-item veto measures, see William J. Shultz, "Limitations on State and Local Borrowing Power," *Annals of the American Academy of Political and Social Sciences* 181 (September 1935): 118–42; and Samuel C. Patterson, "The Political Culture of the American States," in *Public Opinion and Public Policy*, ed. Norman R. Luttbeg (Homewood, Ill.: Dorsey Press, 1968), 275–92. On black suffrage, see Paul Finkelman, "Prelude to the Fourteenth Amendment: Black Legal Rights in the Antebellum North," *Rutgers Law Journal* 17 (1986): 415–46.

30. Elazar, "State Constitutional Design," 10.

31. For a fuller discussion of these trends and a listing of the beginning dates of the state constitutions, see Albert L. Sturm and Janice C. May, "State Constitutions and Constitutional Revision—1984—1985," *Book of the States* 26 (1986–87): 4–15.

32. Sturm, "Development of American State Constitutions," 59 (for the data up to 1979). For the period 1980–85, see Sturm and May, "State Constitutions and Constitutional Revision," 7.

33. Sturm and May, "State Constitutions and Constitutional Revision," 75–76. The 1985 figure does not include the numerous local amendments to the Georgia Constitution.

34. Daniel J. Elazar, "The Principles and Traditions Underlying State Constitutions," *Publius: The Journal of Federalism* 12 (1982): 14.

35. Charles R. Adrian, "Trends in State Constitutions," *Harvard Journal of Legislation* 5 (Winter 1968): 311–13; Allan Nevins, *The American States During and After the Revolution, 1775–1789* (New York: Macmillan, 1924), 114–40. Only Rhode Island and Connecticut retained their original colonial charters as organic laws. These early state constitutions did not rest directly on popular consent, as did the nineteenth-century documents of the populist tradition, because they were framed and adopted by the legislatures. This is one instance when the experience of the federal Constitutional Convention carried into the states. Donald Lutz, "A Theory of Consent in Early State Constitutions," *Publius: The Journal of Federalism* 9 (Spring 1979): 38.

36. Elazar, "State Constitutions," 13.

37. Lutz, "A Theory of Consent in Early State Constitutions," 11–42.

38. Donald S. Lutz, *Popular Consent and Popular Control: Whig Political Theory in Early State Constitutions* (Baton Rouge: Louisiana State University Press, 1980). On the general problem of original intent in both federal and state constitutions, see H. Jefferson Powell, "The Original

Understanding of Original Intent," *Harvard Law Review* 98 (March 1985): 885–948.

39. Elazar, "State Constitutions," 13.

40. Ibid.

41. Lutz, *Popular Consent and Popular Control*, 12–15.

42. Sturm, "Development of American State Constitutions," 60–63.

43. Elazar, "State Constitutions," 20. Twenty new states were admitted before the Civil War and another fifteen existing states rewrote their constitutions in ways that fitted one of these two traditions.

44. James Willard Hurst, *Law and the Conditions of Freedom in the Nineteenth-Century United States* (Madison: University of Wisconsin Press, 1964), 1.

45. Leonard W. Levy, *Law of the Commonwealth and Chief Justice Shaw* (Cambridge, Mass.: Harvard University Press, 1957), 305.

46. As cited in Oscar Handlin and Mary F. Handlin, *Commonwealth: A Study of the Role of Government in the American Economy, Massachusetts, 1774–1861* (Cambridge, Mass.: Harvard University Press, 1947), 66–67.

47. Elazar, "State Constitutions," 21.

48. Daniel J. Elazar, *Cities of the Prairie: The Metropolitan Frontier and American Politics* (New York: Basic Books, 1970).

49. Elazar, "State Constitutions," 21.

50. The civil law inheritance of Louisiana fostered a distinctive constitutional tradition and ultimately produced, at about one-quarter of a million words, the longest state constitution in the nation's history.

51. Morton Keller, "The Politics of State Constitutional Revision, 1820–1930," in *The Constitutional Convention as an Amending Device*, ed. Hall, Hyman, and Sigal, 71.

52. Hurst, *Growth of American Law*, 237–40.

53. On the early nineteenth-century state constitutions see *Democracy, Liberty, and Property: The State Constitutional Conventions of the 1820s*, ed. Merrill D. Peterson (Indianapolis: Bobbs-Merrill, 1966), 3–17, 125–42, 271–85. But see also Fletcher M. Green, *Constitutional Development in the South Atlantic States, 1776–1860*, rev. ed. (New York: Norton, 1966), 285–86.

54. Handlin and Handlin, *Commonwealth*; and Hurst, *Law and the Conditions of Freedom*.

55. David M. Gold, "Public Aid to Private Enterprise under the Ohio Constitution: Sections 4, 6, and 13 of Article VIII in Historical Perspective," *University of Toledo Law Review* 16 (Winter 1985): 410–13.

56. Keller, "Politics of State Constitutional Revision," 72–73.

57. Kermit L. Hall, "The Judiciary on Trial: State Constitutional Reform and the Rise of an Elected Judiciary, 1846–1860," *Historian* 44 (May 1983): 337–54.

58. Keller, "Politics of State Constitutional Revision," 72.

59. Hurst, *Growth of American Law*, 207–8.

60. Keller, "Politics of State Constitutional Revision," 71.

61. Elazar, "State Constitutions," 13.

62. Kermit L. Hall, "Progressive Reform and the Decline of Democratic Accountability: The Popular Election of State Supreme Court Judges, 1850–1920," *American Bar Foundation Research Journal* (1984): 345–70.

63. Lawrence M. Friedman, *A History of American Law*, 2d ed. (New York: Simon and Schuster, 1985), 355–57. For the example of one state appellate court, see Margaret V. Nelson, *A Study of Judicial Revision in Virginia, 1789–1928* (New York: Columbia University Press, 1946). On the changing role of state supreme courts in this period, see Robert A. Kagan, Bliss Cartwright, Lawrence M. Friedman, and Stanton Wheeler, "The Business of State Supreme Courts, 1870–1970," *Stanford Law Review* 30 (Spring 1977): 121–71.

64. James Bryce, *The American Commonwealth*, ed. Louis Hacker (New York: Capricorn Books, G. P. Putnam's Sons, 1959), 1:116.

65. Ibid., 425.

66. Kermit L. Hall, *The Supreme Court and Judicial Review in American History* (Washington, D.C.: American Historical Association, 1985), 37–49.

67. John V. Orth, "The Virginia State Debt and the Judicial Power of the United States," in *Ambivalent Legacy: A Legal History of the South*, ed. David Bodenhamer and James W. Ely, Jr. (Jackson: University Press of Mississippi, 1984), 106–22.

68. Ill. Const., 1870, art. IV, § 22, in *Sources and Documents*, ed. Swindler, 3:291–92.

69. Ibid., art. XI, § 15, in *Sources and Documents*, ed. Swindler, 3:305. For fuller discussion of these developments, see Friedman, *History of American Law*, 349.

70. Elazar, "State Constitutions," p. 22. These traditions, of course, tend to overlap. Oklahoma, for example, has a small population but because of its southern antecedents, it has one of the longest constitutions of the late nineteenth- and early twentieth-century western states.

71. Wash. Const., 1889, art. XII, §§ 18, 20, in *Sources and Documents*, ed. Swindler, 10:310–11.

72. Colo. Const., 1876, art. XVI, § 2, ibid., 2:89; Idaho Const., 1889, art. XIII, § 4, ibid., 3:186.

73. Friedman, *History of American Law*, 351.

74. Cal. Const., 1879, art. XI, § 4. Of course, many constitutions left to the legislature the responsibility for creating these commissions. Others, like that of Nebraska, mandated that the legislature establish "maximum rates of charges," and the Board of Transportation in that state

was to make recommendations to the legislature. See Neb. Const., 1875, art. XI, § 4. These matters are discussed fully in Frank Hendrick, *Railroad Control by Commission* (New York: G. P. Putnam's Sons,1900).

75. Sturm, "Development of American State Constitutions," 67–68. On the competing forces of morality and efficiency that gave rise to the administrative state, see William E. Nelson, *The Roots of American Bureaucracy, 1830–1900* (Cambridge, Mass.: Harvard University Press, 1982).

76. Nelson, *Roots of American Bureaucracy*, 112–14.

77. William Swindler, "Missouri Constitutions: History, Theory and Practice," *Missouri Law Review* 23 (January 1958): 35–37.

78. John W. Mauer, "Southern State Constitutions in the 1870s: A New Perspective" (paper presented at the 1987 meeting of the Social Science History Association, New Orleans). For a general discussion of the reformulation of post–Civil War southern constitutions, see Mauer, "Southern State Constitutions in the 1870s: A Case Study of Texas" (Ph.D. dissertation, Rice University, 1983). For developments in the North before the Civil War, see George Phillip Parkinson, "Antebellum State Constitution-Making: Retention, Circumvention, Revision" (Ph.D. dissertation, University of Wisconsin, 1972), 83, 116–17, 148–51, and 168.

79. J. Morgan Kousser, *The Shaping of Southern Politics: Suffrage Restriction and the Establishment of the One-Party South, 1880–1910* (New Haven: Yale University Press, 1974).

80. As quoted in Keller, "Politics of State Constitutional Revision," 76–77.

81. Elazar, "State Constitutions," 13. The Whig-republican tradition continued to persist in New England, although even there the Progressive tradition made inroads.

82. Sturm, "Development of American State Constitutions," 68–71. On the impact on voter participation, see Hall, "Progressive Reform and the Decline of Democratic Accountability."

83. A. E. Buck, *The Reorganization of State Government in the United States* (New York: National Municipal League, 1938), 7–8, 11; Adrian, "Trends in State Constitutions," 316–30.

84. Keller, "Politics of State Constitutional Revision," 80–84.

85. *Brown v. Board of Education*, 349 U.S. 294 (1954).

86. *A Report to the President for Transmittal to the Congress* (Washington, D.C.: U.S. Government Printing Office, 1955).

87. Ibid., 37, 56.

88. *Baker v. Carr*, 369 U.S. 186 (1962).

89. Sturm, "Development of American State Constitutions," 72–74.

90. *Contemporary Analysis of Mississippi's Constitutional Government*, ed.

Dana B. Brammer and John W. Winkle III (University, Miss.: University of Mississippi Center for Policy Studies, 1986), 15–16.

91. Shirley Abrahamson, "Homegrown Justice: The State Constitutions," in *Developments in State Constitutional Law: The Williamsburg Conference,* ed. Bradley McGraw (St. Paul: West, 1985), 306–35; and William F. Swindler, "Minimum Standards of Constitutional Justice: Federal Floor and State Ceiling," *Missouri Law Review* 49 (Winter 1984): 1–15.

Contributors

Mary L. Dudziak, Associate Professor at the University of Iowa College of Law. University of California, Berkeley, A.B., 1978; Yale Law School, J.D., 1984, M.A., M.Phil., 1986. She has written on legal history for the *Stanford Law Review, Law and History Review,* and *Iowa Law Review.*

Paul Finkelman, Visiting Associate Professor at Brooklyn Law School. Syracuse University, B.A., 1971; University of Chicago, M.A., 1972, Ph.D., 1976. His books include *The Law of Freedom and Bondage: A Casebook, Slavery in the Courtroom* (winner of the Joseph L. Andrews Award from the American Association of Law Libraries), and *An Imperfect Union: Slavery, Federalism, and Comity.* He is coauthor, with Kermit Hall and William M. Wiecek, of *American Legal History: Cases and Materials.* He is the editor of *American Slavery: Major Historical Interpretations* (18 vols.) and *Slavery, Race, and the American Legal System, 1700–1872* (16 vols.). Professor Finkelman has been a Visiting Assistant Professor at the University of Texas Law School and a Fellow in Law and History at the Harvard Law School. He has served on the editorial board of the *Journal of the Early Republic* and the *Law and History Review* and is the Associate Editor of the *Journal of Southern Legal History.*

Lawrence M. Friedman, Marion Rice Kirkwood Professor of Law, Stanford Law School. University of Chicago, A.B., 1948, J.D., 1951, LL.M., 1953; LL.D. (Hon.), University of Puget Sound Law School, 1977; LL.D. (Hon.), John Jay College of Criminal Justice, City University of New York, 1989. His books include *Total Justice, The Roots of Justice: Crime and Punishment in Alameda County, California, 1870–1910* (with Robert V. Percival), *The Legal System: A Social Science Perspective,* and *A History of American Law.* Among the works he has edited are *Law and the Behavioral Sciences* (with Stewart Macaulay) and *American Law and the Constitutional Order: Historical Perspectives* (with Harry N. Scheiber). Professor Friedman has received the James Willard Hurst Prize from the Law and Society Association (with Robert V. Percival), the Scribes Award, and the Triennial Coif Book Award. He has also taught at Wisconsin Law School and St. Louis University Law School.

Stephen E. Gottlieb, Professor, Albany Law School of Union University. Princeton University, B.A., 1962; Yale Law School, LL.B., 1965. Has written for *Boston University Law Review, New York University Law Review, Washington University Law Review, Wayne Law Review, Albany Law Review,* and others. He has also taught at West Virginia University School of Law.

Kermit L. Hall, Professor of History and Law and Chairman of the Department of History, University of Florida. University of Akron, B.A., 1966; Syracuse University, M.A., 1967; Minnesota, Ph.D., 1972; Yale, M.S.L., 1980. His books include *The Politics of Justice, Comprehensive Bibliography of American Constitutional and Legal History* (Choice Outstanding Academic Book in History and Scribe's Award), *The Supreme Court and Judicial Review in American History,* and *The Magic Mirror: Law in American History.* He is coauthor, with William M. Wiecek and Paul Finkelman, of *American Legal History: Cases and Materials.* He has served as the Associate Editor of the *American Journal of Legal History.* Professor Hall has also taught at Vanderbilt University and Wayne State University.

James A. Henretta, Burke Professor of History and Adjunct Professor of Law, University of Maryland. Swarthmore College, B.A., 1962; Harvard University, M.A., 1963, Ph.D., 1968. His books include *Evolution and Revolution: American Society, 1600–1820* (with Gregory H. Nobles), *America's History* (with David Brody, Elliott Brownlee, and Susan Ware), *The Evolution of American Society, 1700–1815: An Interdisciplinary Analysis, "Salutary Neglect": Colonial Administration Under the Duke of Newcastle.* Professor Henretta serves on the Board of Editors of the *Journal of Social History* and has taught at Sussex University, England, Princeton University, the University of California, Los Angeles, Columbia University, and Boston University. He has been a Fulbright Senior Scholar in History in Australia.

Morton J. Horwitz, Charles Warren Professor of American Legal History, Harvard Law School. CCNY, A.B., 1959; Harvard University, Ph.D., 1964, LL.B., 1967. His work includes *The Transformation of American Law, 1780–1860* and articles in the *American Journal of Legal History, Harvard Law Review, University of Chicago Law Review,* and *Yale Law Journal,* among many others. Professor Horwitz has received the Thomas J. Wilson Prize from Harvard University and the Bancroft Prize in American History.

Thomas James, Associate Professor of Education and Public Policy, Brown University. Harvard University, B.A., 1970; Stanford University, M.A., 1982, Ph.D., 1984. His books include *Exile Within: The Schooling of Japanese Americans, 1942–1945,* and *Law and the Shaping of Public Education* (with David B.

Tyack and Aaron Benavot). With Henry M. Levin he has edited *Comparing Public and Private Schools* (2 vols.) and *Public Dollars for Private Schools: The Case of Tuition Tax Credits.* He has taught at Wesleyan University and Stanford University.

J. Morgan Kousser, Professor of History and Social Science, California Institute of Technology. Princeton University, A.B., 1965; Yale University, M. Phil., 1968, Ph.D., 1971; Oxford University, M.A., 1984. His work includes *The Shaping of Southern Politics: Suffrage Restriction and the Establishment of the One-Party South, 1880–1910.* He is the editor, with James M. McPherson, of *Region, Race, and Reconstruction: Essays in Honor of C. Vann Woodward.* He has taught at the University of Michigan, Harvard University, and as the Harold Vyvyan Harmsworth Professor of American History at Oxford University.

Donald S. Lutz, Professor of Political Science, University of Houston. Georgetown University, A.B., 1965; Indiana University, Ph.D., 1969. His books include *Popular Consent and Popular Control: Whig Political Theory in the Early State Constitutions* and *The Origins of American Constitutionalism.* He is the editor of *American Political Writing During the Founding Era, 1760–1805* (2 vols., with Charles S. Hyneman), *Documents of Political Foundation by Colonial Americans*, and *Perspectives on American and Texas Politics: A Reader* (with Kent Tedin) and member of the Editorial Advisory Board for *Publius: The Journal of Federalism.*

Burt Neuborne, Professor, New York University School of Law. Cornell, A.B., 1961; Harvard, LL.B., 1964. Former Legal Director of the American Civil Liberties Union, for which he continues to serve as Special Counsel. His books include *Unquestioning Obedience to the President* and *Emerson, Haber and Dorsen's Political and Civil Rights in the United States* (2 vols., with Norman Dorsen and Paul Bender).

Charles J. Ogletree, Assistant Professor, Harvard Law School. Stanford University, B.A., 1974, M.A., 1975; Harvard Law School, J.D., 1978. Professor Ogletree has served as the Deputy Director, Trial Chief, and Training Director of the District of Columbia Public Defender Service.

Peter S. Onuf, Professor of History, University of Virginia, and Visiting Professor of Modern History, University College, Dublin, 1989–90. Johns Hopkins University, A.B., 1967, Ph.D., 1973. His books include *The Origins of the Federal Republic: Jurisdictional Controversies in the United States, 1775–1787, Statehood and Union: A History of the Northwest Ordinance, A Union of Interests:*

Political and Economic Thought in Revolutionary America (with Cathy D. Matson), and *The Midwest and the Nation: Rethinking the History of an American Region* (with Andrew R. L. Cayton). He has taught at the University of California at San Diego, Columbia University, Worcester Polytechnic Institute, and Southern Methodist University.

Ellen A. Peters, Chief Justice, Supreme Court of Connecticut. Swarthmore College, B.A., 1951; Yale Law School, LL.B., 1954; LL.D. (hon.) from Yale, Swarthmore, and many others. Her books include *Commercial Transactions: Cases, Text and Problems on Contracts Dealing with Personalty, Realty and Services,* and *A Negotiable Instruments Primer.* Justice Peters taught at the Yale Law School for more than twenty years before her appointment to the bench. Among her many professional and public service activities, she has served as a director of the Conference of Chief Justices of the American Law Institute and of the Yale Corporation.

H. Jefferson Powell, Professor, Duke University School of Law. University of Wales, B.A., 1975; Duke University, A.M., 1977; Yale University, M.Div., 1979, J.D., 1982. Professor Powell has written on legal history for the *Harvard Law Review* and the *Yale Law Journal,* among others. He has been a Research Associate at the Yale Law School and taught at the University of Iowa College of Law.

Suzanna Sherry, Professor of Law, University of Minnesota Law School. Middlebury College, A.B., 1976; University of Chicago, J.D., 1979. She coauthored *The History of the American Constitution* and has written on legal history and constitutional law for the *University of Chicago Law Review, Texas Law Review, Constitutional Commentary, Michigan Law Review,* and *Tulane Law Review,* among others.

William M. Wiecek, Chester Adgate Congdon Professor of Public Law and Legislation and Professor of History, Syracuse University College of Law. Catholic University, B.A., 1959; Harvard Law School, LL.B., 1962; University of Wisconsin, Ph.D., 1968. His books include *The Guarantee Clause of the U.S. Constitution, Sources of Antislavery Constitutionalism, Equal Justice Under Law* (with Harold Hyman), and *Liberty Under Law.* He is coauthor, with Kermit Hall and Paul Finkelman, of *American Legal History: Cases and Materials.* He serves on the Editorial Board of the *Law and History Review.* He has also taught at the University of Missouri, Columbia.

Index of Cases

General Index

Chicago, 57, 125
Child labor, 273, 404–5
Christianity, 121, 126, 133
Christian liberty, 99
Christian republicans, 91–101
Church and state, 6, 96–97, 117–38
Cincinnati, 125, 128
Cincinnati Bible case, 132
Citizenship, 19–21, 84 (n. 7), 95, 101
Civil law, 169
Civil liberties, 157, 240, 275, 291–92, 310, 403, 410
Civil religion, 122, 132
Civil rights, 189, 218, 224, 233, 234, 275, 292, 403, 410
Civil Rights Act of 1866, 232, 261 (n. 103), 343
Civil Rights Bill (U.S.) of 1874, 242 (n. 7)
Civil Rights Cases, 235, 263 (n. 122)
Civil rights lawyers, 294–97
Civil War, 9, 124, 128, 132, 388
Clemens, Gaspar Christopher, 237, 240
Clerical establishments, 109
Clerical republicans, 97
Clifford, Nathan, 232, 258 (n. 92)
Clinton, De Witt, 58, 378–79
Coalter, John, 169
Coffeyville, Kansas, 225, 236
Coke, Lord, 68, 207 (n. 8)
Colorado, 54, 272
Colorado Constitution of 1876, 404
Commercial republic, 83 (n. 2), 397, 398–99
Common folk, 92, 109
Common law, 4, 7, 11, 16 (n. 43), 159, 163, 165, 169, 178, 189–95
Common School Journal (1852), 126
Common school movement, 120–33, 136, 138 (n. 2)
Commonwealth, 78, 83 (n. 2), 398
Communitarianism, 78, 149, 396, 402
Compromise of 1850, 294
Comstock Law, 306
Confederacy, 10, 51, 219, 390, 406
Congress, 9–11; under Articles of

Confederation, 375; and veto power, 93
Conkling, Roscoe, 64
Connecticut, 7–8, 13 (n. 9), 16 (n. 43), 23, 28, 31, 43 (n. 49), 46 (n. 74), 54, 58, 97–98, 121, 189–95, 304–38, 372, 413 (n. 35)
Connecticut Birth Control League, 308
Connecticut Constitution of 1818, 190
Connecticut Election Law of 1715, 41 (n. 22)
Connecticut Supreme Court, 191, 304–5, 312, 320–21, 324–25, 334 (n. 82), 372
Connecticut Supreme Court of Errors, 309–12, 323
Conscience, rights of, 11, 13 (n. 60), 117–47
Conscientious objector, 117
Conservatives, 100, 109, 409
Constitutional amendments. *See* individual amendments
Constitutional Convention, Philadelphia, 4–5, 8–9, 13–14 (nn. 16, 17), 339, 396
Constitutional conventions, state, 52–55, 59–60, 70–73, 80, 87 (n. 44), 388, 394, 409
Constitutionalism, 149, 397, 400. *See also* Interpreting state constitutions
Constitutions. *See* State constitutions
Continental army, 30, 45 (n. 70)
Contraceptives. *See* Birth control
Contract clause, 11, 167
Contractual individualism, 78
Conway, Thomas W., 213, 242 (nn. 5, 7)
Cooley, Thomas M., 77
Corporations, 77, 401, 403, 405. *See also* Laissez-faire
Council of Appointment (New York), 69–70
Council of Censors (Pennsylvania), 33, 48 (n. 98)
Council of Revision (New York), 68, 69
Court of Admiralty, 199